WITHDRAWN

D1602768

The Confabulating Mind

The Confabulating Mind

How the brain creates reality

Armin Schnider

Professor and Chairman
Division of Neurorehabilitation
Department of Clinical Neurosciences
University Hospital of Geneva, Switzerland

OXFORD
UNIVERSITY PRESS

OXFORD

UNIVERSITY PRESS

Great Clarendon Street, Oxford OX2 6DP

Oxford University Press is a department of the University of Oxford.
It furthers the University's objective of excellence in research, scholarship,
and education by publishing worldwide in

Oxford New York

Auckland Cape Town Dar es Salaam Hong Kong Karachi
Kuala Lumpur Madrid Melbourne Mexico City Nairobi
New Delhi Shanghai Taipei Toronto

With offices in

Argentina Austria Brazil Chile Czech Republic France Greece
Guatemala Hungary Italy Japan Poland Portugal Singapore
South Korea Switzerland Thailand Turkey Ukraine Vietnam

Oxford is a registered trade mark of Oxford University Press
in the UK and in certain other countries

Published in the United States
by Oxford University Press Inc., New York

A catalogue record for this title is available from the British Library
Data available

Library of Congress Cataloging in Publication Data
Data available

Typeset by Cepha Imaging Private Ltd., Bangalore, India
Printed in Great Britain
on acid-free paper by
Biddles Ltd., King's Lynn, Norfolk

ISBN 978–0–19–920675–9 (Pbk.)

10 9 8 7 6 5 4 3 2 1

To my family

Preface

Few topics in neuroscience can look back on a history of more than a century. Confabulation, the recitation of events and experiences that never happened, is such a topic. Hardly any other subject has received as many interpretations and hypotheses as confabulation. Many ideas, based on clinical observation, were initially formulated in German and French, then partially forgotten, only to reappear in the modern English literature. Writing a book about such a topic is a fascinating adventure, which requires one to proceed from the stage of 'having an idea' to an in-depth analysis of the literature. Throughout the book, I have tried to integrate the old and the new literature, to translate the old German and French literature as literally as possible, and to provide readers with sufficient information for them to take part in the adventure.

Writing this book would have been impossible without the tolerance and support of my family. My wife Andrea not only shared countless ideas with me, but also typed the whole manuscript. My son Patrick repeatedly renounced our soccer match.

Then, there were the scientific advisors. I am deeply indebted to Morris Moscovitch, who reviewed the whole manuscript – a humungous effort from which the book has profited immensely. Thedi Landis read every chapter and helped me smooth out edges here and there. Many specialists and collaborators have reviewed parts of the book and helped me avoid unnecessary misconceptions: Gianfranco Dalla Barba, John DeLuca, Joaquín M. Fuster, Asaf Gilboa, Michael Kopelman, Béatrice Leemann, Sandra Barcellona-Lehmann, Daniel L. Schachter, Wolfram Schultz, Tim Shallice, Larry R. Squire, and an American professor of anatomy. Thanks to them all.

I am also grateful to the Swiss National Science Foundation, which has supported my research over the years, and the friends and collaborators who have helped me conduct the research. Their names can be found in the References.

Writing a book is particularly motivating when the best publisher takes charge of it. I thank Martin Baum of Oxford University Press for his encouraging evaluation and unfailing support of the project, Carol Maxwell for immediate and precise responses to inquiries, and Anna Reeves for careful production editing.

Armin Schnider

Thônex, August 2007

Contents

Chapter 1

The reality of Mrs B

Mrs B was a 63 year-old, well-groomed, noble person with a strong character – and a psychiatrist with a long professional experience. She had grown up in Poland and moved to Switzerland as a young doctor, where she married a state official. Now, she walked slowly down the ward, holding a cane and chatting with patients. The ward was the Division for Neurorehabilitation at the University Hospital of Geneva, a familiar environment for a psychiatrist, and Mrs B appeared to feel at ease – except that she considered it inappropriate that a student was following her all the time and that the nurses seemed to keep a constant eye on her.

She was used to having discussions; many people asked her questions these days. At first sight, this discussion, too, appeared quite unremarkable:

'Would you please explain what you call your 'malady'?'
Mrs B tried to make it simple: 'My malady – that was a rupture of a vessel in my left leg.'
'Do you still work?'
'Yes, I do.'
'Where do you work?'
Mrs B, with no hesitation: 'Presently, I have a position at the outpatient clinic in Geneva.'
'In what sector, what speciality?'
'In physiotherapy.'
'You are a specialist in physiotherapy?'
Mrs B, slightly annoyed and briefly hesitating: 'I am not a specialist in physiotherapy, I am a psychiatrist.' And then, after a deep breath: 'Right now, there was a position available down there, and when I finished working in psychiatry, I went there to work in physiotherapy.'
'Okay … You said you had visitors this morning?'
'Yes, my mother and my brother.'
'They came this morning?'
'Yes.'
'What's on your programme for today?'
Mrs B did her best to explain: 'Tonight, I will give a reception at my home.'
'And who will be there?'
'There will be my colleagues, my family from Poland, and the physiotherapists who care for me.'
'How old are you?'

> Mrs B, with her reading glasses slowly gliding down her nose: '40 years', and then, with an amused giggle: 'That is – a bit more … almost 50!'
> 'And do you know what you will do this afternoon and tonight?'
> 'Yes. I will go home now and prepare the reception. Then, my family and friends will arrive towards 6 p.m.'

Admittedly, an unremarkable interview. Unless one knows that Mrs B was not in our Neurorehabilitation Division to practice psychiatry; she was hospitalized because she had suffered a devastating haemorrhage from a vessel in her head. She was now severely amnesic, unable to retain any significant information in memory. With this in mind, let us again go over the interview:

> 'My malady – that was a rupture of a vessel in my left leg.'

Mrs B had had repeat hip surgery during the last 19 years, but now, the vessels in her left leg were perfectly fine. The idea of the rupture of a vessel was obviously correct; except that this time, it was a vessel in her head.

> Presently, I have a position at the outpatient clinic in Geneva.... I am not a specialist in physiotherapy – I am a psychiatrist.... Right now, there was a position available down there, and when I finished working in psychiatry, I went there to work in physiotherapy.

Mrs B had indeed been a psychiatrist until her early retirement 15 years ago, but she had never held a position as a psychiatrist at our hospital. Of course, she had never worked as a physical therapist; but she had had many therapy sessions after her hip surgery 15 years ago.

> 'Have you had visitors this morning?' – 'Yes, my mother and my brother.'

She often received visits from her husband and her children, but she had had no visits that morning, when she underwent therapies, and she had definitely not had a visit from her mother or brother this morning; they had died 13 and 15 years ago.

> 'How old are you?' – '40 years.... That is – a bit more … almost 50!'

Mrs B was 63 years old.

> 'Tonight, I will give a reception at my home.... There will be my colleagues, my family from Poland, and the physiotherapists who care for me.'

Of course, nobody expected Mrs B to give a reception tonight, now that she was hospitalized. But, as the wife of a state official, she had given many receptions until 15 years ago, including a reception for Polish officials.

Mrs B was not lying, at least not intentionally. She believed what she said. She was greatly concerned about tonight's reception and repeatedly left the unit in order to prepare for it. But her story was not true, either, at least not now. Her story was fabricated, bringing together bits and pieces of her past into a new tale, a fable – she was confabulating!

Her life changed during a vacation three months previously when, out of the blue, she was hit by the most intense headache ever experienced, rapidly followed by loss of consciousness – a typical subarachnoid haemorrhage, a bleeding into the pain-sensitive space between the skull and the brain. A CT-scan revealed the cause, the most frequent one: a ruptured aneurysm, that is, a quasi-explosion of an abnormal, thin-layered bulge from the wall of an artery. In the case of Mrs B, it had affected the vessel most frequently involved: the anterior communicating artery, a delicate vessel at the base of the skull which connects two main arteries at the inner side of the brain and irrigates a small but critical area of the brain, the basal forebrain. Rupture of an aneurysm in this area often destroys surrounding tissue: the cortex at the base of the brain (just above and behind the eyes), which is called the orbitofrontal cortex, plus the basal forebrain (Figure 4.3c). If the bleeding is very severe, blood may enter the liquid-filled ventricles within the brain, as was the case with Mrs B. The accumulation of fluid then additionally compresses the brain from the inside.

Mrs B was lucky to have rapid neurosurgical care. A fine tube was introduced into the ventricular system to release pressure, and two days later, the aneurysm was fixed with a coil put in place by means of a catheter introduced in the groin and pushed all the way up to the aneurysm of the tiny vessel below the brain.

Mrs B slowly regained consciousness. For four weeks, she remained apathetic, hardly saying a word or initiating an act. After five weeks, she was transferred to our neurorehabilitation unit. Within two weeks, she became active and started to talk. After an initial confusional phase with disorganized behaviour, incoherent speech and inversion of her day and night rhythm, attention improved and her behaviour became increasingly consistent.

Now, three months after the haemorrhage, Mrs B caught the eye of the outsider only by her considerate demeanour, her careful gait and possibly her heavy make-up, which she corrected every time she returned to her bedroom. She had a façade of grande dame, perfectly disguising her devastating memory disorder.

Unfortunately, her recovery complicated things enormously, and our team, used to such situations, soon became aware of it. Although discussions about daily events made it clear that Mrs B did not retain any significant information in memory – she immediately forgot therapy sessions and the identity of collaborators – she did not appear to be aware of her confused memory. When asked about her memory, she acknowledged having a bad memory and seemed to be concerned about this, but she could not indicate any specific situation of failure. She became depressed, and required treament, without being able to indicate a reason. In no case would she consider the possibility that her ideas were inappropriate, that she was not a psychiatrist on our ward, and that she did not have to give a reception in the evening. The confabulations themselves were not the problem. The real problem was the conviction behind the confabulations, the degree of truthfulness they attained in her thinking. Mrs B acted according to ideas, which were taken from her remote past, but which were dangerously inappropriate guides for present behaviour.

There was no problem with her conviction that she was a staff physician in our clinic. It simply meant that the neuropsychologist could not start a therapy session before reporting last night's emergency admissions. Or Mrs B might suddenly leave a therapy session stating that she had to look after an emergency admission to the clinic. She would then leave the room, walk aimlessly around the unit and desperately search for the patients she had to take care of. To her family, it meant that she might all of a sudden rise from the chair in the cafeteria and leave them with the idea that she had to resume work. To me, it meant that she would occasionally stop me in the hallway to express her satisfaction with her work in our unit and apply for the prolongation of her contract as a psychiatrist. Normally, I would assure her that her job was not in danger. When I responded that I was not her superior but her doctor, and that she was a patient, she would insist: 'No, no, I know that you are professor Schnider, my boss' (my name happens to be very similar to the name of a psychiatrist who had been her superior in the past).

Much more dangerous were the confabulations that made her leave the unit every once in a while, with no warning. If she was caught before leaving the building, she reacted vigorously and insisted that she had finished work and had to return home to prepare a reception. So, supervision by a student was organized who accompanied Mrs B during the day. Although he was briefed about the intensity of Mrs B's beliefs, he was considerably shocked when she started to beat him with her cane, simply because he did not let her go into the hospital's kitchen. She, by contrast, was convinced that this was the place where she had to prepare tonight's menu. Similarly, her husband was stunned when Mrs B slapped him during a brief visit to their home: finding the fridge almost empty, she suspected him of removing the food that she had already shopped for tonight's reception.

The situation grew dangerous when Mrs B failed to be picked up before she left the hospital on her own. In other confabulating patients, such a disappearance might not be dangerous; they return home or go to their workplace. Mrs B, however, also had deficient attention – she could not concentrate on several things at a time – and a visit to town together with the occupational therapist had shown that she would not pay attention to traffic lights. When Mrs B left the hospital, she was at real risk of running into trouble.

In marked difference to this profound confusion about her present situation, her accounts of her remote past were consistent and correct. She correctly recalled memories from her childhood, her life in Poland, school and professional life, her arrival in Switzerland, and her family life up to her 40s. She always recognized old friends of the family and her children, now 30 and 35 years old. When asked about them, she would refer to them as if they were still children with whom she intended to go to the cinema or the zoo. She correctly recalled the names of her grandchildren, six and eight years old, but then talked about adventures with them that she had in fact lived with her own children 20 years ago.

In contrast to the correct accounts of the remote past, she appeared to be unaware of events from the last 15 to 20 years. She had not integrated the death of her parents and brother 9, 10, and 13 years ago, nor of her retirement 15 years ago. She was completely unfamiliar even with highly dramatic recent events, such as the terrorist attacks of 11 September 2001, 19 months before her cerebral haemorrage. When asked about such events, she just indicated that she did not know. Also, when asked about invented events and facts using plausible names ('What happened in Mimushina, what's a water knube, who is Princess Lolita?') she would acknowledge ignorance rather than confabulate.

She recognized long-standing celebrities on photographs; if she did not recognize a celebrity, she would admit it rather than confabulate. When she was shown photographs of strangers that she had never seen, she would say so. This was completely different for portraits of clinic collaborators who she had seen regularly for weeks and months, but whom she failed to recognize by their name. When shown such photographs, she either denied familiarity or confabulated an identity in relation to her perceived reality at that moment. For example, she recognized the neuropsychologist's portrait as the one of her horse-riding school's stable-girl, and my portrait as the one of her riding teacher: that day, she was convinced that she had been horse riding in the morning (Schnider *et al.* 2005a).

The conviction that she had to go to work or to give a reception persisted for months. We wondered whether a change of environment would have an influence on the content of her confabulations. On different days, the neuropsychologist accompanied Mrs B to places that she had known for many years: her grocery store, the medical library at the university, or a public park where she had often been with her children 20 years ago. Mrs B recognized all places and correctly recounted personal events associated with them; these places, on their own, did not evoke confabulations. At the end of each visit, Mrs B was asked about her plans for the day. Her common response was, not surprisingly, that she would now return to her work at the clinic or to her home to prepare tonight's reception. Only after the visit to the park, where they had talked about her children, did she respond that she would go to the movie with her children this afternoon; in her idea, her children were ten and twelve years old (in fact, they were 30 and 35 years old). It appeared that the discussion about past visits to the park with her children now induced a false idea of reality. Could the mere thinking about a past reality induce a false percept of the 'now'?

We tried to explore this phenomenon further. Mrs B's husband provided us with photographs depicting personal events: a dinner at a restaurant, a promenade by the lake, a visit to the cinema with her grandchildren, a visit to the opera, the grocer's, or an art exhibition. On ten different days, Mrs B was shown one photograph and asked to recall as many details as possible and to think about things that did or might have happened on the occasion. Our interest was not to know how many details she recalled, but to have her concentrate fully on the depicted situation and think intensively about it. After five minutes, the picture was put aside. Then, one minute later, the examiner asked her: 'By the way: where have you been today?' Amazingly, on nine out of ten test sessions, she named the event that had been discussed, as if it had really just occurred.

It thus appeared that, when Mrs B retained a vague memory, the gist of a discussion or of a thought, she would not spontaneously feel whether this memory referred to a mere thought or to a real event – she failed to monitor whether a thought had its source in true reality or in thinking.

This result was obtained about three months after the haemorrhage, when all tests indicated that Mrs B did not retain any information in memory beyond five to ten minutes. In this period, she was extremely amnesic. She was still very severely amnesic after six months with lowest scores in all memory tests, but discussions with her suggested that she now retained at least some bits of information from day to day. In this period, the procedure did not evoke confabulations anymore. We concluded that, when a person has some memory capacity, a five-minute discussion is no longer sufficient to implant a false reality in thought. Nonetheless, the observation suggests that the environment does influence the content of confabulations.

After she returned home, she needed the permanent assistance of a housemaid while her husband was at work. She confabulated less often but the topics remained fairly stable. She would frequently wake up in the morning and believe that she had to go to work; often, she prepared herself to leave the house. During the day, in company, she confabulated less but increasingly resented being under supervision. She continued to believe that she had to prepare receptions in the evenings and on several occasions surprised her husband with full menus prepared for several people.

After 17 months, a notable change occurred. Mrs B started to complain that her memory was bad and sought information when she was unsure about where she was or what she had to do. When questioned about her plans, she would rather acknowledge ignorance than produce a confabulation. She still occasionally asked her husband in the morning whether she had to go to work, but easily accepted a negative response. The idea that she had to give a reception completely disappeared. Daily supervision was reduced and Mrs B stayed alone at home during much of the day.

Mrs B's case is a particularly striking example of reality distortion in memory: she confabulated events that had not taken place, falsely recognized people, and confused current reality with elements from the past. Yet none of these malfunctions of memory appeared to be random. Every false idea had a plausible trace in her past. But the most striking aspect of her memory problem was the conviction she held in her inappropriate plans: She was absolutely convinced about her perceived reality and acted according to it. Nothing and nobody could make her change her mind about where she was and what she had to do.

What is it that motivates patients like Mrs B to make up false stories about their recent doings and to produce plans for the future that are completely incompatible with their current status? What is it that prevents them from acting and thinking in accord with true ongoing reality?

Chapter 2

The history of confabulation

If the Internet and search engines had existed one hundred years ago, the terms 'confabulation, amnesia, disorientation' would have produced the response 'Korsakoff syndrome'. Sergei Sergeievich Korsakoff, a Russian psychiatrist born in 1854, was not the first to describe confabulations, but his persistence in promoting the peculiar memory disorder that he had observed in many alcoholic patients was second to none. He called the disorder 'polyneuritic psychosis or cerebropathia psychica toxaemica'. The term described the thought disorder (psychosis) in association with peripheral nerve inflammation (polyneuritis) giving rise to muscular weakness, all of it due to a poison (toxin), in most cases alcohol. Confabulations were called 'pseudo-reminiscences'.

Only a few years later, in the early 1900s, 'confabulations' and 'Korsakoff psychosis' were established entities. Karl Bonhoeffer (1901), in his classic monograph on 'The acute mental diseases of the habitual drinker', defined Korsakoff psychosis as the combination of

- ◆ a severe defect of learning,
- ◆ loss of memory for recent events,
- ◆ loss of orientation, and
- ◆ a strong tendency to confabulation (Bonhoeffer 1901, p. 119).

The term had been proposed by Friedrich Jolly, director of the Clinic for Psychiatry and Nervous Diseases at the famous Charité in Berlin. He had deemed it

> justified to link the whole peculiar appearance of the mental disorder [occurring in polyneuritis] with the name of the author who has the merit of bringing it to public attention.... Korsakoff symptom complex or, more concisely, Korsakoff syndrome.
>
> Jolly (1897, p. 595)

He noted that a similar disorder could be observed in senile dementia, after traumatic brain injury, and in general paralysis, the chronic encephalopathy resulting from syphilis. Bonhoeffer (1904), late successor of Jolly, suggested a further distinction. He proposed to use the term '*Korsakoff psychosis*' for cases in which the combination of symptoms was due to the abuse of alcohol, and to call it '*Korsakoff syndrome*' or '*Korsakoff symptom complex*' if it was due to other causes. Among these other causes figured arsenic or lead poisoning, the symptoms of senile dementia (Alzheimer's disease), syphilis, tumours, strangulation, carbon monoxide intoxication or cerebral commotion (traumatic brain injury). Thus, by 1901, Korsakoff's wish of 1890 had come true:

> The strange psychic disturbance, together with the manifestations on the part of the peripheral nervous system and the whole organism, provide the disease with such a characteristic picture that any physician, who has seen fully developed cases, must admit that it is absolutely desirable to separate the disease as a distinct entity.
>
> Korsakoff (1890a, p. 692)

Korsakoff's work

Bonhoeffer's monograph was published in 1901, 14 years after the start of a series of articles by Korsakoff.[1] The initial articles were written in Russian, followed by articles in German and French. In his doctoral thesis of 1887, entitled 'The disturbance of psychic activity in alcoholic paralysis and its relation to the disturbance of the psychic sphere in multiple neuritis of non-alcoholic origin', he described 20 patients and suggested that the psychic disturbance and the neuropathy had the same cause (summarized in Victor and Yakovlev 1955). In 1889, in an article entitled 'A few cases of peculiar cerebropathy associated with multiple neuritis', he added some new cases and made the observation that the psychic symptoms might occur without the neuropathy (summarized in Victor and Yakovlev 1955). His third article, written in 1889 in Russian, has come to fame because of its translation to English by Victor and Yakovlev (1955). In this article entitled 'Psychic disorder in conjunction with multiple neuritis (psychosis polyneuritica s. cerebropathia psychica toxaemica)', Korsakoff drew a detailed picture of the memory disorder, which, as he clearly stated, might occur in the context of many diseases, such as 'postpartum affections, typhoid, and the like'. The manifestations were manifold: they encompassed increased irritability, agitation, confusion, and, finally, 'a characteristic disturbance of memory – a peculiar form of amnesia'. In many patients, considerable confusion appeared:

> The patient begins to tell implausible stories about himself, tells of his extraordinary voyages, confuses old recollections with recent events, is unaware of where he is and who are the people around him ... Together with the confusion, a profound disorder of memory is nearly always observed ... [It is] an extraordinarily peculiar amnesia, in which the memory of recent events, that which just happened, is chiefly disturbed, whereas the remote past is remembered fairly well.
>
> Victor and Yakovlev (1955, p. 397f.)

[1] In his German and French articles, Korsakoff spelled his name both Korsakoff (1889, 1890a) and Korsakow (1890b, 1891).

Korsakoff also noted that in some patients, 'even the memory of remote events may be disturbed'. In such cases, he often observed that

> the patients confuse old recollections with the present impressions. Thus, they may believe themselves to be in the setting (or circumstance), in which they were some 30 years ago, and mistake persons, who are around them now, for people who were around them at the time.
>
> Victor and Yakovlev (1955, p. 398)

Regarding what he called 'confusion', Korsakoff explained:

> This confusion does not involve what the patient perceives at the present moment but affects only the recollection of the past events ... When asked to tell how he has been spending his time, the patient would very frequently relate a story altogether different from that which actually occurred; for example, he would tell that yesterday he took a ride to town, when in fact, he has been in bed for two months ... On occasion, such patients invent some fiction and constantly repeat it, so that a peculiar delirium develops, rooted in false recollection (pseudo-reminiscences).
>
> Victor and Yakovlev (1955, p. 399)

In his article, Korsakoff laid out a whole panoply of symptoms and signs encompassing acute confusion, disorientation, anterograde amnesia, retrograde amnesia, and confabulations resulting from diverse illnesses, of which alcoholism was just one. The same was true for his first article in German, published in 1890 (Korsakoff 1890a), where he summarized the cases of two patients described before in Russian ('My work has only scarcely been reported in German'), to whom he added four new observations. All of them had severe generalised illness and weakness; most were in a confusional state. Only two produced fairly stable confabulatory responses to questions, at least for a few days. Clearly, this was not yet Korsakoff syndrome as we know it.

The memory disorder came out more clearly in an article written in French, where Korsakoff (1889) described in detail a 37 year-old alcoholic Russian writer with a severe amnesia: 'He recounted things about himself that never happened, ... explained in detail where he had been the day before, details that were but the product of his imagination' (p. 503). Korsakoff gave an interpretation:

> He not only recalls facts, but also things said in his presence, possibly even his dreams, and all of this is now part of his consciousness; all of it presents but a chaos because, if he remembers something, he cannot decide whether it happened in reality or whether he dreamed it: The trace left by a real incident is only little different in intensity from the one left by a dream or an idea.
>
> Korsakoff (1889, p. 514)

This interpretation of pseudo-reminiscences has resurfaced in the modern literature under the term 'reality monitoring' or 'source monitoring', which will be discussed in Chapter 7.

Korsakoff (1889, p. 518) summarized his observations in this patient as follows:

1. Recent perceptions disappear almost immediately from memory;
2. The trace of an event nevertheless 'continues to exist in the unconscious, continues to guide the chain of ideas of the patient';
3. The memory of remote things which happened before the illness is sometimes perfectly preserved;
4. The different types of memories are not extinguished similarly easily…. The memory of habits persists for the longest period.

He concluded by giving an interpretation of the preservation of old memories, an interpretation which amazingly resembles at least one modern account – the Multiple Trace Theory (p. 225):

> The more associations being established between one impression and others, the more easy it becomes to recall it, because chances increase that the excitation will find on its way a group of neurons that have perceived the impression.
>
> Korsakoff (1889, p. 525)

Two years later, Korsakoff (1891) finally devoted a full article to the 'Illusions of memory (pseudo-reminiscences) in polyneuritic psychosis'. He described them as a:

> situation in which a patient conceives of an event that he has not really experienced but that has only come to his mind, as if it had really happened to him.
>
> Korsakoff (1891, p. 391)

He had observed that in some patients, false memories persisted in a very stable fashion, 'giving rise to more or less fixed delusion'. There were many causes for pseudo-reminiscences: They might occur in paranoia, melancholia, mania, progressive paralysis, and senile dementia, but also in polyneuritic psychosis. In the latter case, Korsakoff made a further observation:

> In polyneuritic psychosis, the pseudo-reminiscences are very often, if not always, rooted in real memories and thus appear as illusions of memory. As a consequence, their character differs between the patients. Patients who have been passionate hunters will talk about their adventures, like hunting, fishing and the like…. In many patients with polyneuritic psychosis, and independent of the diversity of their previous habits, one may encounter extraordinarily constant pseudo-reminiscences which always relate to funerals, deaths and the like.
>
> Korsakoff (1891, p. 394)

To make this point clear, Korsakoff described in detail a 53 year-old businessman who had contracted typhus, and was treated with leeches and lots of wine.

After an initial phase with high fever and obtundation, his general condition and memory improved, but pseudo-reminiscences occurred: 'Apart from other fantasies, which also emanated from the intermingling of old memories with current impressions, he repeatedly said that somebody had died and that there was a body somewhere that needed to be buried' (Korsakoff 1891, p. 396). This idea persisted for weeks, having 'the character of a completely fixed delusion which persistently imposed itself upon his consciousness'. An initial attempt to treat this delusion was undertaken by the relatives:

> The relatives hoped that it might give comfort to the patient if they gave him the opportunity to visit the house where he demanded to go. He was led to the street, which he had mentioned. At this house, he called the concierge and asked him about the whereabouts of the defunct. The concierge was of course astonished and replied that nobody had died in this house. The patient then returned to his home, contemplated for a long time and then modified his delusion in the following way: He now said that the deceased had already been buried, but that it was up to him [the patient] now to pay the rent for the apartment and the costs of the funeral.
>
> Korsakoff (1891, p. 396f.)

This idea persisted, and the patient

> was upset if he was told that it was not true …. Almost every day, the patient demanded to be escorted to the house so that he could pay his dues. His entourage had a very hard time not to give in, because he would turn exceedingly petulant.
>
> Korsakoff (1891, p. 398)

When Korsakoff explored the delusional ideas in more detail, he 'realised that the patient, despite his conviction to remember each and every detail, in reality only had very vague ideas about the allegedly deceased'. Nonetheless, the relatives provided Korsakoff with information about a period dating back seven to eight years, whose details indicated that the delusions were based on real events in the patient's past.

The last part of the case description is interesting as it reveals a concept of behavioural treatment that is still valid nowadays: it is often easier to accept such a patient's false reality than to argue about it. In Korsakoff's words, the concept reads like this:

> The patient became stronger and demanded even more vigorously to be led to the house. His relatives used a ruse: They prepared the concierge of the house to say that the owner of the apartment, which the patient looked for, had moved to another house – the house where the physician lived who had previously treated the patient. The patient went there and looked for his presumed creditor. He was directed towards one of the apartments, where he rang the bell and explained that he wanted to pay his debts. Here, too, it was prearranged what had to be answered; so, he was told that the man he sought was not at home but had given order that the money should

be received. The patient paid and quieted down for a couple of days. But after some time, he demanded again to meet the owner of the apartment to pick up the deceased person's bequest. He went there several times, rang and asked to see Mr. Medynzeff [owner of a house close to where the patient had rent an apartment seven to eight years previously]. He was finally told that Mr. M. had left the country. Only then did the patient calm down and cease to talk about this matter.... Around this period, the patient's memory and judgement had normalised to the point that he resumed his professional activities.

Korsakoff (1891, p. 398f.)

Korsakoff appeared to be impressed by the fact that 'whatever related to [the patient's] delusional idea consistently incited him to actions and did not get out of his mind' (p. 400). These ideas, which did not represent real events, provoked

the feeling of a reminiscence, ... rooted in the memory of some true events.... We may thus understand our patient's delusion as having emanated from illusions of memory.

Korsakoff (1891, p. 400f.)

Following the description of a second patient, presumably with psychotic delusions, Korsakoff (1891, p. 409f.) summarized his insights – and his vision – in a compelling list of ten points:

1. In polyneuritic psychosis, there are often illusions of memory with ensuing delusion.
2. This delusion can have the character of persistently changing confused speech, but it may also be monotonous and very stable.
3. One of the most typical contents of the delusions and the illusionary memories in polyneuritic psychosis is the topic of somebody's death, of deceased people, and of funerals.
4. Sometimes the pseudo-reminiscences and the resulting delusional ideas seize the patient's attention in a powerful way and then produce the picture of partial madness.
5. The pseudo-reminiscences in polyneuritic psychosis almost always root from the remains of some true memories.
6. The 'traces' of memories most likely reflect the continued function of nervous elements, albeit in extremely weak intensity.
7. It is accordingly possible to assume that latent traces unify into stable, associated groups.
8. Pseudo-reminiscences most likely emanate from connections of 'traces' within the unconscious sphere of the psyche into fairly stable associative groups. These stable associations, arisen in the unconscious sphere, can later become conscious and feign true memories.
9. It is very likely that the emergence of such associative groups, which may produce false memories, requires defects within the processes involved in the

association of ideas, whereby connections lacking some elements in the chain of associations become possible, elements which must not be missing under normal conditions of mental processing. Therefore, pseudo-reminiscences occur most often in those psychoses, which are associated with alteration of the processes of mental association.

10. Research on the connections among latent traces and the influence of latent (unconscious) traces on the flow of ideas might help to explain many interesting phenomena concerning normal and pathological psychology.

Korsakoff's synthesis of the characteristics of the memory disorder and the visionary deductions on the associative processes occurring in memory were astounding. Most of the patients that he described were confused and disoriented, had severe memory failures and inconsistently confabulated during limited periods of agitation or clouded consciousness in the course of acute illnesses – anything but a coherent amnesic state. From reading his case series, one gets the impression that Korsakoff derived his conclusions essentially from a few patients presenting a chronic course with a prolonged confabulatory phase and disorientation. It is not clear whether Korsakoff made the distinction between an acute confusional state and stable amnesia, but his synthesis remains amazingly perspicacious. His idea that confabulations (pseudo-reminiscences) resulted from a defect in the unconscious association of ideas has survived today, although nowadays this failure would be called a defect of constructive processes in memory.

Kraepelin's falsifications of memory

Falsifications of memories had been described under diverse headings and in various diseases before Korsakoff (Marková and Berrios 2000). Emil Kraepelin – nowadays considered the father of modern psychiatry, then a psychiatry trainee in Dresden – had used this term (*Erinnerungsfälschungen*) to describe three different disorders (Kraepelin 1886, 1887a, b): 'Simple falsifications of memory' would nowadays be called fantastic confabulation; 'associative falsifications of memory' stood for diverse complex phenomena, in particular misidentification syndromes, in which a patient feels inadequately familiar with strangers; 'identifying falsifications of memory' would nowadays be called déjà-vu, the strange feeling that one has already experienced exactly the same situation before. Of interest here are the simple falsifications of memory, a belittling term for a devastating derangement of thought, in which

constructs of fantasy with haphazard content – just as they are produced in the course of imaginations – enter consciousness just like that with the pretension of reminiscences

> .... The patients recount, mostly in the manner of fleeting ideas, a lot of adventures, stories from their life, namely, long journeys, wild pranks, meetings with famous and high-standing personalities, with the recounts lacking any relation with real events.
>
> Kraepelin (1886, pp. 831–3)

Kraepelin described twelve patients, five of them diagnosed with general paralysis (syphilitic encephalopathy). The first patient, representative of the whole group, was a 42-year-old man who was quoted as follows:

> From my period as Peter the Great, I have just received some of the nicest furs, including one which I will dedicate to His Highness the Emperor because I will become his chief of cabinet ... I make a number of heritages ... From England, I will receive my belongings as the King of England, Wilhelm of Orania 1618 and as the King of Spain and Italy ... I was a very happy emperor of Russia as Peter the Great ... I was Frederick the Great's twin brother of 3 February 1712 ... I also was with Christ on the cross ... I have already been Adam in Paradise, Hercules and Alexander in the battle of Gaugamela.

Kraepelin noted:

> Like that, the patient sometimes talks for hours with no interruption, wrapping up all his historical reminiscences in the form of personal experiences. It is very easy to guide him from one such memory illusion to the next
>
> Kraepelin (1886, p. 834)

Although most of his patients produced such fantastic, implausible confabulations, some still displayed

> a rich flow of ideas, masked by the remnants of an earlier higher education. One may start to doubt in such cases, to what degree the stories might indeed be true
>
> Kraepelin (1886, p. 838)

Kraepelin described very similar confabulations in four patients with 'chronic, incurable psychosis' and a man with senile dementia, and noted that mania could present with falsifications of memory 'resembling the ones observed in milder forms of general paralysis'. The most important cause clearly was general paralysis, the chronic brain disease following syphilis, in which, as he remarked, 'discrete cloudiness of consciousness and lack of correcting critique' (Kraepelin 1886, p. 841) favoured the formation of memory falsifications. He noted: 'The disease, in which the described conditions are by far most frequently realised, is paralytic dementia' (Kraepelin 1887a, p. 214).

In his legendary, multi-volume *Textbook of psychiatry*, Kraepelin (1910) emphasised the similarities between the demented form of general paralysis (paralytic dementia), Korsakoff psychosis in alcoholics, Korsakoff syndrome after brain trauma, and the memory disorder accompanying arteriosclerotic or senile 'mental disturbances' (presbyophrenia). After many years of experience, his description of paralytic dementia was particularly vivid. Although most patients had a severe learning deficit and disorientation, the lack of judgement evolving into insanity with 'silly blissfulness' appeared to be even more characteristic. Fleeting delusions of grandeur, paranoid delusions and hallucinations were common. Patients feared that they would die, be hanged, or be attacked by robbers. A patient might think that

> he was very beautiful and strong, could lift 400 kg, procreate a prince … that he was noble, a general, king of Berlin, professor for all domains, has 28 first names … 1000 elephants and three millions in his account. Every afternoon, he has his wedding, to which he invites all knights.
>
> Kraepelin (1910, p. 401)

A patient phoned his family to tell them about a great discovery he had made and then jumped out of the window in an attack of panic. Confabulations were abundant and associated with amnesia:

> The patients often start to fabulate in a senseless manner, talk about meetings with the emperor, the receipt of money, of a visit they have made the same morning. In some cases, the amnesia with or without falsifications of memory is so pre-eminent that a picture resembling Korsakoff disease results.
>
> Kraepelin (1910, p. 401)

The stories could be provoked by suggestive questions:

> The amenability of the memories to external incitement is only part of the general suggestibility in our patients' thinking. The evoked mental images are not strongly rooted and do not have a decisive influence on their ensuing thoughts and acts.
>
> Kraepelin (1910, p. 346)

Kraepelin's patients had a most pervasive derangement of thought with incoherent thinking and a profound lack of the sense of critique, and they produced fantastic, implausible confabulations, unlike the ones described by Korsakoff. Despite these differences, Kraepelin (1910) warned: 'It may occasionally be of considerable difficulty to distinguish, from the clinical picture alone, a terminal Korsakoff psychosis with advanced imbecility from [paralytic dementia]' (p. 183). This distinction rested much more upon other indices – clinical course, physical signs, and laboratory findings – than the mental picture (Kraepelin 1926).

As to the mechanism of falsifications of memory, Kraepelin (1886) suspected that

> the true fond of memories [should normally] provide the weapons to control fantasy with the sense of critique.... [In the patients] the sense of critique, which guides the weapons that should distinguish between fantasy and reality, is put out of order.
>
> Kraepelin (1926, p. 838)

Nowadays, these 'weapons' are called 'monitoring'. Indeed, as we will see in Chapter 7, many modern authors interpret confabulations in terms of defective monitoring processes. We will see in the next chapter that Kraepelin later replaced the term 'simple falsifications of memory' by 'confabulation' and then ardently promoted another mechanism, namely, that confabulations served the purpose of filling gaps in memory (Kraepelin 1909).

Contested novelty

Plausible confabulations, similar to the ones described by Korsakoff, had also been reported before. Kalberlah (1904) quoted 'the often cited cases' that Wille apparently reported at a meeting in 1878. The quotation given by Kalberlah (*Archiv für Psychiatrie und Nervenkrankheiten*, vol. 8), however, does not lead very far: the only reference to Wille in this volume can by found in the proceedings of the meeting, where Wille is listed as one of the excused members. Be that as it may, Kalberlah described in some detail the four patients of Wille, all of them having suffered traumatic brain injury. After two to four weeks, two of them 'tried to fill their defects in memory with voluntary fantastic narratives that they presented with such vividness that, without a doubt, they were subjectively entirely convinced about their veracity' (Kalberlah 1904, p. 425). Three of the patients recovered within six months; 'only one case remained mentally confused, full of delusional ideas'.

Perhaps Kalberlah quoted Wille so extensively to avoid blame for the type of non-feasance that most authors bitterly resent: not being justly quoted. Theodor Tiling, director of the 'madhouse' (mental home) at Riga, Latvia, reproached exactly this to Korsakoff in 1892. In his article 'On the amnesic mental disturbance', Tiling (1892) bitterly complained about Korsakoff for having written in 1891 that he, Tiling, had falsely stated in an earlier article (Tiling 1890) that the psychic disorder seen in alcoholic paralysis could not occur in other diseases.

Korsakoff's remark was formally correct. Tiling (1890) had indeed only described patients with alcoholic neuritis and stated that 'only alcoholic neuritis is regularly associated with the characteristic amnesic mental disorder' (p. 246). However, Korsakoff's remark was also unfair: Tiling's goals had been to differentiate alcoholic neuritis from other neuropathies, to emphasise the association between the amnesic disorder and the neuropathy, and to fight off the idea that 'the mental disorder and other cerebral symptoms [constituted only] fortuitous complications, caused by alcoholism' (p. 233). Perhaps it would have been better for Korsakoff to support Tiling's statement. In the years to come, the search for 'polyneuritic psychosis' was so eagerly pursued that many authors used the term 'Korsakoff symptom complex' for any type of mental confusion occurring in combination with muscular weakness, e.g., to describe 'disturbed memory for recent events, confusion, and fearful agitation' in association with pregnancy and labour (Von Hösslin 1905, p. 544). Irrespective of whether Korsakoff's remark of 1891 was justified or not, by 1892 he was already the reference for the memory disorder which now bears his name.

Tiling (1892) countered Korsakoff's remark by the description of three patients with typhus, senile forgetfulness, and brain trauma, all of whom filled gaps in memory with excuses and jokes – 'a wild mixture of true memories'. His first patient was a 45-year-old woman, sick with typhus, febrile, and vomiting for weeks. After two months, she had agitation and disorientation, which were particularly marked during the night. She mixed recent events and confused time and place. At three months, her general condition improved although she had severe muscle wasting. She rapidly forgot the date and the names of people but seemed to be aware of this difficulty, 'She realised her inability to remember the date and names and often remarks 'oh, my memory is so weak, but everything will be okay.' She tried to fill the gaps also with stereotyped questions and jocular remarks, such as, 'Ain't it true, you will soon let me return to Moscow', or: 'Well, seems I will soon be up again, I guess you let me get up tomorrow?' (Tiling 1892, p. 533).

Tiling acknowledged that the features of this case corresponded to neuritis multiplex, as described by Korsakoff, but he profoundly disagreed with Korsakoff on the presumed toxic mechanism. His main argument was that the same mental disturbance could also occur in old age and after head trauma. In this context, it is interesting to note that the idea of a toxic mechanism continued to haunt the minds of clinicians: Benon and le Huché (1920) suggested an alcoholic-toxic origin of the Korsakoff syndrome following traumatic brain injury, and in 1939, Tarachow (1939) suggested that haemolysed blood might act as the toxic agent causing Korsakoff syndrome after subarachnoid haemorrhage.

Tiling (1892) took his attack even a step further by questioning the very novelty of Korsakoff syndrome:

> In earlier articles, Korsakoff has even claimed that the psychosis can occur entirely in the form of confusion, where the amnesia does not play any significant role … although in most cases the amnesia will become evident after an initial state of agitation and confusion. One has to object to these claims, that there is nothing characteristic [to this disorder]. The described manifestations may appear in the context of many psychoses.
>
> Tiling (1892, p. 556)

He then explained:

> In all cases, one has to wait for the cessation of the confusion and agitation before it is
> possible to establish pure amnesia, with no falsification of consciousness by delu-
> sional ideas. But Korsakoff has described cases in whom the initial confusion and
> agitation continued until their death, and in these cases, in my opinion, the diagnosis
> remains undecided.

Tiling (1892, p. 556)

It appears that Tiling made the distinction between three disorders: delusional ideas during a confusional state, pure amnesia, and a continued delusional state.

His second case was a 76-year-old woman with increasing forgetfulness over six to seven years who was eventually institutionalized. The patient appeared to be comfortable with her stay at the hospital, but did not know where she was and did not become acquainted with the personnel. She seemed to be embarrassed by questions about her family. She would immediately forget what had been said, but tried to conceal the defect in her memory with little jokes or excuses, and to avoid questions which she could not answer with conventional phrases that she used quite skilfully: 'Wait a moment, what was it? – I have totally forgotten; it was certainly nothing important' (Tiling, 1892, p. 559).

Brain autopsy revealed the typical features of a degenerative disease, in view of the clinical history most likely Alzheimer's disease.

The main case of the article was the third one, giving rise to a particularly elaborate discussion. It was the case of a 31-year-old policeman who, while riding in a drunken state, fell from his horse and had to be resuscitated. One or two days later, he came out of coma. After one month, mental disturbances appeared in the form of loud, convoluted gibberish and motor agitation, and the patient 'notably wanted to leave the clinic'. Tiling described him as bold and direct, negligent, highly euphoric and devoid of any insight into his state of health; the memory for the past was preserved up to a certain point in time, events of the last weeks were freely mingled, and he was totally disoriented with regards to place and time' (p. 560).

In response to questions, the patient contrived elaborate stories reflecting his conviction to be on duty or to have been hunting the day before. 'He repeats this hunting story a number of times and often leaves his bedroom to do business ... On another occasion, he believes to have had a fight at a brothel' (Tiling 1892, p. 561). Seven weeks after the accident, the patient recited all events in an orderly fashion and indicated that his head had been full of wild thoughts, that he had seen pictures of sensuous clarity that could impossibly be true and real (p. 561). He continued to make false statements about invitations that he pretended to have received and he lacked a sense of critique.

Tiling (1892) summarized his observations as follows:

> Thus, the mental disturbance consisted in a haphazard shuffling of real experiences and in the total inability to maintain orientation, once regained … His recollection was falsified by the intermingling of remote and recent events. Everything that was available in his memory lacked chronological order.

Tiling concluded:

> Such a complicated state cannot be explained by the sole disturbance of memory; instead, the other mental capacities were also impaired in many ways … Apart from the forgetting of facts, all affects and interests, as well as his sense of critique were weakened … Insight and self-critique have suffered … After all, the lack of memory is the most obvious feature because it is the inability to retain facts and their chronological order which is most troubling.
>
> Tiling (1892, p. 563)

Tiling was probably the first to make a distinction between a confusional state, amnesia, and stable delusional ideas – the term that he used to describe confabulations. No one before him so prominently described the loss of temporal order in thinking. He may also have been the first to posit mental failures in addition to amnesia as a necessary condition for confabulations to occur – a precursor of the executive hypothesis of confabulation, one of the most influential theories into our days.

Bonhoeffer's résumé

In his monograph *The acute mental diseases of the habitual drinker*, Karl Bonhoeffer (1901) separated acute and chronic disease states and added the distinction between different forms of confabulation. He distinguished a first phase with an acute confusional state, the 'delirium tremens', from a subsequent chronic delirium, Korsakoff psychosis. He noted that patients in the acute delirium tremens often had visual hallucinations, in particular animal visions, which could easily be induced by suggestion. Memory for earlier personal events was typically preserved but 'the sense of the temporal order is severely impaired during the delirium' (1901, p. 31). 'The confusion of place and environment, and to a certain degree also time, is a constant finding – [the patients are] disoriented' (1901, p. 35). He also recognized another typical feature:

> Spontaneously, too, the delirious person has a strong tendency to produce momentary confabulations [*Augenblickskonfabulationen*] … These confabulations out

of embarrassment [*Verlegenheitskonfabulationen*] are in no way different from the false memories observed in other psychoses with severe memory defects, such as, Korsakoff psychosis and senile memory weakness ... This type of confabulation has to be separated from false memories generated on the basis of hallucinations, [which often have] a fantastic content and stable character.

Bonhoeffer (1901, p. 32)

According to Bonhoeffer, this phase, in which the patients also had a peculiar urge to move, normally lasted for three to five days and was followed by deep sleep. Complications such as pneumonia and gastrointestinal problems were frequent and mortality could be as high as 24 per cent. Bonhoeffer seemed to deplore that after 8 to 14 days at the hospital, most patients had to be dismissed: 'At that moment, the obvious residues of the delirium have disappeared but the drinker is entirely unable to resist alcohol' (Bonhoeffer 1901, p. 118).

Bonhoeffer noted that only three percent of the acute deliria evolved into a chronic delirium – Korsakoff psychosis – with 'gross defects of learning, loss of the memory for the recent past, loss of orientation, and a strong tendency to confabulate' (1901, p. 119). In this state, hallucinations were much less frequent. Confabulations might contain elements from the delirious phase. Bonhoeffer distinguished two forms of confabulations in the chronic stage of the disease:

1. *Confabulations out of embarrassment* [*Verlegenheitskonfabulationen*], which are direct consequences of the memory loss. A comparison with cases who do not confabulate despite learning deficits reveals that a second element is necessary [for the occurrence of confabulations, namely] a certain attentiveness and mental agility [*geistige Regsamkeit*]. The patients try to hide a gap in memory, exposed by a question, by means of an ad hoc confabulated pretext ... The patient is convinced about the reality of his story.
2. Confabulations going beyond the state of emergency created by the memory failure. The patient spontaneously recounts adventures [for example, that] he has seen a tiger, crocodile or that he has been to Africa or India ... These *fantastic confabulations* may dominate the clinical picture. They resemble delirious, dream-like states, but also fantastic delusions of grandeur.

Bonhoeffer (1901, p. 133f.)

Thus, Bonhoeffer suggested that confabulations out of embarrassment or momentary confabulations required – in addition to a loss of memory – the preservation of a mental function: preserved 'mental agility'. This was, so to say, the opposite of the dysexecutive hypothesis, first proposed by Tiling (1892), which supposed that the occurrence of confabulation required defective mental control processes in addition to a loss of memory. In contrast, Bonhoeffer interpreted fantastic confabulations as the remnants of hallucinations in the confusional state.

The course of the disease was described as often protracted, whereas the neuritis recovered within a few months:

> It may take years until orientation is regained. In any case, recovery takes several months, once the amnesic symptom complex has fully developed. Recovery may proceed to the point where the patients can be sent back to their families. [But] I have never seen full recovery … Even in cases with favourable outcome, a memory impairment persisted which could mostly be directly demonstrated during the examination and in any case revealed itself in daily life as a forgetfulness interfering with a professional activity. A few patients tried to resume their old profession after leaving the hospital but soon revealed themselves as insufficient.
>
> Bonhoeffer (1901, p. 143)

Bonhoeffer also gave some advice on memory training for such patients:

> Memory exercises that one may contemplate are useless in the initial phase and therefore have to be avoided. As time goes by and learning capacity improves and the patient starts building up a coherent idea of the situation, one may try to support this process. It is better not to do this with memory exercises but by engaging the patient in simple activities, tidying, cleaning etc.
>
> Bonhoeffer (1901, p. 168)

Bonhoeffer's monograph is remarkable in any sense, not only by the sheer wealth of information, but especially by the smooth integration of his own observations with the literature, the depth and the breadth of the analysis, and the clarity of his statements. He also insisted that Korsakoff symptom complex was not specific to alcohol abuse but might occur in the context of many diseases, a point he made again in a later publication (Bonhoeffer 1904). Other contemporary authors supported this view. Meyer and Raecke (1903), after describing eight patients, concluded: 'Korsakoff symptom complex is not a disease on its own. In any case, it is not exclusively an alcoholic psychosis.'

Traumatic Korsakoff syndrome

The similarity between the chronic alcoholic delirium and the memory disorder sometimes occurring after traumatic brain injury came out very clearly in Kalberlah's (1904) article 'On the acute concussion psychosis, together with a contribution on the aetiology of Korsakoff symptom complex'. He described a 43-year-old construction worker, who had fallen five metres from a pile of bricks to the floor. For days, he was severely obtunded, then agitated, especially during the night. After two weeks, he was disoriented, did not know where he was and believed that he had been at home the day before. He gave precise accounts of his family life, the names and birthdays of his children. He had anosmia: that is, he had lost the sense of smell and did not perceive odours anymore, a sign highly indicative of a contusion at the base of the frontal lobes, the orbitofrontal cortex (anosmia results from disruption of olfactory fibres sheared between the orbitofrontal cortex and the skull). A few days later, the patient appeared talkative, completely disoriented, with severe memory impairment. Although he did not remember the accident and the time following it, he had a 'tendency to fill these gaps with confused, contradictory stories' (Kalberlah 1904, p. 411). This state, described in detail, continued for almost two months. The patient had no insight at all and his talkativeness was considered most annoying. He denied having had an accident and tried to prove the correctness of his statements by asking for his [note]books (p. 403). Even his wife could not convince him of the reality of his accident.

> By all means, the certainty and decisiveness, as well as the liveliness and apparently plastic, deeply felt conviction, with which he produces his weird confabulations, are remarkable. He loves to broadly expose his stories, to recount many names and details ... and always wants to prove the veracity of his point by seeking his papers. If one were not perplexed by the many temporal contradictions, one would easily take his stories for true.
>
> Kalberlah (1904, p. 415)

After more than two months, orientation improved and the patient appeared less and less convinced about the veracity of his confabulations. Shortly after, confabulations disappeared despite persisting amnesia. After almost four months, the patient left the hospital. His behaviour remained very problematic, characterized by lack of reliability, obtrusiveness, talkativeness, exaggerated self-esteem and insulting remarks. He was readmitted two months later, five months after the accident.

In his conclusions, Kalberlah recalled the main observations of this case: disorientation for almost two months; no hallucinations; severe learning deficit; and retrograde amnesia, which was initially extended but then shrank to a period of two years before the accident. As to the confabulations, Kalberlah resumed:

> They mostly turned around his occupation as a mason and his medical history and for the most part seemed to be rooted in real experiences and events and essentially served to plausibly fill the amnesic gaps. He was hardly ever spontaneously confabulating, and his stories never appeared senseless, absurd or adventurous but always remained within certain possible boundaries. However, they were always of remarkable plastic coherence and liveliness and produced with obvious inner conviction.
>
> Kalberlah (1904, p. 421)

Kalberlah's paper has the merit of sorting out the elements of Korsakoff symptom complex after traumatic brain injury and of precisely describing the clinical course and the transition out of the confabulatory state despite persistent severe amnesia. He also cogently described the disturbing personality disorder, which is nowadays recognized as a characteristic sequel of severe orbitofrontal contusion. In addition, he pointed out the plausibility and pervasiveness of the confabulations with disorientation, the sense of veracity associated with them, and the dominance that they held in the patient's thinking, repeatedly motivating his active search for materials to prove the truthfulness of his stories.

The sole traumatic cause – as opposed to some toxic mechanism – of this form of Korsakoff syndrome was not universally accepted. Also, future definitions of the Korsakoff syndrome were adapted to include features typical of traumatic brain injury, but different from alcoholic Korsakoff psychosis. Sixteen years after Kalberlah, Benon and LeHuché (1920) extensively described the case of a 28-year-old corporal of the French army during the First World War. During a holiday, he had an accident with his bicycle and suffered traumatic brain injury with two days of coma. After two weeks with somnolence, urinary incontinence, and severe confusion, the typical manifestations of Korsakoff syndrome appeared. The most impressive one, listed first by the authors, was *confabulations*. These were described as

> extremely developed, rich and varied … If one talks to him about his accident and how this could happen to him, he immediately gives numerous imaginary details: 'Yes, I jumped three times from a plane, and I think it was on the first one that I hurt myself … We chased a plane. There were six of them, and I shot down four; the fifth one hit me. I fell from 4000 metres above ground. My tank was penetrated. I jumped towards another French plane but failed to catch it and fell from 3000 meters. I descended with my parachute and my straw hat.
>
> Benon and LeHuché (1920, p. 318)

Sometimes, the patient would change his story and think that he fell from a car. The patient, held at a military hospital, considered himself to be on military duty. And he acted accordingly:

> One morning, he says spontaneously to the sergeant on duty:… 'Let's go! We leave today for machine gun training. The general has told me to do so in the hallway in the morning at three o'clock.'
>
> Benon and LeHuché (1920, p. 318)

The second feature mentioned after the confabulations was anterograde amnesia, which was described as 'more or less complete'. Under this heading, the authors again described false ideas: The patient believed that he had received a letter announcing a visit of his fiancée or other family members. On other occasions, he believed that he had to go to work. Disorientation, too, was listed under 'amnesia' but was not considered a serious finding:

> He knows approximately the year (very often says 1915 instead of 1916), the month (may say interchangeably June, May, April); he does not know the day of the month ... Sometimes he correctly recalls the name of the hospital and the town.
>
> Benon and LeHuché (1920, p. 318)

Finally, there was retrograde amnesia, covering four or five days before the accident, whereas the evocation of more remote events was perfect: 'The observer detects neither errors of time nor errors of place' (p. 319). The third feature of the patient's disorder was false familiarity with people:

> He [pretends to] know every person approaching him. He recognizes the physician treating him from the 65th front regiment. The medical student accompanying the physician is recognized as a man from his own company ... If one asks him for a proof, he immediately provides it in the form of imaginary and fantastic recitations that he insists are true. He gets upset or ridicules people raising doubts [about the veracity of his stories]; more often, he will simply turn conversation to another topic.
>
> Benon and LeHuché (1920, p. 319)

A final characteristic was that the patient was 'usually euphoric, as it is typically the case in Korsakoff syndrome'.

Relying on their experience with patients having traumatic brain injury, Benon and LeHuché (1920) added some features to the classic description of Korsakoff syndrome: 'The characteristic signs of Korsakoff syndrome are the amnesia of fixation, confabulation, false recognition or paragnosia, euphoria, intellectual excitation, etc.' (p. 321). They proposed to separate Korsakoff psychosis, 'a malady of memory', from mental confusion, 'an alteration of perceptions and sensations in general' (p. 322). They did not trust in a traumatic mechanism alone. Rather, they suspected alcohol abuse as a causative agent:

> Without a doubt, the majority of posttraumatic Korsakoff syndromes occur in subjects whose organism has undergone alcoholic impregnation. Is alcoholism a predisposing factor, and the cranial trauma the momentary cause? ... [And what about] infectious elements ... especially when there are injuries of the head or body? The facts are clear; their aetiology is obscure.
>
> Benon and LeHuché (1920, p. 321)

Benon and LeHuché's (1920) case, and in particular Kalberlah's (1904) article, established Korsakoff syndrome as a sequel of traumatic brain injury, be it alone or in conjunction with some additional influence. Both articles highlighted the pervasiveness of the confabulations with disorientation and the dominance they held in the patients' thinking, repeatedly motivating their behaviour. However, they did not speculate about the mechanism of the confabulations. Kalberlah called them confabulations out of embarrassment, serving the purpose of filling gaps in memory.

Pick's suggestion of suggestibility

Indeed, by 1905, this mechanism was so largely accepted that Arnold Pick (1905) made it part of the definition of confabulation. In a review 'On the psychology of confabulation', he wrote:

> Whereas the clinical facets of the filling of gaps in memory by falsifications of souvenirs – a sum of partially disparate processes, which I want to summarize for brevity as confabulation – have been intensively studied, there has been only little consideration of the psychological foundation of this phenomenon.
>
> Pick (1905, p. 509)

Pick noted a dissociation between the defect in memory and confabulation: 'This observation alone allows one not to consider the lack of memory as an essential cause of confabulation' (p. 510). He perceived a number of conditions for the occurrence of confabulations after brain trauma (p. 511f.):

- increased suggestibility, induced by the trauma;
- clouding of consciousness;
- weakness of judgement.

He suggested that confabulations only occurred if these conditions were met. He quoted other authors who had arrived at the conclusion that the central motivation to confabulate laid in a patient's 'compulsion to fill the gaps in his memory … The pseudo-reminiscences are explained by the unconscious desire to fill the gaps in memory' (p. 514). Pick quoted Höffting to explain the cause of this desire:

> Any emerging sensation or imagination will push the desire for imaginations in a certain direction, according to the laws of association. Thus, if the energy of consciousness is not weakened, any imagination will set in motion a series of images'. Thence arises the desire to broadly fill the gaps in memory.
>
> Pick (1905, p. 515)

In a later article, introduced as a complement to this first one, Pick (1921) reaffirmed the crucial role of suggestibility for the occurrence of confabulation. Suggestibility would create a tendency to fill gaps in memory with plausible material. Pick likened this process to other physiological processes such as the filling of the blind spot in vision. He did not explain the mechanism of the suggestibility itself, stating only that it was 'arising in the most diverse ways' (Pick 1921, p. 316). Although Pick's article was no easy read, and certainly no model for a coherent argument, it conveyed at least some ideas about how Pick figured the workings of suggestibility, a process he considered to be very fast. He quoted Jakob Segal's (1916) 'On the imagination of objects and situations' to explain that the quality of a memory is often attained before an imagination has reached its full clarity.

> 'Even before the situation appears clearly in one's mind, the warmth, familiarity, recognition, the knowledge that one has experienced the event in the past, is already and instantaneously there' (Segal 1916, p. 467). This is so important for [our discussion of confabulation] because it helps us understand how the suggestion alone – be it autosuggestion or suggestion by others – that one has already experienced something, may suffice to produce the character of a memory which then attaches itself to whatever imagination arises from fantasy.
>
> Pick (1921, p. 318f.)

In the introduction to the paper, Pick (1921) even speculated about the qualities characterizing a memory as a personal memory. He referred to Linke's (1918) 'Principles of perception', and the idea of an 'individuality index' in thinking, a term denoting in this context something like the intensity with which a memory or thought is perceived as an individual part within the flow of memories.

> The experiences imagined in fantasy – the material of confabulations – attain by the attribution of a defined temporal position also immediately the seeming features of a natural individuality index which thereby imposes itself on the sick person as a pertinent element of the experience. The experience thus obtains for [the patient] the quality of a memory; an act imagined in fantasy has turned into one relating to a [real] memory.
>
> Pick (1921, p. 314f.)

Pick's ideas derived from his profound knowledge of the psychological literature rather than scientific, let alone experimental, evidence. Nonetheless, his latter statements vaguely foreshadowed the idea of defective 'source monitoring' and of a defective preconscious process, which normally filters upcoming thoughts according to their relation with ongoing reality. We will discuss these mechanisms of confabulation in Chapters 7 and 8. Pick's insistence on the role of suggestibility and gap-filling for the production of confabulations was so overwhelming that his idea of an inappropriate individuality index of confabulated memories soon sank into oblivion – a fate probably supported by the complexity of the manuscript. Pick thought that his considerations particularly pertained to confabulation out of embarrassment. In his previous article (Pick 1905), he had made the distinction between spontaneous and provoked confabulations, noticing that spontaneous confabulations were less frequent. Such distinctions did not appear to be essential for him; on the contrary, he was convinced that 'it should not be difficult to demonstrate the effectiveness of this mode of filling gaps in memory for other cases [of false memories]' (Pick 1921, p. 317). Notably, he thought that 'the whole question of confabulation [was also] of medico–legal importance' (p. 319), a notion we will return to in Chapter 6.

Fine distinctions

The question of whether there were distinct types of confabulations, so insignificant for Pick, was at the centre of Moll's work. In a review on the alcoholic Korsakoff syndrome, to which he added some brief case vignettes, Moll (1915) proposed a very fine-grained distinction of confabulations. In his discussion of the chronic amnesic stage he listed four symptoms:

1. impairment of impressionability;
2. disorientation, which he considered a direct sequel of the first symptom;
3. anterograde and retrograde amnesia; and
4. 'fabrications or fictions', which he considered a very striking part of the syndrome. 'These are false statements, inventions made by the patient, who is convinced at the time of their truth.'

Moll distinguished five types of fabrications (p. 428f):

1. Random fabrications: The patient tries to fill out the amnesic gap by an invention ad hoc;
2. Distorted recollections of real facts, pseudo-reminiscences;
3. True recollections of real facts, incorrectly oriented in place and time; this is especially seen in those cases where the chronological faculty has suffered;
4. Fabrications based on hallucinations, mostly found in the acute stage;
5. Remnants of dreams.

Most notably, Moll observed that

> the contents of these false statements are usually within the bounds of the conceivable; the influence of former habits and of emotional complexes is evident

> Moll (1915, p. 429)

Like earlier authors, he did not discuss whether he considered the five forms of fabrications as different manifestations of a common cognitive disorder or whether he had observed dissociations between them.

Mechanisms beyond gap-filling

Van der Horst (1932) was likely the first to claim different mechanisms for two forms of confabulations, which he considered to be independent:

> If a patient with Korsakoff syndrome does not remember what has happened just before and is embarrassed by this, then it is conceivable that he tries to fill these gaps (the so-called *out-of-embarrassment confabulation* [*Verlegenheitskonfabulation*]), but it is not intelligible how one might deduce from this amnesia the *productive confabulations* which are so common in Korsakoff patients.

> Van der Horst (1932, p. 68)

He observed that these patients were badly oriented regarding time and place, failed to estimate the time passed, and often had a peculiar amnesia for the time when an event occurred: 'The event itself is well remembered, but the temporal label has been lost (p. 70).... The impressions, experiences, lose their temporal tag' (p. 73)'. He suggested that this defect induced an inability to experience continuity in time: 'If one fails to put the present [*das Heute*] in the right order, it will not take long until it becomes difficult to maintain the order in the past' (Van der Horst 1932, p. 77). Van der Horst did not provide strong evidence for his claim – he very briefly alluded to six patients that he had examined and who had such diverse diagnoses as syphilis, Alzheimer's disease, uraemia (renal insufficiency), traumatic brain injury, and post alcoholic polyneuritis. Despite this the paper has become a classic; Van der Horst is considered the father of the 'temporality hypothesis' of confabulation.

Up to this time, studies on confabulation had consisted of clinical observations of single patients or series of patients. Williams and Rupp (1938) were probably the first to use a more systematic approach including what they called an 'improvised battery of test questions ... about 50 in number, covering salient facts regarding birth place, parents, school, marital and occupational experiences as well as orientation ... Confabulatory tendencies were elicited by questions inquiring about the patient's activities and experiences during the period of amnesia', Williams and Rupp (1938, p. 397).

The series was comprised of 13 patients with diverse diagnoses (Korsakoff psychosis, intracranial neoplasm, cerebral arteriosclerosis, acute syphilitic encephalopathy, general paralysis), of whom seven confabulated. Although no precise results were provided, the authors concluded that the development of confabulation had three conditions:

> 1. A basic factor in the development of confabulation is the memory disturbance ... The involvement of memory must be of such degree that recent memories are more or less completely disturbed ... [However] if the remote memories are

almost completely destroyed, confabulation seemingly does not occur though other pertinent factors for the development of confabulation are present.

2. In addition to the retrogressive amnesia, lack of insight is necessary to the development of confabulation.

3. [However] the interreaction of memory involvement and the lack of insight is not adequate to evoke confabulation. The other requisite factors pertain to the personality organization of the individual … [Confabulating] individuals had distinct tendencies toward intraversion … in the sense that they were persons who had great resistance to imparting to others their innermost thoughts … They were individuals who were incapable or unwilling to observe themselves objectively … an exaggerated tendency to self deception… Also they did display extraversion tendencies. They are superficially very sociable, the sort of persons who can strike up conversation with a stranger readily … With the development of impaired memory, such individuals are thrown into a dilemma to retain that position of balance they have valued between tendencies toward extremes of intraversion and extraversion with their overtone of indifference to or rejection of body consciousness. They solve this dilemma by confabulation.

Williams and Rupp (1938, p. 397ff.)

Thus, for the first time, personality was considered an essential factor for the generation of confabulation; whether this concerned the premorbid or morbid personality, was not specified. Regarding the plausibility of confabulations and their source, they observed that

at first glance the confabulatory productions appear to possess a vividness and colourfulness suggestive of a flight of imagination into the realm of the bizarre and fantastic … [that] suggests a verbal realization of long-standing desires. Such, however, is not the case for after verification of the facts from trustworthy relatives and acquaintances, it is apparent that these vivid experiences are actual incidents, which have occurred in the life of a confabulator. In each instance, no matter how bizarre or unusual the content of the confabulation, it has been possible to show, that at some time or other in the course of the patient's life the confabulatory experience has actually occurred and never has the confabulation been a pure fiction emanating from the imagination. Much of the vividness of the confabulation arises from the juxtaposition in time of a colourful past contrasted with an uneventful present.

Williams and Rupp (1938, p. 401)

Williams and Rupp also commented on Van der Horst's (1932) idea about the loss of a temporal tag:

Van der Horst's statement that severe disturbances in time perception occur in these cases appears … substantially correct. That such a disturbance in itself is sufficient to produce confabulation, we are inclined to doubt. Inability to measure passage of time in the present, and to allocate past experiences in time is commonly encountered in those patients suffering from a memory disturbance on an arterio-sclerotic or senile basis. Yet, these patients do not consistently confabulate.

Williams and Rupp (1938, p. 403)

Thus, in contrast to Van der Horst, Williams and Rupp, like many authors before them, considered the chronological confusion of memories in confabulations as a characteristic rather than a cause of the confabulations. In their view, the real cause of confabulation was to be searched in the memory disorder and the personality pattern, a combination they suggested as a definition: 'Confabulation may be defined as the tendency of individuals of a particular personality pattern with incomplete memory loss, to substitute retained for forgotten experiences irrespective of time sequence' (1938, p. 404).

The model of Williams and Rupp is interesting in that it demanded a delicate balance between deficits and personality traits: there had to be amnesia, but not too much, introversion, but also extraversion, and lack of insight. At the same time, the model was compatible with Van der Horst's idea of temporal confusion in memory and with the memory-gap-filling account: 'The confabulator fills in the memory gaps with events of yesteryear as if they were but of yesterday' (Williams and Rupp 1938, p. 402).

Satisfaction by gap-filling

Gap-filling was indeed the most popular account of confabulation at the time, although it had never been specifically tested nor specified. Almost 20 years after Williams and Rupp, Flament (1957) gave a new twist to the meaning of gap-filling. He described a 41-year-old woman with traumatic brain injury following a fall from a horse. After initial confusion, the patient confounded people, falsely recognizing her hospital neighbour as her daughter, and severely confabulated. For weeks, her confabulations turned around two topics, namely, an imagined stay in Congo, where she had never been but had friends, and about her five children, although in reality, she had only one child. Flament also heard implausible stories: the patient talked about an airplane accident during which she allegedly was ejected from the plane, made a free fall of 1000 metres, and landed on a big cactus. She recovered from her confabulatory state within two months. Based on this observation, Flament proposed the distinction between two forms of confabulations: classic compensatory confabulations and confabulations having fantastic characteristics.

In this classification, the '*classic compensatory confabulations*' were described as being

> usually induced rather than spontaneous … The material of this fallacious construction of the present and of this pseudo-evocation of the recent past are representations which very often are memory fragments of a subject's real experiences in the past. But, due to the disorder of the 'temporalization of the contents of consciousness' which many, based on Van der Horst's work, accept as fundamental to this syndrome, these representations would be deprived of their 'temporal tag', and the memories of the events that they emanate from are loosened from the chronological context

within which these events have been experienced and memorized … In most con-fabulatory behaviours, the role of imagination concerns the encompassing scenario and its artificialities but hardly ever the creation of the material for the confabulation, which mostly emanates from past personal experiences. Hence comes the 'plausibility' noted by most authors and the 'compensatory' character attributed to the confabulation … Considering this plausibility as the consequence of a certain 'intentionality', similar to considering that the patient 'fills gaps in his memory', might imply some contradictions if this 'intentionality' were meant to be deliberate and situated at the level of consciousness. Indeed, most often, there is no clear consciousness at all of the severe dysfunction of memorization and rem-embrance. In general, the subjects give proof of total ignorance about the situation. In these conditions, it is difficult to ascertain an intentionality in this 'compensatory' property of confabulation.

Flament (1957, pp. 137–8)

Flament suggested that compensatory confabulation related primarily to fragile memories and offered the 'hypothesis according to which … the quan-tity of confabulatory activity is by and large complementary to the amount of possible remembrance' (p. 141). As we will see in Chapter 5, this hypothesis does not hold.

The second type of confabulation, more perplexing, was the one with a *fantastic character*, composed of unreal, imaginary productions. With respect to his patient claiming a fall from an airplane over 1000 metres, Flament (1957) suspected: 'The circumstances of the [patient's] real accident are rather humiliating and upsetting. A stupid accident which the patient is responsible for' (p. 144). He suggested that in such a context

compensatory confabulations might serve a different purpose: By means of its more or less rewarding contents on behalf of the subject, confabulation of this type might compensate not only for a lacuna in memory but in part for a personal situation of inferiority and regression created in a general sense by the consequences of the trauma … In most instances, these mechanisms are unconscious, related to mechanisms of defence (negation, rationalizations) normally considered in psychoanalysis.

Flament (pp. 144–5)

Flament's interpretation of confabulation, in particular fantastic confabula-tion, thus transcended the simple notion of 'filling gaps in memory': confabu-lations not only fill gaps in memory but also provide satisfaction. As we will see in Chapter 7, this idea has recently been revived and received some support.

One may wonder at this point about the influence of psychoanalysis and the 'pleasure principle' on the interpretation of confabulations. Indeed, this influence was negligible. An exception was a study by Betlheim and Hartmann (1925) who sought to explore 'to what extent one may find in the realm of organic disorders phenomena that correspond to the psychologically well characterized and well-known processes of repression, deferral, and compression' (p. 257). They requested three confabulating patients with Korsakoff syndrome to learn and repeat a number of sentences: 'Apart from short harmless pieces of prose and a poem, we had them learn by heart short narratives of rough sexual content' (p. 276). The result was clear:

> The offensive parts are replaced by words that we know as typical symbols from dream analysis (climbing stairs, stab, and shoot as symbols of coitus; knife and cigarette as symbols of penis), ... a deformation, which deprives the learned material of its offensive character and renders it more harmless.
>
> Betlheim and Hartmann (1925, p. 283)

The authors 'emphatically emphasised that in all [their] trials it was only the crudely sexual material which underwent symbolic disguising' (p. 284). The study clearly showed that confabulating patients may be as reluctant as anyone else to use all too explicit terminology.

Definition by exclusion

Coming back to serious matters and the distinct forms of confabulations, Talland (1961, 1965) deserves mention. In his extensive review on confabulation in the Wernicke–Korsakoff syndrome, he, too, made the distinction between plausible confabulations and the fabrication of fantastic stories (Talland 1961). He started out with a simple definition: 'Confabulation is a false verbal statement about facts' (p. 362). He then set out to examine the properties of confabulation in order to refine the definition. He excluded deliberate falsification as a characteristic of confabulation but admitted that 'in a very wide sense confabulation always fills gaps, but not in the sense that the patient is aware of those gaps' (p. 364). He agreed that confabulation typically 'draws on some actual incidences in the patient's past, displacing them in their temporal sequence or in their social and geographical context ... Its area of reference is principally, even though not exclusively, the self' (Talland 1961, p. 365). But what about those confabulations described as 'fantastic confabulation, which involve the supernatural, the clearly fictitious or the historic past?' Talland proposed to set apart such confabulations:

> It seems advisable to restrict confabulation to the reproduction of personal memories outside their actual context or to their distortion within realistic limits, and to apply a second term, fabrication, to the more fantastic and incongruous material ... In the acute phase totally incoherent talk ought probably to be attributed to delirious fantasy.
>
> Talland (1961, pp. 365–6)

Notably, Talland (1961) found that these two phenomena could not be distinguished on the basis of the patient's conviction: 'The tone of conviction is no reliable measure of verdicality; the patient's rock-like certitude can be very misleading' (p. 366).

Based on these considerations, Talland now suggested a remarkably refined definition of confabulation:

> Confabulation is a factually incorrect verbal statement or narrative, exclusive of intentional falsification, fantastic fabrication, random guesses, intrinsic nonsense, the chaotic themes of delirium and hallucinations, and all systematic delusions other than those arising from the patient's disorientation in his experienced time.
>
> Talland (1961, p. 366)

He then added that in the context of the alcoholic Korsakoff syndrome, confabulation, defined in this way, would occur primarily in the acute phase, having then the following characteristics:

1. Confabulation is typically, but not exclusively, an account, more or less coherent and internally consistent, concerning the patient.
2. This account is false in the context named and often false in details within its own context.
3. Its content is drawn fully or principally from the patient's recollection of his actual experiences, including his thoughts in the past.
4. Confabulation reconstructs this content, modifies and recombines its elements, employing the mechanisms of normal remembering.
5. This material is presented without the awareness of its distortions or of its inappropriateness.
6. It serves no other purpose, is motivated in no other way than its factual information based on genuine data.

What about the mechanisms of confabulation? Could gap-filling be an explanation? Talland's unequivocal response:

> As an explanatory formula, the gap-filling model is patently incorrect if it implies a deliberate substitution of some appropriate but incorrect information for the correct one … If the gap-filling formula is meant to refer to an unconscious process of substitution, it explains nothing.
>
> Talland (1961, p. 368)

The often documented displacement of memories in time, also acknowledged by Talland, did not serve as an explanation, either:

> Such temporal signs as are attached to memories in normal cognitive functions are indeed largely destroyed in the amnesic syndrome. This loss, however, is more probably an effect than a cause of the amnesic disturbance.
>
> Talland (1961, p. 380)

So, could suggestibility be a relevant factor? Talland did not retain this element, either: his chronic patients proved absolutely resistant to hypnosis and did not fall for suggestive questions such as the interviewer asking in a jovial tone: 'Now didn't we meet over a drink last night?' So, what cause remained for confabulation? Talland proposed the following explanation:

> Confabulation as a symptom in the Korsakoff syndrome can properly be regarded as secondary to the amnesic derangement ... The amnesic deficit creates an occasion for the occurrence [of confabulation], and dispositions characteristic of the individual patient will determine its presence, rate and quality.
>
> Talland (1961, p. 381)

Korsakoff syndrome coming of age

Talland's article (1961) provided an erudite review of the old literature and integrated many previous observations, but in the end, the account nevertheless appeared somewhat helpless, devoid of convincing evidence – an explanation based on the exclusion of previous ones. there was another remarkable inconsistency: Talland explicitly excluded fantastic fabrications from his definition of confabulation, qualifying them as 'erratic flights into the realm of fancy' that occurred in the early phase of the disease when the patients were delirious and suggestible. His analysis focused on confabulation in the chronic Korsakoff syndrome, but in this phase, confabulation appeared to be extremely rare: 'The majority of our 28 chronic Korsakoff patients furnished no evidence of confabulation, in the wider or narrower sense of the term; a few repeatedly discoursed in a manner which would qualify for that definition' (Talland 1961, p. 372). Thus, Talland's article appeared to be about a phenomenon that he did not really observe in his patients.

The term Korsakoff syndrome had long been used to describe diverse diseases. Scheid (1934) had already commented:

> The cases that Korsakoff subsumed under the term 'polyneuritic psychosis' were characterized only by some crude features: the polyneuritis [and] an amnesia with falsifications of memory. Even nowadays, one finds under the collective term 'Korsakoff psychosis' myriad presentations; it would be impossible to say which one is 'the typical Korsakoff'.
>
> Scheid (1934, p. 346)

He then went on to describe in detail a 48-year-old American schoolteacher who suffered alcoholic Korsakoff psychosis during a stay in Germany. The main part of the paper contained a meticulous description of the patient's behaviour on his journey back to New York by ship, on which Scheid accompanied him. At that stage, the patient was severely amnesic and partly disoriented, but not actively confabulating. Although Scheid repeatedly included confabulations in his considerations on the 'pathopsychology of Korsakoff syndrome', his observations were limited to the severe amnesic state.

A few years later, a 'psycho-pathologic essay' on Korsakoff syndrome by Bernard (1951) also conveyed the idea that stable, spontaneous confabulation was not considered a standard feature of alcoholic Korsakoff syndrome: 'Most often, [confabulation] needs to be provoked. Indeed, it is intermittent. It emerges but in response to an inducing question' (p. 99). This description was very different from the dramatic behavioural aberrations with weird confabulations, guiding the patient's spontaneous behaviour for weeks or months, that Korsakoff had described. It seems that by 1960, the alcoholic Korsakoff syndrome – Bonhoeffer's 'Korsakoff psychosis' – hitherto the most frequent cause of amnesia with confabulation and disorientation, was only rarely accompanied by significant confabulation. A few years later, Victor, Adams and Collins (1989), in the first edition of their classic monograph of 1971, did not even retain confabulation in the definition of Korsakoff amnesic state:

> Confabulation, an ill defined symptom that has traditionally been accepted as an integral feature of Korsakoff psychosis, was neither consistently present in our patients nor essential for the diagnosis … In general, confabulation was a prominent symptom in the early stages of the disease, but it was not present in every patient, and even when present, it could not be consistently elicited. On the other hand, confabulation was present only rarely in the chronic, stable stage of the illness, irrespective of how broadly one defines the term.
>
> Victor, Adams and Collins (1989, pp. 43 and 50)

As we have seen, Bonhoeffer (1901) had already indicated that only three percent of the alcoholic patients being hospitalized with an acute delirium went on to have chronic Korsakoff psychosis; but when this happened, it could last for months. Would a decrease in the number of malnourished alcoholic people have helped to reduce the incidence of chronic Korsakoff syndrome? There may be another factor: Korsakoff psychosis was long considered to be of toxic origin. It was only towards the end of the 1930s that a deficiency in vitamin B1 (thiamine) began to be regarded as a possible mechanism (Minski 1936). It was also in this period that punctiform haemorrhages in the brain, as described by Wernicke, started to be universally accepted as the common pathological basis of both the physical signs of alcohol consumption (unsteady gait, oculomotor disturbances) and Korsakoff psychosis. Nowadays the term Wernicke–Korsakoff syndrome (WKS) denotes this combination of somatic and memory disturbances due to vitamin B1 (thiamine) deficiency.

In an initial study on the efficacy of thiamine substitution for the treatment of Korsakoff psychosis, Bowman and colleagues (1939) defined the disorder as the 'triad consisting of gross memory defect for recent events, disorientation, and confabulation' (p. 570): 55 patients received this diagnosis. It is interesting to read what outcome measure was chosen:

> The disappearance of confabulation and disorientation has been taken as the criterion of recovery. Memory defects of varying degree remained in nearly every case, whether the onset of the psychosis was insidious or with acute manifestations, and irrespective of the treatment given.
>
> Bowman *et al.* (1939, p. 571)

It seems that vitamin B1 substitution was already initially recognized as being particularly efficacious for mending confabulation and disorientation rather than the amnesia itself. It might be a consequence of this efficacy that nowadays, in the diction of many, the term 'Korsakoff syndrome' – which has replaced Korsakoff psychosis – simply denotes amnesia, especially if it occurs in the context of chronic alcohol abuse, but irrespective of the presence of confabulation or disorientation. A recent review of the syndrome by Kopelman (1995) reflects this change of concept:

> The Korsakoff syndrome is defined as a disproportionate impairment in memory, relative to other aspects of cognitive function, resulting from a nutritional (thiamine) depletion.

Many infections and other severe diseases, which presumably induced a state of malabsorption and caused the syndrome in many of Korsakoff's own patients, also virtually disappeared from the literature after the first half of the twentieth century.

From toxicity to anatomy

Most causes of Korsakoff syndrome – alcohol, infections, brain trauma, senile forgetfulness – did not lend themselves to conclusions about an anatomical basis of confabulations. The toxic origin was widely accepted and even proposed as an essential ingredient of traumatic Korsakoff syndrome (Benon and LeHuché 1920). The history of Korsakoff syndrome after subarachnoid haemorrhage, nowadays the most consistently reported cause of severe confabulation, is an example of speculations made in the absence of adequate technologies. Subarachnoid haemorrhage was recognized as a cause of Korsakoff syndrome more than 30 years after the description of the syndrome in alcoholic patients. Flatau (1921) was the first to give a precise description of the psychic disorder:

> [It is] very close to the so-called Korsakoff syndrome, but accompanied by psychomotor excitation, present in numerous patients. Although the patients respond to

questions, they are disoriented with respect to time, place and entourage. They do not remember when they have fallen sick and give false responses as they forget what they have just said … Facts of the remote past are better preserved in their memory. In addition, they manifest a tendency for confabulation. Sometimes they tell imaginary stories about their pretended voyages … Their responses are often incoherent, with rapid transition from one topic to the other.

Flatau (1921, p. 1080)

Some patients were described as violently agitated: 'In one of my cases I was obliged to put her in a house for the mentally ill. This excitation lasted several weeks … Even after several months, the patient presented a certain mental disorientation' (Flatau 1921, p. 1080). As to the cause of the haemorrhage, Flatau thought that 'exceptionally, the haemorrhage arises from an aneurysm' – a point on which present-day neurosurgeons would be considerably more affirmative.

Subsequent authors mentioned the occurrence of Korsakoff syndrome but did not feel compelled to describe their patients' mental disorder in any detail. Goldflam (1923), in a review on subarrachoid haemorrhage, described the occurrence of 'certain psychic disturbances in almost all cases of subarachnoid haemorrhage [encompassing] disorientation … deliria, motor restlessness, confabulation, as they most closely correspond to Korsakoff syndrome. This psychosis can last for weeks' (p. 173). Hall (1929) described three patients, of whom one had 'smiling euphoria, together with unblushing accounts of what he had done, which where quite imaginary' (p. 1026) for several weeks. Another patient 'would at any time, when asked what she had had for dinner, give a detailed account of an ordinary plain dinner, with particulars elaborately filled in, despite taking nothing but liquid food'.

The idea that a localised lesion might account for this type of Korsakoff syndrome continued to be disregarded. Cubitt (1930) described a 57-year-old man with subarachnoid haemorrhage, proven by lumbar puncture, who presented 'definite Korsakoff psychosis' from the second day on: 'There was complete disorientation as to place and time, fairly good memory for past events, but fabrication of recent occurrences … His mind seemed to run on his army days' (Cubitt 1930, p. 212). He died after seven days and the autopsy showed a 'large clot of blood at the base of the brain in the region of the circle of Willis … there was one fusiform aneurysm, and one small, thin-walled saccular aneurysm containing blood'. Yet there had to be more to his Korsakoff syndrome than this finding: 'In spite of negative Wassermann reaction [a serologic test for syphilis],… [it] seems probable that the changes in the membranes and vessels of the brain were due to syphilis' (Cubitt 1930, p. 212).

Nine years later, Tarachow (1939) reported three new cases with Korsakoff syndrome after subarachnoid haemorrhage, taken from a series of 105 patients. A 15-year-old girl started to present mild euphoria, lability of mood, memory defect, confabulation, and disorientation five days after the haemorrhage. After four weeks, she ceased to confabulate. Quite a different course was observed in a 33-year-old woman who was in a restless stupor for about a month and then developed a hypomanic syndrome with:

> the classical features of the Korsakoff psychosis ... She was completely disoriented in time; there were marked defects of retention, recall and general knowledge. Confabulations were glib: 'A lady gave birth. I heard that a woman had to give birth to a baby and they had to give some medicine, some powder. I stay out in the park and read. I am living here, in this apartment house. I am a tenant. I read, sew, wash, do things for the children'.

> Tarachow (1939, p. 892)

The patient's condition improved after two to three weeks. In a third patient, 'aphasic symptoms and evidence of disorientation and clouding, at times of Korsakoff psychosis' lasted for five weeks.

Tarachow's (1939) article was less remarkable for the case descriptions than for the pathophysiological conclusions:

> It is doubtful whether it is possible to make a correlation between definite localizable changes in the brain and the Korsakoff mental picture.... It is quite possible that haemolysed blood acts as a toxic agent

> Tarachow (1939, p. 895)

Tarachow's conclusion may also have been influenced by his extraordinarily careful review of all hitherto reported causes of Korsakoff syndrome, listed on more than two pages in the introduction of the article and documented with almost 50 references. This was no way of extracting precise brain–behaviour relationships on the basis of such an analysis. But then, there was also no technology available at the time to localise the brain damage or the site of an aneurysm in survivors of the haemorrhage.

In this respect, no significant progress was made in the coming years. Fourteen years after Tarachow, Walton (1953) described six patients from a series of 312 cases of subarachnoid haemorrhage, who where severely disoriented and 'wildly confabulated' for two days, several weeks, or up to eleven months. Walton, too, was impressed by the vast number of diseases that could cause Korsakoff syndrome, motivating him to make the following flat statement:

> The mechanism by which these varied neurological conditions may all give rise to a similar psychiatric syndrome is still obscure ... There is certainly no evidence that a localised cortical lesion, say in the frontal lobe, can be the cause; the absence of

clinical features of focal cerebral damage in [our six] cases may be added to the already abundant evidence which confirms this suggestion.

Walton (1953, p. 527)

He also rejected hydrocephalus or a lesion in the hypothalamic region as possible explanations and instead concluded:

The available evidence suggests that the Korsakoff syndrome in cases of subarachnoid haemorrhage is usually a reaction to diffuse cerebral damage

Walton (1953 p. 529)

It was only with the advent of new imaging technologies – angiography in the beginning – that the particular importance of ruptured aneurysms of the anterior communicating artery and the role of damage in the area of the ventromedial frontal lobes (including basal forebrain area) were recognized for the occurrence of amnesia and confabulation in this disease (Lindqvist and Norlén 1966). Of course, new imaging technologies have also profoundly altered the interpretation of confabulations occurring in many other brain diseases, which were previously considered to be diffuse. However, that story is for later.

Summary

Since the early descriptions of confabulations in the 1880s up into the 1960s, an incredibly rich literature on false productions from memory by patients suffering from diverse illnesses has accrued. Korsakoff was the first to draw attention to a consistent syndrome composed of anterograde and retrograde amnesia, confabulation, and disorientation. Most patients had chronic alcoholism, others had severe infections presumably inducing malabsorption. The syndrome was soon also described in patients recovering from severe brain trauma and patients with senile dementia; it was much later recognized as a sequel of subarachnoid haemorrhage. A toxic origin was widely accepted; the anatomical basis appeared to be diffuse.

Different manifestations of confabulations were described: fantastic, implausible and incoherent 'falsifications of memory' in syphilitic and psychotic patients; fleeting and superficial confabulations that patients with diverse diseases, including senile dementia, produced in response to questions; and stable confabulations dominating the behaviour of chronic alcoholics and patients with traumatic brain injury or subarachnoid haemorrhage. Many authors insisted on the plausibility of the latter confabulations and their roots in the patients' real past.

Classifications varied. Authors used terms like 'out-of-embarrassment, compensatory, momentary, fantastic, provoked, spontaneous' to describe the character of the confabulations they had observed. Table 2.1 summarizes these classifications and the supposed mechansims. Although gap-filling was the most commonly assumed mechanism, sometimes even used as part of the definition, the list of hypotheses was long. Most current theories – dysexecutive, monitoring, temporality, constructive deficit, or personality traits – were anticipated on the basis of clinical observation alone.

Table 2.1 Forms and suggested mechanisms of confabulations reported between 1886 and 1961. 'Confabulation types' indicates the nomenclature proposed by the respective author. Terms provided in brackets reflect my interpretation of the proposed mechanisms according to modern nomenclature.

Author	Aetiologies	Confabulation type	Proposed mechanism
Kraepelin (1886, 1887a)	General paralysis (syphilis) Psychosis Senile dementia	Simple falsifications of memory	Deficient sense of critique, failure of the weapons distinguishing fantasy from reality [failure of source- and self-monitoring]
Korsakoff (1889, 1890a, 1890b, 1891)	Alcohol Infectious diseases (typhus etc.)	Illusions of memory (pseudo-reminiscences)	Inability to decide whether memory relates to a real event or a dream [source memory failure]; Defect in the unconscious association of ideas [defect of constructive processes]
Tiling (1892)	Alcohol Traumatic brain injury Senile forgetfulness	False recollections	Intermingling of remote and recent events [temporal order failure]; Disturbance of memory and impaired other mental capacities [amnesia and executive failure]
Bonhoeffer (1901, 1904)	Alcohol	Momentary confabulations out of embarassement	Gap-filling, requires intact mental agility
		Fantastic confabulations	Generated on the basis of hallucinations

Table 2.1 (continued) Forms and suggested mechanisms of confabulations reported between 1886 and 1961. 'Confabulation types' indicates the nomenclature proposed by the respective author. Terms provided in brackets reflect my interpretation of the proposed mechanisms according to modern nomenclature.

Author	Aetiologies	Confabulation type	Proposed mechanism
Pick (1905, 1921)	–	Confabulations, provoked more common than spontaneous	Unconscious desire to fill gaps in memory [gap-filling], suggestibility and clouded consciousness and weak judgement [monitoring deficit], inappropriate individuality index [temporal order, filtering deficit]
Kraepelin (1910)	General paralysis, Alcoholic Korsakoff syndrome, senile dementia	Confabulations	Filling gaps in memory
Moll (1915)	Alcohol	Fabrications, fictions: – random fabrications – distorted recollections (pseudo-reminiscences) – true recollections of real facts, incorrectly oriented in time – fabrications based on hallucinations Remnants of dreams	Filling gaps in memory [Temporal order deficit] Hallucinations
Bleuler (1923)	Alcoholic Korsakoff syndrome, general paralysis etc.	Confabulations	Filling a void in memory
	Schizophrenia	Hallucinations of memory	Generation of an image of memory, not based on a real event

Table 2.1 (continued) Forms and suggested mechanisms of confabulations reported between 1886 and 1961. 'Confabulation types' indicates the nomenclature proposed by the respective author. Terms provided in brackets reflect my interpretation of the proposed mechanisms according to modern nomenclature.

Author	Aetiologies	Confabulation type	Proposed mechanism
Van der Horst (1932)	Diverse	Out-of-embarassement confabulations	Filling gaps in memory to avoid embarassement
		Productive confabulations	Loss of temporal tag [temporal order deficit]
Williams and Rupp (1938)	Diverse	Confabulations	Memory disturbance and lack of insight and personality
Flament (1957)	Traumatic brain injury	Classic compensatory confabulations	Memory weakness, disorder of temporalization [amnesia and temporal order deficit]
		Fantastic confabulations = unreal, imaginary productions	Rewarding in a situation of personal inferiority
Talland (1961)	Alcohol	Plausible confabulations = personal memories outside their actual context	Amnesia and dispositions characteristic of the individual [personality traits]
		Fabrication = fantastic confabulation	Delirious fantasy

Chapter 3

Types of confabulation

The review of the old literature in the previous chapter has shown that confabulations may come in different flavours, varying with regards to intensity, mode of evocation, sense of veracity, behavioural consequences and associated features. Many authors tried to cover these aspects in their definition of confabulation: many distinguished different forms of confabulation; some also assumed different mechanisms. Nowadays, the term 'confabulation' is not only used to denote false products from memory (*mnestic confabulations*), but also those emanating from false perceptions of bodily states or the outer world and other failures (*non-mnestic confabulations*). In this chapter, definitions of confabulation and current classifications will be reviewed. A classification respecting known dissociations will be presented and ways to explore confabulation will be proposed.

Definitions of confabulation

The previous chapters should have made clear what this book is about: unintentional, false productions from memory in cerebral disease states and what they tell us about correct productions from memory. The book is about false memories as described in the previous chapters, irrespective of whether they were labelled pseudo-reminiscences, confabulations, illusions of memory, simple falsifications of memory, or fabrications. Among these terms, confabulation is nowadays most widely used. It is interesting to review some definitions of this term for two reasons. First, it is revealing to see how authors adapted the definition so that it fit the observations in their patients. Some definitions made limitations regarding the aetiology and assumed specific mechanisms. Second, confabulation was eventually used to describe any type of unintentional, objectively false statement. Some authors interpret confabulation as a disorder in its own right, irrespective of its originally synonymous meaning with pseudo-reminiscences, illusions of memory and the like. Of course, such a view has a profound impact on the suggested mechanisms of confabulation (DeLuca 2000).

Confabulation derives from the Latin word *confabulari*, first documented in the writings of Roman playwrights Titus Plautus (254–184 BC) and Terentius Afer (195–159 BC) in the second century BC. Originally, it meant nothing more than 'to gossip, to chat with somebody' or 'to discuss something with somebody' (Georges 1913–1918). Possibly, the author who introduced the term in medical writing had the different meanings of the word 'fabula' in mind; its primary meaning was 'the chat, dialogue, tattle of people', but it also meant 'the saga, fairy-tale' and 'fiction' (Georges 1913–1918). Academicians of the nineteenth century were usually proficient in the use of Latin language. It is tempting to fantasize that the medical use of the term arose during a discussion in which two savants confabulated – that is, chatted – about the nature of pseudo-reminiscences.

Although we may never know the precise circumstances of confabulation's baptism in medical writing, we know that the term was introduced in the German literature in the sense of Korsakoff's pseudo-reminiscences around 1900. Carl Wernicke (1900) used the term in the first edition of his *Principles of Psychiatry* and defined it as follows:

> [confabulation denotes] the emergence of memories of events and experiences which never took place.
>
> Wernicke (1900, p. 139)

He observed confabulation in schizophrenia, senile dementia, and paralytic dementia, but also listed it as a cardinal symptom of polyneuritic psychosis, i.e., alcoholic Korsakoff psychosis (Wernicke 1900, p. 297). One year later, Bonhoeffer (1901) made the distinction between momentary and fantastic confabulations without regard for the definition of confabulations. In 1901, the term was apparently already established.

Indeed, according to Wernicke's definition, the term confabulation was nothing more than a substitute for 'pseudo-reminiscences', defined by Korsakoff as the 'situation in which a patient conceives of an event that he has not really experienced, but that has only come to his mind, as if it had really happened to him' (Korsakoff 1891, p. 391).

Pick (1905) proposed a definition which assumed a mechanism. He defined confabulation as 'the filling of gaps in memory by falsifications of memories', whereby he conceived of the falsification process as 'a sum of partially disparate processes.' As we saw in the previous chapter (p. 27ff.), his pathophysiological considerations were much more elaborate than suggested by this bold definition. Indeed, no one has ever handled the gap-filling idea more delicately than Pick.

It seems that the term was adopted particularly willingly in the German literature. At least, this is what Philippe Chaslin (1912), head of one of the psychiatry wards at the Salpêtrière in Paris, suggested in his textbook on the *Elements of Mental Semiology and Clinics*. He entitled one paragraph 'Perversions of memory. False memories, pseudo-reminiscences (the Germans'

Confabulation) [Confabulation des Allemands]' (Chaslin 1912, p. 92). He then described the case of a woman, institutionalized because of senile dementia, who produced 'enormous errors of memory'. She refused to sit down at table, indicating that she was waiting for her husband, a was angry with her children, saying that it was totally inappropriate for them to start eating before the head of family had arrived. In reality, her husband had died several years before. Chaslin considered these errors of memory very severe

> because they go beyond possible things or are completely invented. They strongly resemble the games of imagination occurring in dreams and the fantastic elucubrations of certain idiots ... The Germans call this type of error confabulation.
>
> Chaslin (1912, p. 94)

It seems that French clinicians understood 'the Germans' term' confabulation in the sense of Bonhoeffer's (1901) fantastic confabulation, and it is very likely that they were impressed by the statements that famous Germans like Kraepelin had made about confabulation.

Emil Kraepelin introduced the term confabulation in his famous textbook on psychiatry in the early 1900s, when it replaced his earlier 'simple falsifications of memory'. In the sixth edition, Kraepelin (1899) used the term 'fabulation' to denote the form of 'falsification of memory' which he had often observed in general paralysis, in the course of dementing processes, and occasionally in mania: 'Entirely free inventions of seeming reminiscences, which have absolutely no corresponding counterpart in the past' (p. 123f). He did not yet comment on its mechanism. This changed in later editions, in which he replaced 'fabulation' by 'confabulation' and left no doubt anymore about its mechanism. He described confabulation as

> the recitation of freely invented experiences ... Gaps, caused by severe memory failure are filled spontaneously or upon incitation with false memories ... Obviously, [this process results from] the desire to create an image of the past which has left no real traces.
>
> Kraepelin (1909, p. 263)

Confabulation would occur in general paralysis, 'Korsakoff mental failure', and presbyophrenia (senile dementia). Kraepelin's concept of confabulation as the recitation of entirely invented, fantastic and implausible events was clearly coloured by his long experience with patients having general paralysis or schizophrenia.

Eugen Bleuler (1923), another famous figure in the history of modern psychiatry, defended a similar concept of confabulation:

> Confabulations are free inventions conceived as [real] memories. They fill a void in memory and often appear to be downright dedicated to this purpose. They often

> transmute from one moment to the other; we can even provoke and steer them, whereas hallucinations of memory do not change more than delusional ideas.
>
> Bleuler (1923, p. 81)

In Bleuler's concept,

> hallucinations of memory (in the narrow sense, as confabulations would deserve this name, too) [were] deceptions of memory which create an image of memory out of nothing, devoid of any connection with a real event, that is, which provide a fantasy with the value of truthfulness ... Hallucinations of memory almost exclusively occur in schizophrenics.
>
> Bleuler (1923, p. 80)

His description of 'hallucinations of memory' was very similar to the 'simple falsifications of memory' that Kraepelin (1886) had observed in patients suffering from general paralysis or schizophrenia, and which he later also called 'confabulations' (Kraepelin 1909).

Bleuler limited the usage of the term confabulations to organic aetiologies like alcoholic Korsakoff syndrome and general paralysis (syphilis), where he observed them most often.

> Unfortunately, the term confabulation is also used for vivid hallucinations of memory and half-conscious fantasy products by schizophrenics. But we need a term [like confabulation] in the above sense, because, applied in this way and restricted to non-delirious states, it is a sign of organic psychosis. It would be wise not to apply the term to other anomalies.
>
> Bleuler (1923, p. 81)

Kraepelin's and Bleuler's concept of confabulation was influenced by aetiological considerations, and both were unambiguous about its mechanism. Given their overwhelming impact on modern psychiatry, it comes as no surprise that their definition of confabulation as 'gap-filling' has survived into our days. The *Diagnostic and Statistical Manual of Mental Disorders DSM-IV* (American Psychiatric Association 1994), the 'bible' for current psychiatric diagnosis, does not explicitly define confabulations but clearly retains the gap-filling idea: 'Confabulation, often evidenced by the recitation of imaginary events to fill gaps in memory, may be noted during the early stages of an amnestic disorder but tends to disappear with time.' All the subtlety of Pick's gap-filling account is gone.

While many authors included the presence of amnesia in their definition, the question of whether psychotic thinking should be included or not has remained controversial. Williams and Rupp (1938) included it: 'Confabulation as an associated symptom is often found in cases of psychosis, in which loss of memory on a structural basis is a prominent feature' (p. 395). As we saw in Chapter 2, these authors included a suspected mechanism in their definition of confabulation: 'Confabulation may be defined as the tendency of individuals of a particular personality pattern with incomplete memory loss, to substitute retained for forgotten experiences irrespective of time sequence' (Williams and Rupp 1938, p. 404).

Talland (1961) specifically excluded fantastic fabrication and psychotic thinking in his famous definition:

> Confabulation is a factually incorrect verbal statement or narrative, exclusive of intentional falsification, fantastic fabrication, random guesses, intrinsic nonsense, the chaotic themes of delirium and hallucinations, and all systematic delusions other than those arising from the patient's disorientation in his experienced time.
>
> Talland (1961, p. 366)

Although he suggested that in the context of the Wernicke–Korsakoff syndrome, confabulation, defined in this way, would occur primarily in the acute phase, this definition effectively excluded confabulation in the acute delirium. Also, the 'simple falsifications of memory' which Kraepelin (1886) described in syphilitic patients would not be considered confabulations in Talland's definition.

Talland (1965) is the author of yet another famous definition of confabulation, which we have already seen on p. 35:

> Confabulation is: (a) typically, but not exclusively, an account, more or less coherent and internally consistent, concerning the patient. (b) This account is false in the context named and often false in details within its own context. (c) Its content is drawn fully or principally from the patient's recollection of his actual experiences, including his thoughts in the past. (d) Confabulation reconstructs this content, modifies and recombines its elements, employing the mechanisms of normal remembering. (e) This material is presented without awareness of its distortions or of its inappropriateness, and (f) serves no other purpose, is motivated in no other way than factual information based on genuine data.
>
> Talland (1965, p. 49f.)

Berlyne (1972) considered Talland's definition as 'thorough but cumbersome', although he seemed to agree with the main idea:

> The falsifications of delirious states require specific exclusion, and the presence of the basic memory defect needs special mention. Hence confabulation can be defined as 'a falsification of memory occurring in clear consciousness in association with an organically derived amnesia'. This description is brief, avoids a complicated descriptive element, includes both momentary and fantastic forms, and excludes memory falsifications not associated with organic memory defect and those due to delirious states.
>
> Berlyne (1972, p. 38)

The difficulty with such exclusive definitions is, of course, that it may be terribly difficult in practice, when listening to a patient producing strange stories, to reliably establish or exclude things such as 'intrinsic nonsense, the chaotic themes of delirium, systematic delusions' and other manifestations of psychotic thinking. The correct application of Talland's and Berlyne's definitions requires that the examiner already knows the cause and the mechanism of a patient's production of false stories. Nevertheless, Berlyne's definition of confabulation as 'a falsification of memory occurring in clear consciousness in association with an organically derived amnesia' has become a classic and is a useful working definition for the disorder described in the previous chapters – under the condition that one does not apply his exclusion criteria too strictly.

Recent definitions have been more inclusive. Moscovitch (1995) defined confabulation as

> A symptom that accompanies many neuropsychological disorders and some psychiatric ones, such as schizophrenia ... What distinguishes confabulation from lying is that typically there is no intent to deceive and the patient is unaware of the falsehood. It is an 'honest lying'. Confabulation is simple to detect when the information the patient provides is patently false, self-contradictory, bizarre or at least highly improbable ... Just as often, however, the tale fabricated by the patient is coherent, internally consistent, and relatively commonplace. It is identified as a confabulation only by consulting with a patient's friends or relatives or by cross-checking it with information provided by the patient on other occasions.

> Moscovitch (1995, p. 226f.)

The definition made no assumption as to the cause or mode of evocation of confabulations. Indeed, it did not even require the presence of amnesia, and like many other definitions, it did not include the production of false memories by healthy subjects.

Dalla Barba's definition also focused on pathological states:

> Confabulation is a symptom which is sometimes found in amnesic patients and consists in involuntary and unconscious production of 'false memories', that is the recollection of episodes, which never actually happened, or which occurred in a different temporal–spatial context to that being referred to by the patient.

> Dalla Barba (2002, p. 28)

Although all these definitions tried to grasp the core features of a relatively delimited class of disorders – falsifications of memory in pathological brain states – they were influenced by the authors' specific observations. Many were partly incompatible with others. This led several authors to complain that confabulation was 'an ill-defined symptom' (Victor *et al.* 1989) or 'another such word which rarely receives adequate definition' (Whitlock 1981). The story gets even more confusing. In the realm of memory, the term has also been used to denote memory falsifications in figurative memory tests, e.g., the intrusion of elements not contained in an originally presented design (Bender *et al.* 1938). More importantly, however, the term has often been applied to domains other than memory to describe objectively false statements about percepts, or true statements about false percepts.

Confabulations beyond memory

Even though the term confabulation entered the clinical literature as a new designation of pseudo-reminiscences, its meaning also suits other phenomena. Objectively false statements do not necessarily result from a defect in memory but may also be based on hallucinations, incomplete or false perceptions. Since the 1960s, a number of authors have used the term confabulation to designate such failures. In the clinical literature, the term is normally applied to false statements if it is assumed that a subject is unaware of the falsehood of his statements. This may be difficult to verify and also depends on the degree to which a subject is pushed to give a response. Based on this more inclusive definition, confabulations have been described in many disorders.

Patients with hemispheric brain lesions and hemiplegia, that is, paralysis of one side of the body, may be unaware of their paralysis (Weinstein and Kahn 1950). Babinski (1914, 1918) introduced the term *anosognosia* for the unawareness of hemiplegia. The term was soon also used to denote unawareness of hemianopia (Babinski 1918), as previously described by Anton (1898) and others. Anosognosia is often associated with confabulations about the state of the paralysed side (Weinstein and Kahn 1950; Feinberg *et al.* 1994). Patients may be unaware of why they are in the hospital or refer to episodes that have nothing to do with their present paralysis.

Patients who become acutely blind may deny this state and confabulate things they pretend to see. This is called Anton's syndrome, in reference to an early article by Anton (1898) describing a patient presenting this peculiar behaviour. The article also contained the description of two patients who were unaware of their deafness and explicitly denied it.

Similar denial has been described in patients presenting with aphasia (loss of language capacity) (Lebrun 1987), prosopagnosia (inability to recognize the individuality of faces) (Young *et al.* 1990) and many other disorders (Vuilleumier 2004). In particular, anosognosia has also been documented repeatedly in demented patients (Michon *et al.* 1994; Dalla Barba *et al.* 1995; Starkstein *et al.* 1996). Anosognosia is used nowadays to describe unawareness of disease in general. It has repeatedly been linked with confabulation (Weinstein and Kahn 1950; Feinberg and Roane 1997b). We will come back to anosognosia in Chapter 5, which discusses disorders related to confabulation or associated with it.

Patients with visual recognition failures (visual agnosia or optic aphasia) may give false names to seen objects (Geschwind 1965; Poeck 1984) and sometimes even try to use the objects as if they were the ones for which the name was given (Schnider *et al.* 1994a). Such erroneous naming has also been labelled confabulation (Geschwind 1965).

Some patients may falsely recognize and have an intense feeling of familiarity with people they have never seen before the onset of their brain disease. Such false recognition or false familiarity, normally termed *misidentification*, has also been observed in patients with Korsakoff syndrome (Benon and LeHuché 1920). Other patients fail to recognize people that they should be familiar with, typically family members. They recognize their features ('looks exactly like my wife') but consider them impostors of the family member. This is called *Capgras syndrome* (Benson and Stuss 1990; Signer 1992; Feinberg and Roane 1997a). Still other patients have a somewhat similar disorder regarding places. If hospitalized in another town than their home town, they may fail to accept this fact and insist that the hospital is still the one they have always known, typically near their home. They may invent elaborate explanations to justify this interpretation. This disorder is called *reduplicative paramnesia* (Pick 1903a; Signer 1992). These types of confabulation, which presumably result from reasons other than failures of memory, will be discussed in Chapter 5.

Defined in such a broad sense, confabulation is a term that might also be applied to many behaviours of healthy people. In particular, the healthy brain may also produce falsifications of memories. Indeed, confabulations can also be induced in healthy subjects when they are pushed to retrieve memories with more details than those they have actually stored (Burgess and Shallice 1996). Nonetheless, in the scientific literature the term confabulation has typically been used to describe false productions in pathological brain states, whereas false productions by a healthy brain have more often been called 'false memories' (Loftus 1979/1996; Brainerd and Reyna 2005). As it is possible that such falsifications of memory share some characteristics or even mechanisms with certain confabulations occurring in brain damaged subjects, they will be discussed in Chapter 6.

Confabulation is a term that can justly be applied to many weaknesses and failures of cognition, both in the diseased and the healthy brain. This book is concerned primarily with unintentional incorrect productions from memory – mnestic confabulations – also described as 'pseudo-reminiscences, illusions of memory, simple falsifications of memory, or fabrications' in brain diseases and as 'falsifications of memory' in healthy subjects.

Forms of confabulation

From the observations described in Chapter 2 it might appear that the existence of diverse, at least partly independent forms of mnestic confabulations, would be an accepted fact. Far from it! The dissociation of confabulatory phenomena, even the separation between mnestic and non-mnestic forms, is still contested and some authors have proposed theoretical frameworks, which attempt to cover all forms of confabulation, including those emanating from faulty perception and those produced by healthy subjects (see Chapter 7).

Table 2.1 (p. 42–44) summarized the categorizations of mnestic confabulations suggested by the classic authors cited in Chapter 2. The extremes in this table were the very early authors, Korsakoff (1891), Kraepelin (1886, 1910) and Tiling (1892), who made no distinction at all among the various forms of confabulatory phenomena, and Moll (1915), who distinguished five different forms. These ranged from random fabrications to distorted recollections, true recollections of real facts falsely oriented in time, fabrications based on hallucinations and those based on dreams. Moll's classification continued to be occasionally cited but had no tangible impact on theoretical concepts of false memories.

Most authors, who did make a distinction, separated two forms, which normally reflected the different degrees or types of confabulations they had observed in their own patients. The most common distinction, initially proposed by Bonhoeffer (1901, 1904), was the one between momentary confabulations produced out of embarrassment and fantastic confabulations. In this dichotomy, 'momentary' confabulations were those that were normally produced in response to questions, apparently to fill a gap in memory, and which were always plausible. Momentary confabulations were also called 'out of embarrassment' confabulations (Bonhoeffer 1901, 1904; Van der Horst 1932), classic compensatory confabulations (Flament 1957), or simply 'confabulations' (Talland 1961). By contrast, fantastic confabulations, also termed fabrications (Talland 1961), described implausible confabulations relating to unreal, imaginary events; they also included delirious fantasy (Bonhoeffer 1901, 1904; Flament 1957).

A slightly different classification was proposed by Van der Horst (1932), who shared the idea of out of embarrassment confabulations. As their counterpart, he suggested 'productive' confabulations, a term describing memories displaced in time of whose veracity the patient was absolutely convinced. Thus, Van der Horst's dichotomy did not cover completely fantastic confabulations having no basis in reality.

Even though the classic authors, or at least their precise claims, have mostly been forgotten, the idea of there being different forms of confabulations, separable within a dichotomy, has survived. However, as the following discussion will show, authors had to adapt the definitions of terms like 'momentary, fantastic, provoked and spontaneous' to make them fit their observations, which varied according to pathology.

In the more recent literature, Berlyne (1972) has often been credited not only for his definition of confabulation, but also for his distinction between momentary and fantastic confabulations. As we saw in Chapter 2, several earlier authors had proposed this distinction (Table 2.1). Berlyne explicitly referred to Bonhoeffer (1901) when introducing the distinction. He described memory falsifications which he had observed in seven patients presenting a chronic Korsakoff syndrome and 62 patients with dementia from diverse aetiologies, primarily senile and arteriosclerotic dementia. He excluded memory falsifications deriving from illusory or hallucinatory experiences in states of clouded consciousness. Among the 62 dementia patients 15 produced what Berlyne considered momentary confabulations, and eight patients produced fantastic confabulations.

Although Berlyne concluded that his study 'confirmed the existence of two forms of confabulation in the Korsakoff syndrome, as postulated by Bonhoeffer' (Berlyne 1972, p. 33), the case reports illustrating both types of confabulation do not appear as convincing as he might have liked them to be. The first patient, a 46-year-old chronic alcoholic with devastation of recent memory, was described as saying that he had been brought to the hospital by two sick berth attendants and a Petty Officer and that he was serving on a motor torpedo boat (he had in fact been an officer on such a boat). He also said that the war was on and the invasion of Europe was imminent. Berlyne classified these confabulations, which went on for two months, as momentary confabulations. A second patient, a 53-year-old housewife who had suffered traumatic brain injury, declared six weeks after the accident that she was in the Royal Air Force and that her accident had occurred while flying in France. At other times she talked of the accident as if it had happened whilst she was driving a car. In addition, she referred to travels to Egypt, mentioned two accidents, and claimed to own a boat and a car and to have trained airmen. Berlyne also mentioned that occasionally, true memories were intermingled with these falsifications, which continued for three months. This patient's confabulations were classified as fantastic, although their content and circumstances of production appear comparable to the first patient. Similarly, the confabulations of a 72-year-old demented woman were considered fantastic. She stated that she had just been playing cricket for the ladies' eleven, that she was a doctor in charge at Manchester University and that her son was a Field Marshall.

Berlyne's article looks less like the analysis of original observations than an attempt to revive the old distinction previously made by Bonhoeffer (1901, 1904), but also by Flament (1957) and Talland (1961). In this respect, his article was a success, and reintroduced the distinction between two forms of confabulation, which Berlyne characterized as follows:

◆ *Momentary (or embarrassment) confabulation* was described as

> brief but not cliché-like, in so far as the replies are not stereotyped. It is autobiographical in content and refers to the recent past. Invariably, it has to be provoked. The content is a true memory displaced in its time context. Habitual or affectively stamped activities form its usual theme. Its content may vary from minute to minute and can be extended by questioning. Frequent contradictions, telescoping of events.

◆ *Fantastic (or productive) confabulation* was described as a much less common phenomenon.

> The content of the confabulation shows less change than momentary confabulation and the grandiose theme is sustained. Not associated with suggestibility. Autobiographical but entirely invented. Unlike momentary confabulation, it is not rooted in true memory. The principal content is invariably grandiose and seems to be related to wish fulfilment and prestige seeking. It seems to be a distinct entity having nothing in common with momentary confabulation except its appearance against the background of organically induced memory impairment.

> Berlyne (1972, p. 33)

The latter statement, that the two forms of confabulation had 'nothing in common' was particularly stark, albeit hardly supported by the data.

Kopelman (1987) referred to Berlyne's article to introduce another distinction: that between *provoked* and *spontaneous confabulation*. Pick (1905) had used this terminology to refer to the evocation of the confabulations, irrespective of their content. He had stated that spontaneous confabulations often disappeared while confabulations could still be provoked by questioning. Kopelman's distinction appeared to be more divisive. He roughly likened spontaneous confabulations to Berlyne's (1972) or Bonhoeffer's (1901) fantastic confabulations, whose qualities he summarized as 'spontaneous, sustained, wide-ranging, and grandiose; and it is readily evident in the subject's every day conversation' (Kopelman 1987, p. 1482).

Kopelman's study did not further explore spontaneous confabulation but provided original data on provoked confabulation, a term he used synonymously with momentary confabulation. Sixteen patients with chronic (amnesic) Korsakoff syndrome in the context of prolonged, heavy alcohol abuse, 16 patients with Alzheimer's disease, and 17 age-matched healthy controls were explored. All subjects heard one of the two Wechsler Logical

Memory stories (Wechsler 1945). These are highly condensed short stories with a definite number of information elements ('Anna Thompson of South Bristol, employed as a cleaner in an office building …'). Confabulations were defined as intrusion errors adding irrelevant or inaccurate material or changing the sense of the passages when recalling the stories from memory. Five of the sixteen patients with Alzheimer's disease produced such provoked confabulations when immediately recalling the story. Eight of the sixteen Korsakoff patients produced confabulations both on immediate recall and when retested 45 minutes later. Most interestingly, healthy controls, too, produced confabulations, especially when tested after one week. In his conclusions, Kopelman again juxtaposed the two forms of confabulations.

Spontaneous confabulation was described as 'a pathological phenomenon, which is relatively rare and may result from the superimposition of frontal lobe pathology on an organic amnesia (Kopelman 1987, p. 1486)… Spontaneous confabulation may reflect an extremely incoherent and context-free retrieval of memories and associations' (p. 1482).

Provoked confabulation was described as 'common in amnesic patients when given memory tests, resembles the errors produced by healthy subjects at prolonged retention intervals, and may represent a normal response to a faulty memory' (Kopelman 1987, p. 1486).

In this description, spontaneous confabulation was clearly a different, not simply a severer, form of confabulation than provoked confabulation.

The article has the merit of introducing a reproducible, clearly defined method for testing provoked confabulation. It also clarified the distinction between two forms of confabulation which can be separated on the basis of solid clinical features. However, one might criticize Kopelman's characterization of spontaneous confabulations as 'sustained, wide-ranging, grandiose' as widely transcending the core meaning of the word. This classification thus looks somewhat like a replacement of Bonhoeffer's (1901) and Berlyne's (1972) fantastic and momentary/embarrassment confabulations rather than a new concept. Indeed, the two classifications were often used synonymously, with spontaneous confabulation denoting the fabrication of grandiose, wide-ranging and fantastic stories and provoked confabulations denoting momentary confabulations in response to questions. A clear distinction between these forms of confabulation was challenged (Dalla Barba 1993a). Several authors simply considered spontaneous/fantastic confabulations a more severe expression of the same disorder as provoked/momentary confabulations (DeLuca and Cicerone 1991; Dalla Barba 1993a; Fischer *et al.* 1995).

Although many authors used the same terminology to classify confabulations, they did not necessarily mean the same thing. Some used the terms momentary and provoked to describe elaborate confabulations when recalling a story, others to describe single word intrusions in word list recall. Some based their classification on observations of spontaneous behaviour, others used questionnaires and memory tests. In any case, the varying classifications and the usage of similar terms with different meanings have not facilitated the communication between researchers in the field. In addition, diverse studies explored one form of confabulation (e.g., intrusions) but extended their conclusions to other forms of confabulatory behaviour, without providing empirical evidence for such an association.

All sorts of confabulations in Mrs M

Our own studies have shown us the difficulty of applying one of the known dichotomies to our patient groups. The first patient entering our studies was Mrs M, a 62-year-old woman who was hospitalized when she suddenly became confused (Schnider *et al.* 1996a). She no longer knew where she was and what she had to do. At the hospital, a very marked memory disorder and disorientation were found. Computed tomography scan showed a small infarct in the knee of the right internal capsule, an area containing fibre packages projecting from the thalamus to the prefrontal lobes. We will have a closer look at this lesion in Chapter 4 (Figure 4.4).

Her amnesia persisted but Mrs M remained unaware of it. She thought that she was hospitalized for regulating her diabetes, which she had had for several years. Her behaviour during weeks of neurorehabilitation was remarkable. She persistently failed in memory tasks, unable to recall the information that she had learned before. Most amazingly, however, in addition to a few correctly recalled items (words, pictures), she regularly produced a large number of items that had not been part of the task; she confabulated them. These intrusions did not appear to be random but were mostly items that had been presented in previous tests, not necessarily memory tasks. In a word learning task containing 16 words, she only recalled 4 words after 40 minutes. In addition, however, she produced many words that had been presented in a parallel version of the same memory task three months previously. Similarly, when presented with a series of pictures from which she had to choose those that had been presented in the memory task, she inappropriately felt familiar with all items, that is, also the distracters that had not been presented in the task. Thus, she had severe false recognition. Only when she was forced to strictly limit her choice to one of four items with only one of them being part of the task, were all her choices correct. When we used a conceptually very simple task, in which she was presented with a continuous series of pictures or words among which she had to detect repetitions (Sturm and Willmes 1995), her performance was virtually perfect. In other words, she was able to store and recognize new information but failed to access this information normally. The most striking feature was that, in all tasks demanding free recall of information she produced many intrusions, which could mostly be traced back to material presented in previous, partly unrelated tasks.

In addition to these intrusions, clearly provoked by our memory task, she also made spontaneous comments that amazed us. Thus, whenever she saw one of the clerks of the clinic, she remarked that she knew her: 'We have been working together at the hospital; we cleaned the operating theatre', referring to a job she had held some years ago at another hospital. While this misidentification persisted for weeks, others were fleeting, dependent on the context. When I asked her after some weeks whether she knew me, she replied: 'Of course, you made physiotherapy with me this morning and showed me pictures composed of dots.' She had really had physiotherapy, but of course with a professional therapist. I had indeed conducted a perceptual priming test with her, in which I had shown her degraded pictures of objects and animals, but this was three weeks earlier. If anything, it was clear that Mrs M had more of a chaos than a gap in memory.

She surprised us even more with her behaviour, which occasionally appeared to be entirely inappropriate and which she justified with confabulations. One morning, she stood with packed suitcase in front of the night's nurse and explained that she was to leave the hospital, as it had been arranged by the doctors. The nurse, insecure in the face of Mrs M's conviction, had a hard time convincing her to stay until the physicians arrived. When Mrs M was at home again, she repeatedly prepared a glass of urine in the morning and passed at her daughter's apartment to say goodbye. She was convinced that she had an appointment with her doctor for a control of her diabetes. Most of these appointments were invented. During this period, she was disoriented regarding the time, underestimating the year by two to five years, and regarding her situation, convinced that the medical problem attracting so much attention was her diabetes. In contrast, when asked about past events, her accounts were entirely correct up to three years previously; her confabulations only concerned the last two to three years. Her plans for the day were always plausible. The confabulations were never fantastic or bizarre, except that they were incompatible with her current health status and hospitalization.

Both the intrusions in memory tasks and the confabulations associated with inappropriate behaviours, but also the false recognitions and misidentifications appeared to relate to real events from her past. Experimental investigation showed that although Mrs M retained information in memory very well, she was unable to decide when, where, and from whom, she had learned lists of words. We therefore suspected that all confabulatory manifestations in this patient, as well as her lack of insight, were due to the loss of a 'temporal tag' of memories (Schnider *et al.* 1996a). There appeared to be no need for distinguishing between different forms of confabulation.

Provoked versus spontaneous confabulation

A study on confabulation, in which we also included a group of non-confabulating amnesic patients, proved the latter conclusion premature (Schnider *et al.* 1996b). The patients had such diverse aetiologies as subarachnoid haemorrhage, traumatic brain injury, olfactory meningeoma, chronic alcoholic Korsakoff syndrome, hypoxic brain damage after cardiac arrest, and multiple strokes. They all had severe amnesia as measured by their inability to recall freely the words of a list presented 40 minutes previously.

In agreement with the trend of the time to separate provoked and spontaneous confabulations, we inteded to study these two confabulatory phenomena. However, while provoked confabulations were easy to measure as the number of intrusions in a verbal learning task, there was a difficulty with spontaneous confabulations. Without a doubt, Mrs M had spontaneously confabulated, but her confabulations had never been 'sustained, wide-ranging, or grandiose'. How could we determine the spontaneity of confabulations? The most reliable criterion appeared to be that patients – at least occasionally – also acted according to their confabulations. So, for patients who confabulated in discussions, it was verified with the team – nurses, therapists etc. – whether they occasionally also acted according to their false ideas or justified inappropriate acts with confabulated explanations. Patients doing so were classified as 'spontaneous confabulators' (Schnider *et al.* 1996b).

Some examples may help to visualize the latter behaviour. A 58-year-old woman, who had suffered rupture of an aneurysm of the anterior communicating artery, paced up and down the ward during most of the day trying to convince us that, in reality, she was at home. During a neuropsychological examination, she suddenly rose from the chair and left the room saying that she had to watch after her children who were playing on the terrace (all her children were adults by the time). On another occasion, she left the session with the idea that she had to feed her baby – who was 35 years old at the time. A 45-year-old tax accountant with extensive traumatic orbitofrontal contusions repeatedly and inadvertently left the unit. If he was picked up before leaving the hospital, he would explain that a taxi was waiting for him to bring him to a business meeting. On other occasions he indicated that he was going to meet a friend to do woodwork in the forest, an old pastime of his. It was very difficult for the personnel to convince him that he had to stay at the hospital (Schnider *et al.* 1996b). A dentist, hospitalized in room 105, called the hospital's telephone desk and asked to be connected with his wife, allegedly hospitalized in room 105 (Ptak and Schnider 1999). On several occasions, he inadvertently left the hospital in the steadfast conviction that patients were waiting for him at his clinic. He would then normally turn up at his clinic. Mrs B, described in Chapter 1, is another example of a behaviourally spontaneous confabulator.

All patients were hospitalized for neurorehabilitation at the time of the study. Only those who were out of a confusional state were included. Patients with a severely disturbed attention with high distractibility, incoherent and fleeting ideas, disturbed or even inversed sleep–wake cycle and an insufficient memory span for numbers (limit, 5) were excluded. Patients with dementia were also excluded. Five patients were classified as spontaneous confabulators, and ten patients as 'non-confabulating amnesics' (i.e., no spontaneous confabulation, irrespective of the presence of intrusions).

Based on our observations in Mrs M and on the prevalent idea at the time, our working hypothesis was that provoked and spontaneous confabulations simply reflected different degrees of the same disorder and that spontaneous confabulators just had a more severe 'lack of the temporal tag' in memory.

This was not what we found (Schnider *et al.* 1996b). The production of provoked confabulations (intrusions) was independent of whether the patient produced behaviourally spontaneous, that is, spontaneous confabulations. Figure 3.1 illustrates this. In this graph, intrusions by spontaneous confabulators are indicated with black bars. Patients whose intrusions are indicated by grey columns never acted according to confabulated, inappropriate plans and never justified inappropriate actions with confabulations. The patient at the far right is Mrs M, our initial patient. As described before, she produced many intrusions in memory tasks and intermittently acted according to her confabulations. The patient second from the right, in contrast, produced many intrusions in memory tasks but never had what we have just defined as spontaneous confabulation. On the other side of the spectrum is the patient on the far left of the graph, who produced no intrusions in memory tasks but acted very intensively according to totally inappropriate ideas. This patient is the mother who was convinced that she had to feed her baby.

Further exploration supported the validity of this distinction. We found a mechanism for provoked confabulations, somewhat resembling gap-filling (Chapter 7), which had no predictive value for spontaneous confabulation. Conversely, the mechanism found for spontaneous confabulation (Chapter 8) had no predictive value for provoked confabulations. A dissociation was

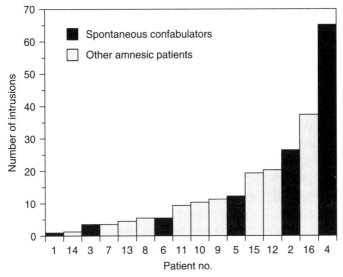

Figure 3.1 Provoked confabulations (total number of intrusions in the California Verbal Learning Test [Delis *et al*. 1987] produced by spontaneous confabulators and non-confabulating amnesics. There is a double dissociation between the number of intrusions and the production of spontaneous confabulations. No healthy control subject produced more than four intrusions. With permission from Schnider *et al*. (1996b).

also found regarding the anatomical basis of the two disorders: provoked confabulations were not associated with a specific lesion location, whereas spontaneous confabulation was only found in patients with lesions of the posterior orbitofrontal cortex or structures directly connected with it (Schnider *et al*. 1996b, c; Schnider and Ptak 1999).

Subsequent studies helped to better delineate this disorder. We found that such behaviourally spontaneous confabulations had some specific qualities and occurred in a relatively fixed combination with other symptoms. We have called this combination of symptoms the '*syndrome of spontaneous confabulation*' (Schnider 2001). Although its elements will be worked out in the following chapters, it may be useful to list its main characteristics here:

1. *Confabulations*: patients confabulate when asked about their recent activities or their plans for the day. Their confabulations can mostly be traced back to elements of real events in their past; they often refer to previous habits. They are convinced about the veracity of their false ideas and occasionally act according to them.

2. *Disorientation*: patients are disoriented regarding time, their current situation, and mostly also to place.

3. *Amnesia*: patients have severe amnesia as measured with delayed free recall. Recognition memory may be relatively spared.

4. *Insight*: patients are normally unaware of their memory deficit and often explicitly deny having a memory problem.

We have used the term 'spontaneous confabulation' to describe this sort of confabulation, in default of a more precise term available in the literature. Behaviour-consistent or behaviourally spontaneous confabulation would be more precise terms, as they emphasize the spontaneity of the behaviour associated with the confabulations. Another recent proposition has been to name them 'spontaneous confabulation (with action)' (Metcalf *et al.* 2007), thus emphasizing our operational criterion that patients intermittently act according to their confabulations. In the following, the term *behaviourally spontaneous confabulation* will be used.

Revised classification of confabulations

Attentive readers may be somewhat perplexed at this point. I hope that by now they believe that intrusions in a memory test (provoked confabulations) and behaviourally spontaneous confabulations are independent disorders. Both deserve the designation as confabulations. Readers hopefully agree that the classification as provoked versus behaviourally spontaneous confabulations makes sense, but it is also obvious that this classification only refers to two precisely defined confabulatory phenomena. Where, readers may ask, are the fantastically combined bits and pieces of historical data characterizing the simple falsifications of memory that Kraepelin (1886) had observed in his syphilitic patients – confabulations that had no impact on the patients' behaviour? Where are those strange stories that patients made up when questioned by Korsakoff (1889, 1891, 1955 [original 1889]), Tiling (1892) and others? Where are the fantastic confabulations revealing the patients' idea that they had jumped out of airplanes (Benon and LeHuché 1920) and landed on cactuses (Flament 1957)?

The answer to these questions may be disappointing: There is no current classification that covers all of these forms of confabulations. Current classifications either propose dichotomies based on an author's observations or consider confabulations an entity requiring no further distinction. The latter attitude certainly cannot be upheld when caring for confabulating patients. Somehow, the dissociations presented above have to be accounted for.

Based on the cases described in Chapter 2, the dichotomies suggested by other authors, and our own studies, I propose to distinguish the following four **forms of confabulation**:

1. *Intrusions* in memory tests (Kopelman 1987; Schnider *et al.* 1996b). Alternatively, they might be called *simple provoked confabulations*, a term which also covers occasional distortions when a subject is pushed to recall the details of a story.

2. *Momentary confabulations*. These describe false verbal statements (rather than intrusions or distorsions of single elements) in a discussion or other situation inciting a patient to make a comment. The incitement can be provided by any situation in which a person feels compelled to say something. Thus, the confabulations can be provoked by questions or spontaneous in a discussion. In that respect, momentary confabulations incorporate the provoked (discrete) versus spontaneous (severe) dimension as used by Pick (Chapter 2, p. 28) and recent authors (DeLuca and Cicerone 1991; Fischer *et al.* 1995). In contrast to fantastic confabulations (see point 3 below), momentary confabulations are conceivable and inherently plausible, although they may be incompatible with a subject's current health status and living circumstances. The confabulations can range from a simple statement to an elaborate, fully invented story. Thus, momentary confabulations also encompass the spontaneous confabulations described by Kopelman (1987), that is, sustained, wide-ranging confabulations readily evident in everyday behaviour (p. 55). It also includes the semantic confabulations that patients sometimes make in response to questions probing semantic memory (Dalla Barba 1993a; Moscovitch and Melo 1997; Dalla Barba *et al.* 1998). This definition of the term is considerably wider than Bonhoeffer's (p. 22) or Berlyne's (p. 55). Momentary confabulation is the most commonly described form of confabulation, documented extensively in Chapter 2. It may be the only confabulatory phenomenon noticed in a patient, but it may also be a feature of behaviourally spontaneous confabulation. At this point, it is unclear whether the propensity for verbal expression of false memories has a mechanism of its own. This form of confabulation is therefore meant to encompass a phenomenon whose independence or associations are yet poorly understood. I suggest not using the terms out of embarrassment or embarrassment confabulations, as these terms assume a mechanism.

3. *Fantastic confabulations*, which have no basis in reality, as described most dramatically by Kraepelin (1886, 1887a) in patients with paralytic dementia and psychosis. These confabulations were nonsensical, logically inconceivable,

and were not accompanied by a corresponding behaviour (p. 15). Fantastic confabulations have also been described as an acute, transitional phenomenon in patients who later produced intense momentary confabulations in accordance with their actions, i.e., in the context of behaviourally spontaneous confabulation (Benon and LeHuché 1920; Flament 1957). The distinction between fantastic confabulations with some inherent plausibility and elaborate momentary confabulations may be delicate, as Berlyne's (1972) somewhat arbitrary classification of his patients' confabulations showed (p. 54f.). Thus, similarly to momentary confabulations, this form of confabulation encompasses a phenomenon whose independence is questionable.

4. *Behaviourally spontaneous confabulation* occurring in the context of severe amnesia and disorientation. The term emphasizes the agreement between the patient's spontaneous behaviour and the verbal expression of his concept of reality: the confabulations and disorientation. The spontaneity here refers to the generation of the underlying concept of reality rather than the production of the confabulations. In discussions, all our behaviourally spontaneous confabulators produced momentary confabulations relating to autobiographical memory, which were often intensive and florid, but sometimes very discrete. Some patients did not produce any confabulation relating to semantic memory. Behaviourally spontaneous confabulation constitutes a syndrome composed of the confabulations, amnesia, and disorientation. Therefore, I have also used the synonymous term 'syndrome of behaviourally spontaneous confabulation' (Schnider 2001, 2003). This syndrome is similar to the variant of the original Korsakoff syndrome in which patients acted according to their confabulations (Korsakoff 1891). The separation of this form of confabulation from momentary and fantastic confabulation is necessary because there are patients who produce the two latter forms of confabulations but never act according to them. The mechanism, which will be discussed in Chapter 8, does not apply to these confabulations.

Evaluation of confabulations

Intrusions (provoked confabulations) in memory tests are by definition easy to identify. Kopelman (1987) measured provoked confabulations as the number of intrusions in logical memory testing. We used the number of intrusions in word list learning (Schnider *et al.* 1996b). These procedures are straightforward and easy to reproduce. However, neither the relevance of these measures beyond scientific exploration nor their intra-individual variance has been determined.

In most instances, the detection of more elaborate confabulations poses no problem either. The bulk of the literature characterizes confabulation as a phenomenon readily revealing itself in a discussion with a patient. Patients rarely spontaneously report false events and few display actions consistent with spontaneously generated, inappropriate ideas, as characteristic of the syndrome of behaviourally spontaneous confabulation. Patients spontaneously tattling absurd fantasies lacking any relation with reality, as reported by Kraepelin (1886, 1887a), are an extreme rarity, occurring in severely demented and confused patients. The discussion with patients about past events, their recent doings and their plans is the most commonly used method of exploring confabulations. Occasionally, confirming the presence of confabulations requires verification of the responses with family members.

Several attempts have been made to formalize the exploration of confabulations and to quantify them. Most procedures were used in studies on the mechanisms or qualities of confabulations and were never validated with regards to their sensitivity or specificity for sorting out a distinct clinical disorder. In most studies, patients had to respond to questions supposed to provoke confabulations in susceptible patients.

Several studies used elaborate questionnaires and interview protocols. Williams and Rupp (1938) mentioned that they had used an improvised battery of approximately 50 questions concerning personal history and orientation (Chapter 2, p. 30). In addition, they tried to elicit confabulatory tendencies by questions about the patients' activities and experiences during the period of amnesia. Unfortunately, they did not provide more specifics about this 'improvised battery of test questions'. Also, they described no results and drew their conclusions without reference to the results of this questionnaire.

More recent questionnaires not only probed the patients' tendency to confabulate in response to questions regarding different categories of knowledge and orientation, but also asked questions to which healthy subjects normally responded by saying 'I do not know.' These questions were designed to measure the patients' tendency to fill gaps in memory. In addition, some studies tested the patients' suggestibility.

Mercer et al. (1977) were among the first to use such an approach. They devised an interview with 41 questions, divided into four main categories:

1. Questions probing overlearned issues associated with remote memory (e.g. patient's birthplace, the last grade completed in school);

2. Questions drawing on recent memory, essentially questions of orientation (the reason for the current hospitalization, location of the hospital, day of the week);

3. Questions that could be answered by drawing on cues in the room (the present weather, the name of the interviewer); and

4. Questions that frequently provoked an 'I don't know' response from non-neurological patients (the winner of last year's Super Bowl).

The questionnaire thus comprised aspects of personal, situational, and temporal orientation, as well as questions probing mental control, i.e., the ability to resist the tendency to fill a gap in memory. This questionnaire was given to 11 patients with diverse aetiologies of amnesia such as hypoxic encephalopathy, alcoholism, hydrocephalus, or dementia. No details regarding their behaviour or the time since brain damage were reported. Two patients were classified as severe confabulators, four as mild confabulators, and five as non-confabulators. As it turned out, the distribution of error types, that is, confabulations, in response to the four types of questions, was consistent among the groups. In particular, severe confabulators did not respond more often to 'I don't know' questions than mild confabulators. Unfortunately, the study does not allow us to draw any conclusion about the usefulness of this questionnaire for diagnosing clinically relevant confabulations because the classification of patients as severe, mild, or non-confabulator was made on the basis of the questionnaire itself; no independent measure of confabulation was used.

Mercer *et al.*'s (1977) study contained an interesting extension. After termination of the interview, three questions to which the patient had responded by 'I don't know' were selected and again asked with the indication that the response inadvertently had not been recorded. The examiner thus tested whether confabulations depended on a patient's suggestibility. As it turned out, severe confabulators did not change their response more often than mild confabulators.

The same battery was used in a study by Shapiro *et al.* (1981), co-authored by Mercer. Seven patients having diverse types of brain damage, such as, right posterior communicating artery or anterior communicating artery aneurysm rupture, trauma, or anoxia were classified as severe or mild confabulators based on the number of confabulations produced in this battery. They then passed a *confabulation-cue test*, designed to elicit confabulations in a structured setting. Patients were shown 20 black and white drawings, each of them containing three major components depicting a situation, e.g., a man in a boat with a fishing rod. After presentation of the picture, the examiner verbally described the picture and the patient was asked to repeat the description. After three to ten minutes of distraction, the patient was again asked to describe the picture. In case of an incorrect response, one of the three components was again presented as a cue. If the patient again failed to give a correct description of the picture, his response was cued by the presentation of two major components. For half of the pictures, the cue was verbal, for the other half, it was the renewed visual presentation of the components.

In agreement with the classification of the patients based on the confabulation battery, severe confabulators gave more confabulatory descriptions after three to ten minutes than mild confabulators (Shapiro *et al.* 1981). Cues helped both groups to reduce confabulatory responses. This decrease was less marked in mild confabulators due to a floor effect. An interesting observation was that two severe confabulators perseverated on their confabulatory responses from one picture to the other. An additional patient tended to perseverate on elements of pictures presented several days previously. This study thus showed that two ways of eliciting confabulations – a verbal confabulation battery and the forced recall of visually presented designs – were equally capable of provoking confabulations and classifying the patients as severe or mild confabulators. However, this study does not allow assigning any specificity to the tasks for classifying confabulations; severe and mild confabulators might just have differed by the degree of overall cognitive impairment.

The questionnaires by Mercer *et al.* (1977) and Shapiro *et al.* (1981) were devised to study the pattern and the mechanisms of confabulations, but they have never been introduced in clinical practice. This was different for Dalla Barba's *confabulation battery*, which was first applied in single case studies (Dalla Barba 1993a, b) and is nowadays regularly used in clinical research and practice. It was initially developed to study the pattern of confabulations in two patients, one having dementia due to Binswanger's encephalopathy (a type of vascular dementia), the other recovering from severe traumatic brain injury (Dalla Barba 1993a). The battery has 95 questions from 7 domains:

1. 20 questions on personal semantic memory (age, date of birth, current address, number of children etc.);

2. 15 questions probing episodic memory;

3. 10 questions on orientation in time and place;

4. 15 questions probing general semantic memory, such as, knowledge about famous facts and people of the past and the present;

5. 15 questions concerning linguistic semantic memory, that is, word definition;

6. 10 questions of semantic knowledge, normally provoking an 'I don't know' response by normal subjects (e.g. 'What did Marilyn Monroe's father do?');

7. 10 questions of episodic type but normally answered by 'I don't know' (e.g. 'Do you remember what you did on March 13 1985?').

Dalla Barba (1993a) found that one patient made confabulations both relating to specific episodes and general knowledge (semantic memory), whereas the other patient confabulated only on questions probing episodic memory. Despite its fairly widespread use, the battery's reliability for predicting specific behaviours or diagnosing a mental disorder with a distinct mechanism or anatomical basis remains unknown. Nonetheless, it allows one to describe more precisely and quantitatively the pattern of a patient's momentary confabulations in response to questions.

A somewhat different approach for studying the conditions eliciting confabulations was taken by Moscovitch and Melo (1997). Rather than asking specific questions, they requested a group of subjects to provide memories evoked by a cue-word, the so-called *Crovitz paradigm*. In their study, they used two lists of words. The list of 'personal cue words' was presented to the subjects with the instruction to think of a personal event or experience evoked by this cue word. Words such as 'angry, brake, dog, letter, make, throw etc.' were used. The second list of 'historical cue words' was used to demand the detailed description of historical events that occurred before the subjects were born. The list contained words such as 'assassination, battle, fire/natural disaster, miracle, saint, train etc.' Responses were scored on a scale ranging from three points for a detailed description specifying time and location of an event to 0 point if nothing was provided. If an event could not be verified, or if the details describing the event were inaccurate and the subjects persisted in their inaccuracy, then the story was considered a confabulation. These confabulations were classified either as errors related to time or to content. The main question was whether confabulations concerned only episodic memory (personal cue words) or also semantic memory (historical cue words).

Seventeen amnesic patients with diverse aetiologies were included in the study (Moscovitch and Melo 1997). They were classified either as confabulators or non-confabulators, 'depending on their behaviour in real life and on their performance on [the] tests that elicited confabulations' (p. 1019), and more specifically, 'depending on whether the number of confabulations produced in either the personal or historical condition was equal to, or greater than, two standard deviations of the scores of the control subjects' (p. 1022). Eight patients were thus classified as confabulating amnesics, nine as non-confabulating. Given that in this study, similar to that conducted by Mercer *et al.* (1977), the experimental task was also used to classify the patients, its discriminative power for clinically pertinent confabulatory behaviour cannot be judged. Amazingly, however, a review of the list of patients (Moscovitch and Melo 1997, p. 1020) suggests that the procedure might have some predictive value for the lesion location: Most confabulating amnesics had lesions including, among other areas, the ventromedial frontal lobes, whereas most non-confabulating amnesics had thalamic, temporal, or diffuse cortical lesions. With respect to the main question of the study, the conclusion was that these patients' confabulations involved both episodic and semantic memories and that distortions of content were at least as common as distortions of time. It is likely that these conclusions particularly reflected the requirements of the paradigm and pertained to the behaviour of this specific patient population. Members of the same research group later confirmed – in agreement with many clinicians working in the field – that 'confabulations are most apparent when autobiographical recollection is required' (Gilboa and Moscovitch 2002, p. 316).

All of these methods, mostly designed for scientific investigation, have been useful for quantifying and classifying momentary confabulations, that is, false verbal statements in response to questions. However, none of them measured the degree of conviction or the behaviour associated with the confabulations. Thus, none of these methods allows sorting out behaviourally spontaneous confabulation.

Diagnosing behaviourally spontaneous confabulation

Diagnosing the syndrome of behaviourally spontaneous confabulation is usually straightforward, as in patients like Mrs B (Chapter 1). Her behaviour left no doubt that her false ideas about her imagined duties were spontaneously generated, and not only fabrications in response to questions. Fully developed behaviourally spontaneous confabulation constitutes an obtrusive clinical problem, where patients confabulate about their current situation and repeatedly act according to their false ideas about the present. The real challenge in caring for such patients is the behaviour emanating from their false idea about current reality – their attempts to leave for imagined meetings etc. – rather than the confabulations. The intensity of inadequate behaviour and of the verbal output – the confabulations – may vary and occasionally dissociates. In the clinical setting, the intensity of supervision needs to be adapted to the intensity of the patient's inadequate behaviour.

In a research setting, however, it is critical to classify patients correctly. The diagnosis of behaviourally spontaneous confabulation can be tricky when one of the components – confabulations, inadequate behaviour – is discrete or if behavioural observation is not possible. By definition, behaviourally spontaneous confabulators – like any other confabulating subject – make false statements when reporting their memories: they also produce momentary confabulations. The critical point is, however, to verify that the confabulations reflect a false concept of reality, which is spontaneously generated rather than the product of a discussion. At least occasional acts in agreement with or explained by confabulations are strong indicators of such mental spontaneity. We used the presence of occasional actions in accordance with the confabulations as an operational criterion in our studies.

The intensity of the patients' verbal output may vary. Some patients mainly confabulate in response to questions or when explaining an action, for example, why they want to leave the hospital; others spontaneously report events and experiences that never took place, or at least not at the indicated time. Hospitalized patients may spontaneously report that they have been at work in the morning or that they have had dinner at home. Very often, such stories concern the patient's previous habits. Occasionally, it may be impossible, just from hearing the patient, to decide whether a story is really invented. One of our patients fooled us when he described in vivid details how he had passed new year's eve with his family at home (Ptak and Schnider 1999). Only inquiry among the nurses reassured us that, in fact, he had passed the night at the hospital, as planned. It can be wise to verify even a credible story with a family member or custodian.

The presence of confabulations is sometimes easier to substantiate when asking a patient about his plans for the day: it may then become clear that his ideas disregard current reality. The patient just mentioned explained with full conviction that he had an appointment with a neurosurgeon in the afternoon because he needed brain surgery. Even the scar on his head did not comfort him that, in reality, he had already had surgery. Rather, he desperately searched for the (fictive) letter confirming the appointment (Ptak and Schnider 1999).

Unfortunately, even the indication of most inappropriate plans, flagrantly false in the face of true reality, does not prove behaviourally spontaneous confabulation. The case of an 82-year-old woman, who had suffered bilateral medial temporal destruction due to herpes simplex encephalitis, exemplifies this difficulty. She was severely amnesic and very concerned about this. Within eight weeks, she regained orientation as to the circumstances of her memory disorder ('You know, I had this virus in my brain') and the place where she was, knew the year and the month, but remained disoriented regarding the day of the week and the date. Up to this time, she had never confabulated but rather complained about her bad memory, and she had never shown proclivity to leave the unit to enact inappropriate plans – an unproblematic patient, very unlike a spontaneous confabulator. So, I was quite surprised when she responded to my question about her plans for the weekend that she would have dinner with her mother at home, where she would also sleep. She admitted some doubt concerning this plan when I inquired about her conviction, but she definitely gave up the idea only after we had calculated her mother's age to be at least 108 years. Indeed, the patient had a retrograde amnesia extending over almost 40 years and was unaware of her mother's death many years ago. In this period of her disease, she regularly confabulated when asked about her activities during the day; she often recounted fictive walks to town. Sometimes, she spontaneously described therapies that she pretended to have had with a collaborator of the clinic who happened to be present at our discussion, but she never spontaneously acted according to such ideas. Direct inquiry usually revealed that she was not fully convinced about what she said. 'You know, I was pretty sure, but I might be wrong', was the typical answer. Based on the above classification (p. 63f.), this patient produced (intense) momentary confabulations in discussion, but no behaviourally spontaneous confabulations.

This example shows that the confabulation of inappropriate plans is not specific for behaviourally spontaneous confabulation; indeed, it is quite common in delirious and severely demented patients. Conversely, the following case demonstrates that very scarce confabulations in response to questions do not exclude the syndrome. This case concerns a 57-year-old man who had suffered rupture of an aneurysm of the anterior communicating artery with ensuing severe amnesia. The patient was apathetic for several weeks. Even though he was subsequently alert and active throughout the day, he remained moderately disoriented. In discussions, he provided very short responses, which were only occasionally patently wrong. Further testing, which will be explained in Chapter 8, indicated a pattern of memory failure compatible with behaviourally spontaneous confabulation. However, nothing like that was obvious in my brief exploration of the patient, who impressed me primarily by his passivity. Thus, I felt compelled to concede that this patient was an exception to the rule and was not a behaviourally spontaneous confabulator despite the pattern of his memory disorder. No sooner had I reached my conclusion that the nurse caring for the patient vehemently interrupted me. It turned out that for several days the patient had repeatedly appeared at the nurses' office in the morning saying that he now had to go to work or that he had an appointment with his wife.

This patient's confabulations were in no way spectacular and he stopped such behaviour a few days later. He was a craftsman normally going to work in the morning and one might speculate that the morning hours particularly strongly cued his habit of going to work. Be this at it may, this patient was a very discrete confabulator both in terms of verbal production and actions. Close observation nonetheless confirmed intermittent behaviour and confabulations which were incompatible with his current health status and signalled the presence of behaviourally spontaneous confabulation.

The example shows that observation by people having a steady contact with a patient may be necessary to diagnose safely or exclude discrete, possibly only intermittent, behaviourally spontaneous confabulation. Such continuous observation by experienced people is often not feasible, e.g., when the patient has returned home. We have encountered this difficulty when following up our first group of patients (Schnider *et al.* 2000a). In this situation, the questions listed in Table 3.1 have proved useful for screening for continued behaviourally spontaneous confabulation. We have asked these questions of relatives

Table 3.1 Questions useful for screening a patient for behaviourally spontaneous confabulation. The questions were addressed to the patients' custodians and family members. Positive responses were followed by detailed analysis of the patient's behaviour.

1. Confusion of information

Does the patient confuse people? Does he/she, for example, take strangers for familiar people?

Does the patient confuse dates? Does he/she believe at the wrong time or on the wrong days that he/she has appointments or that specific events take place? Examples: Meetings with friends or business partners, visits from friends, dinner with friends, medical appointments.

Does the patient confuse places? Does he/she believe to be in another place than he/she really is?

Are there other types of confusion? Please specify.

2. Verbal accounts by the patient

Does it occur that the patient inappropriately tells that he/she has to complete business work?

Does it occur that the patient inappropriately indicates that he/she will meet friends or business partners (indication of false appointments)?

Does the patient inappropriately indicate he/she will meet family members or expects their visit?

Does the patient occasionally indicate other things that cannot be true? Please specify.

3. Behaviour and actions

Does it occur that the patient prepares himself for business meetings, which do not take place in reality? Examples of actions: Selection of clothes, preparation of files, phone calls, actively informing others about such meetings, or actual attempt to leave for the meeting.

Does it occur that the patient prepares himself for a meeting with family members or friends, which do not take place in reality? Examples: Selection of clothes, wrapping of gifts, setting the table for visitors, informing others about such visits, or actual attempt to leave for such a meeting.

Does the patient perform other actions that refer to things or situations, which do not actually take place (for example medical appointments)? Please specify.

or custodians living with the patients. Positive responses were followed by detailed investigation of the patients' behaviour.

Another indirect indicator of the possible presence of behaviourally spontaneous confabulation is the testing of orientation. As we will see in Chapter 8, disorientation may result from the same disorder in memory as behaviourally spontaneous confabulation (Schnider *et al.* 1996c).

Summary

The term 'confabulation' appeared in the medical literature around the year 1900, with the same meaning as the old terms 'pseudo-reminiscences, illusions of memory, or falsifications of memory'. Wernicke (1900) defined it as 'the emergence of memories of events and experiences which have never taken place'. Over the years, diverse definitions have been proposed, often adapted to the observations made in specific groups of patients. Berlyne's (1972) is among the most popular definitions of confabulation: 'A falsification of memory occurring in a clear consciousness in association with an organically derived amnesia.' The term was eventually also used to denote unintentional, objectively false statements about percepts.

Diverse classifications of confabulations have been proposed, mostly reflecting the dichotomy of confabulatory phenomena that authors perceived in their patients. The most common distinction opposing momentary (or embarrassment) confabulations and fantastic (or productive) confabulations was initially proposed by Bonhoeffer (1901) and later revived by Berlyne (1972). Another distinction relates to the evocation of confabulations and juxtaposes provoked and spontaneous confabulations (Kopelman 1987). However, none of the current classifications covers all known forms of confabulation. Although the very dissociation between different forms has been challenged, there is sufficient ground for distinguishing at least four forms of confabulation:

1. *Intrusions* or *simple provoked confabulations* in memory tests;

2. *Momentary confabulations* upon some form of incitement, be this questions or the circumstance of a discussion. False statements can range from a simple response to a question to elaborate confabulations. Momentary confabulations are probably not a unitary disorder;

3. *Fantastic confabulations*, which have no basis in reality and are intrinsically nonsensical and illogical;

4. *Behaviourally spontaneous confabulations*, that is, confabulations reflecting a confusion of reality, which underlies currently inappropriate behaviour and statements.

Until now, only the dissociation between forms 1 and 4 rests upon formal scientific evidence (Schnider *et al.* 1996b). Patients may have a combination of momentary and behaviourally spontaneous confabulations, possibly also fantastic confabulations.

It is normally easy to detect confabulations in a discussion with the patient about past events, recent activities, and plans for the near future. Diverse questionnaires and interviews have been proposed, mostly in the context of scientific inquiry, to quantitatively describe the intensity and the pattern of confabulations (Mercer *et al.* 1977; Moscovitch 1989; Dalla Barba 1993a). The validity of these methods for discerning specific brain diseases or for distinguishing between different forms of confabulation remains unknown. The diagnosis or exclusion of behaviourally spontaneous confabulation often requires close behavioural observation.

Chapter 4

Aetiologies and anatomy of confabulation

What are the causes of confabulations? What diseases induce the tendency to retrieve false and distorted information from memory? The classic authors listed chronic alcohol consumption, syphilis, senile dementia, and schizophrenic psychosis as the most frequent causes (Kraepelin 1899; Wernicke 1900; Bleuler 1923). Recent reviewers favoured anterior communicating artery (ACoA) aneurysm rupture (Gilboa and Moscovitch 2002), at least for severe, clinically pertinent confabulation (Johnson *et al.* 2000). In reality, we do not know. There is no study on the incidence of confabulations in a non-selected cohort of brain-damaged subjects, let alone the general population. Authors tend to describe interesting things as they observe them, and it is much more interesting to describe a floridly confabulating and disoriented patient than ten non-confabulating patients. According to Bonhoeffer (1901), only three per cent of patients presenting with an alcoholic delirium went on to have a chronic Korsakoff syndrome. According to Kraepelin (1926), 'at the utmost four to five per cent' of syphilitic patients went on to have general paralysis. Walton (1953) observed only six 'wild confabulators' among 312 patients with subarachnoid haemorrhage. Clearly, clinically pertinent confabulation is a rare phenomenon.

The aetiologies of confabulation have also shifted to new diagnoses as a result of the progress of medicine. Alcoholic Korsakoff psychosis can now be prevented with thiamine; syphilis can be treated with antibiotics so that it does not progress to general paralysis; and the productive symptoms of schizophrenia and other psychoses can be controlled with neuroleptics. However, modern medicine has also brought about new causes of confabulations: more patients nowadays survive rupture of an anterior communicating artery aneurysm, and many more survive herpes encephalitis, which had an extremely high mortality before the advent of antiviral drugs (Whitley *et al.* 1986). Despite spectacular treatment successes, some patients are left with severe cognitive defects, in particular deranged memory.

The ultimate goal of this chapter is to derive an idea about the anatomical basis of the different types of confabulations and to explore whether and how these lesions differ from classic anterograde amnesia – the inability to learn and retrieve new information. In this endeavour, priority will be given to well documented positive studies describing confabulating patients. Such studies prove that the described lesions or diseases can induce confabulations. Negative cases are more difficult to interpret. Certainly, they do not exclude that a given lesion or disease can induce confabulation. Negative cases may also reflect a selection bias: authors studying amnesia often included patients only in the chronic phase, as they had 'pure' amnesia, which was no longer contaminated by the thought distortions characterizing confabulation and disorientation. In addition, many studies only reported the patients' profile on standardised neuropsychological batteries, with no mention of their everyday behaviour. It will be an interesting challenge in the following paragraphs to figure out the types of confabulations to which the different studies referred.

Anatomical target regions

Before embarking on an analysis of the lesions inducing confabulations, it may be useful to review briefly those structures that are of particular interest in the realm of memory and which will be mentioned in the following paragraphs. Figure 4.1 gives a schema of these structures and their main connections.

A central structure, universally accepted as crucial for the formation of memories, is the *hippocampus* with its surrounding tissue – the parahippocampal cortex containing the entorhinal cortex, the main entry to the hippocampus (Van Hoesen 1982; Suzuki 1996), and the perirhinal cortex (Brown and Aggleton 2001). These structures, together with the amygdala and its surrounding tissue, form the medial temporal lobe. Lesions of the medial temporal lobe, especially if bilateral, have long been known to induce severe amnesia (Squire and Zola-Morgan 1991). Many readers will be familiar with the story of the best-known, prototypical patient presenting an extremely severe amnesia after bilateral medial temporal ablation: patient H.M. He was operated in 1953, at the age of 27, because of intractable epileptic seizures. On both sides, the amygdala and the anterior half of the hippocampus with the overlying cortex (Corkin *et al.* 1997) were removed by a neurosurgeon, William Scoville, ignorant at the time of this area's role for memory formation (Scoville and Milner 1957). Since that day, H.M. has been unable to store any new explicit information (Milner *et al.* 1968; Corkin 2002). Although H.M.'s memory capacities were explored by numerous scholars of memory over the decades, confabulation has never been an issue.

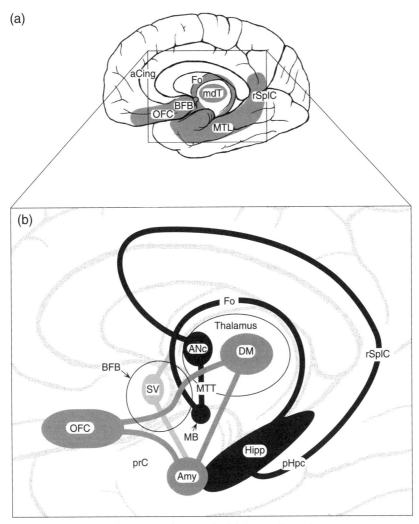

Figure 4.1 Anatomy of anterograde amnesia. (a) Areas whose damage causes amnesia. (b) Main connections within this area. The black loop represents the classic Papez' circuit (hippocampal loop). The mid-grey loop shows the lateral limbic loop (amygdala–dorsomedial thalamus–orbitofrontal cortex). The connections of the septum verum are indicated in light grey. Abbreviations: Amy, amygdala; aCing, anterior part of the cingulate gyrus; ANc, anterior nucleus of the thalamus; BFB, basal forebrain; Fo, fornix; Hipp, hippocampal formation; MB, mammillary bodies; DM, dorsomedial nucleus of the thalamus; mdT, medial thalamus; MTL, medial temporal lobe; MTT: mammillo-thalamic tract; OFC, orbitofrontal cortex; pHpc, parahippocampal gyrus; prC, perirhinal cortex; rSplC, retrosplenial cortex; SV, Septum verum. Adapted with permission from Schnider (2004).

Similarly severe amnesia can occur after medial temporal damage involving the hippocampus and the surrounding cortex due to other causes, such as herpes simplex encephalitis (Cermak 1976; Stefanacci *et al.* 2000), ischaemic stroke with parahippocampal destruction (Victor *et al.* 1961; Schnider *et al.* 1994b), or hippocampal inflammation in systemic lupus erythematosus (Schnider *et al.* 1995). The latter two patients, whom we have described, suffered from their situation and complained about their bad memory. As time went by, they occasionally produced confabulated responses to questions. One of them, who also had very severe retrograde amnesia extending back to his childhood years (Schnider *et al.* 1994b), learned to cope with his memory loss by pretending to recognize people who greeted him, if necessary even by a kind discussion containing invented plans – only to ask his wife immediately afterwards who that person was. These confabulations best corresponded to momentary confabulations in our classification; the patient never acted upon them.

Whereas the role of the hippocampus and medial temporal lobe for memory formation is well established, the role of its connecting structures has remained more controversial. These structures are reciprocally connected with one another by a loop called the *Papez circuit* (Papez 1937) (Figure 4.1b, black loop). The hippocampus projects via the fornix with one fibre package to the mamillary bodies in the posterior hypothalamus. Via another fibre package, it projects to the septum verum, an area containing several nuclei, including the cholinergic nucleus of Meynert and neurons producing other transmitters (Gritti *et al.* 1997), which activate wide areas of the neocortex (Russchen *et al.* 1985). The inferior part of the fornix runs through an area called the basal forebrain, which contains the nuclei of the septum and the ventral extension of the basal ganglia, the ventral or limbic striatum (Nakano *et al.* 2000). The basal forebrain and the fornix may be destroyed to a variable extent by a ruptured aneurysm of the anterior communicating artery or by tumours that may then give rise to severe amnesia, sometimes accompanied by confabulation (Alexander and Freedman 1984; Damasio *et al.* 1985b; Vilkki 1985). The fornix may also be damaged in isolation during surgical procedures to remove tumours or colloid cysts from the third ventricle (Hodges and Carpenter 1991; Aggleton *et al.* 2000). Despite some controversy, amnesia after apparently isolated fornix lesions has been documented in a number of cases (Gaffan and Gaffan 1991; Poreh *et al.* 2006). Confabulation has not been mentioned as a typical feature of isolated fornix damage.

Many past and present students of memory seemed to accept that the *mamillary bodies* in the posterior hypothalamus were crucial for memory formation. Cases with and without confabulation have been described (Benedek and Juba 1941; Kahn and Crosby 1972; Tanaka *et al.* 1997).

Despite widespread acceptance of the mamillary bodies as memory critical structures, no case of enduring amnesia with a lesion strictly limited to the mamillary bodies has – to my knowledge – ever been reported. It is also of note that in the alcoholic Wernicke–Korsakoff syndrome, the mamillary bodies are apparently always destroyed, even in cases who do not have chronic amnesia (Victor *et al.* 1989; Harding *et al.* 2000). One might speculate that the role of the mamillary bodies for memory formation depends on the precise arrangement of fornix fibres in an individual; about half of the fibres do not pass through the mamillary bodies but take a short-cut directly into the anterior thalamic nucleus (Raisman *et al.* 1966; Robertson and Kaitz 1981; Jones 1985), which is the relay station following the mamillary bodies in the Papez circuit.

The mamillary bodies project to the anterior thalamic nucleus via the mamillo–thalamic tract (Jones 1985). These fibres may be damaged in paramedian thalamic infarction, a well-established cause of amnesia. Bilateral infarction may result from the occlusion of one artery, the paramedian artery (also called thalamoperforating artery, thalamic–subthalamic artery) that irrigates the medial part of both thalami in about a third of individuals (Bogousslavsky *et al.* 1988). It has been speculated that damage to this area only results in amnesia if the lesion extends into anterior parts of the thalamus and also destroys the mamillo–thalamic tract on its way to the anterior thalamic nucleus (Von Cramon *et al.* 1985; Graff-Radford *et al.* 1990).

Isolated lesions of the *anterior thalamic nucleus* are extremely rare, thus its role for human memory has not been clearly established (Aggleton and Sahgal 1993). Severe amnesia, accompanied by intrusions and false recognition, was described in a series of 12 patients (Ghika-Schmid and Bogousslavsky 2000). One of them also showed 'spontaneous confabulations' with no specification. The patients made a marked recovery, but significant amnesia persisted.

Animal experiments also suggested that the anterior nucleus is important for memory formation (Aggleton and Sahgal 1993). This nucleus then projects via the cingulate bundle to an area behind the splenium of the corpus callosum, the so-called *retrosplenial or granular cortex* (Robertson and Kaitz 1981). This is the last relay station before closure of the Papez circuit via the entorhinal cortex into the hippocampus. Amnesia following damage to the retrosplenial cortex – so-called retrosplenial amnesia – has been described after haemorrhage from a vascular malformation in this area (Valenstein *et al.* 1987). It was characterized by an inability to acquire temporal information about new stimuli (Bowers *et al.* 1988). One of our patients had amnesia due to a meningeoma arising from the falx (the fibrous plate between the two hemispheres) and compressing the retrosplenial cortex on both sides. She had severely deficient free recall and verbal learning but good recognition. She had no tendency to confabulate (very few intrusions, no behaviourally spontaneous confabulations) and participated in one of our studies as a non-confabulating amnesic (Schnider and Ptak 1999).

While the role of the structures connected with the hippocampal formation, which represents the posterior part of the limbic system, is well documented, the role of more anterior limbic structures – orbitofrontal cortex, amygdala and connected areas – is less clear. These structures are connected through a loop called the *lateral limbic loop*.

Rupture of an aneurysm of the anterior communicating artery (ACoA) is a well-established cause of amnesia (Alexander and Freedman 1984; Damasio *et al.* 1985b; Vilkki 1985). Whether this amnesia results from destruction of the posterior medial orbitofrontal cortex or the underlying basal forebrain with the septum is unclear.

The *posterior orbitofrontal cortex* has reciprocal connections with the amygdala (Porrino *et al.* 1981; Carmichael and Price 1995b; Price *et al.* 1996). Isolated amygdala damage, however, does not induce significant amnesia (Tranel and Hyman 1990; Aggleton 1992). The amygdala appears to be more important for processing the emotional significance of stimuli and for conditioning (Bechara *et al.* 1995). It projects unidirectionally via amygdalofugal pathways to the medial, magnocellular part of the *dorsomedial thalamic nucleus*, the main origin of projections to the prefrontal cortex (Russchen *et al.* 1987; Fuster 1997). As indicated before, paramedian thalamic infarction involves the dorsomedial nucleus and may induce severe amnesia (Von Cramon *et al.* 1985; Gentilini *et al.* 1987; Graff-Radford *et al.* 1990). Confabulation has been described (Gentilini *et al.* 1987; Nys *et al.* 2004).

The orbitofrontal cortex has reciprocal connections with the medial, magnocellular part of the dorsomedial nucleus, thus allowing closure of the loop connecting it with this nucleus and the amygdala – the so-called lateral limbic loop (Morecraft *et al.* 1992; Ray and Price 1993; Gloor 1997; Jones 2007). The position of the dorsomedial nucleus is indicated in Figure 4.2.

Many authors attributed a particular role for the generation of confabulations to the frontal lobes – the *prefrontal cortex*, to be more precise. Some invoked defective 'frontal monitoring processes' to explain confabulation. The notion is very general because the frontal lobes constitute the largest section of the human brain and contain several areas with quite distinct connections (Fuster 1997). Figure 4.2a shows the most common classification of cortical areas by Brodmann (1909), based on cytoarchitectonic distinctions, that is, differences in the composition of the cortical layers. Multiple frontal areas can be distinguished.

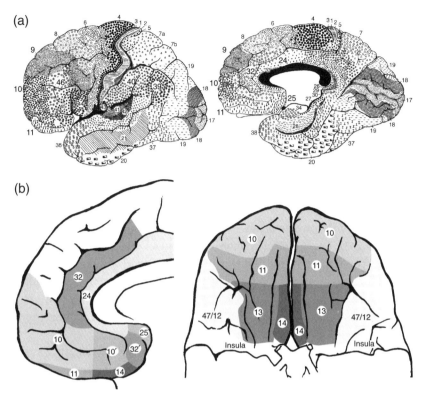

Figure 4.2 Cytoarchitectonic maps of cortical areas. (a) Cytoarchitectonic map by Brodmann (1909). (b) Map of orbitofrontal and ventromedial areas. Adapted with permission from Öngür *et al.* (2003). Simplification approved by Dr J. L. Price.

At least three large frontal areas can be differentiated whose damage induces different types of 'frontal syndromes' (Cummings 1993). The dorsolateral prefrontal cortex – the lateral convexity of the frontal lobes centred on areas 46 and 9 – constitutes the highest degree of association cortex, which is linked with other association cortices (Fuster 1997; Miller and Cohen 2001). Damage to this area does not normally induce classic amnesia, but may interfere with the timely application of memory (Fuster 1997). The patients may fail to store and retrieve precise temporal and contextual aspects of stored information (Shimamura *et al.* 1990; Milner *et al.* 1991; Kopelman *et al.* 1997b). Occasionally, dramatically disorganized use of memory may result from such lesions (Ptak and Schnider 2004). Increased false recognition has also been reported (Schacter *et al.* 1996a).

The medial or paramedian frontal cortex – centred on anterior areas 32 and 24 – contains the anterior part of the cingulate gyrus, an area having strong limbic connections (Carmichael and Price 1995b; Mega and Cummings 1997). Damage to this part of the brain often induces prolonged apathy and lack of drive with an inability to initiate acts and speech, a state called akinetic mutism (Bogousslavsky and Regli 1990; Devinsky *et al.* 1995).

The third component, the *orbitofrontal cortex*, constitutes the inferior surface of the frontal lobes. It has diverse parts with different connections. Brodmann (1909) classified only parts of this area. More complete subdivisions, based on comparative studies of humans and monkeys, followed (Beck 1949). Figure 4.2b shows the simplified version of a modern classification by Öngür *et al.* (2003). Another well-known parcellation was proposed by Petrides and Pandya (1994). The above discussion of connections with the amygdala and dorsomedial thalamic nucleus concerned the posterior medial part of the prefrontal lobes with area 13 and the inferior medial cortex (Figure 4.2b) (Jones 2007). The anterior and lateral orbitofrontal cortex have different connections (Morecraft *et al.* 1992; Carmichael and Price 1996). The area of the posterior medial orbitofrontal cortex and the inferior paramedian frontal cortex, below the corpus callosum, is often referred to as the ventromedial prefrontal area (areas 25, 32' 10' 14 in Figure 4.2b), a description which also includes the deep structures of the basal forebrain.

With this much anatomy in mind, let us now browse the literature to see what aetiologies and confirmed or suspected lesion sites have been associated with the diverse types of confabulations.

Delirium

Confabulations are not necessarily the result of a coherent thought process leading to consistent, but currently inappropriate behaviour, as in behaviourally spontaneous confabulators like Mrs B (Chapter 1). Confabulations and disorientation may also occur when coherent thinking is impossible and memories get jumbled. The acute confusional state or delirium describes a state of chaotic thought processing with lack of attention and impaired awareness of the environment (Kaufer and Cummings 1997; Schnider 2004). Confusion is evident, attention is fluctuating, and the patients may oscillate between alert and drowsy states. Diurnal rhythm is impaired with increased sleeping during the day and agitation with hallucinations during the night. Motor and cognitive performances vary constantly: as the patients are awake, they may participate in a discussion and be oriented. Minutes later, they may turn somnolent and give stereotyped, confused and incomprehensible responses. Formal criteria have been established, but symptomatology varies between patients (American Psychiatric Association 1994). Dementia is similar to delirium in that it affects multiple cognitive domains, but the deficits are more stable, hallucinations are not as common, and attention is much better preserved. We will come back to dementia later in the chapter.

The list of causes that may disturb the brain's concerted functioning is almost endless. Delirium often constitutes a transitional phase in the recovery from acute brain damage, be this brain trauma, subarachnoid haemorrhage, encephalitis, or other causes. It can signal the decompensation of a brain tumour, the beginning of an encephalitis, Wernicke–Korsakoff syndrome, or intoxication. It may also reflect the brain's suffering in cardiac or respiratory insufficiency or anaemia (Lipowski 1985).

Acutely confused patients fail to learn and retrieve information normally from memory, are often disoriented and may give strange responses to questions that can be interpreted as confabulations. Many authors also applied the term Korsakoff syndrome to this state as they described patients having tuberculosis (Béthoux 1935), lymphoma (Környey 1932), leprosy (de Beurmann et al. 1906), pernicious anaemia (Bonhoeffer 1911; Parfitt 1934), incoercible vomiting during pregnancy (Von Hösslin 1905; Ely 1922; Vermelin and Louyot 1936), CO intoxication (Schulz 1908), ventriculo-encephalitis due to cytomegalovirus (Torgovnick et al. 2000), or the brief confusional state following cingulectomy (Whitty and Lewin 1960). Indeed, many of Korsakoff's own patients confabulated only during the acute phase of their disease. Accordingly, Korsakoff's list of diseases that could present with the combination of confusion (pseudo-reminiscences) and neuropathy was impressive: delivery of a macerated foetus, postpartum septic process, faecal impaction, typhus, tuberculosis, diabetes, jaundice, lymphadenoma, necrosis of a neoplasm, alcoholism, poisoning with arsenic, lead, hydrogen disulphide, carbon monoxyde, ergot, spoiled corn, and so on (Victor and Yakovlev 1955, p. 402). For these diseases, Korsakoff's designation as 'toxaemic psychic cerebropathy' (Korsakoff 1890b) appeared entirely appropriate. Even today, the term 'toxic-metabolic encephalopathy' is sometimes used synonymously with delirium. It is interesting to note that in all of the patients described in the above articles, confabulations were limited to verbal expressions produced in response to questions; no behaviourally spontaneous confabulations were reported, with the possible exception of a few aggressive outbursts. In our experience, however, many confused patients have an urge to disappear from the ward during their active hours. It is not always clear whether this urge reflects erratic, random behaviour or a consistent, currently inappropriate action plan based on a confusion of reality, as in patients having behaviourally spontaneous confabulation. Confused patients normally fail to explain the motive of their behaviour.

The *mechanism* of confabulations in delirium has never been formally established. Given the chaotic thought processes characterizing delirium, it is not surprising that memories, too, go wild. It has also been suggested that such confabulations reflected the true remembrance of hallucinations experienced during the delirium (Bonhoeffer 1901; Moll 1915). Patients recovering from coma after traumatic brain injury, a phase called post-traumatic amnesia (Russel and Smith 1961), often start by retaining bits and pieces of information. Indeed, even patients in a severe confusional state may retain some information. We tested a group of patients awakening from coma after different types of brain damage, including subarachnoid haemorrhage (Ptak *et al.* 1998). Almost half of them had to be excluded because they fell asleep during testing. Those that could be tested had significantly superior recall of information presented with a mnemonic aid, namely, the simultaneous presentation of images representing the words that had to be learned. Thus, even severely confused patients store some information. If they retain information as irrelevant as the words used in our study, it is entirely conceivable that they may store some of their hallucinations.

Not only the mechanism, but also the *anatomical basis* of confabulations in delirium is poorly understood. Indeed, a confusional state may just as well result from widespread cortical damage due to hypoxia, metabolic derangement, or encephalitis as from a tiny, strategically located traumatic lesion in the upper brainstem. It is treacherous to draw conclusions about anatomo–clinical relationships from patients confabulating during a delirium. In our studies on provoked and behaviourally spontaneous confabulations, patients were only included once they had emerged from a confusional state and had a normal sleep–wake cycle, were alert during the whole day, and had at least intact focussed attention, as documented with the ability to repeat at least five numbers in the correct order.

In *conclusion*, delirium may be associated with disorientation and possibly all forms of confabulation described in the previous chapter. At present, the mechanism of these confabulations is unknown. Similarly, it is unknown whether the confabulations reflect dysfunction of any specific area of the brain – i.e., the failure of a hypothetical 'final common pathway' of correct memory recollection – or whether they result from disturbed synchronicity in any part of a hypothetical network representing correct memories.

Anterior communicating artery aneurysm rupture

Rupture of an aneurysm of the anterior communicating artery (ACoA) was only recognized as a cause of classic Korsakoff syndrome – amnesia, confabulation, and disorientation – in the late 1950s. Since then, it has given rise to some of the most dramatic descriptions of confabulation. Severe, long-lasting confabulation appears to be rare. Logue (1968) noted confabulation early after operation of an aneurysm in 18 of 90 patients (20 per cent). Only one of them (1.1 per cent) continued to confabulate beyond the confusional state, but 16 patients (18 per cent) had continuing memory impairment. In a comprehensive review, DeLuca and Diamond (1995) estimated that acute amnesia with or without the other elements of the Korsakoff syndrome had an incidence of almost 60 per cent. At the follow-up, the reviewed studies reported a prevalence of these disorders between zero and 15 per cent.

Modern surgical techniques have reduced the incidence of amnesia. Gade (1982) followed 48 patients with rupture of an ACoA aneurysm. In 11 patients, the aneurysm was trapped by occlusion of the ACoA, a procedure also interrupting blood flow in the deep branches of the ACoA, which irrigate parts of the basal forebrain and the anterior hypothalamus. Nine of these eleven patients (82 per cent) subsequently suffered an amnesic syndrome. In 37 patients, the neck of the aneurysm was ligated in an attempt to save the perforating vessels. Only six of these patients (16 per cent) subsequently had amnesia. There was no comment on confabulation. In a more recent review of their data, Bindschaedler *et al.* (1997) observed persistent amnesia in 1 of 56 patients (1.8 per cent) after operation of an ACoA aneurysm, although executive dysfunction was common. It is likely that modern neurosurgical and neuroradiological procedures will help to reduce the frequency of amnesia and confabulation in the context of ACoA aneurysms even further.

Although chronic amnesia and confabulation appear to be rare, rupture and treatment of an ACoA aneurysm have the reputation of producing the most spectacular, long-lasting, and severe confabulatory states. Talland *et al.* (1967) were among the first to provide a dramatic description of this state. A 26- and a 33-year-old man suffered rupture of an ACoA aneurysm and were operated two days apart. Postoperatively, both were confused … and were placed in the same room! This circumstance created occasions for the most fantastic and inconsequential dialogs between the two men. For some weeks, they exchanged complete nonsense in conversation, relating events without regard to factual accuracy or verisimilitude. During that time, they were totally disoriented as to their location, time, their medical histories, and the persons in their surroundings. The patients appeared entirely unconcerned about their condition, but this light-hearted mood continued while confabulation in the sense of fabricating absurd or improbable tales gave way to more plausible errors in temporal or situational placement. One of the patients told of his going to various places the day or night before, places that he had been in the habit of frequenting. He regularly referred to the other patient as an old friend from the army.

In both patients this state lasted for several weeks, and both remained amnesic.

Damasio *et al.*'s (1985b) description was no less spectacular. In particular the description of the first of their five patients established the idea that ACoA aneurysm rupture could be followed by fantastic confabulations. During the acute phase after operation, the patient exhibited bizarre and unusual fabrications. He would interweave current public events with imagined personal experiences. For instance, he believed that he was a spaceship commander at the time of the Columbia space shuttle mission. During that period, he occasionally became a 'space pirate'. When discussing Egyptian President Sadat who had been assassinated one week after the patient's haemorrhage, briefly before the interview, the patient described a personal meeting with the political leader. He believed Sadat had visited him recently in the hospital.

Within a month, temporal orientation and evaluation of reality improved remarkably. In an interview one month later, the patient commented on his experiences in the early phase as follows:

> I was a pirate and I commanded a space ship. Now I realize it's not true. I didn't dream that; it was a total part of consciousness. To me, it was reality at that time. It's embarrassing now.
>
> Damasio *et al.* (1985b, p. 265)

It appears that this patient's fantastic confabulations were limited to the acute phase, possibly as he was still in a confusional state. Evidently, this patient had memorized his own thoughts and confabulations during this stage. His mental condition soon improved, but his memory remained deficient.

Damasio *et al.*'s (1985b) conclusions read like the confirmation of Moll's (1915) proposals, made 70 years earlier, based on a review of the alcoholic Korsakoff syndrome (Chapter 2, p. 29). Damasio *et al.* wrote:

> The patients confabulated freely in a manner best described as wild fabrication ... The fabricated episodes were composed of unrelated memories, some of which corresponded to real experiences and some of which were acquired through reading, conversation, television, and even dreaming... All of these fabrications included some powerful elements of current reality as perceived in the news... The combination of the elements was legitimate, i.e., it respected logic and was within the boundaries of the fictionally possible, but the composition had no basis in reality. Curiously, these fabricated fantasies were subsequently incorporated in memory, at least in part.
>
> Damasio *et al.* (1985b, p. 269)

Confabulations are rarely as fantastic as those described by Damasio *et al.* (1985b), but many patients confabulating after ACoA rupture intermittently act according to their false ideas. Mrs B, described in Chapter 1, is an example of a behaviourally spontaneous confabulator after ACoA rupture. The diagnosis of this type of confabulation requires behavioural observation. While most early studies extensively documented the content of confabulations, especially if they were 'wild and bizarre', only few mentioned the patients' behaviour. Stuss *et al.*'s (1978) study was an exception. Two of their five confabulating patients had suffered ACoA aneurysm rupture. One of them (patient 3 of the series) started to confabulate in the early phase:

> He confabulated spontaneously … During an early interview, he stood up without warning, walked to a window, gazed out at the surrounding buildings, returned to his seat, and informed the examiner that his (the examiner's) boat had been stolen.
>
> Stuss *et al.* (1978, p. 1168)

What is the interpretation of this behaviour? Was this patient still in a confusional state? Was he hallucinating? Did he just produce fantastic confabulations? Or did he act according to an idea – a memory – which was currently inappropriate; so, did he have behaviourally spontaneous confabulation? In this patient, the course eventually confirmed behaviourally spontaneous confabulation, which continued at least for the four months of postoperative follow-up.

The second patient with ACoA rupture is noteworthy as he had a favourable early postoperative course. Within a few months, however, his behaviour changed, he was intermittently incontinent, became disoriented, had impaired memory for recent events, and 'confabulated readily'. He was re-hospitalized seven months after the acute event. Investigations – at the time by pneumo-encephalography, an invasive and painful procedure – demonstrated hydrocephalus, an inadequate accumulation of liquid within the brain's ventricular system. A ventriculo–peritoneal shunt was placed but yielded no significant benefit. The patient was included in the study by Stuss *et al.* (1978) five years later, when his clinical condition was still unchanged. Most clinicians are nowadays aware that confabulation, disorientation, or other behavioural changes, which appear after an initially favourable clinical course following aneurysm rupture, are suspect of a complication – vascular spasms in the early phase, hydrocephalus thereafter. Stuss *et al.*'s (1978) article documented that severe confabulation after ACoA rupture, but also after traumatic brain injury, might continue for many months.

Kapur and Coughlan's (1980) case study illustrated in an impressive way the evolution of confabulation over several months. They studied a 40-year-old building contractor with ACoA aneurysm rupture, operated from the right side. A CT scan one week after the operation showed a left frontal ventromedial lesion. For almost three months, the patient displayed profoundly inappropriate social behaviour. From then on, a severe memory deficit and confabulations dominated the clinical picture. He would claim, first thing in the morning, to have fictitious business appointments, when in fact he was attending a day care centre, and would frequently dress for dinner in the evening in the mistaken belief that guests were coming. In discussion, he would claim to have been engaged in imaginary business appointments and would mix up things from the previous hours and days. He was unable to recall previously presented material correctly but had very good scores at forced-choice recognition tests. Seven months after the aneurysm rupture, confabulation was much less obvious, but still occurred in direct questioning about his recent past. At this time, the confabulations reflected distortions of actual happenings and placing events in the wrong temporal or spatial context.

Kapur and Coughlan (1980) called the initial confabulations of this patient 'fantastic' because they had no clear relationship with the reality of the patient's hospitalization. In the classification used in this book, this patient was a clear behaviourally spontaneous confabulator, who also produced elaborate momentary confabulations which were intrinsically plausible. The authors considered the late confabulations as momentary, because they appeared on direct questioning. These confabulations were not accompanied by a corresponding behaviour. This patient's state of behaviourally spontaneous confabulation lasted almost seven months, during which the content of the confabulations was more and more influenced by the real environment.

Many studies on confabulation included patients with ACoA aneurysm rupture (Mercer *et al.* 1977; Shapiro *et al.* 1981; Moscovitch 1989), but few tried to deduce a specific pattern. Alexander and Freedman (1984) described 11 patients with amnesia after ACoA aneurysm rupture, of which four or five had prolonged, persistent confabulation. They observed diverse stages: all patients presented lethargy and agitation (delirium) in the initial postoperative phase, which normally cleared within one to three weeks. The next stage was dominated by confabulation, confusion of people (reduplication), and denial of illness, with a clear sensorium. This stage was usually transient and cleared within a few weeks. In four patients, however, confabulation was lasting. In the next stage, patients continued to improve over weeks or months, and confabulation, denial, and overt confusion cleared. In this stage, patients were amnesic and unconcerned. The authors also observed a change in personality towards apathy, fatuousness, socially inappropriate behaviour, and unpredictable aggression. The long-term prognosis was not good: no patient returned to his premorbid job, and four of the eleven patients were permanently institutionalized.

A case series by Vilkki (1985) further refined this observation. She described five patients with confusion and disorientation following surgery of an ACoA aneurysm. Three of them regained orientation within a few days, although memory deficits persisted. Two patients, however, continued to confabulate and remained disoriented for at least four months.

Many of the features described by Alexander and Freedman (1984) are nowadays considered prototypical for the amnesia following ACoA aneurysm rupture (DeLuca and Diamond 1995). In reality the *clinical course* may be heterogeneous, ranging from no cognitive deficit or discrete transient amnesia to long-lasting and severe behaviourally spontaneous confabulation. The persistence of amnesia after cessation of confabulation has repeatedly been described (Logue *et al.* 1968; Hanley *et al.* 1994). Our own studies have also illustrated very severe, slowly resolving behaviourally spontaneous confabulation, followed by cessation of confabulation but persistence of amnesia (Ptak and Schnider 1999; Schnider *et al.* 2000a, see also Mrs B's case in Chapter 1).

Concerning the *anatomical basis* of confabulation after subarachnoid haemorrhage, huge progress has been made since the 1950s, when a diffuse toxic mechanism, devoid of any anatomical specificity, was assumed (Tarachow 1939; Walton 1953). Since the 1960s it has been recognized that severe confabulation after subarachnoid haemorrhage most often emanated from the rupture of an aneurysm of the ACoA rather than other vessels (Lindqvist and Norlén 1966). This is true for behaviourally spontaneous and possibly also for fantastic confabulations. In contrast, provoked and elaborate momentary confabulations, without accompanying behaviour, have also been described after rupture and operation of an aneurysm of the posterior communicating artery (Dalla Barba *et al.* 1997a). The insight that ACoA aneurysm rupture was particularly often associated with memory failures meant that anterior limbic structures within the ventromedial prefrontal area (posterior orbitofrontal cortex and basal forebrain) were involved in memory processing, presumably both storage and the control of outflow. However, the precise anatomical basis of amnesia, confabulation, and disorientation after rupture of an ACoA aneurysm has not yet been completely resolved.

Talland (1967) hypothesized that in his patients, damage of the Papez circuit explained the amnesic syndrome. Based on associated clinical features, in particular sexual impotence, he suspected a lesion involving the posterior inferior medial frontal areas and the gyrus rectus (area 14 and medial area 11 in Figure 4.2b). Such claims received support with the advent of CT scans. Alexander and Freedman (1984) analysed the CT scans of their 11 patients, all of whom had infarction in the territory of the ACoA. From reviewing the anatomical connections in this area, they proposed that damage of the septum and its cholinergic projections to the hippocampus was responsible for the particular amnesic syndrome. Using similar evidence from CT scans, Damasio *et al.* (1985b) made a similar suggestion:

> It is our hypothesis that the amnesia results from interference with medial temporal function in the hippocampal formation proper, amygdala, and parahippocampal gyrus caused by the basal forebrain lesion ... Damage to the basal forebrain could lead to significant reduction of cholinergic input to temporal lobe structures and widespread regions of the association cortices.
>
> Damasio *et al.* (1985b, p. 270)

The interpretation, of course, did not explain why the amnesic syndrome following ACoA rupture has behavioural consequences that are so strikingly different from the amnesia following medial temporal lesions. Alzheimer's disease is also associated with degeneration of cholinergic cells in the basal forebrain, but confabulation is not a prominent feature in the early stages. But indeed, recent perfusion studies using single photon emission computed tomography (SPECT) in two patients having isolated basal forebrain lesions demonstrated concomitant medial temporal (hippocampal) hypoperfusion (Abe *et al.* 1998; Hashimoto *et al.* 2000).

A few recent studies tried to make fine distinctions between lesions that produced confabulations after ACoA aneurysm rupture and lesions that did not. Irle *et al.* (1992) analysed the precise lesion extension in 30 patients, who had had ACoA aneurysm rupture one to five years previously. Patients were classified as having a lesion of the striatum (in particular the head of the caudate nucleus), the basal forebrain (diagonal band of Broca, substantia innominata, ventral stratum), the ventromedial frontal cortex (encompassing rectal and orbital gyri, frontal pole, anterior cingulate etc.), or a combination of these. The patients underwent neuropsychological testing. The authors concluded that patients with combined lesions of the basal forebrain and striatum, with or without the ventral frontal cortex, had severe memory deficits, whereas patients with lesions in the basal forebrain or the striatum alone showed virtually no deficit. Intrusions in the memory tests were particularly prevalent in the group having combined lesions of the basal forebrain and ventromedial frontal cortex. The authors' final conclusion has to be taken with care, as it relates only to chronic patients, amnesia, and the provoked confabulations (intrusions) explored in the study:

> Neither basal forebrain nor striate lesions alone are sufficient to produce memory deficits. Combined striate and basal forebrain lesions, however, appear necessary and

sufficient to produce amnesia. Ventral medial frontal lesions appear to add little to the deficit.

Irle *et al.* (1992, p. 478)

Studies with acute patients contradict the very last statement.

The study by Fischer *et al.* (1995) gave much more importance to ventromedial frontal lesion extension than Irle *et al.* (1992). They examined nine confabulatory patients who had had rupture and clipping of an ACoA aneurysm. Five of the nine patients were considered 'spontaneous confabulators', in that they produced 'unprompted grandiose statements in informal conversation and elaborate, extended confabulations to questions' (Fischer *et al.* 1995, p. 22). In the classification used in this book, these would correspond to elaborate momentary confabulations, needing very little to provoke them. An extended case report of one of these patients indicated, however, that behaviourally spontaneous confabulations were included in this group. The patient, a 50-year-old woman, worried during evaluation that her son and daughter were waiting outside in the dark for her and impulsively walked out of the office several times. Throughout her hospital day, she would wander into other patients' rooms, persistently believing she was here to help the elderly. She also produced a significant number of intrusion errors in verbal memory testing. A second group of four patients produced only limited, often superficially plausible confabulations when provoked under questioning. The confabulations by the patient representing this group were defined thus: 'All of his confabulations occurred in response to direct questioning and were relevant to the topic of inquiry' (Fischer *et al.* 1995, p. 25). Thus, despite the inclusion of patients having behaviourally spontaneous confabulation, this study focused on the distinction between abundant and rare momentary confabulations. An analysis of CT scans indicated that the lesions of the severely confabulating patients – called spontaneous confabulators – were more extensive and involved the basal forebrain, ventral frontal lobe, and striatum. The patients producing less elaborate confabulations – called momentary or provoked confabulations by the authors – had lesions restricted to the basal forebrain, except for one who had additional orbitofrontal damage.

Does the production of behaviourally spontaneous confabulation require ventromedial frontal damage, or is basal forebrain damage sufficient? A number of single case studies involving patients having circumscribed lesions within the basal forebrain – for reasons other than ACoA aneurysm rupture – have shown that basal forebrain lesions are sufficient to produce lasting amnesia (Morris *et al.* 1992; Von Cramon *et al.* 1993; Abe *et al.* 1998; Goldenberg *et al.* 1999). In several of these cases, performance in memory tests was distinguished by relatively preserved recognition of previously presented material, but with an increased number of false positives in recognition and abundant intrusions in free recall tests. Most patients were tested after several months, so that the presence of initial confabulation cannot be judged. However, such lesions can obviously also induce severe confabulation: Hashimoto *et al.* (2000) described a 73-year-old woman with a tiny haemorrhage limited to the right basal forebrain: diagonal band of Broca, septal nuclei including the nucleus basalis of Meynert, and nucleus accumbens (central part of the ventral striatum). The patient presented behaviourally spontaneous confabulation and disorientation beyond the confusional state. Of note, the authors observed and examined the patient already in the early phase. After three months, the confabulations, which were pervasive in the first months and associated with striking behavioural aberrations, were described as 'minimal'. Thus, when studying the anatomy of confabulations, it is crucial to know the patients' early clinical course; the absence of confabulations in the chronic phase says nothing about a lesion's propensity to induce confabulation and disorientation.

Notwithstanding this single case, orbitofrontal damage is probably more critical for the occurrence of confabulations after ACoA aneurysm rupture than basal forebrain damage. Gilboa *et al.* (2006) recently analysed the lesions of eleven patients with ACoA aneurysm rupture. Four of them produced 'behavioural and verbal spontaneous confabulations', while seven were classified as non-confabulators (although two of them had been confabulators earlier in the course). Lesion differences between the groups were discrete, but the authors concluded that orbitofrontal damage – in addition to ventromedial damage – was crucial for the occurrence of spontaneous confabulation.

Our own data indicated that more extensive damage of the ventromedial frontal area (posterior medial orbitofrontal cortex and basal forebrain) carries a much higher risk of inducing prolonged and behaviourally significant severe confabulation (behaviourally spontaneous and intense momentary confabulations) than small lesions. Figure 4.3 shows some scans of patients. The patients who had the longest course of behaviourally spontaneous confabulation beyond the confusional state (Figure 4.3a–c) had the most extensive lesions, encompassing large portions of the medial orbitofrontal cortex and at least parts of the basal forebrain. A patient who had a prolonged confusional state with confabulation and disorientation (Figure 4.3d) but stopped confabulating after termination of the confusional state, had a comparable lesion extension; he continued to have severe executive failures. A patient (Figure 4.3e) who had a confusional state with disorientation of six weeks with moderate momentary confabulations and then continued to have moderate

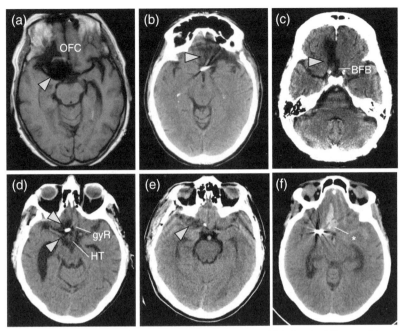

Figure 4.3 Typical lesions after ACoA aneurysm rupture. (a) MRI of a 58-year-old woman who severely confabulated for 12 months (patient 1 in Schnider *et al.* 1996b). (b) 50-year-old journalist, who confabulated for five months (Pihan *et al.* 2004). (c) Mrs B, who confabulated for 17 months (Chapter 1). (d) 35-year-old mechanic who had a prolonged confusional state of almost two months. After termination of the confusional state, he stopped confabulating and regained orientation but continued to have severe executive failures; (e) 56-year-old man who had a six weeks' confusional state and then stopped confabulating. He continued to have moderate amnesia, but with intact orientation and without confabulation. (f) 54-year-old woman who was slightly disoriented for two weeks and then rapidly recovered without producing any confabulations. Her scan shows blood (*) in the area of the orbitofrontal cortex and basal forebrain but does not reveal how much tissue is really damaged. Lesions are indicated by arrowheads. Abbreviations: BFB, basal forebrain; gyR, gyrus rectus (a part of the orbitofrontal cortex); HT, hypothalamus; OFC, orbitofrontal cortex.

amnesia with intact orientation and without confabulation, had small lesions of the transition between the inferior insula and the posterior orbitofrontal cortex. Thus, even though our data are biased in that we only see patients who do not fully recovery after aneurysm treatment, it is obvious that those patients who had an unfavourable clinical course, characterized by prolonged behaviourally spontaneous confabulation and disorientation, had more extended orbitofrontal and basal forebrain lesions (Figure 4.3a–c). The conclusion is compatible with Fischer *et al.*'s (1995) comparison of severe versus mild momentary confabulations.

Prediction of severity and duration of confabulation and disorientation is difficult in the acute stage because the definitive lesion often cannot be correctly appreciated. Figure 4.3f shows an acute scan indicating massive haemorrhage in the area of the posterior medial orbitofrontal cortex. The patient was disoriented for two weeks and then rapidly recovered without producing any confabulations; discrete memory problems and executive dysfunction persisted. In our experience a quite reliable prognostic element has been that those patients who present with behaviourally spontaneous confabulation beyond the confusional state after ACoA aneurysm rupture have a high risk of remaining in this state for many months (Schnider *et al.* 2000a).

In *conclusion*, rupture of an aneurysm of the ACoA may give rise to all forms of confabulations: intrusions, mild or elaborate momentary confabulations, fantastic and behaviourally spontaneous confabulation. Overall, persistent amnesia seems to be a rare complication, and long-standing confabulation is very rare. Nonetheless, rupture of an aneurysm of the ACoA is one of the most consistently reported aetiologies of severe, long-standing behaviourally spontaneous confabulation. The precise anatomical determinants of the different confabulatory manifestations are still unclear. Most studies suggested that more extended lesions, encompassing both the basal forebrain and the orbitofrontal cortex (ventromedial prefrontal area) were more likely to induce severe confabulation. However, the issue has not been completely resolved. It is possible that damage to discrete functional units, which escape detection by current structural imaging, determine whether a patient is simply amnesic, producing momentary confabulation, or having the reality confusion characteristic of behaviourally spontaneous confabulation. In the future, refined functional imaging – seizing the activity of smaller units more rapidly – might help to resolve this question.

Posterior circulation stroke

Rupture of an aneurysm of the anterior communicating artery is certainly the best-known type of stroke producing severe confabulation. In this case, destruction is centred on the basal forebrain and posterior orbitofrontal cortex, that is, the anterior extension of the limbic system. In this section, reports of confabulation after ischemic stroke in the distribution of the posterior circulation – the vertebro–basilar system – will be reviewed. The basilar artery gives rise to the two posterior cerebral arteries, whose branches irrigate the occipital lobes, the medial temporal lobe with the hippocampal area (but not the amygdala), the thalamus, and some other structures. Memory deficits are among the most common manifestations of stroke in this territory.

Bilateral medial temporal stroke involving the hippocampus and the adjacent cortex is a well-known cause of very severe amnesia with incapacity to store new information (Victor *et al.* 1961; Schnider *et al.* 1994b). Confabulation is not normally a feature of this type of amnesia. However, a patient may adapt to his memory deficit by giving invented responses. A patient of ours (Schnider *et al.* 1994b) responded to the question about where he had passed his holidays by saying: 'We like Italy; I think we were in Italy', although he had had no holidays.

Unilateral medial temporal lesions can give rise to severe modality-specific memory disorders, but not normally to confabulation. Von Cramon *et al.* (1988) tested 30 patients two to 24 months after left posterior infarction. Twelve of them had marked verbal amnesia. None of them confabulated, and all had a realistic view of their memory capacities.

Reports of confabulation after posterior cerebral artery infarction are rare. Trillet *et al.* (1980) described 30 patients with ischaemic stroke in the distribution of posterior cerebral arteries. Only a few had CT scans, so that the precise lesion extension was not known in the majority of cases. Eighteen patients (60 per cent) had persistent amnesia. Confabulation was very rare and discrete:

> In only three [of the 18] cases did we think that we could retain a few confabulatory responses, and even then only after insistent induction

> Trillet *et al.* (1980, p. 427)

These reports possibly underestimate the potential of medial temporal infarction to induce an acute confabulatory state. We have recently seen an elderly woman who started to produce intermittent nonsensical confabulations following left medial temporal infarction, somewhat similar to the confabulations described by Kraepelin in his patients suffering from general paralysis (Chapter 2, pp.15ff.). She roamed and justified her urge to leave the unit with ideas that could be classified as behaviourally spontaneous confabulation. Neuropsychological testing revealed severe cognitive deficits corresponding to a chronic confusional state or dementia. The posterior stroke appeared to be the event which had derailed her mental abilities.

It is possible that a more anterior lesion extension, by involvement of the thalamus, increases the likelihood of confabulations. Servan *et al.* (1994) analysed confabulations in 76 patients with an infarct in the territory of the posterior cerebral artery, confirmed by CT scan or MRI. Twenty-one patients (28 per cent) were diagnosed with acute or chronic amnesia, based on their failure to retain three words over three minutes and disorientation in time and space. Amnesia diagnosed this way probably includes confusional states. The fact that the study was retrospective further limited its precision. Among the 21 amnesic patients, five (24 per cent) were reported as 'spontaneously' confabulating. In four patients, these confabulations occurred in the first days after the stroke, accompanied by disorientation and false recognition. One patient, a 57-year-old physician, falsely affirmed knowing the address of the examiners or pretended that the hospital had been transferred to another area. Thus, it appears that these confabulations corresponded to reduplicative paramnesia (pp. 52 and 169f.) rather than mnestic confabulations. Another patient, a 74-year-old man, had signs of a confusional state or dementia. To the question 'Where are we?' he responded: 'You are at Stan Starley, I think ... Stan, this is steel, Starley the geometric form of the instrument from which precisely Starley is made.' The fifth patient appeared to have 'numerous confabulations and false recognitions' for several months, with no further specification.

Although these cases did not convincingly demonstrate stable confabulations of any specific type, they nevertheless differed from the other 16 memory-impaired patients by the presence of confusion, disorientation, and clinically impressive confabulatory phenomena in the acute stage. In this sense, the lesion analysis is interesting. It showed that, while all 21 patients had medial temporal lesions with occipital extension, only the five cases with confabulatory phenomena had an additional uni- or bilateral thalamic lesion, which the authors located in the area of the dorsomedial thalamic nucleus.

Bilateral paramedian thalamic infarction is a well-recognized cause of amnesia, but again, confabulation has rarely been reported. Castaigne *et al.* (1981) conducted a neuropathological study of 28 patients with paramedian thalamic and midbrain infarcts, 24 of them bilateral. Among these patients, only three (11 per cent) were reported as having had amnesia, and only one of them was described as having a global memory defect and confabulation (case 7). Von Cramon *et al.* (1985) studied six patients with bilateral paramedian thalamic infarctions in the chronic phase, twelve months to seven years after stroke. Four of them were amnesic; confabulation was not mentioned. The main merit of this study was that it provided radiological evidence indicating that anterior medial extension of the thalamic lesion was necessary to induce amnesia. Von Cramon *et al.* (1985) concluded that damage to the mamillo–thalamic tract within the thalamus was more important for the occurrence of amnesia than damage of the dorsomedial nucleus. Barbizet *et al.* (1981) had previously arrived at the same conclusion on the basis of a single case. Graff-Radford *et al.* (1990) later supported this conclusion. Among five patients with bilateral paramedian infarction described by Bogousslawsky *et al.* (1988), three had memory impairment. One of them had confabulation in the acute stage, which was not further specified.

Even though the role of the mamillo–thalamic tract is widely accepted, other potentially important structures run through this area. The anterior part of the medial (magnocellular) component of the dorsomedial thalamic nucleus, which is typically also affected, receives afferents from those parts of the amygdala, which project to the same region of the posterior orbitofrontal cortex with which the dorsomedial nucleus has reciprocal connections (Gloor 1997). The anterior part of the magnocellular dorsomedial nucleus is therefore the main thalamic relay station of the lateral limbic loop.

Single case studies occasionally mentioned confabulation. Barbizet et al.'s (1981) patient, a 43-year-old woman, had severe amnesia due to bilateral paramedian thalamic infarction. According to an analysis of the CT scans, the lesion appeared to be centred on the mamillo–thalamic tract and the ventral–oral anterior nucleus of the thalamus; the dorsomedial nucleus was only minimally involved. In the acute phase, the patient produced some confabulations:

> When she was insistently asked about her children, confabulations appeared: she said she had three children (when in fact she had only two). When she was told that she had just given birth to a boy, she replied almost immediately that he was 'at least one year' old; when she was asked whether she was sure about that, she responded: 'Oh yes! We have just celebrated his birthday.'
>
> Barbizet et al. (1981, p. 416)

These confabulations rapidly disappeared.

Guberman and Stuss (1983) described two patients with paramedian thalamic infarction, one of whom remained disoriented, hypokinetic, and apathetic for three weeks and then showed 'a definite tendency toward confabulation' in memory testing, again with no further specifics.

A convincing case of pertinent confabulation after bilateral paramedian thalamic infarction was reported by Gentilini et al. (1987). One of their eight patients, a 66-year-old man,

> revealed a mixture of confabulation and delusion of grandeur. He claimed to live with a woman, sometimes identified as his dead wife, sometimes as a woman in all respects identical to her but whom he just married, and sometimes as his wife's sister (who had never existed). He also claimed that he was very rich, owning eight flats ... He said that he could speak many foreign languages and was a General in the Air Force ... The symptomatology remained unchanged for the month during which he was hospitalized. A few days after he had returned home, he went to the police station asking why his wife had abandoned him.
>
> Gentilini et al. (1987, p. 901)

At seven months, he was perfectly oriented; impaired memory could only be demonstrated with formal testing.

Thus, this patient produced very elaborate momentary or even fantastic confabulations apparently for more than a month. The episode after his hospitalization might correspond to behaviourally spontaneous confabulation. His lesion was indistinguishable from six other patients. It involved the territory of the paramedian thalamic artery and extended on the left side into the territory of the polar artery, i.e., more anteriorly. The authors concluded that damage to the mamillo–thalamic tract was responsible for the memory disorder.

Nys *et al.* (2004) reported a 46-year-old clerk who confabulated for almost two months after paramedian thalamic infarction. He believed that he was living in a sect, although he was actually living alone. During neuropsychological examination, he thought he was participating in a television quiz with the neuropsychologist as the quizmaster. Apparently, he also had visual hallucinations: he saw an audience sitting beside the quizmaster. He often acted on his confabulations. For example, he occasionally wandered around the ward, thinking he was working at the hospital as a physician. Thus, this patient had elaborate momentary confabulations and behaviourally spontaneous confabulation.

The idea that lesion extension anteriorly to the hippocampal formation increased the risk of severe confabulation (Trillet *et al.* 1980) was supported by a single case study by Amarenco *et al.* (1988). Their patient, a 76-year-old painter, had an occlusion of the left *anterior choroidal artery* with infarction of the posterior limb of the internal capsule, the anterior part of the hippocampus, and the amygdala. In the first days, a severe memory deficit and 'important confabulations' were noted: He declared having been secretary under diverse governments (III Republic, Pompidou, Daladier), successively Secretary of culture, Minister of war, of the interior, on other days, he said he was a financial supervisor, then again that he was a great famous writer. There were no false recognitions. When recalling heard texts, he would again produce important confabulations. Three weeks later, the memory disorder and the confabulations had regressed. Thus, this patient produced fantastic confabulations and intrusions in memory testing during the first weeks after his stroke. No associated behaviour was reported.

A case of behaviourally spontaneous confabulation and intrusions in memory tests following an even more anterior lesion was Mrs M, who was described in Chapter 3. Her lesion involved the *knee of the internal capsule*

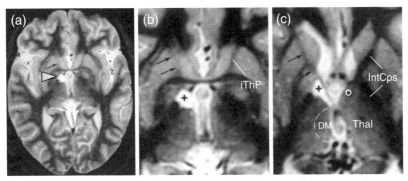

Figure 4.4 Mrs M's lesion. (a) The magnetic resonance image after ten months shows a tiny infarct in the knee of the right internal capsule (arrowhead in a, + in b and c). (b, c) Details of the lesion. There is marked atrophy of the fibres in the anterior limb of the internal capsule (thin arrows), including its inferior part, the inferior thalamic peduncle. This peduncle (thin arrows in b, c) carries the connections of the dorsomedial nucleus of the thalamus with the posterior orbitofrontal cortex. The white circle (o) indicates the anterior thalamic nucleus. DM indicates the approximate position of the dorsomedial thalamic nucleus. Right side of the pictures corresponds to left side of the brain. Abbreviations: IntCps, internal capsule; iThP, inferior thalamic peduncle; Thal, thalamus. Adapted with permission from Schnider et al. (1996a).

and the anterior part of the anterior thalamic nucleus on the right side, presumably due to occlusion of the polar artery. This lesion led to marked atrophy of the fibres projecting from the thalamus to the prefrontal cortex, and in particular to the posterior orbitofrontal cortex, as visible in the magnetic resonance images taken ten months after the stroke (Figure 4.4). Lacunar lesions typically occur in diabetic and hypertensive patients, such as Mrs M. It is possible that this type of lesion also caused the Korsakoff syndrome with confabulations and disorientation, which earlier authors attributed to diabetes (Sittig 1912). Tatemichi et al. (1992) described six patients with such lesions involving the inferior genu of the internal capsule and reported an acute syndrome with fluctuating alertness, inattention, memory loss, and apathy. Although they did not use the word 'confabulation' in their case reports, patient 6 was described as follows:

> During hospitalization ... episodes of confusion were evident. On several occasions, he was found wandering in the hallway with the intention of 'paying his bills'. He described unusual events (e.g., a 'murder in Bermuda') to his wife, who observed

that these reports had a dream-like quality. When questioned later about them, he acknowledged that they were 'imagined'.

Tatemichi *et al.* (1992, p. 1974)

Three months later, all neuropsychological functions were normal. It is possible that this patient produced behaviourally spontaneous confabulations in the early phase, but it is unclear whether they were still present after cessation of the confusional state.

The possible interaction of different memory critical structures for the occurrence of amnesia and confabulations was suggested in a recent case report by Yoneoka *et al.* (2004). Their patient, a 56-year-old businessman, had an abrupt onset of anterograde and retrograde amnesia with disorientation; his conversation contained confabulations. At four and eight weeks, his memory disorder persisted (confabulations and disorientation were not specifically mentioned any more). MRI showed an old lacunar lesion in the right capsular genu with atrophy of the anterior limb of the internal capsule, similar to Mrs M (Figure 4.4). Diffusion-weighted imaging showed that his new lesion involved the anterior medial part of the left thalamus, probably damaging the mamillo–thalamic tract and parts of the anterior nucleus. Thus, in this patient, a lesion, which had caused confabulatory amnesia in Mrs M (p. 57f.), only became manifest as it was 'complemented' by a lesion of the mamillo–thalamic tract on the other side.

In *conclusion*, confabulation after ischemic stroke in the distribution of the posterior cerebral arteries is rare. After medial temporal infarction, no behaviourally significant confabulations have been described beyond the confusional state. Paramedian thalamic infarction appears to produce chronic amnesia only when the anterior medial thalamus is damaged, possibly indicating a particular role of the mamillo–thalamic tract. Non-specified confabulation has been mentioned in a minority of patients. Very few cases producing elaborate momentary confabulations and behaviourally spontaneous confabulation have been reported (Gentilini *et al.* 1987; Nys *et al.* 2004). Their lesions were similar to those of other amnesic patients. An additional case producing these forms of confabulation had a medial temporal lesion involving the amygdala (Amarenco *et al.* 1988). We have observed chronic behaviourally spontaneous confabulation and marked intrusions after right-sided lacunar infarction of the capsular genu and anterior thalamic nucleus (Mrs M, p. 57f.) (Schnider *et al.* 1996a). Overall, it appears that ischemic lesions of more anterior parts of the limbic system or of structures connected with it are more likely to produce behaviourally significant confabulations (fantastic and elaborate momentary confabulations, behaviourally spontaneous confabulation), albeit only in a minority of cases.

Traumatic brain injury

There is no real need at this point to state that traumatic brain injury can induce severe expression of all forms of confabulation. Kraepelin (1910) already included 'insanity in traumatic brain injury' as a cause of Korsakoff syndrome:

> The disturbance of memory uses to be quite conspicuous and often takes the form of Korsakoff psychosis ... Immediate impressions are very rapidly forgotten. Simultaneously, falsifications of memory most commonly appear, sometimes as blends of truth and fiction, sometimes as entirely free inventions. In part, they represent 'confabulations out of embarrassment', recounts of apparently trivial events of the last few days, which can also be incited and influenced by suggestion. Sometimes one can recognize in these stories distorted fragments of true events, whereas others are reminiscent of events deriving from dreams.
>
> Kraepelin (1910, p. 24f.)

Traumatic brain injury was recognized very early as a cause of confabulation. We have seen in Chapter 2 Tiling's (p. 20f.) and Kalberlah's (p. 24f.) descriptions of patients producing behaviourally spontaneous confabulations beyond the confusional state, which lasted for at least two months (Tiling 1892; Kalberlah 1904). Benon and LeHuché's (1920) patient (p. 25f.) initially produced fantastic confabulations and subsequently behaviourally spontaneous confabulations, accompanied by false recognition. Flament's (1957) patient (p. 32f.) produced elaborate momentary or even fantastic confabulations. In the recent literature, traumatic brain injury reappeared regularly as a cause of confabulation and disorientation in case series (Berlyne 1972; Stuss *et al.* 1978; Shapiro *et al.* 1981; Schnider *et al.* 1996b; Moscovitch and Melo 1997). Provoked confabulations (intrusions) were not of much interest to the old masters, when word-list learning was not practised, but of course, provoked confabulations have also been described (Demery *et al.* 2001).

Post-traumatic Korsakoff syndrome is related to *post-traumatic amnesia* (PTA), a term coined by Russel (1932, 1971; Russel and Smith 1961) to describe the early condition of patients recovering from coma after severe head injury: they are usually confused and disoriented, sometimes confabulate, and fail to learn and recall information from memory. Russel likened PTA to disordered consciousness:

> Post-traumatic amnesia (PTA) gives a fair indication of the duration of disturbed consciousness, [whereby] a good indication of full recovery of consciousness seems to be a return of normal orientation, full awareness of the sequence of events, and the ability to store events so that what happens can be recalled at a later date.
>
> Russel (1971, p. 2)

The patients also have retrograde amnesia, which tends to shrink; even if it initially covers several months, it may eventually shrink to only a few minutes before the injury (Benson and Geschwind 1967; Russel 1971).

The duration of PTA is often difficult to determine; patients may remain amnesic for a long period after traumatic brain injury. Russel and Smith (1961) stated that 'the duration of [PTA] is the length of the interval during which current events have not been stored' (p. 16). In Brooks *et al.*'s (1980) words, this definition reads as follows: 'PTA [is] defined as the interval between the injury and regaining continuous day-to-day memory' (p. 530). Using such definitions, many authors established the close link between this clinical state and the duration of disorientation (Artiola *et al.* 1980; Brooks *et al.* 1980; Ellenberg *et al.* 1996). PTA is a significant indicator of severity of traumatic brain injury (Russel 1971; Ellenberg *et al.* 1996). Thus, post-traumatic amnesia starts with the coma and ends when normal orientation has been regained; in between, it comprises the acute confusional state and – if the patient remains disoriented – an ensuing chronic Korsakoff syndrome. In the context of our discussion of confabulation, PTA is important because many studies on what would previously have been called traumatic Korsakoff syndrome have eventually been conducted under the heading PTA.

Confabulations after traumatic brain injury may occur in the acute confusional state and for some weeks after termination of the confusional state, as the examples in Chapter 2 demonstrated. Delayed onset of Korsakoff syndrome was also recognized early on. Aronsohn (1909) described a 50-year-old businessman, 'never infected with syphilis and almost abstinent with regards to alcohol', who became a victim of a serious train accident. He was unconscious for several hours and complained of severe headache, remained confused, and was agitated during the night for several days. Tests of memory and calculation revealed severe deficits, and disorientation persisted. His confusion steadily worsened. After four months, he started to confabulate in a confused or even fantastic way. He was convinced that he would invent a healing potion against mental weakness, earn much money, and become a professor. He pretended to have great earnings. His gait also worsened. Aronsohn attributed this clinical course to continuing degeneration of the cortex. Nowadays, such a patient would have a CT scan, which would probably reveal a chronic subdural haematoma or hydrocephalus, typical complications of traumatic brain injury.

The *frequency of confabulation* after traumatic brain injury is difficult to determine and depends on the severity of the injury. Despite the dramatic descriptions of confabulatory behaviour by the early authors, severe confabulation is a rare phenomenon after traumatic brain injury. Klein and Kral (1933) considered the 'discrete tendency to confabulations' a typical feature of the traumatic amnesic syndrome – apart from logorrhoea (excessive talkativeness), slight euphoria, and lack of insight. 'In any case, confabulations occur only quite sparsely, and strong suggestive pushing is often necessary to obtain them' (p. 165). In Russell's (1971) classic monograph *The traumatic amnesias*, summarizing 40 years of clinical experience with hundreds of patients, confabulations played no significant role, in contrast to disorientation, a determinant of post-traumatic amnesia. Confabulations were primarily portrayed as a phenomenon that might mislead an examiner. Russel (1971) described a 38-year-old patient who had had a motorcycle accident when he tried to avoid collision with a dog. The patient obviously retained this element but insisted that the dog-owner's son had provoked the accident. He fabricated a complex story around this conviction. In reality, the only connection that the young man had with the accident was that he had accompanied the patient to the hospital in an ambulance. Russell's conclusion: 'Care must be taken not to be misled by confabulation.'

Whereas behaviourally dominating confabulation appears to be rare after closed head injury, confabulations can often be elicited in a discussion. Weinstein and Lyerly (1968) studied 101 patients through the course of clinical recovery from acute brain trauma. Eighty-six of these patients had closed head injuries. The authors interviewed the patients repeatedly, enquiring about what had happened to the patients, their main symptoms, activities of the previous day, and specific disabilities and problems. Most were also asked about their jobs and families and to give an account of their autobiography. Patients were considered confabulatory if they invented a story about a past event or gave a distorted version of an actual occurrence beyond omissions and discrepancies in minor details. As it turned out, 60 of the 101 patients confabulated according to these criteria. Most frequent were confabulations about other people, followed by confabulations of great violence to the patient, minor illnesses, play and sports, and work and occupation. The authors did not specify whether these confabulations were only present during the initial confusional state or whether they persisted into the chronic phase.

The *anatomical basis* of confabulation after traumatic brain injury has never been explored formally. There is no prospective study comparing the lesions of confabulating with non-confabulating and non-amnesic brain injured subjects.

Brain injury acts through diverse mechanisms. Penetrating injuries may reach any area of the brain. In an extraordinary case, a stab pushed up the nose and ending up in the left medial thalamus, destroying on its way also the mamillary bodies and the mamillo–thalamic tract, induced severe amnesia

(Teuber *et al.* 1968; Squire *et al.* 1989). A similar unlucky patient, in whom the medial hypothalamus was injured, also had severe amnesia (Dusoir *et al.* 1990). In both cases, no confabulation was reported.

Epidural haematomas are due to the rupture of a meningeal artery and very rapidly compress the brain. Likewise, subdural haematomas, which result from the rupture of bridging veins, may compress the brain, sometimes acutely, in many cases slowly over days or weeks. Epidural and subdural haematomas impair consciousness by compressing the brain and may thus produce a confusional state (delirium) with disturbed attention and disorientation. As discussed previously (p. 84), no reliable anatomical conclusion can be drawn from such observations. A single case reported as having increasing confabulation after a subdural haematoma (Inagaki *et al.* 2003) turned out to have a degenerative disease, probably frontotemporal dementia (Dr Inagaki, personal communication).

Of main interest here is the distribution of brain damage after *closed head injury*. Two mechanisms can broadly be separated. Concussion occurs when the brain is crushed with very high power against the bony and fibrous boundaries within the skull by extreme deceleration or acceleration upon impact. Physical laws alone explain to a large degree the distribution of brain damage (Holbourn 1943). Figure 4.5 shows Courville's (1945) classic depiction of the areas most commonly involved: orbitofrontal area with frontal pole and temporal pole. Orbitofrontal damage is increased by the shearing of the

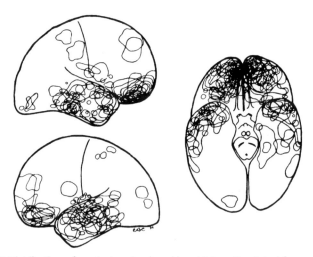

Figure 4.5 Distribution of contusions in closed head injury. Reprinted from Courville (1945).

brain over the irregular bony surface (Adams 1975). To this lesion pattern, the splenium of the corpus callosum (the fibre package connecting the two hemispheres) should be added, often damaged in shearing injury.

The second type of damage is *diffuse axonal injury*, which describes the rupture of axons within brain tissue in closed head injury. Such ruptures, often visible in brain scans as microbleeds, tend to occur primarily at the transition between tissues of different densities: transition between grey and white matter in the cortex, fornix, basal ganglia, the upper mesencephalon, and the upper cerebellar peduncles (Meythaler *et al.* 2001). Accordingly, such patients often have oculomotor disturbances and ataxia. A strategically located lesion in the upper brain stem may induce prolonged coma, although the lesion may appear very discrete.

What lesions, then, cause amnesia and confabulation after closed head injury? Based on the observation of a single patient with provoked confabulations (intrusions in memory tests) for more than nine months, Demery *et al.* (2001) suggested that 'medial temporal lobe damage must be accompanied by ventral frontal lobe pathology to produce the amnestic–confabulatory syndrome' (p. 295): but this conclusion just described the most common lesion distribution in severe closed head injury.

We included several patients with traumatic brain injury in our studies, who were still severely amnesic after termination of the confusional state (Schnider *et al.* 1996b). Overall, patients produced more *intrusions* than healthy subjects. The number of intrusions did not appear to depend on any particular lesion site. The patient producing the second highest number of intrusions – 37 intrusions over all runs of the California Verbal Learning Test (Delis *et al.* 1987) – had no visible lesion in the MRI scan at all, although coma for two days, oculomotor disturbances, and severe ataxia proved the presence of diffuse axonal injury. Based on our data, we would not be able to indicate a specific lesion area for the occurrence of provoked confabulations after traumatic brain injury.

Behaviourally spontaneous confabulation after closed head injury can result from concussion or diffuse axonal injury. In our series, the most common lesion pattern was bilateral orbitofrontal damage (Schnider *et al.* 1996b, c; Schnider and Ptak 1999; Schnider *et al.* 2000a), but lesion patterns may vary. Figure 4.6 shows the acute and chronic lesions of two patients who confabulated for very long periods, one for over five years, the other for 18 months. In the first patient (Figure 4.6a–c), the lesion involved the orbitofrontal cortex and reached up to the level of the thalamus. This lesion thus interrupted the fibres projecting to the whole prefrontal cortex. In this patient, the basal forebrain appeared to be intact, an observation we have also made in

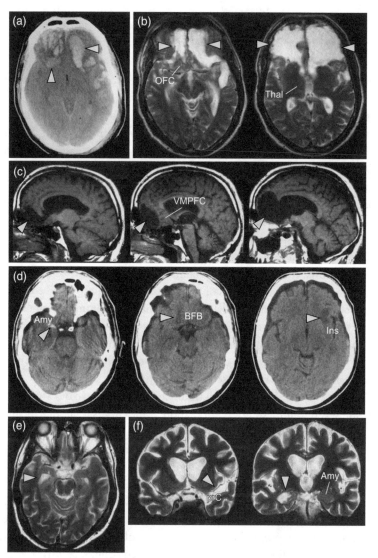

Figure 4.6 Scans of patients with traumatic brain injury. (a–c) 45-year-old man with behaviourally spontaneous confabulations for more than five years. (a) The acute CT scan shows extended bilateral orbitofrontal damage. (b, c) The MRI after three years shows extremely extended orbitofrontal destruction plus left temporal polar damage; (b) axial T2-weighted images; (c) sagittal images from left to right. (d–f) A 45-year-old man who confabulated for 18 months. (d) The acute CT scan shows areas of axonal injury in the right amygdala, right basal forebrain, and left insula. (e–f) The MRI at one-and-a-half years confirms these findings: there is destruction of the amygdala on the right side and of the perirhinal and insular cortex on the left side. Lesions are indicated by arrowheads. Abbreviations: Amy, amygdala; BFB, basal forebrain; Ins, insula; OFC, orbitofrontal cortex; prC, perirhinal cortex; Thal, thalamus; VMPFC, ventromedial prefrontal cortex (most part of posterior orbitofrontal cortex and basal forebrain).

other behaviourally spontaneous confabulators after closed head injury (Schnider *et al.* 2000a). In the second patient, typical diffuse axonal injury was visible (Figure 4.6d–f). There was destruction of the right amygdala and of the left perirhinal and insular cortex, regions projecting to the orbitofrontal cortex.

However, similar to ACoA aneurysm rupture, there are negative cases – patients having extensive orbitofrontal damage but no confabulation or disorientation, sometimes not even amnesia once the confusional state is over. Figure 4.7 shows an example. The lesion would not allow one to predict that this patient, who had a post-traumatic amnesia of approximately two weeks, never confabulated and obtained fully normal neuropsychological results soon after termination of the confusional phase, including normal perform-ance in memory tests.

The duration of behaviourally spontaneous confabulation after closed head injury, once established, is impossible to predict. The cases described in the old literature appeared to confabulate for about two or three months (Tiling 1892; Kalberlah 1904; Benon and LeHuché 1920), similar to most of our patients (Schnider *et al.* 2000a). The examples described in Figure 4.6 show that the confabulatory phase may be much longer.

In *conclusion*, coma followed by confusion with disorientation for varied periods is common after traumatic brain injury. This period has been termed post-traumatic amnesia. Its duration is an indicator of the severity of brain damage. In contrast to disorientation, confabulation has not been mentioned as a dominant feature of post-traumatic amnesia.

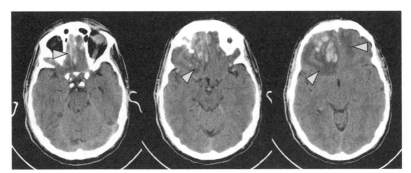

Figure 4.7 Traumatic brain injury without confabulation. This 62-year-old man had extensive orbitofrontal contusions on the right side, visible in the early CT scan. He had a post-traumatic amnesia with disorientation for about two weeks and then rapidly recovered. At four weeks, neuropsychological test results were normal.

Nonetheless, traumatic brain injury is among the well-recognized causes of prolonged, severe, behaviourally spontaneous confabulation beyond the confusional state. Some patients also produced confabulations with a fantastic component, especially in the initial stage. Most of these patients had extended orbitofrontal lesions. However, there are also patients with extensive orbitofrontal lesions, who have intact memory and orientation and do not confabulate. At present, there is no lesion pattern known to reliably predict the occurrence of behaviourally spontaneous confabulation after traumatic brain injury.

Provoked confabulations (intrusions) are common after traumatic brain injury, similar to other types of brain damage. Their occurrence is independent of other forms of confabulation and they do not appear to have a distinct anatomical substrate.

Alcohol and avitaminosis

Chronic alcoholism, together with malnourishment and prolonged disease, was the first generally accepted cause of confabulation, disorientation, and the other symptoms of Korsakoff psychosis. Confabulations were reported in the early phase of the delirium tremens and in the chronic alcoholic delirium, so-called Korsakoff psychosis (Bonhoeffer 1901). Most reports concerned momentary or fantastic confabulations, but behaviourally spontaneous confabulation was also described (Chapter 2). Kraepelin (1910) was impressed by the suggestibility of these patients:

> Oftentimes it is possible to recognize a tie between the falsifications of memory and specific events, delirious or real happenings. A remark by the environment, some new acquaintance can prompt the patient to spin a whole network of weird false memories.
>
> Kraepelin (1910, p. 172)

The link between Korsakoff psychosis and deficiency of vitamin B1 (thiamine) was recognized in the 1930s (Minski 1936). Indeed, many cases previously reported as being due to incoercible vomiting during pregnancy (Von Hösslin 1905; Ely 1922; Vermelin and Louyot 1936) or purulent meningitis with four weeks' refusal to eat (Hanse 1928) would later have been attributed to malnutrition and avitaminosis. At about the same time, Korsakoff psychosis was definitely recognized as a manifestation of *Wernicke's encephalopathy* (Bender and Schilder 1933). This disease typically presents with ataxia of gait, disturbed ocular movements, and mental changes (Victor *et al.* 1989). The Wernicke–Korsakoff syndrome describes this combination of symptoms and signs due to B1 avitaminosis.

Confabulation and disorientation beyond the acute confusional state have always been rare phenomena. Bonhoeffer (1901) estimated that only three per cent of patients presenting with acute delirium tremens would go on to have the full, chronic Korsakoff psychosis. Most patients then remained amnesic. The introduction of thiamine as a treatment has certainly reduced the incidence, but no precise numbers are available. Victor *et al.* (1989) indicated in their monograph on the Wernicke–Korsakoff syndrome that 56 per cent of the patients presenting with Wernicke encephalopathy (the acute somatic manifestation of avitaminosis) were in a global confusional state with profound disorientation, apathy, drowsiness, and a derangement of memory. Of note 14 per cent of the patients were alert and responsive when they were first seen, but had a memory and learning disturbance 'out of proportion to other cognitive functions (Korsakoff psychosis)' (p. 17). The percentage of confused patients appears to be high, but these authors did not include confabulation in their definition of Korsakoff psychosis. They stated that confabulation was a prominent symptom in the early stages of the disease, whereas it was present only rarely in the chronic, stable stage. Most of the described confabulations corresponded to momentary confabulations.

Single cases producing this type of confabulation (Dalla Barba *et al.* 1990; Benson *et al.* 1996), possibly also behaviourally spontaneous confabulation (Kopelman *et al.* 1997a) have continued to be described. We have seen very few patients who continued to confabulate beyond the confusional state. A woman was transferred to us four months after hip replacement, bedridden because of severe muscle wasting and ataxia. Once the diagnosis of Wernicke–Korsakoff syndrome was made and thiamine substituted, she slowly abandoned the conviction that she was on a sailing boat, regained full orientation within four weeks, and finally had an almost complete neuropsychological recovery (Carota and Schnider 2005).

The *prognosis* of chronic Korsakoff psychosis has definitely improved since the introduction of thiamine in the late 1950s. Bonhoeffer (1901) still estimated that most patients with chronic Korsakoff psychosis remained in this state for months, most of them continuing to have amnesia thereafter. Based on the review of 63 patient files, Kauffmann (1913) doubted whether recovery from Korsakoff psychosis was at all possible. Although the files were 'sometimes full of gaps', he found out that only 13 of the 63 patients were dismissed to their home, but none of them was cured: 'In all of these patients, there is weakness of will, lack of initiative, and high-grade loss of mental power; in brief, the characteristic alcoholic insanity' (p. 505). Unfortunately, the author did not make any specific comment about confabulation and disorientation.

In the first study on the efficacy of thiamine, Bowman *et al.* (1939) used a highly variable dosing schema, making it difficult to seize the full potency of thiamine. Also, many patients quit the study unimproved, before they had received the full dose of thiamine. Nonetheless 17 of 51 patients regained orientation and stopped confabulating under this treatment. Most of them remained amnesic. Bowman *et al.* (1939) estimated that the chance of recovery (cessation of confabulations and disorientation, with or without continuing amnesia) was seven times higher with thiamine than without. Lishman (1981) estimated that 25 per cent of patients made a full recovery, 50 per cent a partial recovery.

The *anatomical basis* of alcoholic Korsakoff psychosis has been, and remains, a matter of debate. In an early study covering 16 post-mortem examinations, Gamper (1928) described the areas still disputed nowadays:

> The mamillary body was very consistently involved [and indeed] appears to be the pivotal structure in the whole process … In addition, one regularly finds changes in the tuber cinereum [a part of the hypothalamus, at the bottom of the third ventricle] and its nuclei, including the supraoptic ganglion, and furthermore in the central grey and its nuclear groups within the medial wall of the third ventricle … Among the thalamic nuclei, the parafascicular nucleus [and] the medial layers of the medial thalamic nucleus [are involved] (lateral and anterior thalamic nuclei remain untouched).
>
> Gamper (1928, p. 124)

Gamper did not provide any clinical data, such as the presence of confabulation or disorientation.

Victor *et al.* (1989) were more specific in this regard. In their large series of patients, they found that the medial mamillary bodies were affected in 100 per cent of patients, the dorsomedial thalamic nucleus in 88 per cent, the lateral dorsal nucleus in 68 per cent, and the anterior thalamic nucleus in 35 per cent. Among 43 cases in which the dorsomedial nucleus was available for study, there were five patients who showed no evidence of defective memory once they had recovered from the acute Wernicke encephelopathy, which had included a transient confusional–apathetic state. In these five patients, the dorsomedial nucleus of the thalamus was found to be free of disease. In contrast, the mamillary bodies were affected in all 43 cases. Victor *et al.* (1989) thus concluded that, (1) the mamillary bodies may be significantly affected in the absence of a memory defect, and (2) involvement of the dorsomedial nucleus of the thalamus is essential in the causation of the memory defect (p. 113).

Other authors looking at much smaller case series arrived at different conclusions. Mair and Warrington (1979) repeatedly tested two patients who remained disoriented and amnesic until their death. In neither of the two patients was there evidence of confabulation. On post-mortem examination, there was marked alteration in the medial mamillary bodies. The greater part of the dorsomedial nucleus of the thalamus appeared to be intact although a thin band of gliosis was found bilaterally between the wall of the third ventricle and the dorsomedial nucleus. Mayes and Meudell (1988) made similar observations in two patients, who remained disoriented and severely amnesic for a prolonged period until their death. One of them had been confused and confabulated in the initial stage. At post-mortem examination, the same findings as in the cases of Mair and Warrington (1979) were made: marked neuronal loss in the medial mamillary bodies and a narrow band of gliosis in the medial thalamus, adjacent to the wall of the third ventricle. Apart from the fact that Victor *et al.* (1989) questioned the interpretation of the pathological findings – they were not convinced about the intactness of the dorsomedial nucleus – it is amazing to note that the two latter studies yielded no difference between the patient who initially presented with confabulation (Mayes *et al.* 1988) and those who never confabulated (Mair *et al.* 1979).

A more recent study arrived at yet another conclusion: Harding *et al.* (2000) found that neurodegeneration of the mamillary nuclei and the dorsomedial thalamic nuclei was substantial but similar in their five patients with Wernicke encephalopathy *without* Korsakoff psychosis and the five patients *with* Korsakoff psychosis. In contrast, neuronal loss in the anterior thalamic nuclei was found consistently only in patients with Korsakoff psychosis. For our discussion of confabulation, the article is not very helpful: the word 'confabulation' does not appear at all in the text. Considering the beneficial effect of thiamine on the course of confabulation and disorientation, it is possible that the lesion distribution in amnesic patients who never confabulated differs from those who confabulated initially.

A new approach at elucidating the mechanism of confabulation in Korsakoff psychosis was taken by Benson *et al.* (1996). They observed a 32-year-old alcoholic woman who confabulated for six weeks. She described in detail previous conversations with physicians she had never met, gave or accepted incorrect names for her own children, described recent visitors who had not been there, and gave details of trips she made out of hospital that had not occurred. She was severely disoriented. Measurement of cerebral perfusion using single photon emission computer topography (SPECT) showed hypoperfusion of the anterior cingulum, the orbitofrontal area, and the dorsomedial thalamic nucleus. The patient finally stopped confabulating but remained amnesic. At this stage, SPECT showed normal perfusion of the cingulum and orbitofrontal cortex, while hypoperfusion in the dorsomedial nucleus continued. The authors concluded that dysfunction of the cingulum and orbitofrontal cortex was important for the occurrence of confabulation. Although these conclusions were drawn from visual inspection of the scans rather than quantified image analysis, functional metabolic imaging remains a promising avenue to investigate the anatomical basis of confabulation. New methods will have a better resolution. Currently, diffusion weighted magnetic resonance imaging appears to be most sensitive: a recent study using this technique demonstrated medial thalamic signal abnormalities in the acute phase of Wernicke encephalopathy (Halavaara *et al.* 2003).

In *conclusion*, deficiency of vitamin B1 due to chronic alcoholism, malnutrition or other causes is a well-established cause of all forms of confabulation. The incidence of chronic Korsakoff psychosis beyond the confusional state (delirium tremens) is very low and has probably further decreased since the introduction of thiamine treatment. This treatment has considerably improved the prognosis for recovery from confabulation, disorientation, and amnesia. Nonetheless, vitamin B1 deficiency continues to be reported occasionally as a cause of momentary or behaviourally spontaneous confabulation. The anatomical basis remains contested. The most extensive case series (Victor *et al.* 1989) suggested that involvement of the dorsomedial thalamic nucleus was critical for the amnesia, but the mamillary bodies and more recently the anterior thalamic nucleus remain serious contenders. Whether confabulation and disorientation in Wernicke–Korsakoff syndrome have the same anatomical basis as the amnesia is unknown.

Syphilis

Syphilis has virtually disappeared from the list of diseases causing confabulation in the second half of the twentieth century. Yet there have never been more dramatic descriptions of fantastic confabulations than those by Kraepelin of his syphilitic patients suffering from general paralysis (Chapter 2, pp. 15ff.). In the 1920s, Bleuler (1923) still described such absurd confabulations in his textbook of psychiatry:

> The patient [with paralytic dementia] is not only god, but possibly even an over-god, owns trillions, all the time transports diamonds from India to his house with millions of ships as big as lake Geneva, is hunting on the moon.
>
> Bleuler (1923, p. 191)

Bleuler called the form of paralytic dementia associated with such wild memory falsifications the 'manic, expansive or classical form', quite distinct from the 'simple dementing form', the 'melancholic or depressive form', and the relatively rare 'agitated form'. The patients described by Kraepelin and Bleuler were demented, disoriented, and had severe memory deficits, although 'initially, [the memory deficits were] by far not as severe as in Korsakoff psychosis' (Kraepelin 1910, p. 342). Such states could last for months to years. The patients were highly susceptible to suggestion:

> Imaginations emerging in their mind are not strongly rooted and have no significant influence on prospective thinking and behaviour
>
> Kraepelin (1910, p. 346)

Much less fantastic, behaviourally consistent confabulations were also described. A 50-year-old man described by Meyer (1903) got up during the night and demanded his clothes to leave the clinic and make sure that his fruit would not be stolen. During the day, he 'tended to fabulate'. Autopsy showed the typical features of general paralysis, but making the diagnosis was not obvious at the time. Roemheld (1906) described a woman who was 'forgetful, fabulated, and often pretended untrue things'. Her husband was infected with syphilis. When she was told a story, she would recount it 'very erroneously [and] invent all possible things (p. 707) ... Sometimes, she would even spontaneously tell completely fantastic stories (p. 709).' After two months of iodipin treatment, she 'fabulated less, [was] oriented to time and place ... [but still went] to bed with shoes on ... [She] often meddled into the discussions of others and then often spoke incoherently (p. 708).' After four months, she was 'entirely normal'. Roemheld published the case to demonstrate the similarities between alcoholic Korsakoff syndrome and cerebral syphilis. As to the diagnosis, he cautioned: 'That this case had syphilis of the brain can hardly be doubted ... At the utmost, one might [alternatively] consider a brain tumour (Roemheld 1906, p. 708).

Pfeifer (1928) described eight patients with general paralysis who were delirious, disoriented, and confabulated. Some confabulations were plausible, others fantastic. A patient alleged that he had lifted his parents from their grave and caught crocodiles. Pfeifer tried to deduce the differences between paralytic dementia and alcoholic Korsakoff psychosis. He suggested that in paralytic dementia, personality was more affected, namely, by delusions of grandeur; intellectual capacities, general knowledge, and judgement were more impaired (Pfeifer 1928, p. 280). Karl Jaspers (1973) later criticized such attempts to diagnose syphilis on psychological grounds alone and invoked the high number of false diagnoses that even Kraepelin himself had made before using lumbar puncture: 'Even a disease [like general paralysis] whose somatic manifestations were well known, could not be psychologically diagnosed with certainty' (Jaspers 1973, p. 476). But Pfeifer's considerations showed that, in 1928, paralytic dementia was still a frequent clinical concern.

Why has syphilis disappeared from the confabulation literature? Antibiotics introduced after 1943 have dramatically reduced the incidence of neurosyphilis (Burke and Schaberg 1985) and probably changed its presentation

(Hooshmand *et al.* 1972). Should they also have rendered neurosyphilis less aggressive, without the serious thought disorder inducing confabulations? Neurosyphilis still is a feared cause of dementia, a dementia which is still accompanied by confabulations and hallucinations, whereas delusions seem to have decreased (Mendez and Cummings 2003), possibly also due to the use of neuroleptics. No recent data are available on the duration of such a state of confabulation and disorientation under modern medication.

Lesions in syphilitic general paralysis are diffusely distributed over the whole central nervous system. Brain atrophy appears to be somewhat pronounced in the frontal and temporal lobes (Nelson *et al.* 1993; Mendez and Cummings 2003).

In conclusion, syphilitic general paralysis remains a rare but feared cause of dementia. This dementia may be associated with fantastic confabulations.

Herpes simplex encephalitis

In comparison with syphilis, herpes simplex virus encephalitis has made the opposite career in confabulation research. The diagnosis was unknown in the first half of the last century so that the early reports of Korsakoff syndrome after acute encephalitis are difficult to validate. A 54-year-old woman described by Davis (1932), who produced elaborate momentary confabulations after three weeks of fever, appears unlikely to have had herpes simplex virus encephalitis. Conversely, a 54-year-old physician described by Tsiminakis (1934) had a clinical course compatible with this diagnosis. He did not recognize his own home and confused people: 'He thanked his housemaid – his own wife – for the hospitality during the period of his illness' (p. 323). The patient often insisted that he had to leave to see patients. 'With false promises, he was always made to postpone his decision for a couple of hours.... He was often wondering why no patients turned up. He took comfort in the explanation that it was Sunday' (p. 324). His condition somewhat improved after ten months. Thus, this patient produced behaviourally sponta-neous confabulation in the context of encephalitis, but his brain lesion remained unknown.

This was different in a 50-year-old man described by Friedman and Allen (1969). He had a typical presentation of herpes encephalitis with stupor, muscle twitching and rigidity of the body, followed by coma, from which he slowly recovered within three weeks. Very severe failure of new memory recording, excessive motor activity, loss of sustained goal-directed activity, uninhibited verbal sexuality, impotence, and docility then became manifest. Orientation to time was abolished. He never seemed to be aware of any memory defect and considered himself quite normal. The authors only briefly mentioned confabulation: 'Confabulation, which had been prominent early in his illness, lessened but would reappear in response to direct questioning. His answer consisted of a false statement followed by a long fabrication' (p. 680). He died seven years later from a subdural haematoma following an epileptic seizure. Autopsy showed very extensive destruction of limbic areas, which extended bilaterally from the medial orbitofrontal cortex back to the basal forebrain, the insula on both sides, up to the anterior cingulum, laterally to the perirhinal cortex, the hippocampus and parahippocampal gyrus. Almost the whole left temporal lobe was destroyed. Thus, this very extended lesion apparently produced more or less permanent momentary confabulations.

Damasio *et al.* (1985a) followed a patient for eight years, who had similarly chronic confabulations of this type. Areas of destruction, determined with CT scan, were comparable to the case of Friedman and Allen (1969). The patient had very profound anterograde and retrograde amnesia and remained severely disoriented. Confabulations were present: 'When asked where he was, what he had done recently or what he planned to do next, he readily produced elaborate fabrications that may have involved the examiner and that, in spite of good intrinsic logic, had no basis in reality' (Damasio *et al.* 1985a).

Prognosis of herpes simplex encephalitis improved dramatically with the introduction of acyclovir as an efficacious antiviral drug (Whitley *et al.* 1986). Patients treated rapidly may recover fully, or at least regain independence (Del Grosso Destreri *et al.* 2002). Nonetheless, a substantial proportion of patients are left with amnesia, which may be very dense (Gordon *et al.* 1990; Kapur *et al.* 1994; Stefanacci *et al.* 2000).

The *anatomical determinants* of confabulation after herpes encephalitis have never been explored specifically. Damasio *et al.*'s (1985a) patient, who produced elaborate momentary confabulations, had extensive limbic damage including – apart from the medial temporal lobes – the basal forebrain, parts of the orbitofrontal cortex and the insula. Among three amnesic patients included in a group study by Moscovitch and Melo (1997), only the confabulating patient had visible lesion extension into the ventromedial frontal lobes and basal forebrain.

Unequivocal behaviourally spontaneous confabulation has not been reported in the recent literature and appears to be a rare complication of herpes encephalitis. One of our patients producing such confabulations had MRI-visible bilateral posterior orbitofrontal destruction in addition to medial temporal and temporal pole destruction (one of the 'spontaneous confabulators' in Schnider and Ptak 1999).

We had the unlikely opportunity to observe at the same time two patients with severe herpes encephalitis, who only differed by the production of behaviourally spontaneous confabulations (Schnider and Gutbrod 1997). Both had several months of inpatient rehabilitation. The first patient, A.A., was a 35-year-old female office assistant. The second patient, B.B., was a 53-year-old housewife. Both had very severe anterograde amnesia with no demonstrable recognition capacity, temporally ungraded retrograde amnesia for personal events, and marked semantic memory deficits. Both remained disoriented for at least six months and had similarly severe executive failures, but both were collaborative and soon had essentially normal behaviour. Whereas A.A. was extremely concerned about her memory deficit and constantly complained about it for several months, B.B. did not appear to realize her memory deficits. On the contrary, B.B. often gave advice to visitors of the ward. For months, she denied being hospitalized. In her mind, she was organizing a shooting event – a long-time hobby of hers. This conviction gave rise to the most unlikely situations. As her behaviour was unremarkable and her attitude polite, visitors of the ward would occasionally ask her for the room number of the patients they wanted to visit. She would then explain precisely where the visitors would find the desired shooting booth. Sometimes she walked down the hallway of the ward in search of the participants of the shooting event. There was no absurd, fantastic idea, just a false conviction about reality, evident in her behaviourally spontaneous confabulations and disorientation. Both patients regained almost normal orientation – with continuing difficulties in estimating the date – after about eight months. B.B. then also stopped confabulating.

The two patients also had very similar lesions (Figure 4.8). In both, the anterior half of the left temporal lobe (amygdala, anterior part of the hippocampus and adjacent cortex, temporal pole) was destroyed. In both, this lesion extended medially into the left half of the orbitofrontal cortex. On the right side, damage was less extended; in both, the perirhinal cortex was damaged, whereas the amygdala and hippocampus were not visibly affected. The only obvious difference, already visible in the early CT scans, was more extensive damage of the right anterior insula in B.B. The anterior insula is the main cortical relay for input into the amygdala (Mesulam and Mufson 1982). Thus, B.B. had the left amgdala destroyed and the right amygdala with no or disturbed cortical input. The functional significance of this damage was supported by another observation: for about four months, B.B. had the tendency to take objects into her mouth – a typical feature of the Klüver–Bucy syndrome, which results from bilateral amygdala damage (Poeck 1985). The two most graphic situations of this disorder occurred when she tried to smoke her toothbrush, repeatedly taking it into her mouth and trying to light it,

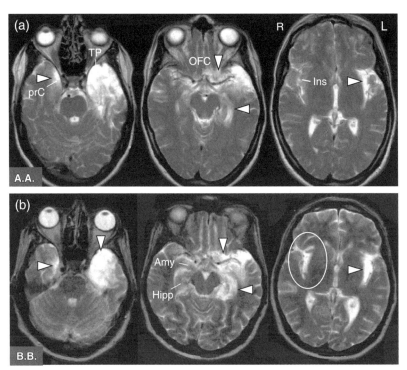

Figure 4.8 Two patients with herpes encephalitis (T2-weighted axial MRI in the chronic phase). (a) Patient A.A. had very severe amnesia and suffered from it; she never confabulated. (b) Patient B.B. had similarly severe amnesia, no insight, and striking behaviourally spontaneous confabulation for several months. The only obvious difference is the additional damage of the right anterior insula (white oval) in patient B.B., which had already been visible in the early CT scans. Abbreviations: Amy, approximate location of amygdala; Hipp, hippocampus; Ins, insula; OFC, orbitofrontal cortex; prC, perirhinal cortex.

and when she drank a bottle of shampoo – with quite unpleasant intestinal consequences. Our hypothesis was that the reality confusion in B.B., as evidenced by disorientation and behaviourally spontaneous confabulations, was due to the more extensive insular damage on the right side, causing bilateral insular–amygdala dysfunction.

It may be added here that herpes simplex encephalitis is not the only type of encephalitis that may produce severe amnesia and behaviourally spontaneous confabulation. We have seen a patient with non-viral, probably autoimmune, possibly paraneoplastic (tumour-associated) *limbic encephalitis*, who had pervasive behaviourally spontaneous confabulation, disorientation, and extremely severe amnesia for months. MRI showed inflammatory changes in the whole limbic system, the posterior medial orbitofrontal cortex, and the caudate nucleus. All hitherto known antibodies and the search for a tumour were negative.

In *conclusion*, antiviral treatment has dramatically improved the prognosis of herpes simplex encephalitis. Many more patients now survive the disease, but some are left with severe memory impairment. Persistent momentary or behaviourally spontaneous confabulations have repeatedly been reported. There is some evidence that the severity and extension of the anterior limbic damage (orbitofrontal cortex, insula, possibly amygdala) determines the occurrence of confabulations, in particular behaviourally spontaneous confabulation. Autoimmune limbic encephalitis may present similar features.

Tumours

Tumours have only rarely been reported as a cause of confabulation. Karl Kleist (1934), in his massive volume *Brain Pathology*, mentioned the association between Korsakoff syndrome – which he called 'time-amnestic syndrome' – and lesions in the vicinity of the diencephalon. In reference to Gamper (1928), whose study on the pathology of the alcoholic Korsakoff psychosis we have already seen on p. 110, Kleist seemed particularly interested in the hypothalamus and mamillary bodies. He had seen Korsakoff syndrome in several patients with proven or suspected traumatic injury of the orbitofrontal cortex, but he also mentioned four patients having tumours of the diencephalon, who had 'time-amnestic' together with delirious and sleep-like manifestations (Kleist 1934, p. 1319). The four patients had huge tumours with various locations in the vicinity of the third ventricle; only one tumour was really centred on the hypothalamus. All had had increased intracranial pressure. None had an isolated Korsakoff syndrome, so that Kleist's anatomical interpretation of his findings appeared to emanate at least in part from his trust in Gamper's study. Gamper (1928) had concluded that alcoholic Korsakoff syndrome was due to hypothalamic damage, in particular of the mamillary bodies. Kleist additionally made an idiosyncratic distinction between 'falsifications of memory' in Korsakoff syndrome and 'confabulations', which he interpreted as the result of a pathological augmentation of fantastic excitation. He had observed confabulatory states in patients with diencephalic lesions, in particular tumours emanating from the hypophysis, but also in a patient with an orbital tumour (Kleist 1934, p. 1328).

Many authors adopted the idea of a particular role of the mamillary bodies for the occurrence of Korsakoff syndrome. Benedek and Juba (1941) considered it 'proven beyond any doubt that the time-amnestic symptom group

[Korsakoff syndrome] is most tightly associated with lesions of the mamillary bodies' (p. 366). Their second patient had severe disorientation and produced 'colourful confabulations'. After his death, a large neurofibroma was found, which filled the third ventricle and compressed the hypothalamus bilaterally; the mamillary bodies were still there. Williams and Pennybacker (1954) reported four patients with tumours of the third ventricle; two of them had had confabulation among the presenting features. After operation, mental failures were even more severe; three of them intensively confabulated and were disoriented, although one of them subsequently improved.

A comparable series of patients was described by Kahn and Crosby (1972). All of their five patients had visual impairment and most had endocrine disturbances as presenting features. Three of them also confabulated and were disoriented. While three of the patients, who had been particularly disoriented, amnesic, and confabulatory before the operation, markedly improved after the removal of the tumour, one patient became seriously confabulatory and disoriented only after the intervention. Although all tumours extended into the anterior part of the third ventricle, Kahn and Crosby (1972) were so convinced about the role of the mamillary bodies – which form the posterior extension of the hypothalamus – that they included them in the title of the article.

Subsequent case reports and reviews of the literature confirmed that Korsakoff syndrome with confabulation was particularly prevalent in tumours of the medial diencephalic region, in particular the hypothalamus. Angelergues (1956) summarized this point concisely:

Among 298 brain tumours with diverse localizations (except frontal and meso-diencephalic), among which 150 had mental disturbances, we found no single case of Korsakoff syndrome … We have observed Korsakoff syndrome in those cases where the tumour concerned the anterior part of the hypothalamus, that is, the whole third ventricle, whereas the more posterior meso-diencephalic tumours produced clinical pictures with lucid stupor or akinetic mutism.

Angelergues (1956, p. 233)

In a magnificent monograph reviewing their own case material and the literature on Korsakoff syndrome, Delay and Brion (1969) arrived at the same conclusion: 'The most frequent aetiology of Korsakoff syndrome caused by tumours is craniopharyngeoma' (p. 58), a tumour usually emanating from the anterior superior hypophysis and infiltrating the third ventricle from below. However they also mentioned a diagnostic problem: many patients described as having a Korsakoff syndrome due to such a tumour also had mental confusion. Indeed, many patients described in the early literature – Kleist (1934) and before – confabulated in a state of impaired consciousness.

In contrast to craniopharyngeomas, colloid cysts of the third ventricle have rarely been reported as a cause of memory disorder and confabulation. These cysts may intermittently interrupt the flow of cerebral spinal fluid and present themselves most typically with headache, sometimes with mental disturbances. Confabulation has been reported in a patient who had marked hydrocephalus and in whom removal was inefficient (Lobosky *et al.* 1984). In the context of amnesia research, colloid cysts and their operation have contributed to the understanding that lesions of the fornix during surgery may induce severe amnesia (Hodges and Carpenter 1991; Aggleton *et al.* 2000; Poreh *et al.* 2006). Typically, the amnesia is not associated with confabulation. One might, therefore, speculate that infiltration of ventral and possibly anterior parts of the third ventricle, as it happens in craniopharyngeomas, is necessary to induce an amnesic–confabulatory state.

One of the most florid confabulators that we have ever observed was a 60-year-old man, who had had surgical removal of a huge craniopharyngeoma, which had caused visual disturbances. After the operation, he suffered extensive bleeding into the tumour cavity. For several months, he was severly amnesic and disoriented, produced wild and incoherent, if not fantastic confabulations, and permanently acted according to such confabulations. Although the ideas guiding his behaviour varied from one moment to the other, he had two recurrent topics in his mind. One idea was that he had to leave the unit to water the flowers at the clubhouse of the ornithological society, which he thought to be located next door. Another idea was that he had to leave to take a hot-air balloon ride. As one may guess, he was hospitalized in our unit during the summer. Discussions with him were extremely incoherent. He would jump from one topic to the other, mixing names, places and events from his past and from the ongoing discussion. Many confabulated ideas recurred a few minutes later in a new combination of ideas constituting another confabulation. He considered himself alternatively at his home or in his office. An impressive moment during an interview was when, ten minutes into the interview, he wanted to verify what person had let me into what he thought to be his office. The nurses were used to not contest his reality and to accept the role of being his office personnel. The problem came two minutes later, when we returned to his room to continue the discussion. He did not allow me to sit down on the chair which I had used just before, stating that he had an important guest who used this chair. Also, he did not allow me to use my writing pad again, saying that this pad belonged to his guest. Amnesia, disorientation, and confabulation continued like that for several months.

Early CT scans showed massive postoperative haemorrhage. A CT scan taken after three month, while the patient was severely amnesic and confabulating, showed a lesion involving the most posterior part of the right posterior orbitofrontal cortex, which corresponded to the surgical access to the tumour (Figure 4.9). In addition, the right half of the hypothalamus was destroyed, anteriorly more than posteriorly. Of course, it is impossible to decide whether the orbitofrontal damage or the hypothalamic lesion produced the severe confabulatory state, but in the latter case, it would be the anterior hypothalamus rather than the mamillary bodies, which would be particularly important.

The observation of another patient supported the idea that the anterior hypothalamus was possibly more important for the occurrence of behaviourally spontaneous confabulation than the posterior hypothalamus (Ptak *et al.* 2001). This 67-year-old retired schoolteacher was admitted because of a two-year history of hyperphagia (insatiable hunger), hyperdipsia (insatiable thirst), and forgetfulness. She repeatedly asked what the date was, but soon forgot the answer. She often produced confabulations and occasionally acted on them. For example, although she had resigned as a committee member of a local party four years ago, she remained convinced that she still held this duty.

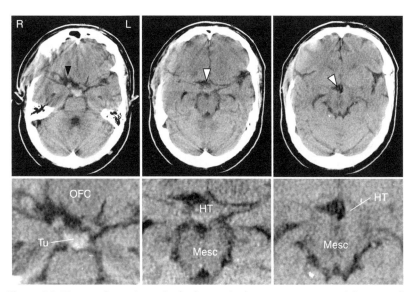

Figure 4.9 CT scan of a patient who had a craniopharyngeoma removed. For several months he was disoriented and produced massive incoherent confabulations, which he often enacted. The scan shows a small area of tissue loss in the right postero-lateral orbitofrontal cortex (surgical access, black arrowhead) and a lesion involving the right anterior half of the hypothalamus (white arrowheads). Abbreviatiations: HT, hypothalamus; Mesc, mesencephalon; OFC, orbitofrontal cortex; Tu, rest of the tumour.

She often prepared herself for work in the morning and searched for the keys, which she had in fact given back at her retirement. She talked about obligations to participate in local party meetings, which were invented. She prepared tea things in the false conviction that friends would come for a visit.

An MRI showed a circumscribed, infiltrating lesion of the paraventricular, particularly anterior hypothalamus (Figure 4.10), consistent with her

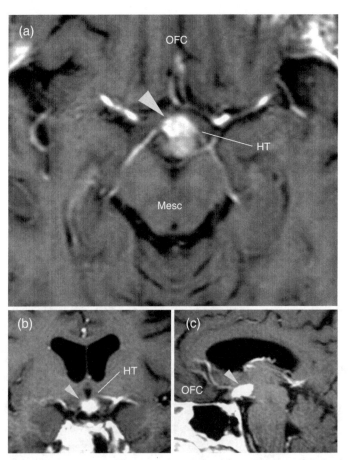

Figure 4.10 MRI of a 67-year-old woman hospitalized for evaluation of endocrine dysfunction (hyperphagia, hyperdipsia) and forgetfulness. She was disoriented and produced behaviourally spontaneous confabulations. The gadolinium-enhanced T1-weighted MRI shows a lesion of the medial hypothalamus (arrowheads). (a) Axial cut; (b) Coronal cut; (c) Sagittal cut. The lesion appears to be particularly dense in the anterior portion of the hypothalamus (a). It turned out to be sarcoidosis. Abbreviations: HT, hypothalamus; Mesc, mesencephalon; OFC, orbitofrontal cortex. Adapted with permission from Ptak et al. (2001).

endocrine dysfunction. Additional examinations confirmed that this lesion was not a tumour but sarcoidosis, a chronic inflammatory process. The patient died six months later. Autopsy showed an infiltration, which now extended over the whole axis of the hypothalamus, including the mamillary bodies (Ptak *et al.* 2001). The minimal conclusion from this observation is that, an isolated medial hypothalamic lesion may suffice to induce behaviourally spontaneous confabulation and disorientation. A more courageous conclusion – based on the early MRI – would be that this state was induced by a lesion which primarily involved the anterior hypothalamus rather than the posteriorly lying mamillary bodies. The anterior hypothalamus has direct connections with the posterior orbitofrontal cortex (Öngür *et al.* 1998; Rempel-Clower and Barbas 1998).

A particularly interesting case illustrating the pervasiveness of confabulation after diencephalic lesions was recently reported by Toth *et al.* (2002). Their 46-year-old patient had a 20 year history of alcohol abuse, but he had always worked. Over six months, his behaviour became peculiar. He repeatedly went to the place where he had lived ten years previously, then did not show up at work because he did not remember where he was employed. At emergency admission, severe amnesia was present, but the patient denied any difficulties. He confabulated and believed that he already knew the examiner from the day before. Orientation was–astonishingly–reported as perfect. There was also mild nystagmus and mild gait ataxia. All in all, the clinical picture was so convincing for alcoholic Korsakoff syndrome that intravenous thiamine was given – to no avail. A CT scan showed why: there was an infiltrating mass centred in the third ventricle with extension into the anterior lateral ventricles and downward towards the fourth ventricle. There was no hydrocephalus. Biopsy revealed a primary central nervous system lymphoma. Under steroids, confabulations ceased and the amnesia improved within three days. Thus, this patient had a clinical presentation indistinguishable from alcoholic Korsakoff syndrome – with severe amnesia, elaborate momentary confabulation, and lack of insight – due to a tumour in the middle of the hypothalamus, which extended into adjacent structures.

In contrast to diencephalic tumours, *orbitofrontal tumours* have very rarely been reported as a cause of Korsakoff syndrome. Kleist (1934) mentioned one case in his series, but the documentation was superficial. In the same concise way as cited above, Angelergues (1956) also commented on frontal tumours:

> Among 80 observations of frontal or fronto-callosal tumours, which did not involve the hypothalamus, among which 54 had mental disturbances, we have noted a Korsakoff syndrome in only one instance and even then it was a degraded form

Angelergues (1956, p. 233)

Indeed, in the article which he summarized so concisely (Angelergues *et al.* 1955), he described the manifestations of frontal tumours extensively: disturbances of consciousness and activation, such as confusional states and indifference; disturbances of mood and character, such as irritability, euphoria and depression; psychotic manifestations such as hysteria; intermittent disturbances like olfactory and other hallucinations. No mention of confabulations.

We have seen one patient, a 67-year-old retired diplomat, who produced behaviourally spontaneous confabulation after resection of a meningeoma of the left olfactory nerve, which had infiltrated the nasal sinuses and compressed the orbitofrontal cortex. Anosmia had been the presenting symptom. After the operation, the patient was in a confusional state for about three weeks. Then his general condition improved but he remained disoriented and confabulated. His social manners were as perfect as one would expect from an experienced diplomat. On one of the physicians' rounds, he was very polite but interrupted the discussion after a minute. He apologized for not being able to offer a cup of coffee, his secretary being absent for the day. Unfortunately, as he indicated, he had no time available for us right now because he had to give a talk at a conference which would start in 30 minutes. Having said that, he opened the door of the bedroom and kindly, but unmistakably, sent us outside. Thus, this patient produced undeniable behaviourally spontaneous confabulation, was disoriented, and failed in memory tasks with particular difficulty in freely recalling information. The thoughts behind his actions were always plausible and typically referred to his late profession. This confabulatory state abruptly ended from one day to the other after about two months.

The postoperative CT scan in this case showed a tissue defect involving the anterior two thirds of the medial orbitofrontal cortex on both sides corresponding to anterior area 14 and medial areas 13, 11, and 10 (Figure 4.11); the posterior medial orbitofrontal cortex and basal forebrain were intact.

In *conclusion*, intense momentary confabulations, which some authors would probably call fantastic confabulations, as well as behaviourally spontaneous confabulations have been described after medial diencephalic tumours involving the hypothalamus. The most common tumour causing such a state was craniopharyngeoma. There is some evidence that involvement of the anterior medial hypothalamus, rather than the mamillary bodies, is particularly critical for the occurrence of behaviourally spontaneous confabulation, which may continue for several weeks to months. Behaviourally spontaneous confabulation is very exceptional after orbitofrontal tumours.

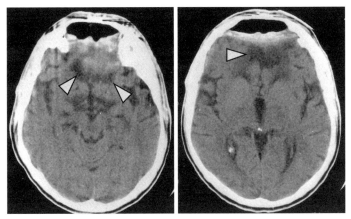

Figure 4.11 CT scan of a 67 year-old diplomat who produced behaviourally spontaneous confabulations and was disoriented after removal of a meningeoma of the left
olfactory nerve. The arrowheads show the border of the surgical cavity. Damage
involved the anterior medial orbitofrontal cortex. The posterior part and the basal
forebrain were intact. Behaviourally spontaneous confabulation was present for only
about two months.

Hypoxia and cardiopulmonary arrest

Ever since a famous case report by Zola-Morgan *et al.* (1986), many scholars of
memory firmly believe that amnesia following cardiopulmonary arrest is the
result of selective hippocampal damage. Zola-Morgan *et al.* (1986) described a
patient who remained amnesic for about five years, until his death, after a
hypoxic episode. No other cognitive deficits were present. Post-mortem examination revealed circumscribed neuronal loss involving the CA1 field of the
hippocampus bilaterally; minor pathology was also found in other structures,
such as the left internal capsule and globus pallidus. The patient never confabulated. Since this publication, many studies advertised patients with hypoxic
amnesia as a model of medial temporal amnesia. But in clinical practice,
outside the laboratories of clean amnesia research, hypoxia is rarely a selective
problem of the CA1 field of the hippocampus (Lim *et al.* 2004).

Hypoxia may produce a whole spectrum of deficits. There are those patients
who have an amazingly perfect recovery with no measurable neuropsychological sequelae. For some reason, some of them go on to develop depression
within a few months. On the other side of the spectrum are those patients who
recover late from a vegetative state and then go on to have devastating motor
and cognitive deficits. As with any form of severe dementia, these patients may

produce elaborate momentary or even fantastic confabulations, and fiercely enact their confusional ideas.

In between are those patients whose primary difficulty concerns memory. Many such patients have been described in the literature; confabulation has not been mentioned as a typical feature (Volpe and Hirst 1983; Zola-Morgan *et al.* 1986; Victor and Agamanolis 1990). In the initial phase, most patients also have significant executive failures and disorientation. They often have fluctuating attention typical of a chronic confusional state. In this stage, we have repeatedly seen momentary confabulations in discussion. These patients were also at risk of suddenly leaving the unit and bringing themselves into danger; transfer to a closed unit was sometimes necessary. In patients who are out of the chronic confusional state and who are not demented, recognition is often well preserved (Volpe and Hirst 1983) and confabulation is normally no concern (Volpe and Hirst 1983; Zola-Morgan *et al.* 1986; Victor and Agamanolis 1990). A possible exception to this rule was the patient described by Cummings *et al.* (1984). This 53-year-old man had severe anterograde amnesia, disorientation and a confabulatory state three month after a cardiopulmonary arrest which had lasted for several minutes: 'He confabulated readily and gave different answers when the same question was repeated' (p. 679). Two months later, amnesia persisted and 'he consistently confabulated answers to questions about his activities and location'. Shortly after, he died of a new cardiopulmonary arrest. At post-mortem, the most striking finding was marked atrophy of both hippocampi. The authors did not attribute significance to small infarcts in the right fronto–parietal cortex and the infero-lateral left thalamus. Dalla Barba *et al.* (1998) observed similar elaborate confabulations, both with regards to episodic and semantic information, in a 57-year-old woman examined one and two months after cardiac arrest.

Despite widespread conviction that hypoxic amnesia is a form of medial temporal amnesia, its *anatomical basis* remains somewhat contested. Autopsies of cases with relatively pure amnesia speak in favour of this idea (Cummings *et al.* 1984; Zola-Morgan *et al.* 1986; Victor and Agamanolis 1990). Volumetry using MRI has also shown preponderant atrophy of the hippocampi (Reed *et al.* 1999), although the severity of amnesia also significantly correlated with cerebral grey matter volume (Allen *et al.* 2006). However, the fact remains that the clinical picture is rarely pure (Lim *et al.* 2004). Accordingly, metabolic imaging studies using FDG–PET, a method visualizing the local metabolization of radio-labelled glucose, repeatedly found hypometabolism of the thalamus (Kuwert *et al.* 1993; Reed *et al.* 1999), sometimes the cingulum and some other structures. No study has specifically explored the functional–metabolic basis of confabulation after hypoxia.

In *conclusion*, hypoxia may lead to very different degrees of cognitive failures. Chronically confused or demented patients may produce all forms of confabulations, including erratic behaviour suggestive of behaviourally spontaneous confabulation. In the absence of a confusional state or dementia, confabulation is rare. Continuing elaborate momentary confabulations for about two months, apparently without accompanying behaviour, have been reported in a patient with selective atrophy of the hippocampus on both sides (Cummings *et al.* 1984).

Schizophrenia and other psychoses

If confabulation is defined as false productions from the memory of a sick brain, then there is no doubt that untreated schizophrenia can cause the most fantastic confabulations. Kraepelin (1886, 1887a) used the term 'simple falsifications of memory' to describe the most fantastic, completely implausible and inconsistent confabulations (Chapter 2, p. 15ff.). Whereas most of his patients had syphilitic general paralysis, some patients very likely had schizophrenia. When schizophrenia started to be recognized as a distinct disorder, the fantastic confabulations by schizophrenics also took on a separate status, distinct from confabulations in alcoholic Korsakoff syndrome or traumatic brain injury (Marková and Berrios 2000). Indeed, authors working in the two medical domains treating these disorders – psychiatrists and neurologists – hardly ever referred to each other.

Wernicke (1900, 1906) has been suspected of having promoted this scission (Marková and Berrios 2000), but this is far from clear. He proposed the distinction between two groups of false memories, based on his observations in schizophrenics: (1) delusional memory interpretation in the form of *retrospective delusional interpretation* [*retrospectiver Erklärungswahn*] or *retrospective delusion of relationship* [*retrospektiver Beziehungswahn*]. In both cases, patients inappropriately adapted and boosted the significance of memories according to their delusional world; (2) *falsifications of memory* [*Erinnerungsfälschungen*] which had two subforms. A positive form, called *confabulation* or *additive falsifications of memories*, was defined as consisting of memories of events and experiences which had never actually occurred. The negative variant consisted of circumscribed gaps in memory with no evidence of impaired consciousness at the time of the presumed event. Of importance for the present discussion is that Wernicke used the term 'confabulation' for the falsifications of memory occurring in schizophrenia, senile dementia, paralytic dementia, and polyneuritic (alcoholic) psychosis. Thus, although he recognized the distinction between truly false memories (confabulations) and delusional misinterpretation of memories, he used the term confabulation to describe active falsifications of memory both in organic brain disease and psychosis.

This was different in Bleuler's (1923) classification. He retained the distinction between different forms of memory falsifications: *Illusions of memory* (*paramnesias*) were defined as 'pathological exaggerations of flaws in memory provoked by affects, as they are also quite common in healthy people' (p. 79). He observed these illusions of memory most often in paranoids and schizophrenics: 'There is no paranoid who would not transform memories according to his delusional ideas' (p. 79). In addition, he tried to make the distinction between *organic confabulations*, whose role it was to fill gaps in memory, and *hallucinations of memory*, which were thought to be products of fantasy, devoid of any link with a real event. Hallucinations of memory would almost exclusively occur in schizophrenics, whereas confabulations were proposed as a sign of organic psychosis. We have seen in the previous chapter (p. 47f.) the difficulties he had in separating hallucinations of memory from confabulations. It seems that the main difference between these falsifications of memories was that confabulations arose in the context of a memory deficit, whereas the hallucinations and illusions of memory of schizophrenics were not necessarily associated with amnesia. Indeed, Bleuler emphasized the relative intactness of memory in schizophrenia:

> The patients mostly reproduce their experiences as well as healthy subjects, oftentimes even better in so far as they indiscriminately store all the details, too ... Thus, the registration of experiences is often very good. But the reproduction may be disturbed.

Orientation, too, was partly preserved:

> A strange finding is that schizophrenics, even in marked delirium and confusional state, mostly have correct orientation in parallel with deranged orientation. Although they consider themselves to be in prison, in hell or in a church, they alternatively know that they are in the bedroom of a psychiatric clinic .... ('double orientation').

> Bleuler (1923, p. 292)

Bleuler's definitions did not make clear in what way the hallucinations of memory in schizophrenics phenomenologically differed from the confabulations of syphilitic or alcoholic patients. Subsequent authors appeared to experience this same difficulty. After reviewing different concepts, Koehler and Jacoby (1978) suggested that

> It might be helpful to call simple false memories occurring in the presence of an organic amnestic deficit 'organic' confabulation, whereas in the absence of such a

disturbance in functional mental illness, the term 'functional' confabulation would appear to be appropriate.

Koehler and Jacoby (1978, p. 418f.)

Leonhard's (1986) summary of 'confabulatory paraphrenia' – his term for fantastic confabulations in schizophrenia – nonetheless highlighted some features which were untypical for other forms of confabulations, and which cogently reflect the impression one has when reading Kraepelin's and Bleuler's patient descriptions:

> Confabulatory paraphrenia is dominated by illusions of memory ... ideas of grandeur. [These] have mostly a fantastic imprint and refer to other countries, parts of the world or even other stars ... The immediate environment is not integrated in the confabulations but is judged correctly.

Leonhard (1986, p. 208)

Of course, the diagnosis of schizophrenia does not solely reside on the observation of fantastic confabulation or illusions or hallucinations of memory, but on many other features (American Psychiatric Association 1994). Nonetheless, any clinician hearing confabulations as absurd as those described by Kraepelin would nowadays suspect the presence of schizophrenia, once a confusional state, and severe dementia were excluded. However, the distinction between the fantastic confabulations produced by acute schizophrenics and the fantastic confabulations produced by acutely confused or severely demented patients remains arbitrary, apart from the distinctive features (delusions versus amnesia) of the underlying diseases. It is doubtful whether a person simply reading the transcripts of such confabulations would be able to make the difference.

Absurd and fantastic falsifications of memories as described by Kraepelin (1886, 1887a, b) have not been reported in the recent literature. In part, this may be due to the insight that many weird ideas of schizophrenic patients reflect delusions rather than false memories (Wernicke 1900; Bleuler 1923; Kopelman 1999), but it is probably also due to the efficacy of antipsychotic drugs, which were introduced in the 1950s and which are particularly effective on the positive symptoms of schizophrenia, such as, delusions and hallucinations.

Confabulation has been a very rare topic in *recent schizophrenia research* and then only concerned provoked confabulations. Nathaniel-James and Frith (1996) conducted a study with twelve schizophrenic patients. They introduced the study as 'an attempt to demonstrate confabulation in schizophrenia'. Indeed, schizophrenic patients tended to spontaneously rearrange original components of heard stories and to produce new ideas considered by the authors to be rather bizarre. This tendency correlated with a difficulty in suppressing inappropriate responses in neuropsychological tests and with formal thought disorder.

Simpson and Done (2002) had two groups of schizophrenics and a non-psychiatric control group recall 15 scripts, of which five contained atypical components, that is, sentences that had no relation with the main story. The authors found that delusional schizophrenics confabulated much more than non-delusional patients and non-psychiatric controls when recalling the stories. There were only fine qualitative differences between the groups.

Salazar-Fraile *et al.* (2004) tested the recall of two stories and the recognition of the source of a story in 33 schizophrenic patients, 35 bipolar I patients, eight schizoaffective patients and seven patients with other psychiatric disorders. They found that none of the two capacities – story recall or source attribution – differentiated between the groups, but they did find a dissociation between the tasks: Confabulations on story recall were mainly predicted by the predominance of positive symptoms (disorganized thought, grandiosity, delusions). In contrast, confabulation about the source was predicted by an electrophysiological measure of surprise (delay in P300 latency) and the dose of antipsychiotics.

Finally, Dab *et al.* (2004) explored the confabulations by five hospitalized schizophrenic patients in several memory tests. They then related the occurrence of confabulations to the patients' performance on tasks of verbal comprehension, encoding, and memory monitoring. All patients had some degree of encoding deficit. The authors found that schizophrenics had a higher tendency to confabulate in story and fable recall than word list recall. Remarkably, these confabulations appeared to be related to the verbal comprehension deficit, rather than a memory monitoring failure.

Thus, these studies confirmed that schizophrenics have an increased tendency to produce provoked confabulations in memory tasks, a tendency associated with disease severity, whereby verbal comprehension deficits possibly play a particular role.

The *pathological basis* of schizophrenic thought disorder – which is characterized by false beliefs and can induce fantastic confabulations, if untreated – is still poorly understood. Pathological studies have repeatedly shown certain degrees of atrophy with enlarged ventricles, most pronounced in the temporal lobes, to a lesser degree also anteriorly and in the area of parahippocampal cortex (Brown *et al.* 1986; Harrison 1999). Atrophy appeared to be due primarily to small size, rather than loss of neurons and neuropil, a finding suggestive of alterations in synaptic, dendritic and axonal organization

(Harrison 1999). A recent review of voxel-based morphometric studies also indicated particularly pronounced volume deficits in the left temporal lobe (Honea *et al.* 2005). Diverse studies described abnormal volumes and neuron counts in the striatum, nucleus accumbens (limbic striatum), dorsomedial nucleus of the thalamus, and lateral nucleus of the amygdala; a recent study confirmed such abnormalities in the striatum and amygdala (Kreczmanski *et al.* 2007). Evidence suggests, however, that morphometry and neuron counts alone will not explain schizophrenia and that dysfunction of transmitter systems, among others dopamine, have to be taken into account (Davis *et al.* 1991; Sawa and Snyder 2002).

An early functional imaging study using PET indicated that activation of the left parahippocampal region correlated with the three subsyndromes of schizophrenia – psychomotor poverty, reality distortion, and disorganization (Friston *et al.* 1992). In a more detailed analysis, the same authors found that disorganization correlated with right ventral prefrontal abnormality, reality distortion with left parahippocampal and striatum abnormality (Liddle *et al.* 1992). One might speculate that these two subsyndromes would be particularly relevant for the production of fantastic confabulations.

In *conclusion*, untreated schizophrenia may be associated with fantastic, illogical and implausible confabulations, which are probably indistinguishable from fantastic confabulations by severely demented or confused patients. According to the early descriptions, schizophrenic confabulation possibly differs from fantastic confabulation in organic diseases by relative preservation of memory and orientation. Diverse studies have demonstrated provoked confabulations in schizophrenia. Pathological changes concern various cortical and subcortical brain areas, in particular the temporal lobes. Recent studies suggested abnormalities in the synaptic, dendritic and axonal organization, but also abnormalities in diverse transmitter systems. These processes are far from being fully understood.

Dementia

Dementia, originally also called presbyophrenia or senile forgetfulness, has long been recognized as an important cause of confabulation and disorientation. Kraepelin (1899) and Bleuler (1923) listed dementia among the most frequent causes of confabulation. The reader may remember Tiling's patient (Chapter 2, p. 20) with increasing forgetfulness over six to seven years, who was embarrassed by questions and would 'conceal the defect in her memory with little jokes or excuses' (Tiling 1892). In our classification, these jokes and excuses would qualify as momentary confabulations. One may also remember Chaslin's patient (Chapter 3, p. 46f.) with senile dementia who refused to sit down at table and start dinner before the head of family had arrived, ignoring the fact that her husband had died several years before (Chaslin 1912). This patient thus acted according to an idea, which was based on remote experiences but inappropriate for ongoing reality. Such confabulations can be considered behaviourally spontaneous confabulations. In this patient, they seemed to be evoked by the long-time routine of preparing dinner for the family.

Similar to delirium, dementia reflects dysfunction of diverse mental capacities typically resulting from damage of multiple brain areas (sole exception: certain types of frontal lobe disease). It has been *defined* as the combined dysfunction of at least three of the following cognitive domains: language, memory, visuospatial capacities (constructive abilities, visual recognition), behaviour and affect (including personality), and cognition (e.g., abstraction, interpretation of proverbs, calculations) and executive functions (Cummings and Benson 1992). Most definitions require the disorder to be sufficiently severe to interfere with daily activities (American Psychiatric Association 1994). In contrast to delirium, dementia is not an acute event, and basic attention is intact. Many of the patients reported in the literature as confabulators would also qualify for the diagnosis of dementia; Kraepelin's patients with general paralysis (Chapter 2, pp.15ff.) are among the most flagrant examples (Kraepelin 1886, 1887a). Comparably to delirium, dementia has countless possible aetiologies. In this section, however, the focus will be on degenerative dementias in which confabulation has been described: Alzheimer's disease and frontotemporal dementia (FTD).

Given the high frequency of Alzheimer's disease in the elderly population, it is amazing how rare reports of confabulation in this disease actually are. Behaviourally dominating confabulation is not a diagnostic criterion of degenerative dementia (McKhann *et al.* 1984; American Psychiatric Association 1994). The incidence of severe, behaviourally pertinent confabulation certainly increases as the disease progresses. Patients with advanced dementia may produce incoherent, even fantastic confabulations. The cause of the dementia is secondary; Kraepelin's patients with paralytic dementia produced most fantastic confabulations. Momentary confabulations were also reported in patients having hydrocephalus (Berglund *et al.* 1979). Some patients try to enact their ideas. If hindered from the execution of their plans – e.g., to leave the hospital – they often react aggressively. Even though most clinicians have seen such situations, there has been virtually no scientific interest in these confabulations. Most of the studies on confabulation in dementia, which will be discussed in the following, have focused on provoked confabulation in mild stages.

In Berlyne's series of demented patients, half of whom had senile dementia, more than a third produced confabulations, with equal prevalence of momentary and fantastic confabulations according to his definition (Chapter 3, p. 54) (Berlyne 1972). According to our criteria, most of these confabulations would correspond to more or less elaborate momentary confabulations.

Behaviourally spontaneous confabulation in dementia has not been reported in the recent literature, with the exception of a case of probable vascular dementia (Dalla Barba 1993a), a type of dementia different from Alzheimer's disease and FTD resulting from multiple vascular defects. This 75-year-old patient was disoriented in time and place and confabulated in response to questions. The author noted that:

> spontaneous confabulation, without grandiose and bizarre content also occurred. So, the patient indicated that he had to go to the general store to buy some new clothes and then actually attempted to leave the hospital room, claiming that there was a taxi waiting for him downstairs.
>
> Dalla Barba (1993a, p. 4)

In our classification, these confabulations would be considered behaviourally spontaneous confabulation. The pathological basis of vascular dementia, however, is unlike Alzheimer's disease or FTD. This patient's confabulations might have resulted from a strategically located lesion, which would by itself have accounted for the confabulations. Such a lesion would be difficult to ascertain among the multitude of tiny lesions normally present in vascular dementia.

A number of studies have looked at ways to elicit confabulations in patients with Alzheimer's disease. In the study described in the previous chapter (p. 55f.) Kopelman (1987) found that 5 of 16 patients with Alzheimer's disease gave examples of provoked confabulations (intrusions) when recalling a logical story. Interestingly, four of these five patients did so only at immediate recall. Two of them also produced 'spontaneous' confabulations according to Kopelman's criteria: sustained, wide-ranging confabulations evident in everyday conversation, i.e., elaborate momentary confabulations according to our classification. One of these patients talked incessantly about her mother, who had in reality died many years ago. She explained to the interviewer that she had to hurry to cook dinner for her mother and that she had been ticked off for being late in preparing the dinner the day before. She also denied having any children, although in fact she had a son (Kopelman 1987, p. 1484).

It is likely that such confabulatory states are more frequent in Alzheimer's disease than the literature suggests. A moving testimony of such a state was provided by Crisp (1995) in describing her own mother who

> mixed up past events with present ones and interweaved fragments of her own life with things she had simply heard about, seen, read, imagined... No matter how fantastic a story seems, carers should take a moment or two to consider whether it may not be literally true or contain substantially true elements.
>
> Crisp (1995, pp. 133–4)

The relative discreteness of confabulatory phenomena in early Alzheimer's disease was suggested by a study by Kern *et al.* (1992), who concluded that their 'findings provided evidence for the feasibility of eliciting confabulatory-type behaviour during clinical assessment' in Alzheimer's disease. Twenty-six patients with mild to moderate Alzheimer's disease (Mini Mental State examination, MMSE, score 18 ± 5) performed a battery of neuropsychological tests specifically designed to assess different types of memory errors. Tests of vocabulary, block design, naming, diverse frontal tests, story recall and other verbal and nonverbal memory tests were used. Novel embellishments in the nonverbal memory task and intrusions in the verbal memory tasks were considered confabulatory phenomena. Not so surprisingly, the patients' performance was significantly inferior to age-matched controls on almost all tasks – after all, they had Alzheimer's disease. It does not appear that the confabulations were the most striking finding in the verbal tasks:

> In general, the recall performance of the AD [Alzheimer's disease] group was characterized by reduced verbal output, limited amounts of accurate information, and an increased proportion of recall inaccuracies and novel intrusions relative to the amount of accurate recall.
>
> Kern *et al.* (1992, p. 179)

A somewhat different approach was taken by Tallberg and Almkvist (2001), who used a questionnaire similar to Dalla Barba's confabulation battery (Chapter 3, p. 67f.) in 15 patients with very mild to moderate Alzheimer's disease. There were a total of 20 questions covering recent and remote autobiographic memory as well as semantic memory. The authors found that the total number of confabulations strongly correlated with the degree of dementia as estimated by the MMSE score (correlation coefficient, $r = -0.8$). Among the more specific tests, memory for recent personal information within the confabulation test ($r = -0.9$) and verbal fluency (FAS test, $r = -0.68$) had very high correlations with the total number of confabulations. In a stepwise regression analysis including age, education, MMSE score, word fluency, item memory, and priming, the MMSE score remained the only significant predictor of the total number of confabulations. Elaborate confabulations occurred more often in moderately than mildly demented patients and were strongly related to deteriorated recent autobiographical memory.

A similar finding was described by Cooper *et al.* (2006). These authors also developed a questionnaire specifically created for eliciting confabulatory behaviours in patients with mild Alzheimer's disease (MMSE 19–26). They found that the number of provoked confabulations in memory testing (recall of a story composed previously by the patient) had the highest correlation with personal episodic memory measures, but not with other measures of cognitive functioning such as executive functions.

What do these studies say about the *anatomical basis* of confabulations in Alzheimer's disease? Deducing brain-behaviour relationships from a progressive disease spreading to multiple brain areas remains speculative. It appears that intrusions and even momentary confabulations can be elicited in the early stages of the disease (Kern *et al.* 1992; Tallberg and Almkvist 2001; Cooper *et al.* 2006). Pathological studies comparing the brains of demented and non-demented individuals indicated that the main pathological changes, in particular the neurofibrillary tangles – a hallmark of Alzheimer pathology – first accumulate in the medial temporal area (hippocampal formation and surrounding tissue) and then spread to other limbic and neocortical association areas (Arnold *et al.* 1991; Braak and Braak 1991). A serial imaging study involving patients with mild cognitive impairment – a disorder not yet qualifying as dementia but predictive of it – also indicated that the early degeneration involves the medial temporal lobe: Patients converting to Alzheimer's disease had a marked, progressive tissue loss as they progressed to full dementia (Apostolova *et al.* 2006). Another imaging study demonstrated considerable early grey matter loss in the neocortex, affecting most significantly temporal and temporo–parietal association cortex, but also lateral prefrontal cortex (Thompson *et al.* 2001). It is likely that provoked and even elaborate momentary confabulations in Alzheimer's disease result from the combined medial temporal lobe and neocortical degeneration. Another potential pathological substrate is the degeneration of cholinergic nuclei in the basal forebrain, which occurs in Alzheimer's disease (Auld *et al.* 2002). Of note, the orbitofrontal cortex is relatively spared in the early course of the disease. This may explain why severe confabulation is uncommon in the early phase.

The case of **frontotemporal dementia (FTD)** might at first sight suggest a more specific anatomical basis of provoked confabulations. This type of dementia is characterized by socially inappropriate behaviour with loss of tact and concern, impaired judgement, and early loss of abstraction and planning. Degeneration primarily involves the frontal lobes, with an emphasis on the orbitofrontal area, and variably extends into the temporal lobes (Rosen *et al.* 2002). The patients may produce confabulations in response to questions, similar to patients with Alzheimer's disease (Nedjam *et al.* 2000). Two studies suggested that such patients differ from patients with Alzheimer's disease in the propensity to produce distorted memories upon questioning. Nedjam *et al.* (2004) tested 22 patients with mild, probable Alzheimer's disease (AD) and ten patients with probable FTD on a number of executive tests and a modified version of Dalla Barba's confabulation battery (p. 67f.). The battery contained ten questions each on episodic memory, semantic memory, and personal plans. Although both patient groups were similarly impaired on the executive tasks, FTD patients confabulated significantly more than AD patients on the episodic memory and personal future parts of the confabulation battery.

Using a different approach, Thompson *et al.* (2005) partially confirmed and refined these observations. They tested 38 patients with FTD and 73 with Alzheimer's disease on diverse cognitive domains including language, visuospatial abilities, memory and executive functions. A general observation was that FTD patients displayed more concrete thought, perseveration, confabulation, and poor organization, which disrupted performance across the range of neuropsychological tests. In particular, misconstructed or confabulatory accounts, such as fictional elaborative elements in story recall, significantly increased the odds for the presence of frontotemporal dementia. By contrast, intrusion of unrelated information in story recall, which had been presented in an earlier test, increased the odds for a diagnosis of Alzheimer's disease. The study suggested a dissociation between elaborate momentary confabulations, somewhat more prevalent in FTD, and provoked confabulations in the form of intrusions, more prevalent in Alzheimer's disease.

What do these data indicate about the *anatomical basis* of confabulation in degenerative dementias? To a certain degree, they suggest that intrusions in a memory task may result from pathology centred on the medial temporal lobes and extending into different neocortical association areas – the pathology of Alzheimer's disease. In contrast, elaborate momentary confabulations appear to be more likely if the degenerative process involves the prefrontal cortex, in particular the orbitofrontal region plus the anterior temporal cortex – the pathology of frontotemporal dementia. Another aspect, however, deserves comment: although the behavioural aberrations with social misconduct, perseverative and stereotyped behaviour, distractibility, loss of personal hygiene, emotional blunting, and loss of insight may be highly impressive in FTD and undeniably prove severe disease of the frontal lobes, confabulation does not figure among the diagnostic criteria of frontotemporal dementia

(Neary *et al.* 1998; McKhann *et al.* 2001). Thus, even severe generalized executive dysfunction does not presage behaviourally pertinent confabulation. There must be something more specific to confabulation than the loss of insight or generalized executive failures.

If it is already difficult to determine the pathological alterations inducing intrusions and momentary confabulations in demented patients, it is certainly no easier to determine the alterations inducing behaviourally spontaneous confabulations. Chaslin's (1912) patient was institutionalized when she refused to sit down at table (Chapter, 3 p. 46f.), an indication that she was in an advanced stage of dementia which made it impossible for her to live at home. As Alzheimer's disease progresses, more and more cortical areas are involved. An autopsy study focussing on pathological changes in the midfrontal gyrus (area 46, Figure 4.2a), inferoparietal (areas 39 and 40) and superior temporal lobe (area 22) indicated that cognitive deficits determined two weeks to two years before death were best explained by the loss of synapses in midfrontal and inferior parietal cortex (Terry *et al.* 1991), but no information concerning the patients' behaviour was provided.

Another pathological study analysed multiple areas of the brain of Alzheimer's patients, most of whom had very severe dementia by the time of death (Tekin *et al.* 2001). The authors concluded that agitation and aberrant motor behaviour was best predicted by the density of neurofibrillary tangles in the orbitofrontal cortex. Of course, it is impossible to determine whether such patients' aberrant motor behaviour, characterized by repetitive activities – pacing around the house, handling buttons, or wrapping strings, sometimes accompanied by strange comments – was the result of a consistent, but currently inappropriate action plan, as is characteristically the case with behaviourally spontaneous confabulation. It appears more likely that such behaviour reflected bouts of more or less erratic behaviour.

At this state of our knowledge, it seems inappropriate to assume a more specific mechanism for the occurrence of confabulations in Alzheimer's disease than the general cognitive decline. It appears premature to attribute such confabulations to dysfunction of a specific brain area. Metabolic imaging studies might provide more consistent data in the future. Conclusions drawn from other, more focal brain diseases such as aneurysm rupture, traumatic brain injury, or herpes encephalitis may simply not apply to a widespread, progressive disease like Alzheimer's. We made this observation when we explored the mechanism of another component of the Korsakoff syndrome, namely, disorientation in Alzheimer's disease (Joray *et al.* 2004). In contrast to the more focal diseases, disorientation had no predictive value for the occurrence of behaviourally spontaneous confabulation in Alzheimer's disease.

In addition, performance on a task which correlated highly with disorientation in focal diseases (Chapter 8) had no predictive value for disorientation in
Alzheimer's disease. In this disease, disorientation was best, albeit weakly,
associated with measures of general cognitive decline.

In *conclusion*, although confabulations are common in degenerative dementia, they do not dominate behaviour in the early stages. Provoked confabulations can be induced in the mild to moderate disease stages and seem to
correlate with general cognitive decline. Momentary or fantastic confabulations and behaviourally spontaneous confabulations occur in advanced stages
but have been rare subjects of recent scientific interest. The precise anatomical
basis of these confabulations remains elusive.

Exceptional causes

Many causes of Korsakoff syndrome listed by the early authors – arsenic or
lead poisoning, carbon dioxide intoxication, etc. (Jolly 1897) – can not be
verified and were possibly associated with confusional states.

A rare cause of fantastic confabulation, difficult to classify, was reported by
Feinstein *et al.* (2000). Their patient, a 'middle aged male of middle-eastern
descent' fulfilled criteria for the diagnosis of *multiple sclerosis*, including findings in the cerebrospinal fluid, evoked potentials, and brain imaging. When
admitted to the hospital, he claimed to be an airplane pilot, whose jet had got
into difficulties, forcing him to eject at 7000 metres. He then explained that his
parachute had not opened and that he recalled floating to earth, describing the
experience as the most beautiful one of his life. He also indicated that he spoke
17 languages and that his father was 137 years old. The content of these tales
remained essentially unchanged over the course of a one-year follow-up. The
patient had disinhibited behaviour with grossly inappropriate sexual
approaches to female nurses. Most notably, however, he was correctly oriented
and achieved an almost normal score on the Mini Mental State Examination
(Folstein *et al.* 1975), a common measure of the severity of many forms of
dementia. The MRI showed confluent periventricular lesions (typical for
multiple sclerosis). It is difficult to make sense of these confabulations, which
resembled those described in the early literature in patients with advanced
paralytic dementia or schizophrenia and other psychoses (Kraepelin 1886,
1887a; Bleuler 1923). The authors considered a conversion or factitious disorder but found no specific argument in favour of such an interpretation.
Although this case was highly atypical for multiple sclerosis, it showed that
fantastic confabulations could occur in the context of normal orientation in a
disorder having the characteristics of hebephrenic psychosis. A similar case of
confirmed multiple sclerosis, a 23-year-old man producing absurd, in part

paranoid stories, was recently described by Gundogar and Demirci (2006). Memory performance – including delayed free recall – and orientation were intact.

Anatomy across aetiologies

The few studies cited in this chapter that specifically examined the anatomical basis of confabulation restricted their analysis to a specific type of brain damage (Angelergues 1956; Fischer *et al.* 1995; Gilboa *et al.* 2006). However, if confabulations have a specific anatomical basis, this basis should hold across diverse aetiologies. Very few studies have looked at this.

Although *intrusions* in memory tests are a very common phenomenon, their anatomical basis has never been explored in a controlled way. Indeed, their occurrence in many types of brain damage makes it unlikely that they have a specific anatomical basis.

Using a modified version of Dalla Barba's confabulation battery (p. 67f.), Turner *et al.* (2007) found that 39 patients with diverse types of frontal lesions produced significantly more confabulations than 12 patients with different non-frontal lesions. Overall, confabulations were rare and mostly related to personal episodic memory and orientation to time and place. The frequency was highest in patients with orbital lesions, followed by patients with medial frontal and left lateral lesions.

Gilboa and Moscovitch (2002) analysed the anatomical basis of severe confabulation. They reviewed 33 studies in which significant imaging or post-mortem findings were reported. Seventy-nine patients produced 'spontaneous', that is, sustained and wide-ranging confabulations that we would call elaborate momentary confabulations in this book. Many of the patients were also behaviourally spontaneous confabulators, but this was not the criterion for entering the analysis. The authors found no evidence for a specific lesion lateralization. They drew two important conclusions: (1) 'damage to the medial prefrontal cortex may be crucial in the production of confabulations' (p. 319); (2) 'lesions of the ventromedial aspect of the frontal lobes are sufficient to produce confabulations, even when damage to other regions is minimal or absent' (p. 323). As we have seen, momentary confabulations occasionally also occur after medial temporal or other non-frontal lesions. Behaviourally spontaneous confabulation may occur after isolated damage to the hypothalamus, in the absence of ventromedial prefrontal damage (Ptak *et al.* 2001, Figure 4.10).

We have explored the anatomical basis of *behaviourally spontaneous confabulations* in several studies (Schnider *et al.* 1996c; Schnider and Ptak 1999). Confabulators were compared with patients having similarly severe amnesia, thereby limiting the analysis to patients having comparable difficulty in accessing their memories. Patients had such diverse causes as ACoA aneurysm rupture, traumatic brain injury, herpes encephalitis, ischemic stroke, and tumours. Patients were only included once they were out of the confusional state. They were then classified either as a behaviourally spontaneous confabulator (criteria, p. 61f.) or a non-confabulator (irrespective of the production of other forms of confabulation), based on the observations by the rehabilitation team. All 'spontaneous confabulators' produced momentary confabulations when responding to questions about their recent doings and plans. None of the patients in the 'non-confabulating amnesic' group produced such confabulations. The studies were conducted in a neurorehabilitation unit which took care of patients suffering from the consequences of acute brain injury, but not degenerative brain diseases. Hence, we could assume that the new brain lesions, rather than some underlying degenerative process, were responsible for the patients' mental difficulties.

Figure 4.12 shows the combined analysis of data from the diverse studies (Schnider 2003). Patients who were amnesic but not confabulating had strongest lesion overlap in the area of the medial temporal lobe (Figure 4.12a). Many had lesions involving neocortical areas, such as, the insula or dorsolateral prefrontal lobes. The lesion overlap was markedly different in the behaviourally spontaneous confabulators (Figure 4.12b). Their lesions mostly overlapped in the area of the ventromedial prefrontal cortex (posterior medial orbitofrontal cortex and basal forebrain). Alternative lesion sites were the anterior medial orbitofrontal cortex sparing the posterior part; the medial hypothalamus (Ptak *et al.* 2001, Figure 4.10), the amygdala on the right side and perirhinal cortex on the left side (Figure 4.6d–f), and the inferior genu of the right internal capsule (Figure 4.4). Thus, all lesions concerned either the posterior medial orbitofrontal cortex itself or structures directly connected with it. In other words, all lesions concerned anterior limbic structures, in contrast to the posterior limbic structures (hippocampal area with adjacent cortex, retrosplenial cortex) damaged in the non-confabulating amnesics.

Making sense of the data – towards a summary

Summarizing the wealth of information contained in the studies cited in this chapter is no easy task. The reports may have shattered some firm beliefs. Some readers may be astonished to see how ubiquitous confabulatory phenomena are. Others may be surprised to see how rare significant confabulations after some of the well-known causes of confabulation actually are, e.g., ACoA aneurysm rupture or traumatic brain injury. In order to interpret these

(a)   Non-confabulating amnesics

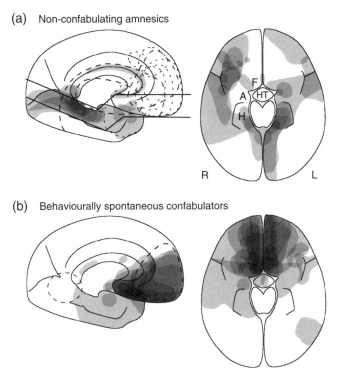

(b)   Behaviourally spontaneous confabulators

Figure 4.12 Anatomy of behaviourally spontaneous confabulation. (a) Lesion overlap of nonconfabulating amnesics. (b) Lesion overlap of behaviourally spontaneous confabulators. Shaded areas indicate lesions of the paramedian cortex (left template) or inferior surface (right template). Dashed lines are used to indicate lesion of the lateral convexity (left template). Adapted with permission from Schnider (2003).

data and to give them anatomical meaning it is important to have the biases, difficulties, and potential shortcomings of this review in mind.

First, this review focused on positive evidence for confabulations in different diseases. This focus might lead to overestimation of the importance of some aetiologies, but there might also be a negative bias in this focus: Most reports came from neurological, neuropsychological, or psychiatric institutions. There were virtually no reports of confabulation from geriatric institutions. I suspect, however, that confabulation is a common phenomenon in elderly demented patients, which has not yet aroused as much interest in geriatric research as in clinical neuroscience.

Second, classification of confabulations and terminology varied among the different authors. Many authors only described their patients' verbal expressions but did not comment on their behaviour in daily life. My classification of the described confabulations might, therefore, at times be inaccurate.

Third, many studies did not comment on the early phase after brain injury. The absence of confabulation in such patients is an unreliable indicator of a lesion's propensity to induce a transient phenomenon like confabulation. These reports might lead to underestimation of confabulation in the respective diseases.

Fourth, medications have influenced the course and manifestations of certain aetiologies, such as general paralysis, avitaminosis, and psychosis. Modern anatomical data from these diseases may not pertain to confabulatory syndromes observed in the untreated forms of these diseases.

Fifth, not all diseases are equally frequent. The frequent reports of significant confabulation after ACoA aneurysm rupture and traumatic brain injury might theoretically also reflect the fact that the ACoA is the most frequent site of aneurysms and that traumatic brain injury is a common cause of brain damage. Nonetheless, the observations presented in this chapter suggest conclusions that cannot be discarded on the basis of different disease frequencies. Tumours, for example, may occur in any part of the brain, but severe confabulation has been observed most consistently when tumours were located in the region of the third ventricle. Also, ACoA aneurysm rupture is far from being the most frequent type of stroke; many more patients suffer ischemic strokes in other parts of the brain – middle cerebral and other arteries. It is not likely that important confabulatory tendencies after these strokes would have gone unnoticed. Thus, the described studies probably give a fairly valid impression of the overall anatomical basis of the diverse forms of confabulation.

Summary and conclusions

The reported data allow some consistent conclusions about confabulations in the different types of brain damage and about their anatomical basis.

There is no cause of brain damage and no known lesion area that always induces significant confabulation.

Overall, behaviourally relevant confabulation is a *rare* phenomenon. Even among the aetiologies generally regarded as the most important ones (ACoA aneurysm rupture, traumatic brain injury, avitaminosis), only a small proportion of patients, possibly three to five per cent, continue to confabulate notably beyond the confusional state.

Behaviourally significant confabulation (severe momentary, fantastic, and behaviourally spontaneous confabulation) is usually a *transient* phenomenon lasting days, weeks, or months. Amnesia often persists.

Provoked confabulations in the form of *intrusions* in memory tests have been reported in virtually all diseases discussed above, independently of the occurrence of other, behaviourally relevant confabulations. Their severity appears to increase together with the severity of cognitive and memory failures (Tallberg and Almkvist 2001; Cooper *et al.* 2006). Provoked confabulations do not appear to have anatomical specificity. It seems appropriate to treat intrusions (provoked confabulations in memory tests) as a non-specific sign of brain dysfunction, distinct from other forms of confabulation.

Fantastic confabulations of two different degrees have been described:

1. Wholly *illogical, nonsensical* confabulations defying any common concept of reality. Such confabulations have been described in the early literature in patients with advanced paralytic dementia (syphilitic general paralysis) and in patients with schizophrenia and other psychoses. In the latter cases, these confabulations were not normally associated with severe memory impairment. Early authors set this type of delusional fantastic confabulations apart from other confabulations and called them *delusional interpretation* (Wernicke 1900) or *'illusions or hallucinations' of memory* (Bleuler 1923);

2. Similar confabulations, fantastic by their lack of connection with ongoing reality but *intrinsically logic* and composed of elements from the patients' real past. Such confabulations were often described in the acute phase of diseases with known potential to induce severe confabulatory states (ACoA aneurysm rupture, traumatic brain injury). Some reported patients stopped confabulating once they were out of the confusional state, others then continued to produce behaviourally significant confabulations.

Elaborate momentary confabulation in the absence of a confusional state or advanced dementia has been described particularly often in diseases affecting the ventromedial prefrontal lobes (posterior medial orbitofrontal area and the basal forebrain), and the diencephalon, in particular the hypothalamus, occasionally the anteromedial thalamus (paramedian thalamic infarction). Specifically, many patients with severe and long-standing confabulatory states had suffered ACoA aneurysm rupture or traumatic brain injury. Fewer cases of similar severity and duration had herpes simplex virus encephalitis or surgery of a craniopharyngeoma. Patients with focal lesions of the anterior cingulate gyrus (Whitty and Lewin 1960) had only very transient states of derealization. Lesions outside the area of the ventromedial prefrontal cortex and diencephalon (hypothalamus, paramedian thalamus) are not normally associated with marked momentary confabulation unless there is dementia or a confusional state.

The anatomical basis of *behaviourally spontaneous confabulation* has been explored across diverse aetiologies and in comparison with non-confabulating amnesics. The area of strongest lesion overlap was the ventromedial prefrontal area (posterior medial orbitofrontal and the basal forebrain, Figure 4.12). Other lesions involved other parts of the orbitofrontal cortex, the anterior hypothalamus, the amygdala on one side and the perirhinal cortex on the other side, and the genu of the right internal capsule. In summary, then, all lesions of behaviourally spontaneous confabulators included the posterior medial orbitofrontal cortex or other anterior limbic structures directly connected with it.

Chapter 5

Disorders associated with confabulation

Since the early description by Korsakoff, confabulation has always been linked with amnesia and disorientation (Bonhoeffer 1904). Some authors observed that their patients felt falsely familiar with other people or places (paramnesic misidentification) and integrated this element in their definition of Korsakoff syndrome (Benon and LeHuché 1920). Lack of insight (anosognosia) was repeatedly portrayed as an integral aspect of confabulation (Williams and Rupp 1938). Conversely, the false statements by anosognosic patients were eventually labelled as confabulations (Weinstein and Kahn 1950). This semantic concordance motivated diverse scholars to postulate a common mechanism for all of these phenomena.

The goal of this chapter is not to provide additional evidence that confabulations are often associated with amnesia, disorientation, false recognition, paramnesic misidentification, and lack of insight. The goal will be to explore the strength and circumstances of the associations and to sort out dissociations. The concepts of paramnesia and anosognosia will be reviewed in more detail, starting with their original descriptions, so that readers can make their own decision about the link with confabulation. Hurried readers may prefer to proceed directly to the conclusions given at the end of each paragraph.

Provoked confabulations first

There have been dramatic reports of patients producing many provoked confabulations (intrusions) in the context of severe amnesia (Demery *et al.* 2001). Mrs M (pp. 57f.) produced abundant intrusions and false positive responses in memory tests, spontaneously confabulated, and was disoriented (Schnider *et al.* 1996a). Her intrusions always consisted of material presented in earlier tasks, even several weeks ago. Such cases are exceptional and documented in single case studies. As we saw in Chapters 3 and 4, group studies clearly demonstrated that intrusions in memory tests dissociate from other confabulatory phenomena. Hence, their association with other cognitive disturbances – amnesia, disorientation, etc. – deserves a separate analysis.

So, are provoked confabulations always associated with *amnesia*? The answer is clearly 'no'. Patients producing provoked confabulation need not have amnesia (Delbecq-Derouesné *et al.* 1990). Even healthy subjects can be pushed to confabulate in memory tests. Burgess and Shallice (1996) asked healthy subjects to retrieve details of recent events, such as the last journey to the coast, yesterday's dinner etc. Being encouraged to provide details, the subjects produced errors. Of course, such 'confabulations' might be considered simple guesses, of which the subjects themselves were not convinced, but this need not be the case. Provided with some 'helpful hints' before the forced retrieval of details about earlier events, healthy subjects – for example witnesses – may confabulate pertinent elements with full conviction (Loftus 1979/1996, 1992). We will come back to the topic of false memories in healthy subjects in Chapter 6. Suffice it for now to conclude that provoked confabulations in the form of intrusions and punctual distortions of recalled memories can also be induced in healthy subjects.

As any clinician knows, intrusions in memory tests are much more common in brain-damaged than healthy subjects. Severity of dementia (Tallberg and Almkvist 2001) or presence of delusions in schizophrenia (Simpson and Done 2002) was found in some studies to predict the number of provoked confabulations. Only one study found an association with personal episodic memory capacity in dementia (Cooper *et al.* 2006).

We have explored this association in a series of 59 patients admitted to neurorehabilitation after diverse types of brain damage, with the exclusion of degenerative dementia (Schnider *et al.* 1997). In this sample of patients, whose common denominator was that they all had brain damage interfering with independence in daily activities, intrusions in memory tests were very frequent. Over all runs of the California Verbal Learning Test (Delis *et al.* 1987), 73 per cent of the subjects made more than four intrusions, the normal cut-off: 47 per cent made more than ten, 15 per cent more than 20 intrusions. The majority of patients (66 per cent) had severely impaired long-delay free recall (≤ 4). The important finding for the present discussion was that some patients with normal learning curves and delayed free recall (uncorrected for intrusions) also produced many intrusions. Over the whole group, there was no significant correlation between any measure of amnesia and the number of intrusions. Amazingly, intrusions did not correlate with false positives in recognition testing, either. Likewise, there was no significant correlation with orientation. Among different measures of executive functioning (verbal and nonverbal fluency, colour-word interference), only the number of perseverations in the nonverbal fluency task (five-point task, Regard *et al.* 1982) significantly correlated with intrusions ($F_{1,50} = 8$; $p = 0.007$), albeit weakly ($r = 0.37$, $r^2 = 0.14$). In comparison, the total number of correctly produced designs also positively correlated with the intrusions, albeit non-significantly.

In *conclusion*, provoked confabulations (intrusions) are more frequent after brain damage but are not reliably associated with amnesia, disorientation, or false recognition. In the remainder of this chapter, provoked confabulation will not be considered any further unless otherwise stated. But we will come back to its mechanism in Chapter 7.

Amnesia

If amnesia is not necessary for provoked confabulations (intrusions) to occur, then what about the other, more serious forms of confabulation? Amnesia has always been recognized as the most stable component of the original Korsakoff syndrome, whereas confabulation and disorientation fluctuated. Amnesia was the main component retained in modern concepts of Korsakoff syndrome, which no longer feature confabulation and disorientation (Victor *et al.* 1989; Kopelman 1995). The early authors had already noted that confabulation and disorientation often resolved in their patients, while amnesia persisted (Bonhoeffer 1901; Kalberlah 1904; Pick 1905), a fact since confirmed by countless observations. Thus, nobody seriously doubts that severe confabulation after brain damage requires the presence of amnesia (DeLuca 1993).

Confabulators have great difficulty in storing new memories, accessing them, or both. They have difficulty in recalling recent events. Studies consistently documented a significant failure of confabulators in memory tasks in which they had to learn a series of words or designs and later to recall them. A possible exception to this rule may have been the fantastic confabulations produced by schizophrenic patients. As we saw in Chapter 4 (p. 128), Bleuler (1923) emphasized his patients' relatively intact, albeit indiscriminate, memory. Bleuler's statement concerned schizophrenia in general and did not specifically refer to confabulating schizophrenics. In any case, the claim is difficult to verify because no such patients have been reported in modern times; nowadays, schizophrenic patients producing fantastic confabulations would rapidly receive neuroleptic treatment. Recent studies revealed significant memory impairment in (non-confabulating) schizophrenic patients, even in periods when they had no delusions (McKenna *et al.* 2000).

Although the association between confabulation and amnesia has never been questioned, a number of authors observed preserved recognition in their patients, even those having the most notorious cause of severe confabulation, rupture of an anterior communicating artery aneurysm (Talland *et al.* 1967; Kapur and Coughlan 1980; Damasio *et al.* 1985b).

So, could it be that confabulators simply failed to access memory in an orderly fashion, even when they had stored normal amounts of information? Could it be that they need not have a gap in memory? We explored the question in behaviourally spontaneous confabulators using a conceptually very simple learning task: a continuous recognition task (Figure 5.1). In this type of task, a series of items is presented, one after the other, with some of them recurring after a number of intervening items (Figure 5.1a). Test subjects are requested to indicate picture recurrences. If there are more than six or seven intervening stimuli before a picture is repeated, the task depends on medial temporal structures, and thus reflects a capacity of long-term memory (Hirst and Volpe 1982; Sturm and Willmes 1995). In our clinical studies, we used a test containing a series of 120 pictures. This series was composed of 80 items, among which eight were selected to recur five times during the run, yielding 80 'distracter' items (first presentations) and 40 'target' items (repetitions). The mean interval between a picture's presentation and its subsequent repetition was 20 items (Schnider *et al.* 1996b).

Describing the task construction is actually more complicated than performing it. Even patients with severe cognitive impairment readily understood the task instructions. It can be solved on the basis of familiarity judgement alone and does not require an effortful search in memory; this type of task, therefore, is relatively insensitive to clinically pertinent memory impairment (Squire and Shimamura 1986). It has the advantage of measuring the ability to put information into long-term memory and subsequently recognize it – that is, learning and recognition – in a pure way, independently of 'strategic' memory demands. We compared the performance of behaviourally spontaneous confabulators with that of other amnesics, who had similar difficulty in the delayed free recall of a word list but never produced behaviourally spontaneous confabulations.

In the initial study (Schnider *et al.* 1996b), we used three versions of the task differing by the type of stimuli (Figure 5.1b). One version was composed of meaningful designs (Snodgrass and Vanderwart 1980), one of nonsense geometric designs, and one of pronounceable but meaningless non-words (Sturm and Willmes 1995). The result is displayed in Figure 5.1c. Two results were important: (1) the performance of confabulators was similar to that of other amnesics, indicating that confabulation does not require a more – or less – severe failure of memory storage. In other words, the breadth of the gap in memory does not distinguish between confabulators and non-confabulators; (2) In all three test versions, there were some confabulators (and other

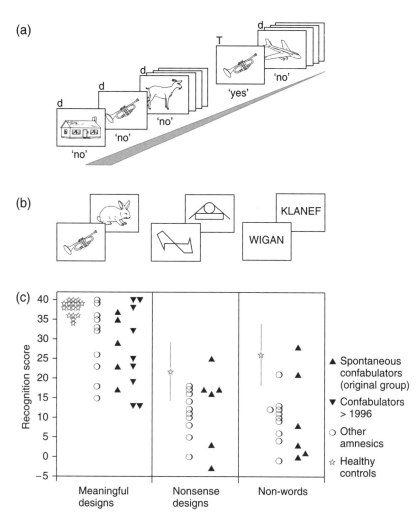

Figure 5.1 Learning and recognition by behaviourally spontaneous confabulators and other amnesics. (a) Design of the continuous recognition task. Subjects had to indicate whether a picture had been seen before during the test run (T, target; correct response: 'yes') or whether it was a first presentation, not yet presented during the run (d, distracter; correct response: 'no'). (b) Type of stimuli used in the three versions: left, meaningful designs; middle, nonsense geometric designs; right, pronounceable non-words. (c) Performance of patients and healthy controls in the three versions of the test differing in the type of stimuli used. Recognition score = hits (true positives) – false-positives. For the task with meaningful designs, results of the original study (Schnider *et al.* 1996b) plus the performance of spontaneous confabulators participating in later studies (confabulators > 1996) are given. The vertical lines in the middle and right part of the graph indicate ± two standard deviations of the mean.

amnesics) who performed in the normal range; they stored the information normally and subsequently recognized the presented information. This means that a gap in memory is not necessary for behaviourally consistent confabulation to occur! Figure 5.1c includes data from spontaneous confabulators participating in a subsequent study (Schnider and Ptak 1999), which confirmed the result. The finding explains why occasional confabulating patients later recall their confabulatory phase (Damasio *et al.* 1985b).

What determines whether a confabulating patient also has deficient recognition memory or not? Figure 5.2 shows a lesion analysis separating those confabulators who had normal recognition performance in this task (version with meaningful designs) and those with impaired performance (same patients as in Figure 4.12b). The main difference appears to concern the posterior ventromedial prefrontal area, in particular the basal forebrain, which was

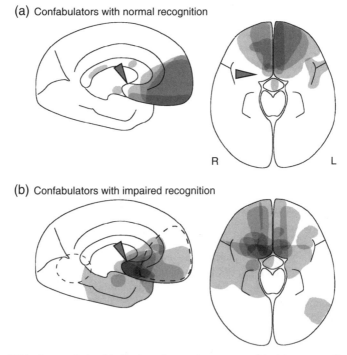

Figure 5.2 Lesion analysis of behaviourally spontaneous confabulators according to their performance in the continuous recognition task explained in Figure 5.1, version composed of meaningful designs. (a) Patients with normal recognition, that is, a performance at least as good as the worst performance by any healthy subject. (b) Patients with impaired recognition. Arrowheads point to the area of the basal forebrain.

much more consistently damaged in the patients with impaired recognition. The data do not allow determining the structure within the basal forebrain whose damage was responsible for the impairment of learning and recognition. Obvious target structures would be the fornix or the septal nuclei. In addition, lesion extension into the posterior limbic system (medial temporal area), which was present in one patient, can be expected to impair recognition memory.

In *conclusion*, relevant momentary, fantastic, and behaviourally spontaneous confabulations are always associated with moderate to severe amnesia as measured with tests of delayed free recall. In behaviourally spontaneous, and presumably also in momentary and fantastic confabulation, learning and recognition – as measured with a continuous recognition task – may be intact. Thus, in terms of simple information storage, confabulation and amnesia dissociate; confabulation need not be associated with a gap in memory! In behaviourally spontaneous confabulation, the extent of basal forebrain damage appears to best predict the degree of recognition memory impairment.

Disorientation

Disorientation describes the inability to place and perceive oneself correctly in time and space. It has at least four dimensions:

1. Disorientation to *time* is the inability to indicate the present day, date, month, year, season, or time of the day;

2. Disorientation to *place* indicates the inability to indicate one's current location, that is, the room, floor, building, town, county, state, country etc;

3. Disorientation to *situation* is the inability to recognize one's present role, including current duties and plans. In a clinical setting, it describes the lack of knowledge about the reason of a hospitalization or consultation, the supporting people (e.g., nurses), the person or organization paying for the hospitalization (e.g. insurance), planned interventions etc;

4. Disorientation to *person* is the loss of knowledge about oneself, that is, one's name, date of birth, age, address, eye colour, family members, profession etc.

Orientation to person is the dimension which is most resistant to brain damage, whereas orientation to time is the most fragile dimension, which normally takes longest to recover (Benton *et al.* 1964; Daniel *et al.* 1987; High *et al.* 1990).

Disorientation was a key component of the classic Korsakoff syndrome (Bonhoeffer 1904) and was mentioned in countless reports on confabulating patients, as summarized in Chapters 2 and 4. Yet, disorientation has always stood behind confabulation and remained its neglected companion. It may have attained its highest visibility in the discussion of post-traumatic amnesia, of which disorientation is a core feature (Russel 1971), while confabulation has rarely been mentioned (Chapter 4, p. 101ff.). Confabulation question-naires usually include questions on orientation (Williams and Rupp 1938; Mercer *et al.* 1977; Dalla Barba 1993a), as if orientation testing constituted a practical way of measuring confabulation rather than the exploration of a independent disorder. Despite this implicitly accepted link between confabu-lation and disorientation, no conjoint hypothesis on the mechanisms of the two disorders has been proposed. Indeed, many hypotheses on confabulation would be difficult to apply to disorientation: how would the satisfaction of filling gaps in memory (Flament 1957), suggestibility (Pick 1905), or person-ality traits (Williams and Rupp 1938) explain the loss of knowledge about one's present situation?

Modern accounts have favoured the lack of memory as an explanation for disorientation. Benton *et al.* (1964) suggested that temporal orientation might be viewed as an index of the integrity of recent memory. Daniel *et al.* (1987) explored the recovery of orientation after electroconvulsive treatment in 32 depressed patients. Such patients remain confused for a variable time after the electrically induced seizure. Disorientation was characterized by backward displacement of events in time. Orientation to person recovered first, then orientation to place, and finally orientation to time. The authors suggested that the subjects' backward displacement during disorientation reflected retrograde amnesia. High *et al.* (1990) came to the same conclusion, based on the study of 84 patients with post-traumatic amnesia. The patients whose disorientation reflected the most extended backward dating of ideas had particularly severe disturbances of consciousness. The authors suggested that the sequential return of disorientation to person, place, and time might be explained by the patients' ongoing retrograde and anterograde memory diffi-culties. Von Cramon and Säring (1982) had a slightly more specific concept. They suggested that orientation to time required that experiences would be stored in memory with a distinct temporal tag. In addition, they suggested that severe amnesia would inevitably induce disorientation.

Thus, all these authors linked disorientation to amnesia; none discussed a potential link between disorientation and confabulation.

In comparison to these modern accounts, the ideas of the old masters appear astonishingly subtle, albeit speculative. Kraepelin (1909) described orientation as the 'clarity of the relation with [our] current environment and the past' and explained: 'The continuous mental processing of events in life renders us capable of constantly giving an account of the situation in which we are and the events leading up to it' (p. 265). He specified different mechanisms for the different dimensions of orientation:

> The temporal order of our experiences evolves from the uninterrupted and all-round association, which is continuously established by memory between all simultaneous and immediately successive events in our consciousness. In this way, all our memories are ordered in a continuous sequence, whose endpoint constitutes the present moment.
>
> Kraepelin (1909, p. 265)

For the other dimensions, he proposed mechanisms beyond memory: 'A clear idea concerning the place in which we are, is partly also tied to the capacities in memory…. [But in addition] we have to attribute an essential role to perception' (p. 266). Orientation to person was seen as dependent on memory, perception and judgement.

Kraepelin (1909) then went on to discuss the reasons for disorientation in different diseases. First, he discussed schizophrenia, called 'dementia praecox' at the time. Wernicke (1900) had already pointed out disorientation as the main characteristic of psychosis: 'There is no [psychotic person] who would not be disorientated in some way' (Wernicke 1900, p. 218). Kraepelin (1909) observed that, for weeks, such patients did not care about where they were, who the persons around them were, and how much time had passed. He called the result of this lack of interest *apathetic disorientation*, which he vaguely distinguished from *stuporous, delirious, and hallucinatory disorientation*, but he warned that 'in the individual patient, the disturbance [of orientation] can never be uniformly deduced, but always requires the coincidence of different causes' (Kraepelin 1909, p. 268). As an example for such coincident causes, he mentioned disorientation in delirium tremens: 'In this case, there are hallucinations and perceptual disturbances' (Kraepelin 1909, p. 268). In contrast, he called the disorientation in chronic Korsakoff psychosis '*amnestic disorientation* … because the disturbance of perception, the hallucinations, the deliria mostly or completely disappear' (p. 268). He continued with other forms: disorientation in senile dementia was seen as a form of amnestic disorientation characterized by particularly severe memory impairment in association with a disturbance of perception, which would interfere with the mental processing of ongoing impressions. Temporal disorientation in paralytic dementia was also seen as a form of amnestic disorientation. Finally, there was *delusional disorientation*. 'In this case it is only the mental processing of impressions, which have been perceived and stored in a basically correct way, that leads to a false idea rather than a lack of knowledge about time and environment,' (p. 270).

Bleuler (1923), too, suggested that a combination of factors was necessary for the maintenance of orientation, finishing the sentence with a most interesting remark:

> Orientation obviously depends on memory (in case of its absence, orientation is impossible), on the perceptions (hallucinations can falsely suggest another room) and on attention (lost in thoughts ... one can arrive at another place than anticipated) ... but there is also an independent function of orientation, whose disturbance needs not be proportional to disorders of other functions.

Bleuler (1923, p. 24)

Jaspers (1973) described orientation as 'a highly complex, but easily discernable capacity of intellectual perception' (p. 145). Similar to Kraepelin, but without direct reference to him, he distinguished four types of disorientation:

1. *Amnestic disorientation* based on immediate forgetting. 'The patients think they are 20 years old, women take on their maiden name, think they are at school ... take the physician variably for a teacher, a court employee, or the mayor.'

2. *Delusional disorientation*, in which fully conscious patients have delusional ideas and conclude from them that time has shifted by three days, although they know that their entourage is writing a different date; they conclude that they are in prison although they know that the entourage declares the house for a psychiatric institution. A special form of this type of orientation was double orientation: The patients are at the same time correctly and falsely oriented. They know exactly where they are, what time it is, and that they are 'insane', but at the same time, [they are convinced that] everything is spurious, that this is the Golden Age, and that there is no time.

3. *Apathetic un-orientation*, in which 'the patients do not know where they are and what time it is because they do not think about it. But they are not falsely oriented.'

4. Disorientation in the context of *disturbances of consciousness*, in which 'patients perceive only bits and pieces. Varying experiences during impaired consciousness, which induce a mass of fantastic disorientations (similarly with dreams), replace the perception of the real environment.'

Even though these authors also expressed views about the mechanisms of confabulation in other writings, none of them proposed a relation between disorientation and confabulation. The concept of 'double orientation' (Bleuler 1923; Jaspers 1973) during psychosis suggests, at least, that *fantastic confabulations* by psychotic patients were normally associated with a measurable abnormality of orientation. Notwithstanding this 'usual' situation, occasional patients producing undeniable fantastic, implausible confabulations–such as Feinstein *et al.*'s patient (2000) with multiple sclerosis (Chapter 4, p. 138)– demonstrate that fantastic confabulations may occur with intact orientation.

Momentary confabulations probably do not require a deficit of orientation. DeLuca and Cicerone (1991) compared nine patients confabulating after anterior communicating artery aneurysm rupture and 17 patients with intracranial haemorrhages in other locations. Their conclusion was that, with the return of orientation, only subjects with aneurysm rupture continued to confabulate . This statement referred to the patients' behaviour during repeated interviews, which covered orientation, recent memory, and personal historical information. The conclusion of continuing confabulation despite resolution of disorientation therefore appears to refer to momentary confabulations. As mentioned, any amnesic subject may at some point in time respond to questions with confabulations, with no specificity for a particular type of brain lesion.

What about the association between disorientation and *behaviourally spontaneous confabulation*? The cases described in Chapters 2 and 4 suggested that there could be a strong association, although modern accounts of disorientation favour a link between disorientation and amnesia. Figure 5.3 summarizes

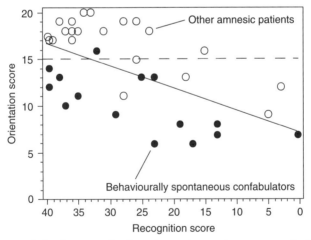

Figure 5.3 Association between disorientation and amnesia as measured with the continuous recognition task explained in Figure 5.1 (maximum score, 40). Orientation was quantified using a 20 item questionnaire (Von Cramon and Säring 1982). There was a significant correlation between the two scores: $r = 0.61$, $F_{1,38} = 10,7$, $p < 0.0002$. The oblique line indicates the regression line. The dashed horizontal line indicates the cut-off for normal orientation, i.e. 15. Ninety-four per cent of behaviourally spontaneous confabulators (filled black circles), but only 15 per cent of other amnesic (open circles) were disoriented according to this cut-off.

the data that we have obtained in the course of our studies on confabulation. The data include the 21 patients of the original study (Schnider *et al.* 1996c) plus 18 patients participating in subsequent studies. All patients had similar difficulty in accessing memories as measured by the delayed free recall in a verbal memory test. All performed the continuous recognition task described in Figure 5.1 as a measure of learning and recognition. On the same day, orientation was explored with a 20-item questionnaire containing 5 questions each for orientation to time, place, situation, and person (Von Cramon and Säring 1982). Of the 39 patients 16 were spontaneous confabulators, while 23 were other amnesics that never produced behaviourally spontaneous confabulations.

Figure 5.3 contains diverse pieces of information, which corroborate the results obtained in the original 21 patients (Schnider *et al.* 1996c). First, the analysis confirms the association between disorientation and amnesia, expressed as the inability to learn and recognize new information. The correlation between orientation and the recognition score is highly significant. The recognition score explains almost 40 per cent of the orientation scores' distribution. That is, severe amnesia, as measured with a continuous recognition task, does indeed predict disorientation. More importantly, however, Figure 5.3 holds information regarding our main question, namely, the link between disorientation and behaviourally spontaneous confabulation. First, the two non-confabulating amnesic patients on the right side of the graph show that the sole combination of severe amnesia and disorientation does not predict behaviourally spontaneous confabulation. Second, while almost all confabulators (15 out of 16, 94 per cent) were disoriented according to the cut-off of this questionnaire, only a small proportion of the other amnesic patients (4 out of 23, 15 per cent) were disoriented. This difference is highly significant (Fisher's exact test, p < 0,0001). Thus, the data indicate that there is a strong association between behaviourally spontaneous confabulation and disorientation, in that confabulators are (virtually) always disoriented. The only exception in this series (one behaviourally spontaneous confabulator with normal orientation score) can be attributed to the fact that orientation scores tend to vary from one session to the next; in clinical practice, it may be advisable to repeat evaluations. The findings are compatible with the idea that in many patients, disorientation results from the same dysfunction as behaviourally spontaneous confabulation. As will be discussed in Chapter 8, we did indeed find such a dysfunction. But the findings also indicate that there are additional dysfunctions (e.g., severe amnesia), which are independent of confabulation, that can induce disorientation.

In *conclusion*, disorientation seems to have diverse mechanisms and is variably associated with the different forms of confabulation. Although it has regularly been linked with confabulation as a part of the original Korsakoff syndrome, its association with momentary confabulation appears to be loose. Fantastic confabulation is virtually always accompanied by a measurable disorder of orientation, but in rare cases, orientation may be normal. Behaviourally spontaneous confabulation is always accompanied by disorientation. Conversely, disorientation – even in association with amnesia – need not be accompanied by confabulation.

False recognition

The term 'false recognition' with no further specification normally describes the erroneous recognition of items in memory tasks; test subjects believe they have encountered a piece of information in a specified previous context when the information has not been presented. False recognition also occurs in healthy subjects having an intact memory. An experimental condition which reliably induces false recall (intrusions) and false recognition, is the Deese–Roediger–McDermott paradigm – the DRM paradigm (Roediger and McDermott 1995; Roediger *et al.* 2001). In the DRM paradigm, which will be discussed in more detail in the next chapter, subjects are presented with lists of words (e.g., bed, rest, awake, tired, dream, wake, snooze, blanket, doze, slumber, snore, nap, peace, yawn, drowsy), all of which are associated with a critical item (sleep), which is not presented. Under this condition, healthy people are very likely to produce the target item – the 'lure' – when recalling the word list and to falsely recognize it among a series of distracters, as if it had been presented. Indeed, they are even convinced about the lure's presence in the word list.

False positives in the DRM paradigm can – in a sense – be considered the price that humans have to pay for the associative power of their memory. Accordingly, brain damage does not necessarily increase false positives in the DRM paradigm. Schacter *et al.* (1996c) observed that amnesic subjects recognized fewer studied items and also fewer related lure words than controls. When the test was repeated five times with the same word lists, both Korsakoff amnesics and 'mixed' amnesics having other aetiologies increased their correct recognition performance. Korsakoff amnesics, who made few false positives in the initial test run, increased their false recognition of related words, ending up at the same level as non-amnesic alcoholic controls (Schacter *et al.* 1998b).

Melo *et al.* (1999) compared three groups of patients using this paradigm. They found that amnesic patients with medial temporal or diencephalic lesions and as non-amnesic patients with frontal lesions produced more false words (intrusions) than controls. At recognition, however, amnesic patients both in the medial–temporal–diencephalic group and in the frontal lesion group had less false recognition than non-amnesic patients with frontal lesions or controls. The authors, therefore, suggested that abnormally high number of false memories in the DRM paradigm were related to three conditions:

1. partial memory for the word lists;

2. the ability to extract the semantic gist of the lists; and

3. a deficit in strategic monitoring processes, a notion that the authors also invoked to explain confabulations.

This paradigm was used in a recent study on patients surviving severe brain trauma, who had mild to moderate verbal memory impairment (Ries and Marks 2006). The patients produced relatively more critical lure items on recall, i.e., words related to the learned word list but not contained in it. Although they recognized fewer studied words, they falsely recognized more critical lures and lures that were only weakly related to the learned word lists. Thus, in contrast to the previously mentioned studies with amnesic subjects, these patients had an increased tendency to falsely recognize items that had not been presented before, apparently in a fairly indiscriminate way.

In these studies, false recognition was not associated with confabulation. Ciaramelli *et al.* (2006) compared patients with ventromedial frontal lesions who confabulated, patients with frontal lesions who were amnesic but non-confabulating, and amnesic patients with non-frontal lesions. Using the standard DRM paradigm, the three amnesic groups had more difficulty in recognizing the presented items and also falsely recognized a lower number of lure items than healthy controls. There was no difference between the three amnesic groups, indicating that the normal weakness of memory exposed by the standard DRM paradigm is not increased in confabulating patients. Only in a modified version of the task with presentation of several word lists, each immediately followed by recall and recognition, did the confabulators falsely recognize more critical lures. Such a procedure obviously enhances overall memory performance. The finding is intriguing but requires further analysis. These studies together did not establish a link between confabulation (other than intrusions) and the normal false recognition induced by the DRM paradigm.

The clinical conditions associated with pathological false recognition have mostly been investigated in single case studies. Mrs M, our initial confabulator with an infarction of the knee of the right internal capsule (Figure 4.4, p. 57), not only produced behaviourally spontaneous confabulations, but also presented reduplicative paramnesia for another person, a high number of provoked confabulations, and striking false recognition. In common memory tests using lists of words or geometric designs, her recognition performance was markedly impaired because of a high number of false positives; she normally felt familiar not only with all items that had really been presented, but also with many items that had not been presented (Schnider *et al.* 1996a). False recognition occurred in all tests requiring distinction between previously presented and new items, irrespective of whether designs or words had been presented and whether the words had been presented in the auditory or visual modality. An impressive example was her recognition of items that had previously been used to test perceptual priming. In this task 16 concrete line drawings depicting animals or objects were repeatedly presented, first in very degraded, unrecognizable form, then in an increasingly more complete presentation. Even patients with very severe amnesia eventually recognize highly fragmented pictures, which they have not recognized initially. In Mrs M, this perceptual priming effect was normal. Two days, one week, and one month after this task, recognition of the items was tested. To this end, each item of the priming task was presented together with three distracters from the same semantic category. For example, the picture of a car, which had been part of the priming task, was presented together with the picture of a sailing boat, motorbike and a helicopter (Figure 5.4). When this test was performed two days after the priming task, Mrs M recognized all items that had been presented in the task, but also selected six of the 48 items that not been part of the priming task. After one week, she chose 36 distracters, and after one month 39 distracters. For all items, she indicated that she was sure about their previous occurrence in the priming task. A simple manipulation allowed correcting these false recognitions. On all three test sessions, Mrs M was again given this recognition task with the indication that her performance had been bad and that indeed, only one of the four simultaneously presented items had been part of the priming task. With this indication, Mrs M hesitated much longer before answering. Amazingly, under this constrained recognition condition, her performance dramatically improved in comparison to the unconstrained, free recognition condition. In the three tests after two days, one week, and one month, she correctly recognized 15, 13, and 14 of the 16 items that had been part of the task, with one to three false recognitions. The same result was obtained when recognition of items presented in other tasks was tested, such as a temporal order judgement task (Schnider *et al.* 1996a). Indeed, further experiments showed that Mrs M was unable to determine when, from whom, and in what room she had learned a word list, that is,

(a)   (b)

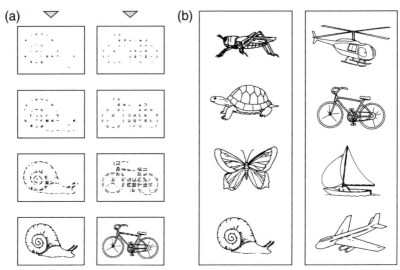

Figure 5.4 Recognition task inducing many false positives in Mrs M. (a) Examples of perceptual priming items (total 16) that the patient had to learn. The perceptual priming effect was normal. (b) Recognition task. Two days, one week and one month after the priming task, the patient was shown 16 series of pictures, each containing an items that had actually been part of the priming task and three distracter items. Mrs M was asked to identify the items that had been presented as 'a dot pattern' during a previous task – the priming task. In this situation (free, unconstrained recognition), she falsely selected almost all items of the recognition task, including the distracter items. When told that only one of the four items in each series had actually been presented (constrained recognition), her performance improved to an almost perfect level.

she had a source memory problem (Johnson and Raye 1998). This failure appeared to be a convenient explanation for all her memory problems, including the behaviourally spontaneous confabulations, intrusions, and false recognition. As discussed on p. 59, subsequent group studies disproved this hypothesis.

Mrs M's behaviour was compatible with the idea that she applied an unduly lenient criterion during recognition – that is, that she failed to 'monitor'. Amazingly, however, she did not display false recognitions when she had to distinguish between illustrious Swiss politicians from more than three years ago and unknown personalities. By contrast, she had difficulty in selecting politicians from the three years preceding her stroke, a period corresponding to the extension of her retrograde amnesia and confabulations. Mrs M only confabulated about the events of the last three years, but not about events dating back more than three years.

Whereas the case of Mrs M might suggest a link between false recognition and serious forms of confabulation, other case studies did not mention such a coincidence. Despite the scarcity of reports on patients displaying marked false recognition, the heterogeneity of this phenomenon clearly emerged. Delbecq-Derouesné *et al.* (1990) described a patient who had suffered rupture of an anterior communicating artery aneurysm with extensive destruction of the ventromedial and orbitofrontal area on both sides with extension into the right lateral frontal and anterior temporal lobes. The report did not contain details on the early clinical course. The patient was examined after eight years. In a number of memory tests, free recall often contained an increased number of intrusions, but overall performance was mostly in the normal range. In striking contrast, recognition performance was random in most tasks due to a high rate of false positive responses. The patient had no insight into his memory impairment. The authors located the problem at the level of retrieval. They suggested that this patient's recognition failure did not result from any lack of knowledge, 'but rather from his inability to distinguish his experience of remembering from another kind of misleading subjective experience triggered by the distracters' (p. 1069). Most notably, apart from intrusions in recall conditions, this patient did not produce relevant confabulations despite strikingly increased false recognition.

The same remark can be made with respect to other case studies. Schacter *et al.* (1996a) described a 66-year-old patient with an ischemic lesion of the right posterior dorsolateral frontal cortex plus smaller lesions of the right thalamus. The patient was studied about six month after the event. He neither confabulated in discussions nor when examined with questionnaires. In a common word list learning task, he produced very few false recognitions. Recall performance was moderately impaired. However, when recognition of previously learned visually or auditorily presented words, environmental sounds, concrete pictures or even non-words was tested, he had significantly increased numbers of false recognitions. Performing a series of experimental manipulations, the authors found in two recognition tasks that false recognition could be eliminated when the distracters were taken from categories that were not represented among the learned items. They concluded that this patient's false recognition emanated from an over-reliance on memory for general characteristics of the study episode, along with impaired memory for specific items. They suspected that the right frontal lobe might be critical for item-specific recognition.

Another often cited patient was described by Parkin and co-workers (Parkin *et al.* 1996, 1999). Their patient had suffered rupture of an anterior communicating artery aneurysm and was left with damage of the left frontal cortex and left caudate. He was investigated several years after the event. His performance in memory tasks was severely impaired. Not only did he recall very few correct items, but he also produced abundant intrusions and had many false positives on recognition tasks (Parkin et al. 1996). The false alarm rate was not affected by increasing the similarity between distracters and targets, and remained even high with non-words. Notably, restricting the number of items that he was allowed to select in recognition tasks did not improve his performance (Parkin et al. 1999). Thus, this patient did not profit from a manipulation comparable to the one which had markedly improved the performance in Mrs M, described above. In contrast, this patient profited when he was given instruction of how to process words contained in a list that he had to learn. In particular, correct recognition increased and false alarms significantly decreased when he was instructed to visually imagine the items. The authors, therefore, suspected that this patient's problem was more consistent with an encoding deficit than a retrieval deficit. By the same token, they explained this patient's failure by 'reliance on a poorly focused event description' (Parkin et al. 1999, p. 260).

Quite a different form of false recognition was reported by Rapcsak et al. (1999). They explored two patients in the chronic phase after brain damage. The first patient had had rupture of an anterior communicating artery aneurysm with damage to large parts of the ventromedial prefrontal area with particularly extended damage of the right frontal lobe. This patient remained severely amnesic and produced many false positives in verbal learning. The other patient had had surgical removal of a right frontal lobe tumour with damage involving the right lateral orbitofrontal cortex, which reached up to the whole right frontal lobe in front of the corpus callosum, whereas the basal forebrain appeared to be intact. This patient did not display amnesia and made neither false positives nor false recognitions in verbal learning. However, both patients presented with false recognition of faces, both unfamiliar and familiar ones. Their rate of false positives decreased when shorter series of faces were presented. False recognition was particularly prominent with distracter faces from the same category (same race and gender). The patients also falsely recognized many unfamiliar faces portrayed like celebrities. These false positives could markedly be reduced when the patients were instructed to call faces familiar only if they could remember the occupation and name of the person. The authors therefore interpreted the patients' false recognition as a 'breakdown of the strategic memory retrieval, monitoring, and decision functions critical for attributing the experience of familiarity to a specific source' (Rapcsak et al. 1999, p. 267). An additional point emphasized by the authors was that frontal executive functions were dissociable. Although both patients had false recognition when processing faces, only the first one had executive failures, whereas the second patient had perfect scores on diverse executive tasks, including the Wisconsin Card Sorting Test, a very sensitive test for frontal executive failures.

Even though these are only a few patients demonstrating pathological false recognition, the data already suggest that false recognition, a seemingly unitary failure, is in fact *heterogeneous*. The examples show that patients with false recognition may or may not display amnesia in common memory tests; they may or may not produce relevant confabulations; they may or may not have other executive dysfunctions. False recognition may concern different materials, like words, non-words, faces, or environmental sounds, either in combination or separately. Modifying task instructions or the amount of information that has to be encoded may or may not influence later false recognition. Modifying task instructions at retrieval may or may not influence the number of false recognitions. Some form of frontal lobe damage or disconnection appears to be common to these patients: All reported patients had lesions involving different parts of the frontal lobes or thalamo–frontal connections, but there was no clear lateralization and no obvious difference between orbitofrontal and dorsolateral frontal lesions.

The importance of frontal lobe damage was also suggested by a study by Alexander *et al.* (2003). They analysed the performance of 44 patients with focal brain lesions on the California Verbal Learning Test. In this task, subjects learn a list of 16 words and are later tested on the recall and recognition of the items. Thirty-three patients had frontal lesions, whereas only eleven patients had non-frontal injuries, a selection inducing a heavy bias for the detection of false memory production following frontal lobe lesions. The main objective was to characterize the memory impairment after frontal lesion. Patients with posterior dorsolateral and posterior ventromedial lesions had overall impaired learning and recall. The most significant impairment was found in the left posterior dorsolateral frontal group. It was also this group which produced the highest number of false positives in delayed recognition testing. It is interesting to note that this is not the same area that is typically damaged in the most pervasive forms of confabulation, namely, the ventromedial (posterior orbitofrontal) area, a finding additionally suggesting the anatomical dissociation between confabulation and false recognition.

Contradicting our observations in Mrs M, in whom behaviourally spontaneous confabulation and intense false recognition coincided, the data that we obtained in subsequent group studies indicated a clear *dissociation* between confabulation and false recognition. In an analysis of the data from 15 behaviourally spontaneous confabulators and 26 non-confabulating patients, who had participated in our studies, I found no significant correlation between provoked confabulations (intrusions) and false recognitions in the California Verbal Learning Test (r = 0.17). Also, false recognitions did not significantly correlate with measures of verbal fluency, non-verbal fluency, or colour-word interference (0.02 < r < 0.17). More importantly, the two groups of patients did not differ regarding the number of false recognitions: Behaviourally spontaneous confabulators made 9.9 ± 5.9 false positives, non-confabulators made 7.2 ± 7.7 false positives (T = 1.2; p = 0.24). Thus, in a group of similarly amnesic subjects (similarly impaired delayed free recall), the amount of false recognitions in a conventional memory task had no predictive value for the occurrence of behaviourally spontaneous confabulation.

A recent study by Ciaramelli and Ghetti (2007) suggested, however, that behaviourally spontaneous confabulators might have qualitatively different recollection. They tested five confabulators and seven non-confabulating patients with comparable memory and executive deficits using recognition tasks. Subjects had to indicate whether they simply felt familiar with the presented items ('Know' or 'K' response) or whether they had a distinct recollection of the items' previous presentation ('Remember' or 'R' response). Although confabulators and non-confabulators did not differ on the number of recognized items and false positive responses, their 'R' responses appeared to be based on different recollective experiences. Non-confabulators and control subjects remembered specific experiences during the items previous presentation. Confabulators tended to explain their recollection by autobiographical memories related to the test items. In addition, and in difference to the non-confabulators and controls, they indicated equally vivid subjective experiences for true and false memories. The authors suggested that remembering states in confabulators might be linked to a deficit in inhibiting irrelevant memories triggered by test items during retrieval attempts. We will come back to this notion in Chapter 8.

There are certain *conditions* in which the occurrence of false recognition does have a predictive value for the occurrence of confabulations. Indeed, it has been the most significant finding of our clinical studies that, under precise experimental conditions, the increase of false positives in a recognition task reliably separated behaviourally spontaneous confabulators from other amnesics. Although this finding and its consequences will be the main topic of Chapter 8, it deserves to be mentioned briefly here. As discussed above (pp. 148ff.), behaviourally spontaneous confabulators did not differ from non-confabulating amnesics in terms of their ability to store information, as measured with a continuous recognition task (Figure 5.1). However, when we repeated the same task with the same series of pictures, arranged in different order, the performance of confabulators dramatically decreased (Schnider *et al.* 1996b). In a subsequent study, we explored the basis of this performance decrease in more detail (Schnider and Ptak 1999). We used two types of continuous recognition tasks as described in Figure 5.1, but with fewer items and more repetitions within the runs, so that the task was even easier for amnesic subjects. In one version of the task we used meaningful designs, in the other version, we used nonsense geometric designs. With both versions, four test runs were made. We found that confabulators and non-confabulators had similar difficulty in recognizing item repetitions within the runs; correct recognition of repetitions even tended to decrease in the two groups across the four runs. In contrast, the number of false positives dramatically dissociated between the two groups of patients. Whereas in the first run of both test versions – meaningful designs and geometric nonsense designs – the number of false recognitions neither significantly differed between the patient groups nor in comparison with healthy controls, spontaneous confabulators dramatically increased their false recognitions from the first to the fourth run. In comparison, non-confabulating amnesics did not differ from healthy controls and had no increase of false recognition. That is, as the subjects became increasingly familiar with the test items, only the spontaneous confabulators started to have increasing difficulty in distinguishing item repetitions within a run from item repetitions across the different runs. This failure was not due to the adoption of a lenient recognition criterion by the spontaneous confabulators, as indicated by the fact that many of them sensed their difficulties as the task went on, became more sceptical about their responses, and even slightly decreased their true hit-rate. The experiment showed that behaviourally spontaneous confabulators had more difficulty in selecting among familiar pieces of information those that were currently pertinent, that is, those that were repeated within – and only within – the ongoing run.

Spontaneous confabulators may also have increased false positives when a continuous recognition task contains closely related items. We presented such a task to Mrs B (Chapter 1) and non-confabulating amnesics (Schnider *et al.* 2005a). In this task, which was very easy for healthy subjects, she saw a series of concrete pictures and words with every item being repeated two items later either in the same modality (word 'fork' followed by the word 'fork') or in the other modality (picture of a bear followed by the word 'bear'). Patients were asked to accept only repetitions in the same modality as true repetitions. In comparison the non-confabulating amnesics, Mrs B had many more false recognitions, indicating that her sense for true item repetition was determined by semantic similarity in the first place, disrespecting the item's modality. The data and their specificity for behaviourally spontaneous confabulation remain to be evaluated. In the meantime, Gilboa *et al.* (2006) have conducted an experiment with comparable logic. They composed a continuous recognition task containing pairs of structurally slightly different, but semantically entirely similar line drawings. Spontaneous confabulators having ventromedial prefrontal damage after ACoA aneurysm rupture had significantly more false recognitions than non-confabulating amnesics with similar lesions.

In *conclusion*, false recognition as measured with conventional memory tasks is neither significantly associated with provoked confabulation (intrusions) nor with behaviourally relevant confabulations. Indeed, false recognition and confabulation dissociate. False recognition appears to be a heterogeneous phenomenon in terms of associated memory or executive failures, modality, possibilities of modulating it, and anatomical basis, which – at least – mostly involves the frontal lobes or their connections. False recognition can presumably result from defective processes at different stages of memory formation and evocation.

Despite this dissociation, there are specific situations in which behaviourally spontaneous confabulators have much higher false recognition than non-confabulating amnesics. Specifically, behaviourally spontaneous confabulators failed to distinguish items of current relevance within a series of familiar items. Likewise, they have been shown to confuse semantically similar items within a continuous recognition task. The pathophysiological implications of these observations will be discussed in Chapter 8.

Paramnesic misidentification

Delusional misidentification, reduplicative paramnesia, and paramnesic misidentification are terms often used interchangeably. They describe a group of mental disturbances characterized by the involuntary attribution of a false identity to and familiarity with other people, places, or situations. There are several links with confabulation: The patients may contrive complex stories – confabulations – to corroborate their false beliefs; some forms of paramnesic misidentification suggest a state of de-realization in thinking – a detachment from reality – that bears superficial resemblance with the reality confusion characterizing behaviourally spontaneous confabulation; misidentification of people or places may occur in patients producing mnestic confabulations; finally, some investigators have tried to interpret paramnesic misidentification and confabulation in terms of a common underlying mechanism (Weinstein *et al.* 1952; Weinstein and Kahn 1955; Benson and Stuss 1990). Thus, there are plenty of reasons to review paramnesic misidentification syndromes and their association with confabulation.

Déjà-vu

The most common form of paramnesia, occasionally experienced by healthy people, is déjà vu. More precisely, it should be called *déjà vécu* (already experienced) rather than déjà-vu (already seen). It can be conceived as a misidentification of the present moment, which is experienced as if it had already been lived in precisely the same way before. In contrast to the type of false recognition discussed in the previous paragraph, déjà-vu induces an instantaneous feeling of familiarity with the present situation as a whole rather than specific pieces of information. The phenomenon is much more frequent in certain brain diseases, in particular epilepsy. Pick (1876), who cited previous authors, gave an early detailed account of the phenomenon. His patient was 20 years old when he started to have 'illusions of memory [*Erinnerungstäuschungen*]', whose frequency dramatically increased after an episode of typhus at the age of 23. During his stay at the clinic, he expressed the strange feeling that he had already stayed at the clinic before; when he read the newspaper, he thought that he had already read all articles before (Pick 1876, p. 570). The patient described his experiences as follows:

> When visiting leisure places or during outstanding festivities and meetings with people, I experienced the whole situation as so familiar that I thought I could certainly claim that I had met the very same localities and the same people in precisely the same circumstances as concerns the season, weather, the people at the site, with exactly the same behaviour, even during exactly the same discussion.
>
> Pick (1876, p. 572)

The patient had other delusional ideas and occasional auditory hallucinations, so that Pick interpreted the illusions of memory as a symptom of psychosis rather than a complication of typhus; the possibility of epileptic fits was not mentioned.

Kraepelin (1887b) discussed the possible mechanisms of the phenomenon, which he called *identifying falsifications of memory*, extensively. He had never personally observed it in patients and suggested that it was 'almost exclusively associated with healthy life' (p. 428). The few mentally ill subjects in whom it had been described were epileptics. At about the same time, J. Hughlings Jackson, who also quoted earlier authors, described the phenomenon in epileptic patients (Jackson 1888). He called it *reminiscences*, one of many manifestations of *dreamy states*. It was also Jackson who later coined the term déjà-vu. A patient who came to autopsy had a cavity in the medial temporal cortex overlying the left amygdala (Jackson and Colman 1898).

The *anatomical basis* of déjà-vu was explored in a number of studies using electrophysiology. Penfield, a neurosurgeon famous for his studies on the effects of electrical cortical stimulation, reported that he could evoke dreamy states, including déjà-vu, by stimulation of the lateral temporal neocortex, in particular the superior temporal gyrus (area 22 in Figure 4.2a) (Penfield and Perot 1963). In a more recent study, Bancaud *et al.* (1994) found that in most dreamy states, there was participation of the amygdala, the anterior hippocampus, and the temporal neocortex, in particular the superior temporal gyrus. Epileptic or electric activity associated with dreamy states often spread from the lateral temporal cortex to the medial temporal lobe or vice versa.

So then, what is the link between déjà-vu and confabulation? Weinstein *et al.* (1950, Weinstein and Kahn 1952) likened déjà vu to what they called 'reduplication for time … the confabulation that a present experience has also been experienced at some time in the past' (p. 808). A similar connection has recently been made by Moulin *et al.* (2005). These authors described two demented patients who had permanent feeling of déjà vécu and provided reasonable justifications for it. The authors called these justifications 'recollective confabulations'. Thus, in this case, confabulations described the patients' false interpretation of their recollections rather than false products from memory.

Déjà-vu has not been associated with mnestic confabulation, but the frequency of dreamy states and déjà-vu has never been formally explored in confabulation. None of our confabulating patients complained about this phenomenon. For our forthcoming discussion of the mechanism of behaviourally spontaneous confabulation and reality in thinking (Chapter 8), the anatomical data on déjà-vu may, nevertheless, be of relevance. They show that limbic activity influences our feeling for the uniqueness of the present moment – the 'now'.

Reduplicative paramnesia

Other forms of misidentification have a stronger overlap with confabulation. This concerns in particular the mental reduplication of places and people. Pick (1903b) described this 'new form of paramnesia' in a 48-year-old businessman with a progressive dementing illness, presumably general paralysis. In an initial attack of 'mental confusion', he did not recognize his wife and took her for a stranger. Soon after, he started to make incoherent statements and could not find the way back to his home. During the hospitalization at Pick's clinic in Prague, which lasted several months, he constantly misidentified certain people and the place. Although he gave a 'fairly precise medical history and remembered even minute details from earlier times' (p. 7), he thought that he was hospitalized at a clinic in North Bohemia. He occasionally admitted being in Prague because all of the people around him believed it, but even then, he thought that it would take him at least an hour to go to the clinic where he was already staying, claiming that 'a part of the people insist that this is Prague, but it takes nevertheless a one hour's journey, even by train' (Pick 1903b, p. 6). With regard to people, the patient recognized Pick but was convinced that there were three people like him: 'There are three professor Pick; one of them [is] chairman of the psychiatric clinic [in North Bohemia], the second one is you (points to the professor), the third one is a legal doctor' (p. 10). In addition, he thought he had two, sometimes three, brothers, all of them having the same name.

In a second article, Pick (1903a) introduced the term *reduplicative paramnesia*, this time in reference to a 67-year-old woman with senile dementia accompanied by paranoid delusions. She also had auditory hallucinations, 'accompanied by lively confabulation, the products of which were often maintained in her memory for a long time' (p. 262), but the most striking delusion concerned her whereabouts. Even though the patient was hospitalized in Prague, she imagined she was in K. and said that she was very pleased to see professor Pick there, too. 'On being questioned further how it was that the entire hospital, as well as the patients came to be in K., she replied that the doctor had so arranged it' (p. 262). In contrast to the first patient, she did not duplicate people in her mind.

The term reduplicative paramnesia has survived into our day and, in the absence of specific qualifiers, denotes the mental reduplication of places. Many patients with this phenomenon have been described, very often in the context of organic brain damage. Benson *et al.* (1976) demonstrated, in three patients with traumatic brain injury, that reduplicative paramnesia may persist beyond the state of severe memory impairment. Ruff and Volpe (1981) described four patients with focal right parietal lesions, which extended into the frontal lobe in three patients. All of them were convinced during the hospitalization that they were either at home or at a hospital near their home. The authors emphasized the specificity of the patients' spatial disorientation; orientation to time was intact. Kapur *et al.* (1988) reported a 71-year-old man admitted because of a peculiar confusion. Being at his home, he was sure that this house was not his real home. He remarked on 'How striking it was that the owners of this house had the same ornaments as he had in 'his' house and what a coincidence it was that there were similar items beside the bed as there were in 'his' house.' (Kapur *et al.* 1988, p. 579). A CT scan revealed a right frontal haemorrhage.

Thus, if reduplicative paramnesia emanates from localized brain damage, the lesion often involves the right hemisphere. Reported lesions involved the right parietal or frontal lobe. We have seen a few cases with right temporo–parietal lesions. Although they were very convinced that they were at another hospital, they did not confabulate on other topics, such as their recent doings, and they never tried to leave the hospital to enact currently inappropriate ideas, as spontaneous confabulators typically do.

Capgras syndrome

Although Pick had already described the misidentification of people, and had actually been its focus (Pick 1903b), Joseph Capgras, a French psychiatrist, is nowadays given credit for the first specific description of this form of misidentification – the 'Capgras syndrome'. At the meeting of the Clinical Society for Mental Medicine on 10 January 1923, Capgras and Reboul-Lachaux (1923a) described a 33-year-old, psychotic woman. She had ideas of grandeur and persecution, believing that her grandmother was the queen of India and that she descended from King Henry IV. She believed she had an immense fortune and incredible intellectual and moral qualities. At the same time, she was convinced that she had enemies who tried to poison her – in summary, a state of fantastic confabulation similar to Kraepelin's descriptions (Chapter 2, p. 15ff). However, the most flagrant topic of her persecutory delusions concerned the substitution and disappearance of people. She was convinced that her children, her husband, the concierge, and all residents had been replaced by impostors. She was even convinced that she herself had been substituted by two or three impostors, so that she remained unjustly hospitalized: 'The captivity which I undergo belongs to another person who is among my impostors' (Capgras and Reboul-Lachaux 1923a, p. 8). The patient was fully convinced about the veracity of her suspicions: She went to a police post to complain and wrote numerous letters to authorities. Considering the wide range of these delusions, the summary of the case description, published by the Society appeared amazingly clear:

> This is not false recognition based on the detection of some unexpected resemblance between one individual and another, but the impossibility to identify a person despite the detection of resemblance.

> Capgras and Reboul-Lachaux (1923b, p. 186)

Possibly as a consequence of this original description of the syndrome in a floridly psychotic patient, Capgras syndrome has long been considered a psychiatric, 'non-organic' phenomenon. Indeed, an immense literature on Capgras syndrome in psychosis has accrued over the years, but there are also numerous reports of patients with organic brain damage. One of them was reported by Alexander *et al.* (1979), who described a 44-year-old man with psychotic features including grandiose and persecutory delusions as well as auditory hallucinations. He then suffered a severe traumatic brain injury, which caused a right frontal subdural haematoma and destroyed parts of right frontal and temporal lobe as well as fronto–polar region. It was only after this event that he started to confuse people. For more than two years of follow-up, during which the patient lived at home, he was convinced that he now lived with a second, different family, virtually identical with his 'first' family, and that they lived in a house just like the one he had lived in previously. He insisted that the two families had identical composition. The wives of both families had the same appearance, came from the same town, and had brothers with the same name; there were five children in both families with the same names and the same sex distribution. In contrast to this profound disorientation regarding his family, orientation to time and place was intact. It is obvious from the title of the article that Alexander *et al.* (1979) sought a common interpretation for reduplicative paramnesia for place and the Capgras syndrome. They suggested that both disturbances required bilateral frontal and right hemisphere pathology.

Such a link had been assumed by previous authors. Weinstein *et al.* (1952) analysed the 'phenomenon of reduplication' in 16 patients with organic brain disease, including meningoencephalitis, tumours in the region of the third ventricle, intracranial metastases, right hemispheric haemorrhage etc. All of them had reduplication for place, defined as 'the confabulation of the existence of two or more places with almost identical attributes, although only one exists in reality' (p. 808). Indeed, all patients located the hospital closer to their home. Five patients had reduplication for person, defined as 'the confabulation that there are two or more persons with almost identical attributes, although only one exists in reality'. Finally, eleven patients had *reduplication for time*, defined as 'the confabulation that the present experience has also been experienced at some time in the past'.

A striking example of the latter type of reduplication was described by Marshall *et al.* (1995). Their 69-year-old patient had had an industrial accident 34 years previously. Following a new brain injury, which caused extensive bilateral frontal contusions, he was repeatedly transferred between three hospitals. From then on, he persistently and strongly believed that he had just recently had another accident. The authors considered this belief 'a confabulation that arises from the particular combination of memory-loss and memory-preservation' (p. 187). But this interpretation did not appear satisfactory: 'His 'confabulation' of an earlier accident is not really a (pure) confabulation. Rather, it is an inference to the best (simplest) hypothesis on the basis of the fragmentary data available to [the patient]' (p. 188). The emphasis of this interpretation lay in the idea that this patient's delusion was a belief held on reasonable grounds, explained by the fragmentary and mutually interfering pieces of information available to his memory. Weinstein *et al.* (1952) had emphasized this aspect, too: 'Reduplication does not appear to be a random manifestation of a confused state or a hysterical reaction following brain injury, but seems to be an orderly pattern of behaviour integrated with brain function' (p. 813). However, their emphasis was on motivational factors, an interpretation they had already offered for confabulations in general (Chapter 7) and which they also proposed for the lack of insight, as we will see later in the paragraph on anosognosia.

Fregoli syndrome and intermetamorphosis

There is another well-known form of misidentification of people: the Fregoli syndrome. Courbon and Fail (1927) briefly presented a 27-year-old schizophrenic women 'of low intelligence' at the meeting of the Clinical Society for Mental Medicine on 11 July 1927. In the context of delusions of persecution and grandeur, 'she had the conviction that her persecutors were 'Fregolis' who incarnated themselves in people around her in order to torture her' (p. 290). At the time, the authors did not have to explain to whom they were alluding. Leopoldo Fregoli (1867–1936) was an internationally renowned actor performing in the big cities of Europe and Argentina. He had an extraordinary ability to impersonate famous personalities and to switch between these roles with incredible smoothness. Thus, the patient of Courbon and Fail (1927) falsely recognized her imagined persecutors in different strangers. The authors concluded that this type of illusion

> is not an agnosia of identification due to an error of an affective judgement, as is the case in the 'illusion of impostors [Capgras syndrome]', which can also occasionally occur with intact intelligence. [The illusion of Fregoli] is a creation of imagination, which can only happen in a sick mind.
>
> Courbon and Fail (1927, p. 290)

Later studies showed that this syndrome, even when it occurred in the context of psychosis, often had an organic component. Christodoulou (1976) somewhat adapted the definition of Fregoli syndrome:

> The patient identifies a familiar person (usually his persecutor) in various strangers and claims that, although these strangers and his familiar person bare no physical resemblance to each other, they are in fact psychologically identical.
>
> Christodoulou (1976, p. 305)

He described seven patients with this syndrome. All of them were psychotic and some had a history of schizophrenia. Importantly, however, he found indices of organic brain disease in six of the seven patients: three had a history of severe head injury, two had had febrile convulsions, one had grand-mal seizures, and two had had severe paroxysmal headaches.

Fregoli syndrome has also been described in patients suffering undeniable organic brain damage. For example, Feinberg *et al.* (1999) described a 61-year-old man suffering from extended traumatic contusion of the right frontal and left temporo–parietal areas. At a time when he still had severe memory disturbance and was unable to sustain a 'mental set' for more than a few minutes, he had varied misidentifications. These concerned family members, co-workers, and even himself. Thus, he claimed that another patient was his younger son, believed to see his older son on television, reported that a man he used to work with was in the hospital as a patient, and identified himself on television as a skater. The authors suggested that these statements by the patient represented confabulations, while at the same time interpreting them as 'over-personalized misidentifications'.

Cases like de Pauw *et al.*'s (1987) demonstrated that the Fregoli syndrome could also result from circumscribed brain damage. They described a 66-year-old woman who suffered an ischaemic stroke destroying much of the right temporal and parietal lobes. She had slurred speech, memory impairment, and disorientation in time and space. Within two months, she recovered from these disturbances but then developed a Fregoli syndrome with delusions of persecution. She was convinced that her married cousin had moved into her neighbourhood with a lady friend and that they were following her in disguise. She vividly described how the couple disguised themselves with make-up, wigs etc. On occasions, she confronted strangers in public and demanded that they revealed their true identity. This delusion subsided with neuroleptic treatment but relapsed two months after discontinuation of the medication. It is noteworthy that even in this case with focal right-sided temporo–parietal damage, psychotic features with delusions of persecution dominated the clinical picture. It is possible that various patients diagnosed in the past with non-organic psychosis, such as schizophrenia, had organic brain damage. The case also demonstrated that frontal damage was not necessary for paramnesic misidentification to occur.

Fregoli syndrome has repeatedly been interpreted as an inappropriate *hyper identification* of people unfamiliar to the patient, who imposes an identity on them (Feinberg *et al.* 1999). The nonsensical explanations used by the patients to substantiate their delusion are not clearly different from the fantastic confabulations described in severely psychotic or demented patients. These confabulations are not explained by the sole misidentification. Vuilleumier *et al.* (2003) reported a 21-year-old woman who had suffered a left lateral temporo–occipital venous infarction leaving a defect in this region. Soon after this event, she realized that she felt familiar with all people around her. She naturally approached total strangers as if she knew them, although she neither remembered their name nor precise meetings with them. She felt deeply embarrassed when the people did not reciprocate her friendly approach.

This hyperfamiliarity occurred in the absence of other delusions, confabulation or other cognitive impairment; in particular she had no difficulty in recognizing truly known faces. The case demonstrates that an inadequate sense of familiarity with unknown people, as it also happens in the Fregoli syndrome, does not by itself explain confabulatory behaviour. In addition, it shows that false familiarity does not require frontal lobe damage.

There is still another form of misidentification of people: *intermetamorphosis* or, to be more precise, the 'illusion of intermetamorphosis and charm'. Courbon and Tusques (1932) described a 58-year-old woman with a nine-year history of depression with ideas of persecution, who had 'sometimes the illusion that people around her transmuted physically and morally into one another' (p. 401). For example, her husband would transiently change his appearance, behaviour, and face and take on the expression of a neighbour. During such metamorphoses, a number of physical characteristics remained unchanged: he never changed his hand, on which one finger had been amputated, nor the grey colour of his eyes. The patient perceived these metamorphoses as if the neighbour were incarnating himself within her husband. There were other episodic illusions: her belongings, objects and animals would change; her clothes were transformed. Familiar people transformed themselves: their ears elongated, women transmuted into men, and young persons transmuted into elderly people. She remained oriented, obliging, and talkative. Nowadays, such a patient would be examined for the presence of temporal-lobe epilepsy. The authors explained the difference between intermetamorphosis and the illusion of Fregoli:

> In the illusion of Fregoli, there is false recognition in the absence of physical resemblance. In the illusion of intermetamorphosis, in contrast, there is both false recognition and false physical resemblance.
>
> Courbon and Tusques (1932, p. 404)

Mechanisms of misidentification and link with confabulation

To determine the aetiologies underlying paramnesic misidentification syndromes, Förstl *et al.* (1991) analysed reports of 260 patients with misidentification syndromes. By far the most frequent one was Capgras syndrome (174 patients), whereas 18 had Fregoli syndrome, 11 had intermetamorphosis, and 17 had reduplicative paramnesia for place. Overall, schizophrenia was by far the most frequent diagnosis (127 cases), followed by affective disorders (29 cases), and organic mental syndromes including dementia (46 cases). Eleven patients had epilepsy 18 had cerebrovascular disease, and 15 had had brain trauma. The frequency of organic diseases, mostly affecting the right hemisphere, was particularly high among the patients with misidentification of place (reduplicative paramnesia). As regards to misidentification of persons (syndromes of

Capgras, Fregoli, and intermetamorphosis), the authors concluded that it could be a manifestation of any organic or functional psychosis.

Fleminger and Burns (1993), whose analysis also consisted of a review of the literature, arrived at a similar conclusion, namely, that delusional misidentification of place was significantly more common in cases with evidence of organic brain disease. Delusional misidentification of persons, by contrast, was more common in cases with a functional diagnosis. A caveat to be considered with such an analysis is, of course, that Capgras and Fregoli syndrome were for a long time considered diagnostic for the presence of schizophrenia, so that no other diagnosis was sought.

There have been many speculations about the *mechanisms* of paramnesic misidentification syndromes. Pick (1903b) appeared to favour an interpretation in terms of a disturbance of temporal and sensory convergence during memory retrieval:

> In my opinion, the disturbance consists in the fact that a continuous and essentially stable sequence of events in the patient's memory belatedly breaks into multiple components whose individual parts, which are fairly well attached in memory, then appear to the patient as a repetition [of the initial event].
>
> Pick (1903b, p. 22)

To explain this problem, he invoked William James' (1890/1983) concept of a 'sense of fusion' necessary to experience an evoked memory as real. Thus, when Pick introduced the term 'reduplicative paramnesia', he not only referred to phenomenology but also to a faulty process in memory retrieval.

Capgras and Reboul-Lachaux (1923a), who were probably unaware of Pick's work, proposed a different mechanism: a derangement of the degree of familiarity. 'In any instance of recognition, there is, more or less, a struggle between two affective elements of sensory or mnemonic elements: the feeling of familiarity and the feeling of strangeness' (p. 13f.). Many modern interpretations propose variants of this idea, using different terminologies: under-personalized versus over-personalized misidentification (Feinberg *et al.* 1999); hypo-identification as opposed to hyper-identification (Christodoulou 1976; de Pauw *et al.* 1987) or – in anatomical terms – a temporal–limbic–frontal disconnection (Alexander *et al.* 1979). The core idea of these interpretations lies in a dissociation between intact perceptual–analytical processes and a faulty sense of familiarity or strangeness.

So what does paramnesic misidentification have to do with confabulation? Many authors used the term 'confabulation' to describe the false statements by their patients. Weinstein *et al.* (1952) defined reduplicative phenomena as material-specific confabulations relating to the identity of persons, places or events. Kapur *et al.* (1988, p. 579) described reduplicative paramnesia as 'one of the more florid types of confabulation'. Indeed, most of the false claims by patients described in this paragraph could be considered momentary confabulations, incited by the circumstances of a discussion; some of them – those produced by floridly psychotic patients – can even be considered fantastic confabulations. Despite this phenomenological resemblance, there are features that distinguish most of these confabulations from those discussed in the first four chapters of this book, the pseudo-reminiscences or mnestic confabulations: most confabulations in paramnesic misidentification syndromes selectively refer to one or several types of misidentifications (people, places) and refer to one sensory modality (mostly visual). In contrast, the mnestic confabulations discussed in the previous chapters relate to personal, autobiographical memories and plans for the future. Thus, despite semantic congruence, it is likely that confabulations in paramnesic misidentification differ from confabulations referring to autobiographical memories and plans (pseudo-reminiscences) in the same way as perceptual processes differ from episodic memory. Even though in the healthy brain, these processes work in concert (Fuster 1995), they are subserved by largely separable neural systems. Treating misidentification and confabulation as a single package risks obfuscating pathophysiological and anatomical differences that would be clinically important, for example, in devising a rehabilitation programme. As Marshall *et al.* (1995) wrote: 'It would be of considerable interest to know whether reduplication of place [and presumably other types] could be interpreted in terms that are somewhat more specific than "confusion" and "confabulation"'(p. 189). It looks very much as if it could.

Accepting this distinction does not mean that paramnesic misidentification cannot occur together with mnestic confabulations. In fact, persistent misidentification of people and places by confabulating patients has already been described by the early authors (Benon and LeHuché 1920; Victor and Yakovlev 1955; Flament 1957). We have seen patients producing elaborate *momentary confabulations* during a confusional state or with severe dementia, who misidentified people, the location, and their own situation. The demented elderly lady with left medial temporal infarction described on p. 95 claimed that she was in Africa hunting wild animals and that collaborators of the clinic were hunting partners; only to claim 30 minutes later that she was a member of the hospital's supervisory board and the nurse was the hospital's pastor. Like that, ideas might come and go in rapid succession. In non-confused, non-demented patients producing momentary confabulation, consistent misidentification is rare.

Behaviourally spontaneous confabulators may present misidentification even when they are out of the confusional state. These misidentifications typically refer to people or places and may be stable or variable. Mrs M, the patient with a lesion of the right capsular genu (p. 57f. Figure 4.4) consistently mistook a specific clerk of the clinic for an earlier professional colleague without making any other confabulation about this person. Unfortunately, we never had a chance to check whether our collaborator resembled the patient's earlier colleague. Mrs B, described in Chapter 1, had more variable, but also striking misidentifications. She never gave a false identity to a real stranger. In contrast, collaborators of the clinic, whom she had repeatedly seen, were given an identity corresponding to the activity that she falsely thought to have had on a given day. The patient with limbic encephalitis mentioned on p. 117 felt falsely familiar with most people on the ward and often hugged other people. This state lasted for several weeks.

Misidentification of place is common among behaviourally spontaneous confabulators. They hold the pervasive conviction to be at a location other than the hospital. A 58-year-old woman with anterior communication artery aneurysm rupture, who left the examination to feed her baby (p. 59, Figure 4.3a), was convinced she was at home. She repeatedly wanted to prove this fact to us. Before opening the door to her hospital bedroom, she explained that she would now show us her living room, for which she had just received new furniture. When she entered the room and realized that there were hospital beds rather than her furniture, she was outraged by the fact that not only the wrong furniture had been delivered, but also the whole living room had been exchanged without her permission. Another patient with a similar lesion (Figure 4.3b) maintained that he was in Bordeaux despite all the evidence to the contrary and despite acknowledging that the town that he saw did not resemble Bordeaux. Thus, reduplicative phenomena may be very pervasive in behaviourally spontaneous confabulators. Indeed, given the strong conviction that behaviourally spontaneous confabulators hold in their false ideas and plans, there is probably always a certain degree of paramnesic misidentification. This misidentification always refers to the present circumstances, mostly also to place and often to people. The patients just mentioned clearly expressed the products of misidentification; in other patients, reduplicative phenomena only emerge when testing orientation. When using tests of orientation as a measure of reduplicative phenomena, it appears indeed that the mechanism accounting for behaviourally spontaneous confabulation also explains misidentification phenomena in these patients, as we will see in Chapter 8.

In *conclusion*, paramnesic misidentification syndromes (reduplicative phenomena) have often been described in schizophrenia and other 'non-organic' psychoses, but also in diverse types of structural brain damage. Focal lesions producing such syndromes mostly involved the right temporal, parietal or frontal lobes in isolation or in combination. Frontal damage is not necessary. Although the different misidentification syndromes dissociate, in that patients may have one type of misidentification but not the other, the precise anatomical or functional basis of this dissociation is unknown. The confabulations offered by the patients to corroborate their false beliefs may be conceived as momentary, in some cases even fantastic confabulations. However, in contrast to the mnestic confabulations discussed in the previous chapters (pseudo-reminiscences), which referred to events in the patient's past or future, the confabulations in paramnesic syndromes describe the products of an erroneous identification process, in most instances referring to the outer world. These two groups of confabulations should therefore be considered as largely independent entities.

Fleeting misidentifications may accompany momentary or fantastic confabulations, especially in confused and demented patients, but the association is loose. In contrast, reduplicative phenomena referring to person, place and personal situation are common in behaviourally spontaneous confabulation, although patients often do not express them spontaneously. Evidence that will be presented in Chapter 8 indicates that the mechanism explaining behaviourally spontaneous confabulation can also explain reduplicative misidentification as revealed in tests of orientation. Conversely, reduplicative phenomena have repeatedly been described in otherwise correctly oriented patients with no evidence of behaviourally spontaneous confabulation. It is likely that paramnesic misidentification syndromes may result from diverse mechanisms.

Anosognosia

The term 'anosognosia' was coined by Joseph Babinski, a French neurologist. At a meeting of the French Neurological Society on 11 June 1914, he described two women with left hemiplegia (Babinski 1914). Both appeared to ignore the existence of their hemiplegia. When asked to move their left arm, one of them behaved as if the question had been addressed to someone else, whereas the other simply said: 'That's it [*voilà; c'est fait*].' The patients explicitly denied being paralysed. Babinski specifically mentioned that none of them had hallucinations, fabulation, or confusion. For this disorder, he wanted to introduce a new term: 'I think it is allowed to use a neologism to designate this state and to call it anosognosia' (Babinski 1914, p. 846). In addition, he wanted to introduce a new term to make the fine distinction between the unawareness of hemiplegia (anosognosia) and the indifference about it:

> I have also seen some hemiplegics who, without ignoring the existence of their paralysis, seemed to attach no importance to it at all, as if it were an insignificant malaise. Such a state could be named anosodiaphoria (indifference, lack of concern).
>
> Babinski (1914, p. 846)

He suspected that anosognosia was a particular manifestation of right hemisphere lesions.

The ensuing discussion immediately enlarged the scope of the disorder. Pierre Marie, a famous name in French neurology, mentioned that a similar psychic trouble could not only be found in affections of the nervous system but also in visceral affections. Gilbert Ballet, whose name was later attached to an ocular motor disorder, remarked that he had also seen unawareness of disease in patients with brain tumours, 'who not only stop complaining about headache ... but who also affirm not to have any visual problem although they are completely blind' (Babinski 1914, p. 847). Henry Meige, whose name is associated with a movement disorder, described his observations of patients who had partially recovered from hemiplegia but 'persist in their inertia and neglect to make movements, which, however, would again be possible. Nothing seems to incite them to execute [the movements] spontaneously' (Babinski 1914, p. 848). For this disorder, he proposed the term 'functional motor amnesia'. Nowadays, this behaviour would be called motor neglect.

The discussants at the meeting of 1914 were apparently not aware of Gabriel Anton's work. Anton, professor of neurology and psychiatry at Graz, Austria, had described two patients who were unaware of their deafness and one who was unaware of her blindness (Anton 1898). Two cases were particularly well studied. One of them, a 56-year-old woman, suffered from generalized pain when walking, and 'almost all nerve tracts were enormously pressure sensitive'. When Anton examined her, she had difficulty in naming objects. Most importantly, she was almost completely blind, but seemed to be unaware of it. When shown objects, she would give them some random name.

> The patient was unaware of this loss of vision. The defect did not incite further reflection or conclusions, nor sorrow or loss of pleasure. This at a time when the absence of a verbal denominator, that is, of the memory of a word image [the anomia], obviously caused pain to her.
>
> Anton (1898, p. 93)

The patient eventually lost her ability to localize sounds, then also suffered left hemiparesis, before she died. At autopsy, vessel walls were 'very thick and dehiscent', a finding suggesting nowadays – together with the clinical course – a diagnosis of giant-cell arteritis. There was widespread damage to the white matter of both hemispheres. In particular, the occipital lobes were severely damaged.

The second well-documented case of Anton – case three of the series – concerned a 69-year-old woman who was hospitalized because of confusion.

> Soon after her admission, it was noted that she did not understand spoken words and never reacted to them, be it by turning her head or by giving an answer. Similarly, [she did not react to] loud clapping of the hands, shouting, or intense noises near her ears.

At the same time, she had word-finding difficulties. Most notably, however,

> Even in discussions she never became aware of the fact that she did not hear nor understand questions ... She was repeatedly asked in written form whether she could hear and then wholeheartedly and indifferently affirmed that she heard well.
>
> Anton (1898, p. 106f.)

She died of purulent bronchitis. At post-mortem, there was softening [ischaemic necrosis] of the first temporal gyrus with varying extension into the second temporal and angular gyrus on both sides. Thus, this lesion involved primary and secondary auditory cortex and some surrounding tissue on both sides.

In the German literature, *Anton's symptom* became the term describing the unawareness of a neurological deficit. Otto Pötzl, director of the German Psychiatric Clinic in Prague, described two patients who denied their left-sided hemiplegia (Pötzl 1924). When asked to move the left extremities, they would either not react or move the right extremities. One patient repeatedly tried to stand up from his bed although he always fell to the floor. The other patient would spontaneously grasp her left hand and claim that it was a stranger's hand. Both patients died of a new stroke. Post-mortem showed destruction of the right supramarginal gyrus in the inferior parietal lobe, with additional damage or degeneration of thalamic nuclei. Pötzl called this unawareness of the left-sided hemiplegia 'Anton's symptom' and remarked in a footnote: 'After termination of this work, I found that Babinski, who – as we know – referred to Anton's symptom as anosognosia, described a number of cases, in whom the picture occurred with left-sided hemiplegia' (Pötzl 1924, p. 118). Nowadays, the term 'Anton's syndrome' is only used to describe the unawareness of blindness.

If Pötzl was not aware of Babinski's work until 1924, it is only fair that Babinski did not know about Anton's work in 1918. Indeed, Babinski still did not refer to Anton when he again reported on anosognosia at the meeting of the French Neurological Society on 5 December 1918 (Babinski 1918) – as he did not refer to Anton in a new communication in 1924 (Babinski and Joltrain 1924). He still wanted to limit the use of the term anosognosia to the unawareness of hemiplegia:

> Despite the relative preservation of intellectual functions that would allow them to respond to most requests, these patients appear to have no notion at all of their paralysis and they absolutely do not complain about their handicap, which they appear to ignore ... There appears to be here a special psychic perturbation: It is as if the subject had absolutely no interest in his paralysed arm, was incapable of focusing attention on it, did not retain – so to say – the memory of it.
>
> Babinski (1918, pp. 365f.)

It was again Pierre Marie who contested the specificity of the disorder: 'I do not think that the psychic trouble described by Monsieur Babinski should be considered a phenomenon specific to hemiplegia, and particularly, to left-sided hemiplegia' (Babinski 1918, p. 366). He insisted that most patients with hemianopia were unaware of the fact that half of their visual field was missing. Similarly, he explained that most patients who had lost sensation on the side of the body corresponding to a cerebral lesion had no idea about the existence of the paralysed half of their body. 'This is a general psychic phenomenon described by many observers but which deserves no less to be studied in detail' (Babinski 1918, p. 366).

Even when adopting the broad concept of anosognosia – or lack of concern – that Pierre Marie advocated, it may appear strange that anosognosia is discussed in this book. The 'confabulations' by anosognosic patients concern their present state of disease; they do not reflect pseudo-reminiscences and illusions of memory for which the term confabulation was originally introduced. So, why a discussion of anosognosia? According to its Latin root (Chapter 3, p. 45), the word 'confabulation' can obviously be used to describe any type of false statement, including the false statements about one's health status that characterize anosognosia. This semantic congruity was taken by some authors to link the two phenomena and to seek a common explanation for anosognosia and confabulation (Pötzl 1924; Weinstein and Kahn 1955; Feinberg and Roane 1997b; Hirstein 2005). Let us therefore look at the different forms of anosognosia, their associations and dissociations, and their relevance for confabulation.

Pötzl (1924) used the term confabulation to describe the fabrications by blind patients with progressive paralysis (syphilis), who were unaware of their blindness but pretended to see. He pushed the idea of a commonality much further by suggesting a common, super-ordinate mechanism for anosognosia and Korsakoff psychosis:

It appears possible to conceive of Korsakoff psychosis as a disorder of the construction of a range, a sphere for the localization of the most recent events, in which self-awareness of the disorder is lacking. Instead of the absent sphere of time and the localizations that would belong into it, the specific activators for the build-up [of this temporal sphere] would be deviated towards the sphere of a remote past and the memories of those times. Such an interpretation of Korsakoff psychosis would, however, constitute a real progress only if it were possible to pin down specific structures … I have only mentioned this idea here because it shows that Anton's symptom [anosognosia] cannot be explained as a consequence of Korsakoff psychosis, but that Anton's symptom and Korsakoff psychosis might possibly emanate next to each other and in an independent fashion from a particular basic mechanism, of which both disorders would be special instances.

Pötzl (1924, p. 166)

In the English literature, the idea of a link between anosognosia and confabulation was taken up and strongly promoted by Weinstein and Kahn. In the introduction to their first study on anosognosia (Weinstein and Kahn 1950), they mentioned the fact that denial of illness, which had mainly been described with regards to left hemiplegia and blindness, had also been reported with reference to right hemiplegia, paraplegia, hemiballismus (a movement disorder), alexia (inability to read), auditory agnosia (inability to understand the meaning of heard sounds), and deafness. They then went on to describe the anosognosia of 22 patients with brain tumours, of whom 16 had raised intracranial pressure. Anosognosia concerned not only neurological symptoms, such as hemiplegia, blindness, or memory loss, but also incontinence, sexual impotence, vomiting, or the fact that a patient had had an operation. All of these patients also produced confabulations, which were not offered spontaneously but could be elicited in questions. The confabulations were of three types:

1. denial of defect;
2. accounts of supposed events or accomplishments which were incompatible with the serious illness;
3. remarks related to what the patient felt was an inadequacy in his life situation.

All patients were disoriented to time, 19 also to place. Ten patients had hallucinations. One may therefore wonder whether these patients were not in a confusional state. Without providing details, Weinstein and Kahn (1950) suspected that premorbid *personality* was important. Specifically, they suggested: 'The person with anosognosia relates to the environment largely in terms of his needs and feelings. His main need is to be well' (p. 789).

In an impressive compilation of 103 patients, most of them with brain tumours, Weinstein and Kahn (1955) further elaborated on their views. Confabulations were portrayed as a manifestation of *explicit verbal denial*.

According to the authors, 'confabulations were used [by the patients] to amplify the denial and to explain away obvious manifestations of illness' (p. 15). All patients were also disoriented to place and time. The authors again insisted on personality traits:

> All [patients with explicit verbal denial] had previously shown a marked trend to deny the existence of illness. They appeared to have regarded ill health as imperfection or weakness or disgrace ... Attitudes toward work were also consistent. All were characterized as conscientious and responsible people.
>
> Weinstein and Kahn (1955, p. 73f.)

The pathological basis was described as being 'usually of rapid onset as indicated by high incidence of rapidly growing neoplasms, ruptured aneurysms and acute head injuries'. When there was no subarachnoid bleeding or intracranial hypertension, anosognosia appeared to be particularly strongly associated with lesions in the region of the third and lateral ventricles, the diencephalon and midbrain.

> It did not matter which cortical area was involved by a tumour provided that there was accompanying involvement of deeper structures. Thus anosognosia occurred with frontal, parietal or temporal lobe lesions when these invaded the medullary centre of the cerebral hemisphere and the corpus striatum and diencephalon.
>
> Weinstein and Kahn (1955, p. 66)

Despite the many dissociations between anosognosic phenomena and despite such diverse anatomical bases, Weinstein and Kahn (1955) were adamant about the validity of a unitary concept of anosognosia:

> Historically, the tendency has been to divide forms of denial of illness into artificial units of behaviour. This has been manifested, for example, by a classification in terms of the particular symptom or defect that is denied. Denial of hemiplegia, denial of blindness and lack of concern over illness have been treated as separate entities involving dysfunction of different areas of the brain ... Our findings indicate that the various forms of anosognosia are not discrete entities that can be localized in different areas of the brain. Whether a lesion involves the frontal or parietal lobe determines the disability that may be denied, not the mechanism of denial.
>
> Weinstein and Kahn (1955, p. 122f.)

Weinstein and Lyerly (1968) eventually applied a similar interpretation to the mnestic confabulations they had observed in patients having acute brain damage.

> While confabulation is ostensibly the fictitious narration of past events, it is also a condensed symbolic representation of current problems and relationships. The content is determined by the nature of the disability and those aspects of past experience that have been significant sources of identity.
>
> Weinstein and Lyerly (1968, p. 354)

Only few authors subsequently used the term 'confabulation' so explicitly to describe the verbal denial of illness (Feinberg et al. 1994; Feinberg and Roane 1997b; Hirstein 2005). Although anosognosia was also observed in disorders such as aphasia (Lebrun 1987; Alexander et al. 1989) and disturbed face recognition (Young et al. 1990), most studies focused on the denial of hemiplegia and hemianopia. Methods were refined. The degree of unawareness was quantified, ranging from the sole absence of spontaneous complaints about a disorder to the explicit denial even upon demonstration of the deficit (Bisiach et al. 1986). Questionnaires were introduced which allowed quantifying anosognosia by comparing the patient's perception of disease with his objective performance (Cutting 1978; Dalla Barba et al. 1995; Barrett et al. 2005) or with the appreciation by carers (Michon et al. 1994). An amazing number of facts and dissociations appeared from these studies:

1. Overall, unawareness of hemiplegia and hemianopia appears to be equally frequent after right and left hemisphere damage (Cutting 1978; Celesia et al. 1997). More severe degrees of anosognosia with explicit denial of a hemiplegia are more frequent after right hemisphere dysfunction (Bisiach and Geminiani 1991; Adair et al. 1995; Marcel et al. 2004; Baier and Karnath 2005).

2. Even when limiting the analysis to patients with right hemisphere damage, anosognosia for hemiplegia and for hemianopia dissociate (Bisiach et al. 1986; Levine et al. 1991; Feinberg et al. 1994; Jehkonen et al. 2000; Marcel et al. 2004); a patient may be unaware of his hemiplegia but aware of his hemianopia or vice versa.

3. Even the awareness for hemiplegia and hemianopia may dissociate from the awareness of hemispatial neglect (unawareness of left space) (Bisiach et al. 1986; Jehkonen et al. 2000). Similarly, the unawareness of hemispatial neglect may dissociate from the unawareness of illness (Jehkonen et al. 2000).

4. Unawareness of hemiplegia does not correlate with the severity of the hemiplegia or sensory loss (Bisiach et al. 1986; Marcel et al. 2004).

The anatomical basis also varies. For example, anosognosia for hemianopia may result from an entirely different lesion than anosognosia for hemiplegia. Anosognosia for hemiplegia or hemianopia has been described after lesions involving the cortex and reaching into the white matter, but also after deep hemispheric lesions (Bisiach et al. 1986; Levine et al. 1991). An analysis comparing anosognosic and non-anosognosic patients with right hemisphere lesions indicated that anosognosia for hemiplegia demanded damage to the posterior insula, a multi-modal integration area (Karnath *et al.* 2005). For our discussion of confabulation, it is interesting to note that anosognosia for hemiplegia and hemianopia does not require frontal damage.

Considering the many dissociations and the absence of any firm correlations, it is not surprising that there is no generally accepted hypothesis on the mechanisms of anosognosia. Vuilleumier's (2004) designation of anosognosia as 'the neurology of beliefs and uncertainties' refers as much to the investigators as to the disorder. A prominent hypothesis interpreted anosognosia as the failure to *discover paralysis*:

> because proprioceptive mechanisms that ordinarily inform an individual about the position and movement of limbs are damaged, and the patient, because of additional cognitive defects, lacks the capacity to make the necessary observations and inferences to diagnose the paralysis.

Levine et al. (1991, p. 1770)

In this and similar theories, anosognosia was thus seen as a problem of the interpretation of or failure to obtain perceptual information, rather than a problem of memory. A study by Adair *et al.* (1995) on anosognosia during the Wada procedure supported this conclusion. During this procedure, a hemisphere of the brain is anaesthetized by injecting an anaesthetic (barbiturate) through a catheter that is normally placed in the carotid artery. The test is sometimes necessary before epilepsy or tumour surgery to forecast and prevent iatrogenic deficits caused by surgery to functionally critical areas. Using this procedure, Adair *et al.* (1995) found that anosognosia for hemiplegia was more frequent during right hemisphere anaesthesia. Most importantly, the proportion of subjects with right hemisphere anaesthesia who showed anosognosia for hemiplegia was similar during and after the procedure, indicating that the anosognosia reflected a true failure of deficit awareness rather than an inability to recall the deficit. Using the Wada procedure, too, Lu *et al.* (1997) investigated the association between anosognosia and confabulation. Patients practiced to indicate by pointing whether and with what type of material they had been touched. Confabulation was defined as any evident response to no-touch trials, that is, when a patient was not touched but signalled having been touched with a certain material. Anosognosia was assumed if a patient negatively responded to the question: 'Are you weak anywhere?' The authors found that the presence of anosognosia for hemiplegia was independent of the production of this type of confabulation. For our present discussion, it is important to note that even non-mnestic confabulation, e.g., the false indication that one has been touched, does not appear to be associated with anosognosia. In the light of these findings, it appears even more unlikely that there is a link between anosognosia and mnestic confabulations, that is, pseudo-reminiscences and illusions of memory.

Anosognosia for cognitive deficits

A number of studies explored the mechanisms of anosognosia for cognitive or behavioural deficits in dementia. Michon *et al.* (1994) used questionnaires to compare self-evaluation of cognitive capacities by patients with Alzheimer's disease with evaluations made by carers. The difference between the scores obtained in these two questionnaires was used to determine an anosognosia score. They found that this score was correlated with a 'frontal score' including a number of tasks. There was neither a correlation with general cognitive decline as measured with the Mini Mental State Examination, nor with memory function as measured by the Wechsler Memory Scale. They concluded that anosognosia in Alzheimer's disease was at least in part explained by frontal dysfunction but not by the severity of cognitive decline.

Two studies using single photon emission computed tomography (SPECT) indeed indicated that anosognosia in dementia was associated with dorsolateral prefrontal perfusion deficits (Starkstein *et al.* 1995; Derouesné *et al.* 1999). However, diverse studies did not reveal a consistent association between anosognosia and any particular frontal or memory dysfunction or cluster thereof. Accordingly, studies did not converge on a common interpretation of anosognosia for cognitive or behavioural disorders in dementia (Starkstein *et al.* 1995; Derouesné *et al.* 1999; Barrett *et al.* 2005). Also of interest for our current discussion is that, in these studies, the word confabulation did not appear. The only allusion to a link between confabulation and anosognosia was made by Dalla Barba *et al.* (1995), who compared 12 patients with mild to moderate Alzheimer's disease, 12 depressed patients and 24 normal controls. They found that anosognosia concerning memory deficit strongly correlated with the tendency to produce intrusions. The authors' conclusion that 'anosognosia of memory deficit seems indispensable for intrusions' appears somewhat strong. Many of our patients who produced high numbers of intrusions were fully aware of their memory deficit.

Anosognosia for *impaired memory* has been investigated under the heading of *metamemory*, a subject's ability to correctly estimate his or her memory capacities. Independently of the presence of amnesia, patients with frontal lobe damage tend to overestimate their memory capacities (Janowsky *et al.* 1989b; Squire *et al.* 1990). Kopelman *et al.* (1998) asked three groups of memory-impaired patients to self-evaluate their memory capacities. All three groups estimated their memory to be less efficient than healthy controls. Importantly, the groups having frontal lesions or diencephalic disease (alcoholic Korsakoff syndrome, pituitary adenoma) rated themselves significantly higher than patients with medial temporal damage (herpes encephalitis, hypoxia etc.). Self-evaluation was independent of objective memory performance. This finding is consistent with our observations: patients with severe amnesia after medial temporal lesions typically complain about their bad memory and suffer from their amnesia, whereas patients with diencephalic or orbitofrontal lesions often do not appear to integrate the memory failure in their behaviour, although they, too, may suffer from marked depression.

Association between anosognosia and confabulation

What remains for the association between anosognosia and behaviourally pertinent forms of mnestic confabulations? The question has never been formally explored. The early authors (Tiling 1892; Kalberlah 1904) occasionally mentioned their confabulating patients' lack of insight. Williams and Rupp (1938) suggested that lack of insight was necessary for confabulation to occur but provided no specific data for this claim. Our own observations, albeit anecdotal, do not support such a claim, either for momentary or for behaviourally spontaneous confabulation. Two of our patients with extremely severe amnesia after medial temporal damage after stroke (Schnider *et al.* 1994b) or inflammation (Schnider *et al.* 1995), who sometimes produced momentary confabulations, were fully aware of and suffered from their memory deficit. The elderly woman with herpes encephalitis mentioned on p. 70, who sometimes produced quite elaborate momentary confabulations, knew that she had a bad memory and that she had suffered encephalitis from 'a virus in the brain'. Although these are just three examples, they suffice to show that momentary confabulation does not require anosognosia.

No specific data are available on anosognosia in *fantastic confabulators*. Kraepelin (1910) mentioned that many patients with paralytic dementia were concerned about their health status at the beginning of the disease but did not specifically refer to the phase characterized by the production of 'simple falsifications of memory', that is, fantastic confabulations. A remark by Pötzl (1924) appeared to support a partial dissociation between fantastic confabulation and anosognosia for the memory impairment. He had seen 'Anton's symptom' (anosognosia) in many patients who became blind as a result of optic nerve atrophy due to tabes dorsalis, an intermediate stage of syphilis. When such patients went on to have progressive paralysis with dementia, they would often deny being blind and invent visual experiences, especially upon suggestive questioning. Pötzl commented: 'Even in [progressive] paralysis, [Anton's] symptom is independent of the degree of the disorder of memory and learning.

In my experience, it is also independent of the degree of manic excitation' (1924, p. 154). Pötzl's designation as 'manic excitation' corresponded to the fantastic confabulations that Kraepelin and Bleuler had described in such patients.

With regards to *behaviourally spontaneous confabulation*, even the interpretation of anecdotal cases is delicate. The outstanding characteristic of these patients is that they act according to currently inappropriate memories and that they produce confabulations which reflect their false concept of ongoing reality. The patients are not only unaware of the falseness of their ideas, but often even insist on their veracity; it is normally impossible to convince such a patient of true reality. Thus, with regards to the content of their false ideas and confabulations, there is no doubt that these patients do have anosognosia. In contrast, occasional patients are apparently aware of having a memory disorder. Mrs B (Chapter 1) acknowledged having a bad memory but nevertheless fiercely defended the rightness of her plans and imagined duties. The young woman with limbic encephalitis mentioned on p. 70—a lawyer—complained about the 'confusion in her memory' and often cried: 'Everything is mixed up in my head and I forget everything; I don't know what to do.' Despite this insight, she was convinced that the personnel on the ward were colleagues of hers and that she had to leave the unit to go to court. A young man who had suffered rupture of an anterior communicating artery aneurysm and was hospitalized in Bern indicated with no hesitation that he had been in Zurich (110 kilometres away from the hospital) in the morning. When asked whether he was sure about this, he acknowledged that the people had told him that he could not trust his memory: 'I am convinced and feel that I was in Zurich this morning [false idea], but now that you ask me, I realize that I do not know how I went there and how I came back; so, I might be wrong.' Thus, in the course of his hospitalization, this patient had become aware of his having a memory problem, even of having false memories. This insight, however, did not prevent him from trying to leave the unit that same afternoon in the conviction that he was to meet with his friends. He made the statement toward the end of his confabulatory stage.

It appears that in behaviourally spontaneous confabulation – similarly to hemispatial neglect and hemiplegia – the cognitive or mental components subject to anosognosia may vary. Thus, occasional behaviourally spontaneous confabulators are aware of having a severe defect of memory, maybe even of having false ideas, while at the same time totally lacking awareness of the falsehood of the thoughts that guide their behaviour.

In *conclusion,* anosognosia, the unawareness of disease, normally concerns distinct cognitive or somatic domains rather than disease in general. Accordingly, lesion sites and functional associations vary; there is no single brain area that is constantly affected in anosognosic patients. The main link between confabulations and anosognosia is of semantic nature, in that the term 'confabulation' has also been applied to the explicit verbal denial of illness. Such confabulations reflect subjects' false perception or interpretation of their current health status and living situation rather than falsifications of memory.

Anosognosia for memory impairment seems to be associated primarily with frontal and diencephalic lesions. Despite this anatomical concordance, a definite link between anosognosia and mnestic confabulations has never been established. Provoked confabulations (intrusions) and momentary confabulations are not necessarily associated with anosognosia for the memory deficit. Patients presenting behaviourally spontaneous confabulations – and behaving as if they had no memory problem – are always anosognosic regarding the falsehood of their ideas, but not necessarily regarding the presence of a memory deficit.

Summary

In this chapter, we have reviewed a number of disorders that have routinely been associated with confabulation: amnesia, disorientation, false recognition, paramnesic misidentification, and anosognosia. As it turns out, the relation between these disorders and the different forms of confabulation is quite inconsistent.

Provoked confabulations (intrusions) have no consistent association with amnesia, disorientation, or anosognosia. They can also be evoked in healthy subjects having no memory problem. A very powerful way of inducing specific provoked confabulations is the Deese-Roediger-McDermott (DRM) paradigm, in which subjects learn a series of semantically related words that together point to a target word – the 'lure' – which is not present in the list. Under this condition, healthy subjects very often produce the target word and also falsely recognize it. Other than that, there is no significant association between provoked confabulation and false recognition. In amnesic subjects, this effect tends to be weaker.

The more serious forms of confabulation have a more complex relationship. *Amnesia*, commonly considered a prerequisite for relevant confabulation, can be demonstrated in practically all patients with momentary, fantastic, or behaviourally spontaneous confabulation – provided amnesia is defined as impaired delayed free recall. By contrast, if amnesia is evaluated with a continuous recognition task, a conceptually very simple paradigm that only measures storage and recognition of information, then confabulation and amnesia dissociate. While severe confabulators, including behaviourally spontaneous confabulators, may have extremely severe amnesia with no appreciable explicit recognition capacity (Schnider *et al.* 2005a), occasional confabulators perform normally in such a task, indicating that they have no difficulty in storing information. In other words: severe confabulation does not require a gap in memory!

Disorientation, which has also routinely been associated with confabulation, is not necessary for momentary confabulation to occur, possibly not even for fantastic confabulation. Conversely, there is a very close association between behaviourally spontaneous confabulation and disorientation: behaviourally spontaneous confabulators probably always have a measurable deficit of orientation. As we will see in Chapter 8, in many patients, these two disorders may indeed have the same mechanism. But disorientation is also significantly associated with amnesia in that severe amnesia predicts disorientation. Conversely, even the combination of severe disorientation and amnesia does not reliably predict confabulation.

False recognition as emerging in ordinary memory tasks is not normally associated with any form of confabulation. However, under specific experimental conditions, which require the ability to sort out among a series of familiar items those that pertain to the current moment, patients with behaviourally spontaneous confabulation fail. Under such conditions, they have increased false recognition, although in other conditions, they have no such increased tendency. The experimental context leading up to this finding and its neurobiological foundation will be the main topic of chapter 8.

Paramnesic misidentification syndromes – déjà-vu, Capgras, Fregoli, intermetamorphosis, and reduplicative paramnesia for place – are mostly modality-specific. Even though they are accompanied by false statements that may be considered momentary confabulations, they have no consistent association with mnestic momentary confabulations reflecting falsification of memories. There is even less of an association with behaviourally spontaneous confabulation: paramnesic misidentification normally is not accompanied by acts emanating from currently inappropriate ideas. Conversely, however, behaviourally spontaneous confabulators typically present features of paramnesic misidentification: They confuse the hospital with their home and often misidentify people according to their falsely perceived reality. A plausible interpretation is that the mechanism causing behaviourally spontaneous confabulation is also one among different mechanisms of paramnesic misidentification. In contrast to these reduplicative phenomena for places and people, the other forms of paramnesic misidentification (déjà-vu, Capgras, Fregoli, intermetamorphosis) are not part of behaviourally spontaneous confabulation.

The link between mnestic confabulation and *anosognosia* is not consistent. Anosognosia – the unawareness of disease – is highly modular. It encompasses many disturbances that dissociate from each other both regarding the aspect of disease that patients are unaware of and their anatomical bases. Similar to paramnesic misidentification, anosognosic patients make objectively false statements – confabulations – about an incorrectly identified situation, in this case, their current health status. False statements about the past or future, which characterize mnestic confabulations, are not an essential part of anosognosic confabulation unless patients are in a confusional state where both disorders may coincide. Anosognosia does not predict mnestic confabulations. Inversely, mnestic confabulations do not require anosognosia. *Momentary confabulations* may also occur in patients who are fully aware of their memory impairment and suffer from it. The relation with *behaviourally spontaneous confabulations* is more subtle. At first sight, all of these patients show striking lack of insight into their memory impairment. They are consistently unaware of the falsehood of their inappropriate thoughts and plans. However, some patients may be aware of having a memory impairment, rarely even of having false memories. This insight does not protect them from acting according to their false ideas. The observation that anosognosia for impaired memory is particularly frequent after frontal and diencephalic damage – similar to many instances of significant confabulations – may be explained by anatomical proximity and partial overlap of the lesions causing the two disorders.

Chapter 6

Normal false memories

The confabulations discussed in the previous chapters occur almost exclusively in the context of brain disease. To conclude from this that falsifications of memory and confabulatory phenomena require a sick brain would be erroneous. False memories, even those held with full conviction, also occur in healthy people and constitute one of the 'sins of memory' (Schacter 2001). Indeed, an immense literature on false memories has accrued over many decades (Brainerd and Reyna 2005), in particular with regards to their impact on eyewitness testimony (Loftus 1979/1996). Amazingly, with a few exceptions, this literature has gone unnoticed in the clinical realm of confabulation. Conversely, even exhaustive reviews on normal false memories (Brainerd and Reyna 2005) have made their case without any substantial reference to the clinical literature on confabulation.

It would be beyond the scope of this book to bridge the gap between these two fields of research and to provide an in-depth review of normal false memories. Nonetheless, a brief review of normal false memory and a comparison with confabulation in brain disease is interesting, all the more so that some theories have been proposed to explain all types of memory falsifications.

False memory in the DRM paradigm

Under certain conditions, human memory becomes the victim of its own associative power. One of the most powerful paradigms to induce false memories is the Deese-Roediger-McDermott (DRM) paradigm, which we have already seen on page 157f. Roediger *et al.* (2001) presented 55 lists of 15 words (e.g., door, glass, pane, shade, ledge, sill, house, open, curtain, frame, view, breeze, sash, screen, shutter), each of them being associated with a target word not present in the list (e.g., window). When healthy subjects learn such lists of words and later are asked to recall the lists, there is a high probability that they will produce the target words – the lures. Likewise, when presented with lists of words containing the presented words, the lures, and new words, healthy subjects are likely to falsely recognize the lures, as if they had been presented on the studied lists. Subjects are typically as convinced about the lures' presence as about the true words' presence in the word lists (Roediger and McDermott 1995).

Roediger *et al.* (2001) found that the probability of false production of the lure words significantly correlated with the backward associative strength, that is, the associative connections from the study words to the lure items. In addition, there was a significant, albeit weaker, negative correlation between the veridical recall of the words contained in the lists and the production of the lures. Conversely, the frequency of the target words in general language or the concreteness of the words were not critical. Thus, it appears that normal human memory is particularly prone to produce false memories, held with conviction, when the original pieces of information fail to be remembered with precision but convey the gist indicative of another piece of information, which has not originally been presented.

The psychological variables of the DRM effect have been explored in countless studies. Schacter and co-workers explored its *neuroanatomical basis* in a series of studies (Schacter *et al.* 1996b, 1997; Cabeza *et al.* 2001). The most compelling finding – from this author's perspective – was that there was very little difference in brain activation between the recognition of true items (contained in the word lists) and false items (lures); differences were discrete and varied between the studies (Schacter and Slotnick 2004). In an analysis of evoked potentials, Düzel *et al.* (1997) found very similar electrocortical responses when subjects correctly recognized the truly presented words and when they falsely recognized the lures. A recent imaging study with the same logic but using abstract designs yielded a similar result: False recognition of designs that were similar, but not identical with previously presented designs elicited similar patterns of neuronal activity as the originally presented designs (Garoff-Eaton *et al.* 2006). Interestingly, false recognition of items that were clearly distinct from the studied items induced activity in language-processing regions. The overwhelming impression then is that the false memories induced in these studies were associated with highly similar brain activation as the true memories. The discomforting conclusion is that the human brain, with its associative power, may create false memories that have the same apparent veridicality and much the same neurophysiological underpinnings as true memories.

Flashbulb memories

Some readers might possibly dismiss the false memories induced by the DRM paradigm as the product of an artificial laboratory experiment, irrelevant to autobiographical memory. So, let us examine the other extreme type of memory, those crystal clear memories that we all have about very special, personally significant events: the birth of a child, graduation from university, or public events such as marriages of royal celebrities, the sudden death of famous people, or disasters. Many people have strong, vivid, and seemingly precise memories about the circumstances in which they experienced or learned about such events. Brown and Kulik (1977) introduced the term *flashbulb memories* to denote the 'memories for the circumstances in which one first learned of a very surprising and consequential (or emotionally arousing) event' (p. 73). The prime event of their study was the assassination of President John F. Kennedy, an event they compared with the memories of the assassinations of other political and civil rights leaders. The occurrence of flashbulb memories was clearly influenced by the ethnic group to which the test subjects belonged. The authors concluded that a high level of surprise and consequentiality, perhaps also emotional arousal, determined the likelihood that an event would be stored as a flashbulb memory. Innumerable studies in the aftermath of many dramatic public events have thereafter refined the concept of flashbulb memories. The intensity of initial emotional reactions (Pillemer 1984), together with the importance attached to an event (Conway et al. 1994) emerged as the main determinants of flashbulb memories.

The terrorist attacks of 11 September 2001 constituted an event having all these qualities. Many of us know precisely what they were doing and who they were with when they heard about the attacks. Flashbulb memories emanating from this event – definitely the most dramatic event in recent history – have been shown to be long-lasting and very consistent over prolonged periods and in diverse cultures (Curci and Luminet 2006). Sharot *et al.* (2007) recently found that subjects who had been close to the site of the attacks had more emotionally enhanced, vivid recollections three years later than subjects who had been at more distant sites. When retrieving memories for the event after three years, the subjects close to the site had stronger activation of the amygdala in functional imaging than the distant group. The authors concluded that close personal experience was a critical parameter for the formation of intense flashbulb memories.

Even memories of such an event are not impervious to distortion. A personal experience exemplifies this. In a discussion with friends five years after the event, everyone of us recalled numerous details about that day, which were highly consistent among the discussants – with one exception: one of us firmly believed that it was about 10.30 a.m. when we heard the news. In this case, counterevidence was easy to provide: Because of the time lag of six hours between New York and Switzerland, it was obviously already mid-afternoon in Switzerland when we heard the news. It is very likely that the TV pictures diffused for days and weeks after the attacks had transformed this person's memory. Pictures have indeed been found to be very strong inducers of false memories (Loftus 1979/1996). The observation, albeit anecdotal, shows that seemingly precise memories about highly salient events, even when held with strong conviction, may not be correct.

It is likely that events with less of an impact than the terrorist's attacks may induce flashbulb memories that are less stable. Schmolck *et al.* (2000) asked college students three days after the 'not guilty' verdict in the O.J. Simpson trial about the circumstances in which they had heard the news. O.J. Simpson, a football star and actor, was accused of murdering his wife and her friend. The trial was frequently televised, and many spectators expected a verdict different from the jurors'. When the college students in Schmolck *et al.*'s study were again questioned after 15 months, 50 per cent of their recollections of how they learned about the verdict, where they were at the time, how their initial feeling was, etc., were still highly accurate, and only 11 per cent contained major errors or distortions. At that time, rehearsal, interest, and strength of opinion were all predictive of accuracy. When questioned for the third time after 32 months, only 29 per cent of their recollections were highly accurate, whereas more than 40 per cent contained major distortions. As in previous studies, the strength of the emotional reaction when first hearing the verdict was the only predictor of recollective accuracy at 32 months. Clearly, the intensity of this event cannot be compared to the terrorists' attack of 11 September and the memories emanating from it were certainly not as vivid, but the study showed that autobiographical memories may undergo major distortion. Although accuracy scores significantly correlated with confidence ratings, there were also many individuals with low accuracy scores but high confidence in their recollections (Schmolck *et al.* 2000). Thus, being convinced about the veracity of an autobiographical memory does not guarantee its correctness.

How to manipulate eyewitnesses

The production of objectively false memories has had the most dramatic consequences in the realm of eyewitness testimony, as documented in a rich literature accumulated over more than 100 years (Loftus 1979/1996). False statements may not necessarily reflect failures of memory but may result from false or inaccurate perception (Loftus 1979/1996; Wells and Olson 2003; Brainerd and Reyna 2005). The time a witness is exposed to an event, the saliency of significant details, but also expectations and ethnic biases have a striking impact on what a witness perceives or believes they have perceived. No one is protected from false perception: Neither high intelligence nor professional experience reliably improves the registration of details under the stress of observing a criminal act (Loftus 1979/1996).

For our discussion of false memories, it is interesting to look at the circumstances under which the content of, or conviction about, memories may be distorted. This may happen in diverse situations:

1. the type of questioning may significantly alter the way in which we recollect and report our memories;

2. memories may be altered by information received after an event;

3. it is even possible to implant memories of events that never happened.

A number of studies demonstrated how the phrasing of questions influences responses. For example, Harris (1973) found that the question 'How long was the movie?' elicited 30 per cent higher estimates than the question 'How short was the movie?' Loftus and Palmer (1974) showed a film of an automobile accident to 45 subjects. The critical question was: 'About how fast were the cars when they hit each other?' Some subjects were asked this question. For others, the word 'hit' was replaced by 'smashed, collided, bumped, or contacted'. Subjects responding to the 'smashed' version estimated the speed at 40.8 mph, those responding to the 'contacted' version estimated it at 30.8 mph, with the other versions in between (collided, 39.3 mph; bumped, 38.1 mph; hit, 34.0 mph).

Questions such as these implicitly suggest information about an event that is likely to modify the memory of the event. The influence of *post-event information* has been explored in numerous studies. A few examples may illustrate this aspect. In a classic experiment, Loftus and co-workers presented 30 slides depicting a simulated traffic accident to almost 200 subjects (Loftus 1979/1996, 1992). One of the slides showed a car in front of a stop sign. Immediately after studying all slides, subjects answered a series of questions, one of which was critical: 'Did another car pass the red Datsun while it was stopped at the stop sign?' Half of the subjects were asked this question, for the other half, the words 'stop sign' were replaced by 'yield sign'. Twenty minutes after completing the questionnaire, subjects were shown pairs of slides from which they had to select the one they had seen before. The critical pair contained two slides depicting the car stopped either at a stop sign or a yield sign. As it turned out, significantly more subjects who had been asked the critical question with the words 'yield sign' now chose the photograph containing the yield sign. A simple question had transformed their memory of what they had seen during the slide presentation.

Feedback may profoundly influence the conviction about a retrieved memory. Wells and Bradfield (1998) showed a video of a man entering a store to students.

After viewing the video, they were informed of the fact that the man entering the store murdered a security guard moments later. They were then asked to identify the man from a photospread, that is, a series of photographs. Unbeknown to them, the real culprit was absent from the photospread. Under such conditions, normal subjects have a high tendency to select a person (Wells and Olson 2003). In this experiment, too, every participant made a false identification. The critical part of the experiment then followed. After the false identification, the experimenter gave either confirming feedback ('Good. You identified the actual suspect'), or disconfirming feedback ('Actually, the suspect was number ...'), or no feedback. A short time later, the participants answered a number of questions. Amazingly, the subjects who had received the confirming feedback not only inflated their recollection of how confident they were at the time of making their choice, they also had a higher estimate of their view of the culprit and their ability to make out details of his face. Notably, they also had a higher estimate of their ability to easily pick him out of a real line up of suspects and they had greater willingness to testify. A follow-up experiment, in which the culprit was actually shown in a video-taped line up, demonstrated that retrospective certainty was particularly inflated for inaccurate eyewitnesses (Bradfield *et al.* 2002) – quite an uncomfortable prospect for suspects.

The list of *suggestive procedures* in criminal investigation is long (Brainerd and Reyna 2005). It ranges from seemingly harmless behaviours such as the insistence on a yes-no response, the encouragement to fill in pertinent information, or the confirmation of responses to obviously manipulative interventions such as punishment or reward for information, lying about evidence, or the provision of background information about a suspect. Such procedures are particularly efficacious if the memory of an event is inaccurate to begin with or has faded away with the passage of time and when the manipulative information is compatible with the subject's own recollection (Loftus 1979/1996). Thus, the way in which one perceived an event, is questioned, has thought, and answered questions about it can strikingly alter the content of a memory and the conviction about its veracity.

Even the awareness of the fact that one is merely guessing in response to questions does not protect one from creating false memories. Ackil and Zaragoza (1998) asked children in first or third/fourth grade and college students to watch an eight-minute movie depicting the adventures of two brothers at a summer camp. Immediately after watching the movie, participants were asked a series of questions. Some questions suggested elements that had not occurred in the movie: 'The chair broke and Delaney fell on the floor. Where was Delaney bleeding?' In the video, Delaney had fallen off a chair, but clearly had not bled or hurt himself. Half of the participants were told to answer only those questions for which they were certain of the response. The other participants were told to provide an answer to every question and to guess if they did not know the answer; that is, they were pushed to confabulate. One week later, participants had another interview, in which they were asked to indicate for each element whether they had actually seen it in the movie or whether they had only talked about it. As it turned out, the participants who had been asked to guess if they did not know the answers, falsely attributed a high proportion of confabulated items to the video, that is, they thought they had actually seen them in the video. This effect was much stronger in the first graders than in the college students. In a follow-up study with undergraduates, Zaragoza *et al.* (2001) additionally tested the effect of feedback to confabulated responses, which was either confirmatory (e.g., 'That's right, "knee" is the correct answer') or neutral (e.g., 'knee, ok'). When interviewed one week later, subjects attributed significantly more confabulated items to the video, on which they had received confirmatory feedback. There was another interesting finding: Items which subjects had verbally resisted (e.g., 'He wasn't bleeding' or 'I did not see that'), were attributed falsely less often to the movie, but only when the feedback had been neutral. When the feedback had been confirmatory, even verbal resistance in initial questioning had no significant protective effect against false attribution to the movie. After four to six weeks, participants freely recalled 13 per cent of their forced confabulations in the neutral condition and 27 per cent in the confirmatory condition as having occurred in the movie.

The studies mentioned so far explored the manipulation of details and the introduction of fictive elements into the memory of events, but it appears that it is even possible to plant memories of completely invented events. Loftus (1997) asked 18- to 53-year-old individuals to describe four events from their childhood. Three of the events were true, based on information obtained from a close relative. A fourth event, by contrast, was an invented story describing how the subject got lost in a shopping mall around the age of five. Subjects received a booklet containing a detailed one-paragraph description of the event. They were asked to write down what they remembered about the event or to indicate that they did not remember it. One to two weeks later, subjects were again interviewed with the indication that their memories would be compared with those of a relative. Amazingly 25 per cent of the subjects now fully or partially remembered the false event.

Photographs appear to be particularly strong stimuli to create false memories. Wade *et al.* (2002) interviewed 20 persons between the age of 18 and 28 years about four childhood events depicted on photographs. However, one of the photographs was fake, a montage showing the test subject at the age of four to eight years having a hot air balloon ride. Subjects were interviewed on three occasions, which were separated by three to seven days. Whereas the subjects recalled information about more than 90 per cent of the true events, no subject immediately reported memories of the false event when shown the doctored photo initially. Subjects were encouraged to think about the events during and after the interviews. At the end of the third interview, 50 per cent of the subjects recalled the false event either partially or clearly, claiming to remember at least some details of a hot air balloon ride during childhood. Even though the result was impressive, it is interesting to note that confidence ratings for the 'recalled' false event were comparable to the non-recalled true events and on average much lower than for the recalled true events. Thus, in this study, the subjects did not develop high confidence in the planted childhood memory.

Normal false memory and pathological confabulation

The foregoing paragraphs have documented that normal memory has its weaknesses. Memory is never a perfect, let alone objective, rendition of an event or an experience. Memories undergo modifications, making it difficult at times to distinguish between true and imagined experiences. Kraepelin put it this way:

> During storage, the memory regularly undergoes transmutation under the influence of earlier and subsequent experiences ... The feeling of certainty by no means protects from such illusions. Even free inventions may take the form of [real] memories.

> Kraepelin (1921, p. 4)

Almost one hundred years of research have confirmed this statement. The preceding paragraphs have shown that any person with a normal memory may retrieve objectively false memories and make false statements about previous events – anyone may confabulate!

In this sense, normal false memories share a significant quality with most pathological confabulations: they are false statements about past events. Nonetheless, apart from obvious differences in the intensity of the false statements, very significant differences in the mode of evocation of the false memories emerge. While suggestive questioning may indeed influence the way in which healthy people report their memories – and further distort a memory – neutral questioning does not induce blatantly false memory recall in healthy subjects. Neutral questioning is the safest way of obtaining reliable responses from healthy subjects (Loftus 1979/1996; Brainerd and Reyna 2005). By contrast, in all forms of pertinent confabulation – momentary, fantastic and behaviourally spontaneous confabulation – the false statements occur in response to neutral questions such as 'Where have you been this morning? What will you do this afternoon?'

In most situations described in the foregoing paragraphs, in which healthy subjects produced false memories or had false convictions about them, the memories first had to be manipulated or planted. This happened by providing the gist of some target information (the DRM paradigm), by having subjects imagine events, or by manipulating post-event processing, for example in the form of comments on the quality of the answers given by the subjects. Even suggestive questions may conceivably first distort the memory of an event, before it is recollected. The subjects then reproduce the manipulated or induced memories, sometimes with strong, sometimes with moderate, conviction.

There is no evidence that behaviourally significant confabulations have to be planted first. It is true that some patients incorporate elements of events experienced after the onset of brain disease into their confabulations. This feature is by no means universal. In most patients, the overwhelming mass of confabulations is composed of pieces of information acquired before, often long before, the onset of brain disease (see Chapters 1 to 4).

These observations suggest that normal false memories and pathological confabulations might not only differ in severity, but also in their mechanism. A possible interpretation is that most normal false memories result from the normal association of information received during the storage and updating of an event record. This interpretation is fully compatible with current theories on how memories get consolidated (Squire and Alvarez 1995; Nadel and Moscovitch 1997; Dudai 2004; Frankland and Bontempi 2005; Moscovitch *et al.* 2005). It is possible that at times, monitoring processes during retrieval may help to detect and correct false memories (Johnson and Raye 1981; Johnson *et al.* 1993), especially when there is a marked discrepancy between the retrieved memory and new information (Loftus 1979/1996). However, in most described instances, false memories were plausible and preserved the general meaning. It is then difficult to imagine a mechanism by which the brain might retrospectively verify the exactness of a to-be-retrieved memory. In most retrieval situations, monitoring processes may simply have no substrate to work on; there is just the memory trace, which may be partly correct, partly manipulated. There is no need to invoke inefficient or defective monitoring processes at retrieval. Thus, the proposition made here is that most normal false memories are generated during the encoding and re-encoding, rather than the retrieval of memories.

In contrast, significant pathological confabulations probably result from defective processes during the evocation of memories; newly encoded information may modulate, but is not required for the occurrence of confabulations.

Accordingly, very severe confabulation may occur in patients with extremely severe amnesia who have no demonstrable storage capacity, such as Mrs B. (Chapter 1). As discussed in the previous chapter (p. 157f.), the amnesia that most of these patients have may actually protect them from one of the most powerful methods to induce normal false memories, the DRM paradigm (Schacter and Slotnick 2004).

Summary

It has been established that false memories also occur in healthy people and are sometimes held with strong conviction. Even without explicit manipulation, memories for events may undergo significant transformation. Flashbulb memories – the memories for the circumstances in which one first learned of a personally engaging event – appear to be relatively protected from distortions, although modification of significant elements over time has been reported.

Falsifications of memory are of particular importance to eyewitness testimony. Suggestive questioning may modify the way in which memories are reported and may induce new distortions of memories. Weakly established memories are particularly vulnerable. Much research has shown that it is possible, and actually quite easy, to implant fictive elements into the record of an event and to manipulate the conviction subjects hold in their memories.

An analysis of eliciting circumstances suggests that normal false memories mainly result from normal physiological processes at encoding, processes associating the pieces of information constituting the memory of an event. There is no ostensible need to invoke defective processes during the retrieval of memories. Hence, normal false memories might have a different mechanism than pathological confabulations, which mostly reflect erroneous compositions of memories stored before the onset of brain disease.

Chapter 7

Mechanisms of confabulation

The question of whether the different confabulatory phenomena and memory distortions reflect independent disorders or different manifestations of a common underlying disorder – the topics of Chapters 3, 5, and 6 – has mostly remained a matter of opinion rather than data-driven debate. Many theoreticians assumed that the different confabulations and normal false memories represented different flavours of a common disorder and proposed hypotheses that – supposedly – explained all confabulatory phenomena. I hope that by now, the reader has become suspicious of such generalizations and shares the idea that there is simply too much evidence in support of a separation between different forms of memory falsifications – that these falsifications dissociate from each other, have different anatomical bases, and can constitute normal or pathological thought processes.

In this chapter, we enter the real battlefield of confabulation research: the dispute over the mechanism or mechanisms of confabulations.

Many recent authors have listed all theories on the same level – with no discussion of their empirical basis – and implied that they pertained to every disorder called 'confabulation'. Such an approach should be justified, all the more so since it runs counter the current developments in neuroscience and medicine that attempt to analyse cognitive and disease mechanisms in increasingly minute detail and to sort out specific mechanisms.

There is no reason not to apply the same rigour to mental failures, such as confabulations. After all, momentary, fantastic, and behaviourally spontaneous confabulations reflect disease states that normally require some kind of medical or neuropsychological intervention. Some forms of confabulations might profit from rehabilitation that would be counterproductive in another form. Some forms might profit from medication, others not. Thus, the question of mechanisms is more than an intellectual game and deserves a critical, scientifically solid approach.

The goal of this chapter is to present the current theories on confabulation and to analyse their scientific underpinnings. Thus, the theories will be scrutinized regarding the following criteria:

- *Field of application*: What forms of confabulation does a theory try to explain: specific forms of confabulation or all confabulations, with or without normal false memories?

- *Empirical basis*: Is the theory based on an experimental procedure with proven specificity for the types of memory falsifications that the theory covers? Has the experimental procedure been used in controlled studies comparing subjects with the discussed memory falsifications and appropriately matched non-confabulating patients?

- *Concurrent evidence*: Is the experimental procedure sufficiently specific to guide the exploration of the proposed mechanism's neurobiological validity? For example, have imaging studies using the experimental procedure provided concurrent evidence that the mechanism in healthy subjects depends on the brain areas whose damage produces the type of memory falsification to which the theory refers?

As we saw in Chapter 2, confabulation has always prompted speculations about its mechanism (Table 2.1). In the early days, these speculations were derived from careful clinical observation – the common approach to cognitive disorders at the time – rather than experimental evidence. Clinical manifestations of confabulation have not changed, and so many modern theories reiterate the ideas of the old masters. It will be interesting to see in the following paragraphs the ways in which the modern theories have refined the old ideas.

Gap-filling

The idea that confabulating patients simply try to fill gaps in their memory is as old as the interest in confabulation (Table 2.1). Bonhoeffer (1901) proposed this mechanism for momentary confabulations, which served the purpose of avoiding embarrassment. He did not invoke this mechanism to explain more fantastic confabulations (Chapter 2, p. 22). Van der Horst (1932) later shared this opinion and also restricted the gap-filling idea to momentary confabulations. Pick (1905), who made no distinction between forms of confabulation and normal memory distortions, made gap-filling a part of his definition of confabulations. As we saw in Chapter 2 (p. 27f.), his concept was quite sophisticated; he characterized gap-filling as a physiological mechanism akin to the filling of the blind spot in vision (Pick 1921). Nonetheless, confabulations would only occur if there was also increased suggestibility. Other authors, like Kraepelin (1909), were less delicate and proclaimed gap-filling as the one and only mechanism underlying confabulations (Table 2.1). The idea that confabulating patients try to cover up lacunas in memory to avoid embarrassment still appears in a number of present-day references (American Psychiatric Association 1994), neuropsychiatry textbooks, and in medical teaching.

Despite the continued attractiveness of the gap-filling account, there is no controlled evidence in favour of it. As far as the idea has been tested, data failed to support it.

We have already encountered the study by Mercer *et al.* (1977), who were among the first to formally explore suggestibility and the tendency of confabulators to fill gaps in memory (Chapter 3, p. 67f.). They found that severe confabulators had no increased tendency over mild confabulators or non-confabulators to respond to questions which normally drew an 'I don't know' response. Although no details regarding the patients' behaviour in everyday life were given, the confabulations explored in this study were probably of the elaborate momentary type. Thus, momentary confabulation, which is certainly the type most authors referred to, cannot simply be explained by a tendency to fill gaps in memory.

This study also explored the role of suggestibility. At the end of the test, patients were again asked three questions for which they had given an 'I don't know' response before with the indication that the response had not been recorded. This suggestive procedure did not prompt severe confabulators more than mild confabulators to produce confabulated responses.

We explored the tendency to fill gaps with regards to provoked confabulations (intrusions) and behaviourally spontaneous confabulation (Schnider *et al.* 1996b). Fifteen amnesic subjects with diverse lesions and aetiologies were tested. Their common characteristic was that they all had severely impaired free recall in verbal memory testing. Five of these patients were behaviourally spontaneous confabulators; ten were non-confabulating amnesics (no momentary, fantastic, or behaviourally spontaneous confabulations). As already reported in Chapter 3 (p. 60f., Figure 3.1), provoked confabulations were evenly distributed across these two patient groups. Subjects responded to a questionnaire containing 30 questions of general knowledge. Ten questions referred to famous personalities, ten to geographic names, and ten to object and animal knowledge. Unbeknownst to the subjects, half of the questions in each category covered real items ('Who is Prince Charles? Where is Parma? What is an oboe?'), whereas 15 questions referred to non-existent items (Who is Princess Lolita? Where is Dutchinson? What is a vibrasse?). For these latter items, there was no doubt that subjects did have a gap in memory. The interest of the task was to examine whether confabulating patients had an increased tendency to answer these questions.

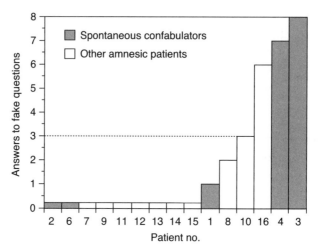

Figure 7.1 Gap-filling. The illustration shows the number of questions relating to non-existent items that behaviourally spontaneous confabulators (dark columns) and other, similarly severe amnesic patients (white columns) answered (total 15 questions). There was no statistically significant difference between the groups. The numbering of patients ('Patient no.') is concordant with the numbers used in Figure 3.1.

The result was negative for both types of confabulations (Schnider *et al.* 1996b). We found that provoked confabulations did not correlate with the tendency to fill such gaps in memory (Spearman's Rho, 0.18). Similarly, the number of answered fake questions (confabulated responses) had no predictive value for the distinction between behaviourally spontaneous confabulators and other amnesics. Figure 7.1 shows that two of five behaviourally spontaneous confabulators did not answer any fake question, whereas two produced many confabulated responses, similar to an otherwise non-confabulating amnesic patient. The groups did not statistically differ.

Thus, neither provoked nor behaviourally spontaneous confabulations reflect an indiscriminate tendency to fill gaps in memory. The negative result may be somewhat surprising with regards to provoked confabulations, as intrusions might intuitively reflect such a tendency. We will see below (p. 212) that the desire to perform well in a task may indeed contribute to the risk of producing intrusions. In contrast, the negative result comes as no surprise with regards to behaviourally spontaneous confabulation. Apart from the fact that spontaneous confabulators need not even have a gap in memory (pp. 148ff.), it is inconceivable how an increased tendency to fill gaps in memory might explain the confusion of reality and strikingly inappropriate behaviour characterizing this syndrome (see for example Mrs B, Chapter 1).

Of course, negative group data do not exclude the possibility that singular patients do produce confabulations to cover up memory gaps to avoid embarrassment. Talland's (1965) remark about alcoholic amnesics may apply to other aetiologies, too: 'Amnesic patients are not all paragons of virtue. They are as apt as others to tell a deliberate lie'(p. 43). We have seen patients with very severe amnesia after bilateral medial temporal damage, who eventually responded to questions about their recent doings with vague but plausible answers, although they had no clue of what they had actually done. They were fully aware of their amnesia. They would not insist on the veracity of their momentary confabulations. Clearly, they had developed a strategy to avoid being embarrassed by questions they could not answer. Occasionally, patients seem to resort to gap-filling as a way of dealing with what they recognize to be implausible scenarios or inconsistencies in their knowlege. Notwithstanding such single cases, in which gap-filling appears to be the obvious explanation for momentary confabulations, controlled data from groups of patients have established that gap-filling is no generally valid account for confabulation.

Personality and motivation

In the original gap-filling account, memory impaired patients simply had the urge to fill the gaps in their memory. As we saw in Chapter 2, diverse authors pushed their interpretation beyond this neutral notion; gap-filling reflected a specific personality pattern and became a rewarding behaviour in its own right. Williams and Rupp (1938) included 'a particular personality pattern' – characterized by a delicate balance between intraversion and extraversion – in their definition of confabulation (Chapter 2, p. 30ff.). Flament (1957) considered fantastic confabulations as compensatory, in that they 'might not only compensate for a lacuna in memory but in part for a personal situation of inferiority and regression created in a general sense by the consequences of the trauma' (Flament 1957, p. 144). The evidence he provided in support of this idea was a woman who thought that she was ejected from a plane and had made a free fall of 1000 metres; in reality, she had suffered brain injury when falling from a horse (Chapter 2, p. 32). According to present-day norms, it is not evident in what way her fantasized landing on a cactus could be considered less humiliating than her real fall from a horse.

Diverse investigators have pursued the idea that confabulations serve the purpose of embellishing the real situation of a patient. Of course, there is no a priori reason to limit such an interpretation to mnestic confabulations. Weinstein (1987) suggested that confabulations had a positive, meaningful and motivational aspect in that they constituted a symbolic or metaphorical representation of the patient's current situation. In many instances, confabulations reflected a patient's need to be well. In Weinstein's concept, all forms of confabulation were thought to be due to motivational factors, with their content being determined by the nature of the patient's health problems (Weinstein 1987). This concept applied equally well to mnestic confabulations (Weinstein and Lyerly 1968), false statements in anosognosia (Weinstein and Kahn 1950; Weinstein and Kahn 1955) and paramnesic misidentification (Weinstein et al. 1952). Even though Weinstein's conclusions were based on a mass of clinical observations, he did not proceed to controlled testing of his hypothesis. Also, he attributed no significance to the lesion location for the occurrence of confabulations.

Even though none of these authors mentioned the work of Sigmund Freud or psychoanalysis, it is difficult to disregard a potential influence. Freud (1915/1976) introduced the idea of repression as a defense mechanism keeping information away from consciousness and serving 'no other motive and goal than the avoidance of unpleasure' (p. 114). Repression forms the axiomatic basis of analytical psychotherapy but remains a matter of vigorous debate among cognitive neuroscientists (Erdelyi 2006). Recent behavioural evidence demonstrated that healthy subjects could consciously suppress the normal formation of memories and attenuate their later retrieval (Anderson and Green 2001). Functional imaging showed that this type of suppression was associated with increased activity in a distributed network including, in particular, the dorsolateral prefrontal cortex, and with decreased activation of the hippocampus (Anderson et al. 2004). Even though it is easy to speculate on an association of repression with anosognosia, paramnesia, and confabulation, the association remains unproven. In particular, the concept would have difficulty in explaining the dissociation between these clinical phenomena.

Nonetheless, recent studies have taken up the idea that confabulations reflect 'wishful reality distortions'. Dalla Barba and Cipolotti (1990) suspected that the confabulations by their patient with an alcoholic Korsakoff psychosis 'substituted a lacking autobiographical mnestic trace … a strategy allowing the patient to retain some form of necessary autobiographical recall in order to maintain a self respect' (p. 533). The confabulations occurred only in response to questions, never spontaneously. Conway and Tacci (1996) described a 73-year-old woman who had suffered extensive traumatic brain injury with bilateral contusions of the anterior temporal lobes, the orbitofrontal cortex and bilateral dorsolateral prefrontal cortex. She had severe memory impairment, anosognosia, and a disinhibited conversational style. For many months, she produced confabulations when reciting events from her life, which she repeated in many conversations. Most confabulations related to the patient's family and appeared to excuse behaviour by relatives. One such false belief was that a young close relative had failed to obtain a particular position because his school had failed to forward documents. The authors concluded:

> The confabulations, then, serve the important purpose of providing a basis for [the patient's] explanations of her social environment. The explanations derived from the confabulations make more bearable the largely indifferent attitude of her relatives ... [The patient's] confabulations rewrite her personal history so that both the remote and recent past provide support for her in a difficult period when little external support is present.
>
> Conway and Tacci (1996, p. 333)

The last sentence of the article highlighted – perhaps unwittingly – the problem with such an explanation: 'The fantasies mistaken as memories served the psychodynamically useful purpose of protecting the self in a time of stress and isolation' (p. 337). Why were the fantasies mistaken as memories?

Fotopoulou *et al.* (2004) used a more standardized approach to explore the affective quality – the pleasantness – of confabulations produced by a 65-year-old man who had had surgical removal of an olfactory sheath meningeoma extending into the suprasellar region – an anatomical situation comparable to the craniopharyngeomas discussed in Chapter 3 (pp. 119ff.). One year after the operation, he was still severely amnesic and produced behaviourally spontaneous and provoked confabulations. The authors conducted twelve 'minimally guided' one-hour interviews with the patient and obtained 155 confabulatory statements, which they rated regarding their pleasantness. They found that the patient's confabulations contained significantly more pleasant statements than the confabulations that six healthy men had intentionally generated. The authors, therefore, concluded that motivational factors contributed in parallel with memory and executive deficits to the mechanism of confabulation.

An obvious difficulty with this study was the control group. Can intentionally produced false statements be compared to the confabulations that an amnesic patient produces in an honest attempt to retrieve memories? Another difficulty – or strength – of such an account is that it holds for all forms of confabulations, as previously shown by Weinstein and colleagues (Weinstein and Kahn 1950; Weinstein *et al.* 1952; Weinstein and Kahn 1955). Turnbull *et al.* (2004b), too, rated the confabulations of at least two of their three patients, who had suffered ACoA aneurysm rupture, as more pleasant than reality. Similarly, they found that confabulated places in published cases with reduplicative paramnesia were more pleasant than the real locations of the patients (Turnbull *et al.* 2004a). Given its general applicability to false statements, the idea of a positive emotional bias does not explain the specifics of the diverse forms of confabulations. With regards to confabulations of amnesic patients, it does not explain why the patients have false memories in the first place and then accept them as veridical.

If the positive emotional bias really exists, it might simply be a quality of confabulations reflecting a consequence of the lesion location. Many severe confabulators, in particular behaviourally spontaneous confabulators, have anterior limbic lesions (ventromedial–orbitofrontal area and vicinity). Such lesions often involve components of the brain's reward system. This extension might account for an emotional bias, including an unreflectedly positive, risk-taking attitude (Damasio 1994; LeDoux 1996; Rolls 1999; Bechara et al. 2000; Hornak et al. 2003). In this case, the degree of 'wishful reality distortion' should, of course, differ according to the type of confabulation and the causative lesion.

In *conclusion*, a positive emotional bias has repeatedly been reported in mnestic, mostly momentary confabulations and in confabulations associated with paramnesic misidentification and anosognosia. Particular personality patterns have been postulated but never well documented. The observation of a positive emotional bias itself needs to be confirmed. It is unclear whether such a bias – if it were confirmed – would constitute a causal factor contributing to the generation of confabulations or whether it simply constituted a quality of certain confabulations caused by lesions in areas which are also involved in the modulation of emotions.

Executive hypothesis

The insight that confabulation was not explained by memory failure alone but required additional mental impairments, dates back at least to Tiling (1892). Bonhoeffer (1901) was possibly the only one to postulate that one form of confabulation – momentary confabulations – required the preservation of a cognitive function: 'mental agility [*geistige Regsamkeit*].' Nowadays, the mental impairments invoked by Tiling are called frontal or executive dysfunctions, a term describing the failure of a vast array of capacities known to depend on intact frontal lobes. Executive functions encompass processes such as goal setting, the ability to maintain a mental set, to concentrate on a task but to change set when necessary, the ability to initiate an act but also to inhibit inappropriate behaviour (Fuster 1997). These processes are partly dissociable from one another both functionally and anatomically (Stuss et al. 2002). Processes monitoring the retrieval of memories have also been associated with the frontal lobes. They play such an important role in the discussion of confabulation that they will be treated in separate paragraphs.

The association between confabulation and severe executive failures has been described in numerous case reports (Baddeley and Wilson 1988; Papagno and Baddeley 1997). In some patients, the disappearance of severe confabulations was accompanied by marked improvement of executive functions despite persistent amnesia. The observation was taken to indicate a causal relation between confabulation and executive failures (Kapur and Coughlan 1980; Benson *et al.* 1996; Nys *et al.* 2004).

Even though the relation may have appeared particularly convincing in these cases, it is dangerous to generalize it. A first problem is that the vast majority of patients who have the combination of severe memory impairment and executive failures – as often happens after traumatic brain injury – do not markedly confabulate. This raises a second problem: the specificity of the account. Which are the precise executive failures that would be responsible for the confabulations: specific ones, a combination of some, or a generalized failure? Would different executive dysfunctions account for different forms of confabulation?

The answer to these questions can only come from properly controlled group studies. In the following, the available studies will be reviewed with reference to the different forms of confabulation.

As we saw in Chapter 4, *provoked confabulations* (intrusions) can occur in many diseases and do not seem to have a specific anatomical basis. So it does not appear very likely that all provoked confabulations emanating from the different diseases would result from similar executive dysfunction.

Cooper *et al.* (2006) explored the association between provoked confabulations and executive dysfunction in patients with mild dementia of the Alzheimer type. The patients first constructed a story describing a series of pictures and were asked a few minutes later to reproduce the story. The authors found that the number of intrusions in the delayed reproduction was associated with autobiographical memory impairment, but not with executive dysfunctions. Thus, in Alzheimer's disease of a specified – in this case, mild – degree, executive dysfunction did not predict provoked confabulations.

Cunningham *et al.* (1997) analysed story recall in a sample of 101 patients with miscellaneous brain diseases. Memory performances ranged from normal to severely impaired. Patients were then classified as high, low, and non-confabulators based on the ratio between confabulations and correct responses in the recall of a logical story. The authors found that high-confabulators were significantly more impaired than the other groups on six of the eight reported measures of memory performance. In comparison, they were more impaired on only two of nine measures of executive functioning (Trail making test, part A and B). Thus, on seven of the nine executive measures, there was no difference. Nonetheless, the authors suggested that their study provided 'support for the combined deficit model of confabulation with co-morbid impairments evident in both memory and aspects of executive functions' (Cunningham *et al.* 1997, p. 875). In view of the discrete difference between the groups and a classification procedure, which favoured the detection of more severe executive dysfunctions in the high confabulators (no matching of the groups on a pertinent measure), the study cannot be considered as having established a convincing link between provoked confabulations and executive dysfunction.

In a study already described in Chapter 3, Kopelman (1987) found that the intrusions that amnesic subjects made in story recall after brief intervals resembled those that healthy controls made after prolonged intervals. His suggestion, therefore, was that provoked confabulations reflected a normal response to a faulty memory. Our findings support this view (Schnider *et al.* 1996b). We tested the association between intrusions in a word list learning test – our measure of provoked confabulations – and verbal fluency (Thurstone and Thurstone 1963), figural fluency (Regard *et al.* 1982), and the Stroop colour-word interference task (Perret 1974). The patients had diverse aetiologies but were matched in the sense that they all had severely impaired free recall in verbal learning (same group as mentioned in Chapters 3 and 4; pp. 59ff., 140f.). To our surprise, we found that the number of intrusions positively correlated with verbal fluency and different measures of the verbal memory task (Schnider *et al.* 1996b). That is, provoked confabulations were associated with relatively better performance on the verbal fluency and memory tasks. Correlations with the other frontal measures also tended to support an association of intrusions with relatively better performance, although they fell short of significance. The result suggested that provoked confabulations (intrusions) in amnesic subjects might be the trade-off for increased item recollection from a defective memory and reflect the effort to perform well in the tasks. As seen above (pp. 205ff.), the patients' behaviour in this endeavour remained controlled; they would not indiscriminately respond to questions for which they had no clue of a response – they did not just try to 'fill gaps' in memory.

Diverse investigators suggested a link between *momentary confabulations* and executive dysfunction (Stuss *et al.* 1978; DeLuca 1993), but controlled evidence is scarce. A study by Fischer *et al.* (1995), which was already mentioned for its anatomical virtues in Chapter 4 (p. 91), appeared to provide such evidence. The authors studied nine patients who had suffered rupture of an ACoA aneurysm. Five patients produced elaborate, sometimes grandiose confabulations in an informal interview ('spontaneous confabulations' in the authors' diction), which would be considered elaborate momentary confabulations according to our classification. At least one of them was also a behaviourally spontaneous confabulator. Another group of four patients produced limited, often superficially plausible confabulations (termed 'provoked' by the authors), which would qualify as more discrete momentary confabulations according to our classification. The authors found that the five intense confabulators performed worse on all frontal executive tasks. Despite the small study group, the difference was statistically significant on half of the tasks. Even though the results were solid, the study is difficult to interpret. By including only patients with a specific pathology – in this case ACoA aneurysm rupture – any comparison between subgroups runs the risk of demonstrating differences in general disease severity rather than a specific mechanism of confabulation. As we saw in Chapter 4 (p. 91), the intense ('spontaneous') confabulators also had more extended lesions than the discrete confabulators. Even though the study showed that more extended brain damage after ACoA aneurysm rupture may be associated with more severe executive dysfunction and more pervasive confabulations, the result does not necessarily pertain to momentary confabulations in general.

Moscovitch and Melo's (1997) study had no such limitation. They asked severely amnesic patients with diverse aetiologies to produce autobiographical or historical events evoked by cue words. The authors found that the patients who produced high numbers of confabulations in this task were significantly more impaired on frontal executive tasks and measures of intelligence than non-confabulating amnesics. As the groups did not differ on other tests of memory and naming, the result indeed suggested a valid link between momentary confabulation and executive dysfunction in amnesic subjects, which did not simply reflect a more severe general cognitive impairment in the confabulators.

The association between *fantastic confabulation* and executive dysfunction has never been formally explored. In most acute diseases, fantastic confabulation probably only occurs in the early stage while patients are still in a confusional state (delirium). This state is characterized by severe executive failures. But executive dysfunction is not sufficient, and possibly not even necessary, for fantastic confabulations. As most clinicians know, the majority of patients with severe executive dysfunction, who are out of the confusional state, do not produce fantastic confabulations. Conversely, delusional ideas of psychotic (schizophrenic) patients, which would qualify as fantastic confabulations, need probably not be accompanied by severe executive failures. However, the question has never been formally addressed.

Finally, what about *behaviourally spontaneous confabulation*? Fischer *et al.* (1995) had at least one behaviourally spontaneous confabulator in their series, as evident from a case vignette. It might be suspected, then, that behaviourally spontaneous confabulation was associated with more impaired frontal executive functions. However, as mentioned before, the limitation to one focal pathology does not allow one to conclude on a generally valid association between executive dysfunction and confabulation.

Our study groups did not have this limitation, so that simple effects of lesion size could be excluded. The result was clear: in our studies, behaviourally spontaneous confabulators did not differ from non-confabulating amnesics on any of the tested frontal executive measures (Schnider *et al.* 1996b; Schnider and Ptak 1999). The same result arose when reviewing data obtained from 15 behaviourally spontaneous confabulators and 28 other amnesics, who had participated in our diverse studies: there was no hint of a significant difference between the groups on executive tasks.

Of course, the group of behaviourally spontaneous confabulators as a whole improved on frontal executive functions as they recovered from their confabulatory state (Schnider *et al.* 2000a); many other mental and bodily functions – deranged enzymes, broken bones etc. – improved over the same period. However the association between the course of confabulation and executive functions was not reliable in individual patients. Thus, in our group of patients, who were matched regarding the severity of the amnesia but not regarding the aetiology or lesion site, executive dysfunction neither predicted the occurrence nor followed the course of behaviourally spontaneous confabulation.

In *conclusion*, the association between confabulation and general executive dysfunction varies among the different forms of confabulation. This conclusion is not surprising since the notion of 'executive functions' encompasses diverse processes that are partly dissociable both anatomically and functionally. Provoked confabulations are more frequent in people having cognitive impairments. However in severe amnesia, they do not signal more severe executive dysfunction. Rather, they appear to reflect the patients' effort to recollect as much information as possible from their defective memory; the confabulations are the price to pay for increased item recollection. The severity of momentary confabulations is probably associated with the severity of frontal executive failures, but it is unclear whether this association is causal or whether it simply reflects the severity of general cognitive impairment. The associations of fantastic confabulations have never been formally explored. Behaviourally spontaneous confabulation has no significant association with frontal executive failures. If patient selection is not restricted to a single pathology, executive dysfunction predicts neither the occurrence nor the course of behaviourally spontaneous confabulation in amnesia.

Reality and source monitoring

Possibly the earliest interpretation of confabulations, which even preceded the gap-filling idea, was that the patients confused memories from different episodes in the past and confused the source of memories – that is, whether the memories originated from real or imagined events (Chapter 2, Table 2.1). Kraepelin (1886) attributed 'simple falsifications of memory' (fantastic confabulations) to a defect of the 'weapons distinguishing fantasy from reality.' Korsakoff (1889) attributed pseudo-reminiscences to an inability to decide whether memories related to real events, thoughts or dreams. Bonhoeffer (1901) thought that fantastic confabulations resulted from hallucinations taken as real memories. Other authors were more impressed by the temporal disorder within confabulations. Van der Horst (1932) has received much credit for his proposition that the loss of temporal tags of memories was responsible for productive confabulations – his term for intensive momentary, possibly also behaviourally spontaneous confabulations. However the idea had been advanced before: Tiling (1892) had already characterized 'false recollections' as an intermingling of remote and recent events.

These interpretations are as attractive nowadays as they were a century ago, although terminology has changed somewhat. A prominent theory interprets confabulations as a problem of 'reality or source monitoring'.

Reality monitoring refers to the process of distinguishing a past perception from a past act of imagination (Johnson and Raye 1981). *Source monitoring* encompasses – in addition to reality monitoring – the capacity to distinguish different sources of information and to specify the conditions under which a memory was acquired (e.g., the spatial, temporal, and social context of an event; the media and modalities through which it was perceived) (Johnson *et al.* 1993). Johnson and Raye (1981) distinguished three major categories of imaginations:

1. Re-representation, that is, information reactivated at a later time in the absence of the original external stimulus;

2. Co-temporal thoughts, that is, elaborative and associative processes that augment, breach, or embellish ongoing perceptual experience but are not necessarily part of the veridical representation of perceptual experiences; and

3. Fantasy, that is, novel combinations of information that produce imaginary events.

According to these authors, such internally generated memories differ from externally generated memories by less spatial and temporal contextual attributes, less sensory attributes, and fewer semantic details. Conversely, they have more operational attributes associated with them and coded in the memory trace.

The *source monitoring framework* (Johnson and Raye 1981; Johnson *et al.* 1993) proposes that the brain distinguishes between memories relating to real events and memories relating to imaginations on the basis of these qualities of memories. In addition, the brain uses more extended reasoning processes that take into account the content of particular memories and the relation to other knowledge available to a person, as well as a person's ability to reflect on their own memory, a capacity called metamemory.

The source monitoring framework was not only applied to confabulation, but also to normal memory capacities and failures, as they are relevant for old-new recognition or eyewitness testimony – e.g., the incorporation of fiction into the recollection of an event. In the latter cases, source monitoring was suggested to depend primarily on the information available from activated memory records and to rely on the quality of the information initially recorded about events (Johnson *et al.* 1993). By the way, this is also the conclusion we reached in the last chapter on normal false memories. Confabulations were suggested to be the consequence of a disruption in more extended reasoning processes (Johnson *et al.* 1993).

Our findings in Mrs M, who produced spontaneous, momentary, and provoked confabulations (pp. 57ff.), were entirely compatible with the source monitoring framework. She was unable to indicate when, where, and from whom she had learned information (Schnider *et al.* 1996a). Subsequent testing of additional amnesic patients revealed, however, that several non-confabulating amnesics had the same difficulty, too. We did not publish the data because at the same time, another experiment, which will be explained in Chapter 8, yielded far more specific results. Johnson *et al.* (1997) made a similar observation. They explored a patient who had suffered rupture of an ACoA aneurysm five months before. His confabulations were generally plausible and mainly concerned biographical events. He did not realize that he had had aneurysm rupture but believed that he had fallen and hit his head while standing outside and talking with a friend. The patient underwent a series of experimental tasks, and his performance was compared with that of three non-confabulating patients with frontal damage. In one task, two lists of eight stimuli were presented 30 minutes apart, followed two minutes later by a test in which subjects had to identify items that had been presented. In addition, they had to indicate whether the items had been in the first list or not. It turned out that the confabulating patient had no deficit in temporal discrimination in comparison to normal controls (and also in comparison with Mrs M, p. 58); his performance was significantly better than that of the non-confabulating patients with frontal damage. The experiment was performed four times with different stimuli (words, sentences, faces, paintings), each time with the same result. A different result was obtained in a task in which subjects had to identify the speaker (man or woman) from whom they had heard words just before. In this task, the confabulating patient was as impaired as the non-confabulating patients. Thus, the confabulating patient did not have more difficulty in these source monitoring tasks than non-confabulating patients with frontal damage.

Ciaramelli and Ghetti (2007) recently reported a similar finding. In their source memory task, patients had to indicate whether they had seen words in the upper or lower half of a screen and in red or green. Five behaviourally spontaneous confabulators and seven non-confabulating patients with similarly severe memory and executive failures had similar difficulty in this task.

These negative results are not so surprising. Indeed, numerous studies have documented a difficulty to indicate the temporal order and the context of previously presented information in non-confabulating amnesics and in non-amnesic patients with frontal lobe damage, who did not confabulate (Huppert and Piercy 1976; Hirst and Volpe 1982; Shimamura and Squire 1987; Bowers *et al.* 1988; Janowsky *et al.* 1989a; Milner *et al.* 1991; Shoqeirat and Mayes 1991; Parkin and Hunkin 1993; Kesner *et al.* 1994; Kopelman *et al.* 1997a; Thaiss and Petrides 2003). The conclusion from these studies is clear: the inability to indicate the time when in the past something happened and to indicate the source of this information is not specific for, and does not predict, confabulation. In other words, failure of conscious, elaborate source monitoring is a feature of confabulation, as documented in many patients, but it is not its cause.

This conclusion agrees with results from imaging experiments testing the explicit knowledge about source and temporal order of memories. Such tasks typically activated the lateral prefrontal cortex and other brain areas rather than the ventromedial—orbitofrontal area (Zorrilla *et al.* 1996; Cabeza *et al.* 1997; Johnson and Raye 1998; Nolde *et al.* 1998; Rugg *et al.* 1999), whose damage is often associated with confabulation. A possible exception was a study using positron emission tomography (PET), which showed right medial orbitofrontal activation while subjects retrieved the temporal order of previously experienced events, but not when they retrieved information about spatial context (Fujii *et al.* 2004). The specificity of this finding needs further exploration.

In reviewing their results, Johnson *et al.* (2000) suggested that

> Confabulation requires more than a deficit in feature information … It requires a
> failure in source attribution processes that evaluate the quality of the information

(i.e., that make one aware that information is pure) and that link belief and action to the quality of the information ... the specific reflective processes that are disrupted in confabulating patients and account for their memory distortions need more focal investigation.

Johnson et al. (2000, p. 398)

As we will see in Chapter 8, the failure of behaviourally spontaneous confabulators may indeed be interpreted as a source monitoring failure, but one relating to memories' relation with the present, rather than the past.

Memory reconstruction and monitoring

If there is one aspect on which virtually all students of pathological, mnestic confabulations agree, then it is the idea that confabulations emanate from some defect in the retrieval and reconstruction of memories. For some reason, the brain appears to produce incorrect memories and fails to check that they are false. 'Monitoring hypotheses' feature among the most prominent and influential current interpretations of confabulation. The core idea of these hypotheses is that the retrieval of memories proceeds through a series of processes – from the initiation of memory search to the verification of its content – leading to the production of a correct or a distorted memory.

Korsakoff's (1891) early idea that pseudo-reminiscences resulted from a defect in the unconscious association of ideas (Chapter 2, pp. 10ff.) is nowadays most prominently represented in Schacter *et al.*'s (1998a) *constructive memory framework*. The concept draws from other models on monitoring and remains the most far-reaching account, in that it includes both the construction of the original memory at encoding and the reconstruction of a memory at retrieval. At encoding, the linking together of features comprising a coherent representation of an episode is proposed as critical. Inadequate feature binding would result in source memory failure, that is, the inability to recollect how and when the fragments of a memory were acquired. The retrieval of memories is suggested to involve an initial stage of 'focusing', which leads to a refined description of the characteristics of the episode to be retrieved. Schacter *et al.* (1998a) suggested that poor retrieval focus could result in recollection of information that did not pertain to the target episode or might produce impaired recall of an episode's details. In the subsequent stage, according to these authors, 'a decision must be made about whether the information that is delivered to conscious awareness constitutes an episodic memory, as opposed to a generic image, fantasy, or thought' (p. 291). This phase would be controlled by 'a criterion setting process', which would allow the rememberer to consider perceptual vividness, semantic detail and other kinds of information for determining the origin of the retrieved pattern. The use of lax criteria in this phase would increase the risk of accepting images of fantasies or other internally generated information as evidence of external events that never happened. Thus, the critical processes would be feature binding and pattern separation during encoding plus focusing, pattern completion, and criterion setting during retrieval.

Within this concept, Schacter *et al.* (1998a) attributed false recognition in the DRM-paradigm (Chapter 6, pp. 193ff.) to a failure of pattern separation during encoding, leading to unacceptably high levels of overlap between item representations. The authors noted:

> It is also possible to explain false recognition of semantically related lures by appealing to the notion of 'implicit associative responses' – the idea that people overtly or covertly generate a non-presented lure word at the time of study in response to an associate.
>
> Schacter *et al.* (1998a, p. 295)

Pathological false recognition, as seen after frontal lobe lesions, would reflect a criterion-setting deficit at retrieval, which 'might stem from an inability to form an appropriate or focused description of the study episode. [Conversely,] it is also possible that … false recognition deficit results from failure to encode distinctive item attributes at study' (p. 298).

Schacter *et al.* (1998a) were careful when interpreting confabulation. Notably, they described the relationship between intrusions, confabulation, and false recognition as an unresolved issue and mentioned the heterogeneity of confabulation, which might cover personal experiences or factual knowledge and which might sometimes be bizarre. The authors insisted that 'theories of confabulation need to explain why incorrect information comes to mind in the first place (in addition to why subjects fail to recheck this incorrect information)' (p. 311). One possibility appeared to be that 'focussing processes are impaired in confabulating patients … Another possibility is that the process of pattern completion is itself dysfunctional' (p. 311). Based on anatomical considerations, the authors suggested that 'poor monitoring (resulting from frontal lobe damage) … is not sufficient to explain retrieval of incorrect information; some other functional deficit has to be present' (p. 311).

Thus, the constructive memory framework encompasses diverse stages of memory processing whose failure might be responsible for different forms of memory falsifications occurring in healthy and brain-damaged subjects. Although this model is often cited as a theory explaining confabulation, Schacter *et al.* (1998a) were in fact very careful in laying out alternative interpretations – all of them awaiting specific investigation – and avoided dogmatic statements. The constructive memory framework does not constitute a data-supported theory of confabulation but should be seen as a conceptual guide for the research on false memories, including confabulations.

In contrast to Schacter *et al.* (1998a), who mentioned poor monitoring as just one possible interpretation of confabulation, other authors were adamant about the role of poor monitoring. Mercer *et al.'s* (1977) article has often been cited for this view. As we have seen in previous paragraphs (pp. 65f. and 205), this study did not find evidence for increased suggestibility in severely confabulating patients as compared with mildly confabulating or non-confabulating amnesics. Without providing any additional data or explanation, the authors nevertheless concluded that 'confabulation can be attributed to the coincidence of four factors:

1. The patient believes that a response is required;

2. Accurate memory of the answer is lacking;

3. An over-learned and affectively significant response is available; and

4. The ability to monitor or self-correct is defective (Mercer *et al.* 1977, p. 433)

They then speculated about the nature of this monitoring process, and assumed that:

> under normal conditions, any potential answer about which the respondent is uncertain can be checked against a variety of indices: external information, previous responses in the session, canons of logic and plausibility, etc. ... The confabulator lacks at least the inclination, and quite possibly the capacity, to carry out such monitoring. Thus, a prepotent response erupts and is enunciated without hesitation.
>
> Mercer *et al.* (1977, p. 433)

Later clinical authors repeated this statement, but again without providing any specific data to support it (Shapiro *et al.* 1981). Benson *et al.* (1996) noted that their alcoholic patient, whom we have already seen in Chapter 4 (pp. 111f.), only confabulated during the period in which she failed on many frontal lobe tasks and thus concluded:

> Disordered self-monitoring (a frontal mechanism) appears to be responsible for confabulation. The absence of self-monitoring during the period of confabulation is striking, but as the patient becomes increasingly aware of the memory dysfunction, the level of confabulation decreases.
>
> Benson *et al.* (1996, p. 1242)

None of these authors suggested any specific way of testing 'impaired self-monitoring', with the possible exception of Mercer *et al.* (1977), who, in fact, found no increased suggestibility in confabulators. It appears that in this context, self-monitoring was essentially similar to executive functions. As we have seen above, executive dysfunction, or disorganized thinking in general, may possibly explain certain instances of confabulation, especially during confusional states and in dementia, but it is not a generally valid explanation for any type of confabulations.

Diverse psychological models posited specific monitoring defects in the genesis of confabulation. A particularly elaborate model on the control of recollection was proposed by Burgess and Shallice (1996). They asked eight healthy subjects to provide details about recent events that had occurred to them. The subjects were strongly encouraged to think about the events and to provide specifics. All responses were then classified according to 25 categories. Thus, elements in the responses were classified, for example, as an answer, a reflection of conscious memory search, failed recall, a hypothesis, recall speci-fications, task demand analysis, etc. The categorization process was considered so complex that it was performed by the authors themselves rather than naive judges. The authors then analysed the sequential dependency between the elements of memory produced by the subjects and came up with four sequentially connected levels which they labelled as follows:

1. memories;
2. memory editing;
3. descriptions of recall requirements;
4. mediator (strategic) processes.

Based on this connective sequence, they suggested a model describing their concept of the relationship between memory control processes under inclusion of other cognitive systems (Figure 7.2). In this model, a mental representation is thought to derive from perceptual and cognitive input called an 'input template', which activates key nodes within long-term storage systems. 'Descriptor processes' are thought to specify the type of memory trace that would satisfy the demands of the retrieval task. An 'Editor process' would check that the outputs of the long-term storage systems fit with previously retrieved memory elements in the episode being retrieved and also with the overall task requirements. In cases where the editor would detect incompatibilities either within the recall structure or between the original description and the output representation, a 'Mediator' would resolve the incompatibilities by processes akin to problem solving routines. The Mediator processes would control cognitive (strategic and problem-solving) operations concerning the adequacy or plausibility of retrieved memory elements.

Burgess and Shallice then tried to explain confabulation within this complex system and started with 'the simplifying assumption ... that the same type of process is occurring in all confabulating patients described in the literature'

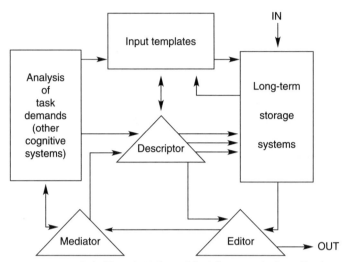

Figure 7.2 Burgess and Shallice's (1996) model of the control of recollection. Reproduced with permission.

(Burgess and Shallice 1996, p. 392). Invoking evidence from diverse clinical studies, they postulated that confabulators have damage to processes in description formation and editing. As regards the descriptor deficit, they suggested that a breakdown of this process would lead to too noisy specification of the to-be-recalled memory, leading to 'too wide a part of the memory store being activated' (p. 394). More catastrophic damage to the descriptor process would lead to recall being stimulus driven. In addition, they postulated that bizarre confabulations should be related to damage of the mediator process.

Burgess and McNeil (1999) later applied this model to a patient presenting striking behaviourally spontaneous confabulation for 12 weeks following rupture of an aneurysm of the anterior communicating artery. He regularly got out of bed in the morning and dressed in formal clothes in the conviction that he had to take stocks. Confabulations around this conviction were plausible and consistent. The authors interpreted this patient's confabulations as a deficit of a descriptor process. The consequence of descriptor failure would be the intrusion of 'input templates' or generic memories. The consistency of the false convictions, which recurred every morning, was explained by 'schematisation of this erroneous memory [occurring] through repetition, which is a phenomenon prevented in unimpaired individuals by the ability to recall alternative, especially conflicting memories' (Burgess and McNeil 1999, p. 179).

This model of memory retrieval is obviously very complex and based on many assumptions. Burgess and Shallice (1996) tried to explain both false memories occurring in healthy people and pathological confabulations, an ambition requiring a far-reaching model. Although Burgess and McNeil (1999) showed that even a specific confabulatory syndrome such as behaviourally spontaneous confabulation could be accommodated within this model, it is important to note that the different processes making up the model were derived from the observation of memory productions by healthy people, rather than controlled experimentation with confabulating patients. Indeed, there are no procedures known to specifically explore the activity of these processes. Strictly speaking, there is no solid scientific evidence that the brain really proceeds through the stages proposed by Burgess and Shallice (1996) when retrieving memories. From this perspective, the model may be considered an interesting conceptual framework that may potentially guide future studies on false memories and confabulations, but as regards the mechanisms of confabulations, it remains a speculation awaiting confirmation by appropriately controlled data.

Strategic retrieval hypothesis

Probably the most comprehensive current model of memory retrieval and monitoring is Moscovitch's 'strategic retrieval model'. In comparison to Burgess and Shallice's (1996) model, it is much more anatomically oriented, attributing specific roles to different structures in the retrieval and monitoring of memories. The model was strongly shaped by observations of confabulating patients (Moscovitch 1989, Moscovitch and Melo 1997) but was also applied to false recall and recognition (Melo *et al.* 1999) and to normal memory distortion, consistent with the idea that 'it should be apparent that confabulation is similar in many ways to the type of memory distortion observed in children and in adults in the laboratory and in real life' (Moscovitch 1995, p. 245).

The model, which is shown in Figure 7.3, proposes two routes of memory activation (Moscovitch and Winocur 2002): a direct route, also called the associative route, in which a cue directly activates the memory. The other route is an indirect one, depending on an effortful search. In this, the dorsolateral prefrontal cortex would first establish a retrieval mode, that is, it would set the goals of the task and initiate a retrieval strategy. After that, the ventrolateral prefrontal cortex would take over and specify the cues needed to gain access to the hippocampal complex and maintain the information until the memory would be recovered. The hippocampal complex is thought to contain an index necessary to elicit the memory. This evocation of a memory engram

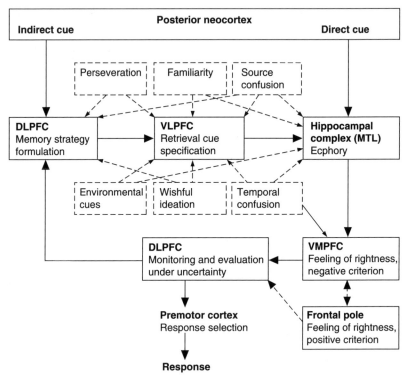

Figure 7.3 Model of the strategic retrieval hypothesis. Components of the original model (Moscovitch and Winocur 2002) are outlined with straight lines. Recent additions to the model (Gilboa et al. 2006) are indicated with boxes having dashed borders. Abbreviations: DLPFC, dorsolateral prefrontal cortex; MTL, medial temporal lobe; VLPFC, ventrolateral prefrontal cortex; VMPFC, ventromedial prefrontal cortex. Redrawn with permission from Gilboa et al. (1996).

from its latent to a manifest, active state is called ecphory. The recovered memory would then be delivered to the ventromedial prefrontal cortex, which would automatically and immediately signal whether the recovered memory traces satisfy the search goals set by the dorsolateral prefrontal cortex and are consistent with the cues in that particular context. The ventromedial cortex would then signal the felt-rightness of the recovered memory. Its role is believed to be inhibitory in setting criteria. In these operations, the ventromedial cortex would collaborate with the frontal pole, which would be more important for signalling acceptance and endorsement of the recovered memory. In cases of uncertainty, the dorsolateral prefrontal cortex would be recruited to engage strategic verification processes thought to involve diverse regions in the frontal and posterior neocortex. These regions would supply relevant information about the recovered memory, such as perceptual characteristics and its compatibility with all the knowledge that would influence the decision to accept or reject the recovered memory. Then, a response would be provided.

Even though the model offers an elegant integration of a large corpus of clinical and experimental data, as well as recent functional imaging findings, it remains controversial in some key aspects. For example, it gives a central role to the hippocampal complex in the reactivation of memory (ecphory), including remote memories – an aspect critical to the Multiple Trace Theory devised by Moscovitch and collaborators (Nadel and Moscovitch 1997; Nadel *et al.* 2000; Moscovitch *et al.* 2005). This structure would be important for re-experiencing an old event with full contextual details. The postulate has been heavily contested and is the object of a continuing debate (Bayley *et al.* 2003 2006; Squire and Bayley 2007).

Another key structure in the model is the ventromedial prefrontal cortex, the area damaged in many severe confabulators. According to the model (Figure 7.3), this area is proposed to set in after the hippocampal complex, that is, after the evocation of the memory trace (post-ecphory). To attribute to this area, together with the frontal pole, the ability to convey the feeling for our memories' rightness would nicely explain the conviction that many confabulators hold in their false memories. But the postulate is speculative in that it lacks controlled experimental evidence.

How could the 'strategic retrieval model' explain confabulation? The basic failure is considered to be one of monitoring:

> Confabulation arises because of deficient strategic retrieval processes at output that are involved in monitoring, evaluating, and verifying recovered memory traces, and placing them in proper historical context. The ventromedial frontal cortex and related structures in the basal forebrain, cingulum, and striatum are the structures that are most likely to mediate strategic retrieval processes and whose damage leads to confabulation.
>
> Moscovitch (1995, p. 247)

The following conditions for confabulation were specified (Moscovitch and Melo 1997; Gilboa and Moscovitch 2002):

1. Faulty output from the associative/cue-dependent retrieval system, as it might also occur in healthy people;

2. Impaired strategic search processes, which would not only account for the errors of omission, which the authors recognized as the most common error type in confabulating patients, but which might also exacerbate faulty output in normal and amnesic subjects;

3. Defective monitoring which would render the confabulating patient incapable of detecting that output from associative/cue-dependent system was faulty.

At this stage, the model made no explicit distinction between different forms of confabulation. In considering that 'models that propose a singular underlying mechanism [of confabulation] are unlikely to succeed in explaining the variety of its phenomena' (Gilboa *et al.* 2006, p. 1411), the model has recently been adapted to include 'contributing factors' such as source-monitoring deficits, perseverations, wishful ideation, and the failure that we have suggested to be responsible for behaviourally spontaneous confabulations (but not other forms of confabulation), termed 'temporal context confusion'. These new components are included in boxes with dash lines in Figure 7.3. The authors did not dwell on how they determined the sequence of these contributing factors within the strategic retrieval model and their hierarchical relation with it.

What is the empirical basis of this model? More than any other model, the strategic retrieval hypothesis was derived from the observation of confabulating patients. We have already encountered the study by Moscovitch and Melo (1997) in Chapter 3 (p. 68) and above (p. 213). The authors asked subjects to provide details about personal experiences and historical events relating to specific cue words. Tested this way, patients classified as 'confabulating amnesics' produced significantly more false details (confabulations) than non-confabulating amnesics. The proportion of erroneous details markedly increased when the confabulating patients were prompted to provide more details than those produced spontaneously, an effect that was not present in non-confabulating amnesics or healthy controls. Confabulations tended to be even more frequent in the historical part of the task. Errors of content were at least as common as a confusion of temporal sequence.

The study had the strength of using a clearly defined test procedure and comparing groups of amnesic patients, but there were also important limitations. In particular, the production of confabulations in the task was an important criterion for classifying the patients as confabulating or non-confabulating. The study was taken to suggest that:

> confabulation is associated with impaired strategic retrieval processes resulting from damage in the region of the ventromedial frontal cortex [which] help initiate and guide search in episodic and in semantic memory and help monitor and organize the output from those systems.

Moscovitch and Melo (1997, p. 1017)

The confabulators were also more impaired in tests sensitive to frontal lobe damage. Thus, the data might also be taken to support the executive hypothesis of confabulation, which has been discussed above (pp. 210ff.).

The strategic retrieval hypothesis was again proposed as the best explanation of data obtained in a more recent study from the same group. Gilboa *et al.* (2006) compared two groups of patients having damage of the ventromedial frontal area due to rupture of an aneurysm of the anterior communicating artery (ACoA) or an infarction in the territory of the anterior cerebral artery. One of the groups was classified as 'verbal and behavioural spontaneous confabulators', the other as 'non-confabulating amnesics'. (We will come back to the difficulty of this distinction in Chapter 8.) Of relevance here are two experiments whose results were taken as supportive of the strategic retrieval hypothesis. In one experiment, subjects were asked to tell four fairy tales and bible stories with as much detail as possible. In accordance with the previous study (Moscovitch and Melo 1997), Gilboa *et al.* (2006) found that three of the four confabulating patients produced more erroneous details than all non-confabulating ACoA patients and healthy controls, whereby idiosyncratic errors, which had no relation to the original stories, were only produced by the confabulating patients. Of note, this experiment only concerned semantic memory. In an additional experiment, in which three confabulating patients were compared with four non-confabulating ACoA patients, the recognition of details from fairy tales and bible stories as well as autobiographical events was tested. Subjects had to read sentences describing details of these stories or events. As it turned out, the three participating confabulators accepted more false statements than the four non-confabulating ACoA patients. The difference was pronounced on the semantic part of the task. In addition, confabulating patients had a higher confidence in their false statements than non-confabulating patients. The authors concluded that confabulation resulted from a failure of the 'monitoring' component within the strategic retrieval hypothesis, thus supporting earlier authors (previous paragraph). However the study did not address the most critical question: what is the physiologic basis of monitoring? How does the brain distinguish between a true and a false memory?

This study, like the previous one (Moscovitch and Melo 1997), had a strong focus on momentary confabulations referring to semantic memory. Indeed, the presence of such confabulations was a criterion for classifying confabulators (Moscovitch and Melo 1997) and an essential argument for favouring the strategic retrieval hypothesis over temporal accounts of confabulation (Gilboa *et al.* 2006). As we saw earlier (p. 205f., Figure 7.1), the production of semantic confabulations is not a distinctive feature of behaviourally spontaneous confabulation (Schnider *et al.* 1996b). With respect to the tendency to invent answers to semantic questions, behaviourally spontaneous confabulators do not differ from other amnesic subjects, who are unselected with regards to lesion location (Figure 4.12). Even very severe spontaneous confabulators, living in a profoundly confused reality, may not produce any confabulation in response to questions referring to semantic memory or their personal remote past. Thus, most of the data provided by Gilboa *et al.* (2006) and Moscovitch and Melo (1997) supported the strategic retrieval hypothesis' standing as an explanation of (intense) momentary confabulation, but they did not pertain to the reality confusion characterizing behaviourally spontaneous confabulation.

In *conclusion*, the strategic retrieval hypothesis is a plausible schema of how the brain organizes memory retrieval. The hypothesis is sufficiently far-reaching to accommodate all forms of confabulation. It has the merit of being precise with regards to anatomo–functional relationships, making it an attractive starting point for scientific scrutiny. Data presented so far have supported the idea that momentary confabulations are associated with deficient monitoring, but have not revealed a way to explore the physiological basis of the monitoring process.

Consciousness in time

The monitoring hypotheses discussed above may have succeeded in conceptualizing the steps leading to the retrieval of memories, but by their wide applicability to both normal and faulty memories, they mostly failed to explain the specifics of confabulations and the dissociations between different forms of confabulations. Dalla Barba (2002) was critical of another aspect:

> To accept the hypothesis of unconscious monitoring mechanisms means falling into … the contradiction of postulating the existence of a type of unconscious consciousness, that is of unconscious monitoring mechanisms endowed with intentionality, which select, evaluate and reject false memories and provide … consciousness with only real memories … [But] on the basis of what criteria does the [unconscious monitoring mechanism] distinguish a true memory from a false one?
>
> Dalla Barba (2002, pp. 31 and 42)

Dalla Barba's own approach built on a peculiar quality of most serious confabulations: their inappropriateness in time. As documented in Chapters 1 and 2, confabulations that are of personal relevance – in that they describe the idea of a patient about his past, present, and future – can mostly be traced back to elements of real events in the patient's past. Indeed, even provoked confabulations often stem from previous tasks, as those produced by Mrs M (Chapter 3, pp. 57ff.). The only exception may be semantic confabulations produced in response to questionnaires and bearing on events having no personal connotation. In the case of behaviourally spontaneous confabulation, the temporally inappropriate application of memories and the execution of habits that are currently inadequate are most evident features.

Talland (1965) had already suggested an erroneous temporal reference in thinking as a crucial aspect of confabulation:

> The source [of confabulation is] predominantly … the patient's actual experiences in an earlier phase of his life. [Confabulation] seems to arise from the disruption of his temporal frame of reference, so that true statements become displaced in their chronological setting, those drawn from different periods become confused. Typically, a memory of their more remote past re-emerges as an event in the present or immediate past.

> Talland (1965, p. 56)

In a sensitive essay, Dalla Barba (2002) described temporality – the sense for one's existence with reference to the past, the present, and the future – as a central component of consciousness. Confabulation entered this discussion with the presentation of some confabulating patients. A 75-year-old patient with vascular dementia, who was disoriented with respect to people, time and space, treated the examiner as though they had known each other for some time before (patient previously described in Dalla Barba 1993b). His confabulations appeared to be influenced by the examiner's Italian accent but they also seemed to be traceable to real events in the patient's past. The patient did not only confabulate in discussions but actually executed his false ideas, for example, when he attempted to leave the hospital in the conviction that a taxi was waiting for him. Another patient, a 52-year-old woman (previously described in Dalla Barba *et al.* 1997b) who had had rupture of an ACoA aneurysm, confabulated heavily when asked about her recent doings, her present whereabouts, and her plans for the next day. However, she never confabulated in learning tasks, nor when answering questions about historical events or the news, leading the author to conclude:

> [The patient] confabulated only when her subjective temporality was involved … She is perfectly aware of her personal temporality but confuses her habits with her real past, present and future … [She] is conscious of a past, present and future which are 'false', in that they do not represent a past, present and future which are consistent with her present situation. What then is [the patient's] confabulatory reality? … It is a matter of a whole confabulatory temporality, which takes, so to speak, the place of real temporality.

> Dalla Barba (2002, p. 197ff.)

The concept is interesting in that it does not ascribe confabulation to a primary distortion of a memory's content or the failure of a distinct retrieval mechanism. 'Confabulation reflects a pathological awareness of personal temporality' (Dalla Barba *et al.* 1997b, p. 425) – in other words, the confabulator is out of phase with reality.

The most compelling evidence that Dalla Barba put forward to formulate his hypothesis, were definite (Dalla Barba 1993b) or probable (Dalla Barba *et al.* 1997b) behaviourally spontaneous confabulators. As we will see in Chapter 8, our data on behaviourally spontaneous confabulation are compatible with this characterization of confabulations. In addition, we found that behaviourally spontaneous confabulators often have a disturbed sense of time, independent from memory: behaviourally spontaneous confabulators, in comparison with similarly severe amnesics and healthy controls, failed to normally discriminate between visually presented, temporally overlapping intervals in the range of one second, unless the intervals' length varied by a factor of three (Schnider 2000). Non-confabulating amnesics discriminated the intervals as well as healthy controls. Thus, the disturbed sense of time postulated by Dalla Barba may not only pertain to memory, but constitute a basic characteristic of thinking in behaviourally spontaneous confabulation.

The difficulty with Dalla Barba's (and Talland's) account was that it had no specific experimental basis and that there were no controlled data to support it. The idea was also applied to the momentary confabulations of patients with Alzheimer's disease (Dalla Barba et al. 1999) and frontotemporal dementia (Nedjam et al. 2000, 2004), although the link with these confabulations appeared far less compelling than with the behaviourally spontaneous confabulators described above.

Summary

Over more than a century, many hypotheses have been proposed to explain confabulations. Most models covered all types of confabulation, assuming that all confabulations represented a common disorder. Most models were derived from clinical, some from neuropsychological observations, but only few sought controlled evidence. None brought forward an experimental procedure specific for the proposed hypothesis. Consequently, none of the hypotheses indicated a way to explore the physiology of the cognitive mechanisms whose supposed failure should explain confabulation.

The status of the proposed mechanisms can be summarized as follows:

- A tendency to fill gaps in memory, be it under the influence of increased suggestibility or not, is not a generally valid mechanism of confabulation, although – on the basis of clinical observation – it appears to be the best explanation in some patients.

- Motivation to see things better than they are and particular personality patterns have been suggested as factors contributing to the generation of all forms of confabulation, mnestic and non-mnestic. Controlled evidence is scarce. The hypothesis fails to explain why distorted memories come up in the first place and are then accepted as veridical.

- Executive failures have been found in many confabulating patients, but no association of specific executive failures with specific forms of confabulations has been demonstrated. Provoked confabulations may even be associated with relatively preserved executive functions. Behaviourally spontaneous confabulations are independent of the severity of executive dysfunction.

- Diverse hypotheses on the recollection of memories and the monitoring of this process have been put forward. Most applied to both correct and false memory retrieval. None was specific for any type of confabulation and none of these models provided solid evidence for answering the central question: How – by what physiological mechanism – does the brain monitor the outflow from memory, which is obviously defective in confabulation? And what specific monitoring deficits would explain the different types of confabulation?

- The idea that confabulators' consciousness is determined by a past, present and future displaced in time, has been deduced from case observations but lacks experimental evidence.

With regards the different forms of confabulation, the following conclusions can be drawn:

- *Provoked confabulations* (intrusions) appear to be a normal response to a faulty memory. They reflect a subject's attempt to retrieve as much information as possible from memory and are the price to pay for maximum item recollection.

- *Momentary confabulations* cannot be attributed to one specific mechanism. Executive dysfunction, motivational factors, a poorly guided search in memory, a false sense of time and other disturbances might contribute to different degrees and characteristics of momentary confabulations. Diverse authors favoured an interpretation in terms of impaired 'monitoring', but failed to indicate a way to explore the physiologic basis of monitoring. It may be that the 'one and only' mechanism of momentary confabulation will never be found: In view of the different situations that may evoke momentary confabulations (questionnaires, discussions), the different domains of memory that may be concerned (episodic, semantic memory), the varying associated features (disorientation present or not), the varying clinical course (appearing or disappearing over time), and the varying degree of conviction held in the confabulations, it appears likely that momentary confabulations, in fact, represent the common expression of many different disorders of memory and cognition. These different disorders probably have different mechanisms, which vary according to lesion location and associated cognitive failures.

- *Fantastic confabulations* have never been specifically explored. Their common occurrence in the context of a confusional state (delirium), severe dementia, or psychosis suggests that they reflect a high degree of formal thought disorder with detachment from reality. However, studies are lacking.

- *Behaviourally spontaneous confabulations* have not been the target of any of the above models. The next chapter will – hopefully – demonstrate that the focused exploration of this type of confabulation constitutes a worthwhile endeavour. As seen in this chapter, the specificity of the syndrome has allowed us to exclude gap-filling and executive dysfunction as relevant mechanisms. The idea of faulty temporal consciousness seems to have been derived primarily from the observation of such patients.

The next chapter will specifically deal with behaviourally spontaneous confabulation. We will see that this form of confabulation – but not other forms – is associated with a particular failure to distinguish between memories that pertain to ongoing reality and memories that do not – a disorder of temporality in consciousness. We drew this conclusion from experimental exploration comparing behaviourally spontaneous confabulators and non-confabulating amnesics. Subsequent studies using similar experimental designs in healthy subjects suggested that this failure is probably based on the defect of a pre-conscious orbitofrontal 'monitoring' process, which normally intervenes in the early phase of a memory's 're-construction'.

Behaviourally spontaneous confabulation and reality

Throughout the previous chapters, behaviourally spontaneous confabulation has held a special status. More than other forms of confabulation, it appears to be an honest account of what patients perceive as their reality and their duties. Despite this special status, the reader may wonder why behaviourally spontaneous confabulation is singled out at this point and receives the attention of a full chapter. Re-reading of Chapter 1 may indicate why. Mrs B acted according to plans that related to her past rather than the present, but which she held with similar conviction to that of healthy people adhering to their reality. Her plans were not fantastic or absurd. They represented normal ideas, which attained the status of profoundly inappropriate thoughts and plans only by their inappropriateness in time and context.

Seen this way, behaviourally spontaneous confabulation is more than a model of false statements, that is, confabulation – it is a model of how the brain adapts thought and behaviour to ongoing reality; how it sorts out reality in thinking; how it distinguishes between thoughts that pertain to current reality and thoughts that do not, such as, daydreams and fantasies.

In this chapter, I will summarize our clinical studies on behaviourally spontaneous confabulation and then show how these studies guided our exploration of the normal adaptation of thought to ongoing reality in the healthy brain. The chapter will end with the presentation of a model of memory filtration derived from our clinical, functional imaging, and electro-physiological studies.

The syndrome of behaviourally spontaneous confabulation

Before starting the analysis of the mechanisms of behaviourally spontaneous confabulation, it may be useful to summarize and complement the observations and data spread over the previous chapters. The type of confabulation discussed in this and the next chapter – as far as we have studied it – has the following characteristics:

1. A core feature of behaviourally spontaneous confabulation is the *conviction* that the patients hold in their false ideas about reality and their incorrigibility. The patients justify inappropriate acts with confabulated meetings, professional obligations or other intentions. In most cases, the patients enact previous habits, such as going to work, practising an old hobby or meeting family and friends. These ideas are often vigorously pursued. The real problem in caring for such patients is their urge to enact previous habits; the confabulations simply reflect their profound misinterpretation of current reality. The themes of such acts are often quite monotonous and consistent over time. Extreme incoherence of thoughts and actions is suggestive of a confusional state rather than a stable syndrome of behaviourally spontaneous confabulation.

2. Although the content of the confabulations evoked in discussions varies, they can mostly be traced back to *elements of real events*. All patients make confabulations about recent personal experiences, that is, confabulations that extend to autobiographical memory. There may be a temporal gradient, in that patient's recollection of remote past events may be correct. In Mrs M, this temporal gradient was three years (p. 58); in Mrs B, it was 15 years (Chapter 1); in the patient with craniopharyngeoma surgery described on page 120f., confabulations appeared to have no limitation in time or topic. This patient also confabulated in response to questions about general knowledge, but extension of confabulation to semantic memory is not a consistent feature of behaviourally spontaneous confabulation. Fantastic ideas have been described in acute patients who were presumably behaviourally spontaneous confabulators (Kapur and Coughlan, 1980; Damasio *et al.* 1985b). None of our patients, who were out of the confusional state when tested, produced fantastic confabulations. Fantastic ideas are not a typical feature of behaviourally spontaneous confabulation.

3. The patients always have an *amnesia* characterized by poor access to memories, that is, they have severely impaired free recall. When information storage is measured with a conceptually simple task such as a continuous recognition task, most patients are impaired, but occasional patients store normal amounts of information (p. 147ff., Figure 5.1).

4. The patients always have *disorientation* regarding time, place and situation. Once out of the confusional state, orientation to person – that is, regarding one's own identity – is intact.

5. Features of *reduplicative misidentification* are often present and may reflect the false ideas that the patients hold about reality.

6. Patients always have *anosognosia* with regards to the falsehood of their ideas and plans. Some patients may acknowledge that they have a weak memory and may even have insight into the fact that their memory is unreliable. Such insight does not protect them from enacting currently inappropriate plans and from having false ideas about ongoing reality.

7. Even though most patients have *executive dysfunction*, such dysfunction – even when associated with amnesia – is not predictive of behaviourally spontaneous confabulation. In addition, executive dysfunction does not reliably follow the clinical course of the confabulations (Schnider *et al.* 2000a).

8. Behaviourally spontaneous confabulations have a consistent *anatomical basis*. In all reported cases which were not in a confusional state (delirium) or demented, lesions concerned structures in the anterior extension of the limbic system (Figure 4.12). In most cases, the lesion involved the posterior medial orbitofrontal cortex (ventromedial prefrontal area) with or without the basal forebrain. Other lesions involved the anterior medial or lateral orbitofrontal cortex, the medial hypothalamus (Figure 4.10), the amygdala on one side and the perirhinal cortex on the other (Figure 4.6d–f) or the capsular genu (Mrs M, Figure 4.4). Thus, the lesions always involved the posterior medial orbitofrontal cortex or structures directly connected with it.

9. The *aetiology* of the lesion is not critical. Most described cases had acute lesions, but chronic progressive damage (e.g., sarcoidosis, pp. 121ff.) is also possible. We have observed behaviourally spontaneous confabulation in patients having very diverse aetiologies of brain damage: rupture of an anterior communicating artery aneurysm, traumatic brain injury, herpes simplex virus encephalitis, ischemic lesion of the right capsular genu, sarcoidosis of the hypothalamus, craniopharyngeoma, orbitofrontal meningeoma, or alcoholic Korsakoff syndrome. Critical for the occurrence of behaviourally spontaneous confabulation is the lesion site.

10. Behaviourally spontaneous confabulation represents a *unique syndrome*, which dissociates from other forms of confabulation. There is double dissociation from provoked confabulations (intrusions, Figure 3.1). It also partly dissociates from momentary confabulation: spontaneous confabulators always produce momentary confabulations, whose intensity at least mirrors the degree of the patients' reality confusion. Some patients produce very discrete, others quite massive momentary confabulations.

Conversely, there are also patients who have massive, almost 'spontaneous' momentary confabulations, which they never enact – these patients do not qualify as behaviourally spontaneous confabulators. Thus, behaviourally spontaneous confabulation is not simply a more severe form of the same disorder as momentary confabulations. Finally, behaviourally spontaneous confabulation also dissociates from fantastic confabulations. The latter may be present in the initial confusional state, albeit rarely. Conversely, fantastic confabulations may occur in patients having no behaviourally spontaneous confabulations. A consequence of these dissociations is that the conclusions reached in this chapter only apply to behaviourally spontaneous confabulation, and not to other types of confabulation.

Increased temporal context confusion

The observation that confabulators like Mrs M (pp. 57ff.) produced confabulations that could virtually always be traced back to real events led us to hypothesize that confabulations resulted from a loss of a hypothetical 'temporal tag' of memories; patients would not know when in the past, and in what context, they had acquired a memory (Schnider *et al.* 1996a). The idea had initially been expressed by Van der Horst (1932). As described in the previous chapter, we failed to confirm this hypothesis. When we probed patients' knowledge about when (in which one of two series) they had learned words, we found that non-confabulating amnesics had as much difficulty as behaviourally spontaneous confabulators (unpublished data), a finding also obtained by Johnson *et al.* (1997). In retrospect, the hypothesis had to be wrong. The lack of knowledge about when in the past something happened would not explain the patients' tendency to act according to currently inappropriate plans and their false concept of reality (disorientation). What the patients seem to have lost is the intuitive feeling for the current relevance of memories and their own temporal frame of reference – an idea shared by Dalla Barba (2002). How could this intuitive distinction between memories relating to 'now' as opposed to memories not relating to 'now' be tested?

The task, which eventually proved decisive for our concept of behaviourally spontaneous confabulation, evolved from the continuous recognition task described in Figure 5.1 (pp. 148ff.). What would happen if the patients made the same task again – after an hour or so – but with a different arrangement, newly mixed and with different pictures repeated within the run than in the first run? Would the patients be able to distinguish between repetitions within this second run and familiarity referring to the first run? Figure 8.1 shows the concept of the experimental task.

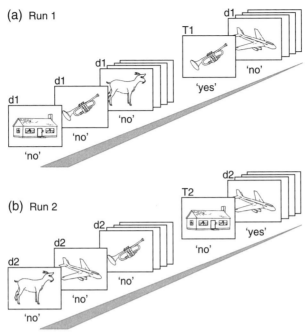

Figure 8.1 Task to measure temporal context confusion in memory (TCC) used in diverse studies (Schnider *et al.* 1996b, c, 2000a). The original task was composed of 80 pictures, among which eight pictures were selected to be repeated five times during the run. Subjects had to indicate picture recurrences within the ongoing run. 'd' denotes 'distracters', i.e., pictures' first appearance within a run; T denotes targets, i.e., repeated pictures within the run. d1 and T1 are stimuli presented in the first run, d2 and T2 are stimuli of the second run. (a) First run demanding learning and recognition. (b) Second run composed of the same 80 pictures but arranged in different order. Subjects had to indicate for each picture whether it had already been presented within the second run, irrespective of familiarity from the first run. 'yes' and 'no' indicate correct responses.

The following formula describes what we wanted to learn from this experiment:

$$\text{Temporal Context Confusion TCC} = (\text{FP2/Hits2}) - (\text{FP1/Hits1})$$

In this formula, FP1 and 2 denote the false positive responses in runs 1 and 2, that is, incorrect 'yes' responses to items that have not been presented yet within the ongoing run. Hits1 and 2 describes the number of true within-run repetitions that are correctly recognized.

It took us nine months to have a sample of five behaviourally spontaneous confabulators and ten other amnesics who had similarly impaired delayed free recall in verbal learning, that is, ≤ 4 in the California Verbal Learning Test (Delis *et al.* 1987). All patients were hospitalized for rehabilitation of severe memory impairment at the time of the study, a situation providing a 'standardized' environment and the possibility to observe them. One of the non-confabulating patients had reduplicative paramnesia but never acted according to false ideas; false statements exclusively concerned her present location. Aetiologies of brain damage in the non-confabulating amnesics were as diverse as those described above for confabulators: medial temporal stroke, anterior communicating artery aneurysm rupture, herpes simplex virus encephalitis, traumatic brain injury, meningeoma of the posterior falx etc.

Figure 8.2 shows the result of the experiment (Schnider *et al.* 1996b). Whereas non-confabulating amnesics tended to have somewhat less temporal context confusion (TCC) than normal controls, all behaviourally spontaneous confabulators had a higher TCC value than any non-confabulating amnesic or healthy control. It appeared that there was a threshold above which patients sufficiently confused reality to act upon it. Although we did not quantify

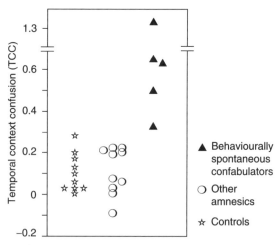

Figure 8.2 Result of the continuous recognition task with two runs. High values of temporal context confusion (TCC) indicate strong performance drop in the second run; TCC of zero indicates that performance was similar in both runs. Non-confabulating amnesics had TCC of similar degree as healthy controls. In contrast, all spontaneous confabulators had a TCC above the highest value of any healthy control or non-confabulating amnesic. In this version of the task, a threshold of TCC = 0.3 appeared to distinguish between behaviourally spontaneous confabulators and non-confabulating amnesics, a rule of thumb since confirmed in many more amnesic patients. With permission from Schnider *et al.* (1996b).

behaviourally spontaneous confabulation, it appeared that TCC reflected the intensity of the confabulators' thought derangement quite well.

Over the years, TCC has proved a clinically useful measure of patients' propensity to act on the basis of false memories, at least in the patient population that was under our care. While most patients included in our studies had very severe cognitive impairments, none had known degenerative dementia or schizophrenia. Of course, there have been some false negative and false positive test results over the years. They will be discussed later in this chapter.

The impression that TCC measured a cognitive function of biological relevance was further supported by an unexpected finding: We found that TCC in amnesic subjects very precisely predicted disorientation (Schnider *et al.* 1996c). Figure 8.3 shows the result of the original study. Whereas performance in the first run of the task, that is, new learning and recognition (item recognition), significantly but relatively weakly correlated with orientation (r = 0.54, Figure 8.3a), TCC had a correlation of r = 0.9 with orientation (Figure 8.3b). This correlation was obtained when the total orientation score was used, which was composed of five questions each for orientation to time, place, situation, and person (Von Cramon and Säring 1982). All patients were correctly oriented to person. TCC had comparably high correlation with orientation to time, place and situation ($0.78 \leq r \leq 0.84$). In contrast, item recognition significantly correlated only with orientation to place and situation ($0.55 \leq r \leq 0.57$), but not with orientation to time (r = 0.38). As we saw in Chapter 5, the inclusion of more patients over the years also markedly

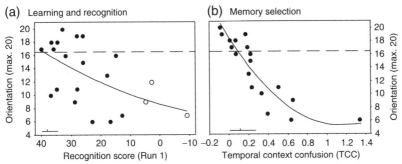

Figure 8.3 Mechanism of disorientation. (a) Relation between orientation and information storage (recognition score) that is, performance in the first run of the continuous recognition task (Figure 5.1c). (b) Relation between orientation and temporal context confusion (TCC) as measured by the performance drop in the second, as compared to the first run of the task. The black horizontal bars in the lower left part of the figures indicate normal values. With permission from (Schnider *et al.* 1996c).

strengthened the correlation between storage capacity and confabulation (Figure 5.3). The finding indicated that increased TCC, which was so strongly predictive of behaviourally spontaneous confabulation, was also implicated in disorientation to time, place, and situation. Conversely, while disorientation could also result from severe learning and recognition failure, behaviourally spontaneous confabulation had no strict association with storage failure (Figure 5.1c). As we will see later (p. 248), TCC also closely followed the clinical course of behaviourally spontaneous confabulators.

At the time, I considered the performance drop in the second run – as reflected in increased TCC – 'a failure to recognize the temporal order of stored information, resulting in erroneous recollection of elements of memory that do not belong together' (Schnider et al. 1996b, p. 1365). The terminology was influenced by the conclusions drawn from the observation of Mrs M (Schnider et al. 1996a), but the term did not correctly describe the requirement of the task. Indeed, the task does not demand the ability 'to recognize the temporal order of stored information'. Given the long series of pictures (120 pictures), it would be impossible to indicate the temporal order of the stimuli. What the task demands is the ability to develop the feeling for those memories that are of current relevance, that is, the memory for an item's previous occurrence within the ongoing rather than the previous run. Healthy subjects who performed the second run 45 minutes after the first run – as it was done in our clinical studies – did so intuitively with no particular effort; for healthy subjects, the task constitutes no challenge.

In these studies, TCC was only calculated in patients who had demonstrated significant recognition capacity in the first run, as determined with signal-detection theory (d' > 1.64). The concern was that the performance of patients, who had random recognition, would reflect strategy and momentary behavioural inclinations rather than the workings of memory. The fear may have been unwarranted. Mrs B (Chapter 1) performed at chance in runs 1 and 2. Nonetheless, we repeated testing eight times over the weeks of her hospitalization. Although her performance was mostly random, the analysis of the pooled data yielded a TCC of 0.45, a value highly predictive of behaviourally spontaneous confabulation. Thus, Mrs B had increased TCC in implicit memory, despite random explicit recognition (Schnider et al. 2005a). At 18 months, after termination of the confabulatory state, TCC was below the 'threshold' of behaviourally spontaneous confabulation.

Suppression of currently irrelevant memory

These initial studies demonstrated that behaviourally spontaneous confabulation and disorientation were associated with a failure to sort out memories of current relevance. Why should confabulators have this difficulty? One possibility seemed to be that the patients fail to mentally represent new, incoming information with normal saliency in thinking, so that associations of old, firmly established memories intrude into ongoing thinking and behaviour. A difficulty with this interpretation was that it would not explain why many patients with extremely severe amnesia with no measurable storage capacity – and thus unable to represent new, incoming information with normal saliency in thinking – do not present behaviourally spontaneous confabulation (Schnider *et al.* 1994b, 1995; Stefanacci *et al.* 2000; Corkin, 2002). An alternative possibility was that behaviourally spontaneous confabulators fail to suppress activated memory traces and mental associations which do not refer to current reality.

We tested these alternatives with two versions of a task having the same logic as the task used in the previous studies (Schnider *et al.* 1996b, c) (Figure 8.1). However, the runs were easier (fewer items repeated more frequently), so that more patients achieved significant recognition scores in the first run, and there were more runs.

The task was intended to be analysed in the following way (Schnider and Ptak 1999): if the difficulty of spontaneous confabulators emanated from an inability to mentally represent incoming information with sufficient intensity, confabulators should have particular difficulty in all runs to recognize item repetitions, because they would not have encoded the items strongly enough on the previous presentation within the run. Thus, the confabulators would have a low hit rate in all runs. Conversely, if their difficulty consisted of an inability to suppress activated memory traces as they lost their relevance (at the end of a test run), they should have more and more false recognitions from one run to the next. That is, they should produce increasingly more false positive responses. Since such a hypothetical suppression capacity might depend on the time allowed for forgetting, we made four runs with increasingly longer intervals. The second run was made immediately after the first one; the third run was made five minutes after the second one; the fourth run thirty minutes after the third one. Two versions were developed: one used meaningful designs, the other had meaningless geometric designs.

Six new behaviourally spontaneous confabulators, who had not been involved in the earlier studies, participated in the study (Schnider and Ptak 1999). Three of them had had rupture of an anterior communicating artery aneurysm, one herpes simplex encephalitis, one sarcoidosis involving the hypothalamus (Figure 4.10), and one had removal of a craniopharyngeoma (Figure 4.9). Their lesions strongly overlapped in the posterior medial orbitofrontal area (scans included in Figure 4.12). Their performance was compared to twelve non-confabulating patients with similarly deficient delayed free recall in verbal learning.

Figure 8.4 shows the result, which was essentially the same for the meaningful designs and the meaningless geometric designs (Schnider and Ptak 1999). In both versions, spontaneous confabulators and non-confabulating amnesics

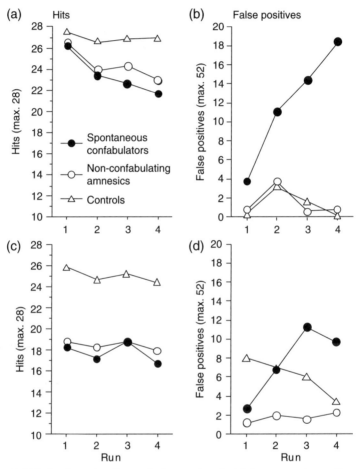

Figure 8.4 Mechanism of reality confusion, explored with four runs of a continuous recognition task. Run 2 was performed one minute after the first run, run 3 was made five minutes after run 2, run 4 was made 30 minutes after run 3. (a, b) Task with meaningful designs; (c, d) Version with meaningless geometric designs. In both versions, behaviourally spontaneous confabulators and non-confabulating amnesics had significantly fewer hits than the controls, but they did not differ from each other (a, c). In contrast, in both versions, spontaneous confabulators differed from both non-confabulating amnesics and normal controls by their steep increase of false positives from run to run (b, d). With permission from Schnider and Ptak (1999).

had similar difficulty in recognizing picture repetitions, as reflected in a lower hit rate than controls (Figure 8.4a, c). Thus, weak retention of incoming information with subsequent difficulty in recognizing its reappearance is common to amnesia in general but does not distinguish between behaviourally spontaneous confabulators and non-confabulating amnesics.

The result was completely different with regards to false positive responses (Figure 8.4b, d). In both versions of the task, behaviourally spontaneous confabulators produced increasingly more false positives from run to run. The result was particularly striking with the meaningful pictures: In this version, the confabulators increased their number of false positives even after a 30-minute break between the third and the fourth run (Figure 8.4b). The specificity of this finding was supported by the observation that the number of hits tended to decrease in the same interval, indicating that the increase of false positives did not reflect a more lenient 'search strategy' or less stringent 'monitoring' during recognition. On the contrary, confabulators increased false positives despite increasing uncertainty about their choice. In this version, non-confabulating amnesics produced exactly the same number of false positives as healthy controls. When runs were immediately repeated (run 2), they had a few false positives, a finding compatible with the way in which healthy people perceive ongoing reality: We do not perceive the present moment as a strictly separate event but rather as part of a continuum.

The conclusion from this study was that behaviourally spontaneous confabulation resulted from 'an inability to suppress activated memory traces and associations at the right time ... [Thus, it appears that the healthy brain] represents ongoing reality by suppressing mental associations that lack current behavioural relevance' (Schnider and Ptak 1999, p. 680).

Although this statement correctly described the findings of the study, the concept which I derived from the findings, was probably incorrect. I conceived of 'suppression' as a mechanism which would inactivate memory traces. The concept is shown in Figure 8.5. The idea was that real incoming information – perceptions – would lead to inhibition of those activated memory traces that did not relate to current reality anymore. Retrospectively, it is clear that the model was wrong: such a model would not allow daydreams and fantasies to dominate thought; the model would not allow creative thinking. As we will see later on, suppression of (the interference of) currently irrelevant memories is better described as 'filtering' of up-coming memories according to their relation with ongoing reality.

Clinical course and rehabilitation

Caring for a full-blown behaviourally spontaneous confabulator is a gruelling experience, which brings any rehabilitation team to its limits. The patient,

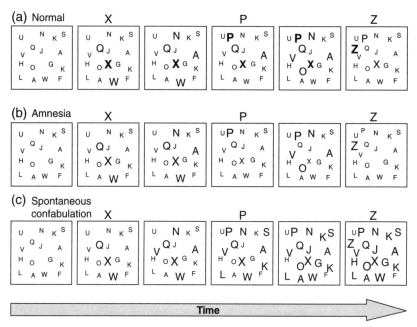

Figure 8.5 Early, probably incorrect model of 'now representation' and suppression in thinking (Schnider 2000, 2003). Any letter is meant to indicate an event (X, P, Z) or memory trace (letters within squares). The size of the letters indicates their saliency in thinking. (a) In a healthy person, new incoming information (the reality of 'now') is thought to attain high saliency in cortical representation (X) and to provoke mental associations. Some of these associations may lack connection with ongoing reality; they may be fantasies. The next piece of incoming information (P, later Z) again attains high saliency and provokes mental associations. In addition, previous associations, which do not refer to current reality, are suppressed (deactivated). (b) In common amnesia, a new event attains high saliency and provokes mental associations. In contrast to healthy subjects, however, previously encountered information cannot be normally retained (encoded). Thus, 'now' is unequivocally represented in thinking, but the information is subsequently forgotten. (c) In behaviourally spontaneous confabulation, new information is thought to provoke mental associations, just like in a healthy brain. However, when new pieces of information are processed (P, Z), those associations, which no longer refer to the current reality, fail to be inactivated. Any activated memory trace, pertinent or not for ongoing reality, may thus guide thinking and behaviour. The model would not allow fantasies and daydreams to dominate thinking. With permission from Schnider (2000).

who is in our division as I write these lines, leaves her bedroom unremittingly and makes all efforts to leave the unit to go back to her work as a lawyer – day in, day out, even during the night. Discussions and treatment sessions upset her – she has to go back to work. In this phase, there is no other way than to close doors and try to calm down the patient with medication.

But there is a phase when neuropsychological and behavioural interventions become feasible.

At the time of our early experimental findings, the prevalent idea was that confabulations varied only with regards to severity and that a combination of amnesia and executive failures determined the appearance of confabulations (Stuss *et al.* 1978; Kapur and Coughlan, 1980; DeLuca and Cicerone, 1991; Fischer *et al.* 1995). Hypotheses invoking failures of monitoring and constructive memory processes were just being formulated. Based on such accounts, the common rehabilitation approach to confabulation was to do memory training with patients, to train reorientation by repeated questioning, and to provide memory aids. Patients were trained to use diaries and notebooks. The goal was to teach them to respect a schedule and to find pertinent information at the right place. Another goal was to have them take notes whose belated study would provide evidence to the patients that their thoughts were false. Isolated cases responding to this approach have been published (DeLuca and Locker, 1996; Burgess and McNeil, 1999; Dayus and van den Broek, 2000; Del Grosso Destreri *et al.* 2002). In our experience, some patients do profit from such an approach: they accept a diary and rapidly learn to refer to it for information. Other patients, however, never refer to the booklet and cannot be trained to use it. Mrs B, for example, never used her diary. The utility of a memory booklet – or other memory aids, such as a pager system, which has proved highly efficient for diverse memory disorders (Wilson *et al.* 1997; Wilson *et al.* 2001) – has never been explored systematically in confabulating patients.

Our experimental findings suggested that another behavioural adaptation – this time on the side of the caregivers – might be helpful when dealing with behaviourally spontaneous confabulators. Assuming that the patients fail to suppress the interference of currently irrelevant memories (Schnider and Ptak 1999), it appeared potentially counterproductive to impose knowledge about true reality upon them. Indeed, it seemed more logical to avoid confrontation with the patients about their false convictions, an idea already expressed by Korsakoff (Chapter 2, p. 13f.) and Bonhoeffer (p. 23). The personnel of our clinic nowadays accept a patient's false convictions as long as they do not lead to dangerous behaviour. Thus, rather than contradicting a patient who believes that he has to leave for a business meeting, he will be told that the meeting has been postponed. Rather than trying to convince a confabulating woman that the baby she wants to feed is 35 years old, she will be told that she has already fed her baby. Of course, such reactions by caregivers do not prevent all conflicts with patients, but they often attenuate them. Nonetheless, hospitalization in a closed unit is often necessary. In our clinic, we have installed an automatic door-locking system, which is activated when a patient wearing a magnetic device approaches the door. Even so, the burden on caregivers and families of behaviourally spontaneous confabulators is enormous.

Fortunately, in most cases, the severe reality confusion characterizing behaviourally spontaneous confabulation is temporally limited, although such a state may last for many months, as in the case of Mrs B (Chapter 1). We followed up eight of our initial confabulators for more than three years (Schnider *et al.* 2000a). All of them severely confabulated after termination of the confusional state. Seven patients eventually stopped confabulating and regained correct orientation. These patients were able to return to their home, whereas the continued confabulator had to be institutionalized. Specifically, we made the following observations:

The *duration* of behaviourally spontaneous confabulation depended much more on the lesion site than lesion size (Figure 8.6). Patients with lesions of the orbitofrontal cortex, which spared the posterior medial part (Figure 8.6a), stopped confabulating within about three months. Patients having lesions that destroyed the ventromedial prefrontal area with the posterior medial orbitofrontal cortex plus the basal forebrain confabulated for longer periods, in this study up to one year (Figure 8.6b). Mrs B (Chapter 1), who had a similar lesion (Figure 4.3c), confabulated for 18 months. Two patients confabulated for even longer periods (Figure 8.6c). One of them had traumatic brain injury with destruction of the amygdala on the right side and of the perirhinal cortex and anterior insula on the left side (no. 7 in Figure 8.6; same patient as in Figure 4.6d–e). This patient stopped confabulating after about two years and was then able to live independently at home (his wife had left him) and to attend a day-care facility. The other patient had extremely extended orbitofrontal damage, which left the most posterior medial orbitofrontal area and basal forebrain intact, but extended so far dorsally that it interrupted all likely projections to the prefrontal cortex (no. 8 in Figure 8.6; same patient as in Figure 4.6a–c). Five years after the traumatic brain injury, this patient lived in a nursing home.

Most patients remained amnesic after termination of the confabulatory state. Two of the eight patients (numbers 1 and 2 in Figure 8.6) obtained normal neuropsychological results after termination of the confabulatory state. Both had orbitofrontal lesions sparing the most posterior medial part. One of them (no. 2) had full social integration working in a carnival. The other (no. 1), 52 years old, appeared somewhat 'peculiar' at the end of his hospital stay, despite normal neuropsychological results. It was difficult to stop a conversation with him. Within one year, this patient, a previous engineer, lost his job, where he was considered a simple executor rather than a creative person, and his wife left him. Thus, many behaviourally spontaneous

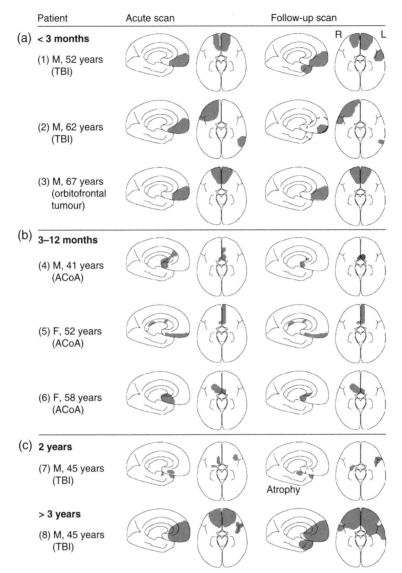

Patient — Acute scan — Follow-up scan

(a) < 3 months

(1) M, 52 years (TBI)

(2) M, 62 years (TBI)

(3) M, 67 years (orbitofrontal tumour)

(b) 3–12 months

(4) M, 41 years (ACoA)

(5) F, 52 years (ACoA)

(6) F, 58 years (ACoA)

(c) 2 years

(7) M, 45 years (TBI)

Atrophy

> 3 years

(8) M, 45 years (TBI)

R   L

Figure 8.6 Impact of lesion extension on the duration of behaviourally spontaneous confabulation. Lesion reconstructions in the acute and chronic phase (after at least one year) are shown; there is very little difference. (a) Patients who confabulated for the briefest period after termination of the confusional stage. Their lesions involved anterior orbitofrontal cortex but left the posterior medial orbitofrontal cortex intact. (b) Patients who confabulated for prolonged periods had lesions involving the posterior medial orbitofrontal (ventromedial cortex) and basal forebrain. Mrs B (Chapter 1) had a similar lesion (Figure 4.3c) and confabulated for 18 months. (c) One patient who confabulated for two years had amygdala damage on the right side and perirhinal and anterior insular damage on the left side (Figure 4.6d–f). Another patient, who still confabulated after five years had extremely extended prefrontal destruction (Figure 4.6a–c). Abbreviations: ACoA, rupture of an anterior communicating artery aneurysm; TBI, traumatic brain injury. With permission from Schnider *et al.* (2000a).

confabulators eventually regained the ability to adapt their behaviour to ongoing reality and to lead a relatively independent, albeit professionally unproductive, life at their home, despite continuing amnesia.

In this group of patients, recovery from behaviourally spontaneous confabulation, irrespective of the persistence of amnesia, was paralleled by normalization of TCC (Figure 8.7). All patients who had stopped confabulating had again normal or near-normal values. The two patients, who continued to confabulate for several months, were retested after one-and-a-half years. Both still had increased TCC. After three years, one of them (no. 7 in Figure 8.6) had stopped confabulating, accompanied by normalization of TCC. The other patient continued to confabulate (patient 8 in Figure 8.6); his TCC remained abnormally increased. Further analysis showed that cessation of behaviourally spontaneous confabulation was accompanied by the control of false positives in the second run of the task. Thus, it was the recovered ability to 'suppress' currently irrelevant memories which was decisive for recovery from behaviourally spontaneous confabulation (Schnider *et al.* 2000a).

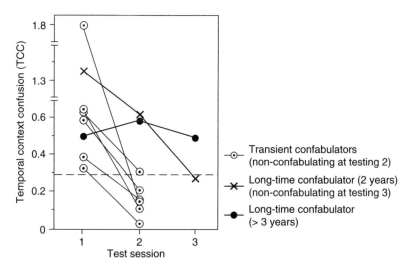

Figure 8.7 Relation between the clinical course of behaviourally spontaneous confabulation and the measure of temporal context confusion (TCC). At session 1, all patients were confabulating. At session 2, all but two patients (no. 7 and 8 in Figure 8.6) had stopped confabulating. These two patients were again examined at session 3 after three years; patient 7 had ceased to confabulate, patient 8 was still confabulating. The dashed line indicates the worst performance of any healthy control or non-confabulating amnesics involved in the original study. With permission from Schnider *et al.* (2000a).

The cessation of behaviourally spontaneous confabulation was sometimes fairly abrupt, at least in the few patients we could observe in this phase. Mrs B (Chapter 1) markedly changed her behaviour within one week after 18 months, although she still occasionally confused reality, thinking in the morning that she had to go to work; but she would now accept corrections with ease. Some patients realized this transition. One patient spontaneously remarked that he had the 'strange feeling of switching between two realities' shortly before he stopped confabulating. Another patient, already mentioned on page 188, realized towards the end of his confabulatory state that he could not trust in the veracity of his own ideas. DeLuca and Locker reported a similar observation (1996). No systematic inquiry into this transitional phase is available, however.

The *structural basis of recovery* from behaviourally spontaneous confabulation is unknown. As Figure 8.6 shows, lesions did not markedly change over time in our patients. It seems likely, then, that other areas, presumably also in the anterior limbic system, eventually convey the suppression capacity necessary to maintain a correct idea of ongoing reality. What these areas precisely are, is unknown. In any case, the observation that virtually all patients eventually stop confabulating indicates that the system may be redundantly organized. This conclusion would also be compatible with the observation that only a minority of patients having damage to anterior limbic structures, including the posterior medial orbitofrontal cortex, go on to have behaviourally spontaneous confabulation beyond an initial delirium (Chapter 4).

The state of behaviourally spontaneous confabulation is so severe that many physicians are tempted to try *medications*. However, no controlled study on the efficacy of medication is available. Circumstantial evidence, which will be explained in Chapter 9, has led us to try dopamine antagonists, that is, neuroleptics. Results have been mixed. In an initial patient, who had suffered rupture of an anterior communicating artery aneurysm, risperidone, a modern neuroleptic, had a dramatic, dose-dependent effect on behaviourally spontaneous confabulations and disorientation. The effect was observed within three to six days at low doses (Pihan *et al.* 2004). Performance in verbal memory and executive tasks was not influenced. Of note, this patient's performance in the first run of our task was normal, demonstrating preserved ability to store new information.

In Mrs B, who had extremely severe amnesia with no demonstrable storage capacity (Schnider *et al.* 2005a), risperidone was tried after four months with no obvious effect on her problematic behaviour (Chapter 1). At 12 months, quetiapine, another neuroleptic, was tried with a discrete beneficial effect on behaviour: she insisted less on leaving her home and on going to work and had fewer conflicts with her housemaid. We have observed similar effects in other patients with severe accompanying learning and storage deficits. It is possible that only the rare patients having relatively intact learning capacity have the potential of building up a consistent image of true ongoing reality under the tonic dopaminergic inhibition induced by neuroleptics. Patients having severely deficient learning capacity may simply fail to build up a coherent idea of ongoing reality and therefore do not profit from medication. However, since the effect of dopamine antagonists can be estimated within a few days and with low doses, brief therapeutic trials may be warranted and can easily be repeated some weeks later if treatment response is unsatisfactory.

Scope and limits of the TCC measure

Even though TCC has proved to have high predictive value for the occurrence of behaviourally spontaneous confabulation in amnesic subjects, there have been real and seeming false positive and false negative results. Some of these can be explained; others raise interesting questions awaiting focused investigation.

A critical source of *seemingly false results*, both positive and negative, is the erroneous classification of patients. Intense confabulations in a discussion – even if they appear 'spontaneous' – do not prove that a patient has the reality confusion characteristic of behaviourally spontaneous confabulation. The essential criterion is the accordance between confabulation and behaviour. Whereas severe behaviourally spontaneous confabulation is readily diagnosed, discrete cases with minor reality confusion may be difficult to ascertain. All our patients were hospitalized at the time of study so that we could observe their everyday behaviour. It is likely that chronic patients eventually adapt to their environment. Imagine, for example, a farmer hospitalized after ACoA aneurysm rupture, who would get up in the morning telling the nurse that he had to milk the cows. This would be considered an obviously inappropriate enactment of a habit betraying behaviourally spontaneous confabulation. Imagine the same farmer at home, getting up in the morning and saying that he had to milk the cows. Now, he would be considered well adapted to reality. The questions proposed in Table 3.1 have been helpful for us when we followed up our initially confabulating patients (Schnider et al. 2000a). But the transition from a state marked by behaviourally spontaneous confabulation to a state with discrete reality confusion may be difficult to verify. As we have seen, Mrs B (Chapter 1) still occasionally thought in the morning that she had to go to work, although she now accepted corrections. Even if TCC appears to have a threshold beyond which patients enact inappropriate plans (Figure 8.2), there is likely to be a continuum between the state of severe, incorrigible reality confusion with inappropriate actions and ideas, and discrete, correctible reality confusion. Orientation appears to be a useful continuous measure of the reality confusion reflected in increased TCC in amnesic patients (Figure 8.3). Behaviourally spontaneous confabulators have some degree of disorientation.

False negative results may reflect a patient's strategy to cope with the interference sensed in the runs following the first one. Our first patient presenting a false negative result was an undeniable confabulator having suffered rupture of an anterior communicating artery aneurysm (Ptak and Schnider 1999). He was also amnesic and severely disoriented. Despite these clinical findings, TCC was normal. It appeared that he responded to the feeling of interference by an extremely conservative strategy, distrusting any instance of familiarity with an item. The task was repeated a few days later. This time, the patient was repeatedly informed in both runs about the fact that both the recognition of true repetitions and the rejection of items, which had not appeared in the ongoing run, yet, would be counted. This time, the hit rate was comparable in both runs, whereas false positives significantly increased in the second run (Ptak and Schnider 1999). The case also showed that stringent self-monitoring in a memory task does not protect against false ideas dominating the behaviour of these patients.

False negative cases have been rare. More often, we have obtained *false positive* results in patients who had suffered typical anterior limbic lesions, but who had only discretely impaired or normal explicit memory, including delayed free recall. The woman with ACoA aneurysm rupture, whose CT scan was shown in Figure 4.3f. had presented an initial confusional state, then rapidly recovered her memory capacities, regained correct orientation, and never confabulated despite increased TCC. She strongly perceived the interference in the second run of the task. Another patient with similar results indicated that she had difficulty distinguishing between dreams and real events. Such patients did not enter our studies because they were neither amnesic nor confabulating. In any case, it appears that increased TCC in the presence of normal explicit memory does not predict behaviourally spontaneous confabulation or disorientation. Intact access to memories may apparently override the effect of the memory confusion measured with TCC.

In this context, it is important to note that TCC does not correlate with amnesia. We tested 59 patients with varying degrees of amnesia, ranging from mild to very severe according to the California Verbal Learning test (Delis *et al.* 1987) and our TCC task. For cross-validation, 26 patients were also tested with a similarly designed verbal list learning task composed of ten words, in which delayed recognition was tested by the presentation of the target word

Table 8.1 Predictors of amnesia. Correlation of performance in the first run of a continuous recognition task (Figure 5.1, Run 1) and temporal context confusion in the second run (TCC) with performance in the learning trials, long-delay free recall (LDFR) and recognition in the California Verbal Learning task (CVLT) and a ten-word verbal learning task.

	Run 1	TCC
CVLT (N = 59)		
Learning	0.30 *	– 0.21
LDFR	0.37 **	– 0.15
Recognition	0.48 ***	– 0.17
10-word test (N = 26)		
Learning	0.29	– 0.17
LDFR	0.40 *	– 0.14
Recognition	0.61 ***	– 0.29

Levels of significance: * $0.05 > p > 0.01$; ** $0.01 \geq p > 0.001$; *** $p \leq 0.001$.

together with two semantic foils. Table 8.1 shows the result (Schnider *et al.* 1997). Both verbal learning tasks had significant correlations with performance in the first run of our recognition task, that is, with information storage capacity. In contrast, TCC did not correlate with any component of the verbal memory tasks. Thus, the ability to store and recognize information, which is particularly dependent on the medial temporal lobes, is predictive of the occurrence of clinically manifest amnesia. In contrast, the control of interference induced in the second run of the task (TCC), which depends on the anterior limbic system (orbitofrontal cortex), is predictive of the behavioural features of an amnesia – behaviourally spontaneous confabulation and disorientation – but not of the amnesia itself.

Other groups have also described increased TCC in confabulating patients (Gilboa *et al.* 2006; Ciaramelli and Ghetti 2007). However, Gilboa *et al.* (2006) also found increased TCC in six of their eight non-confabulating patients. All patients had ventromedial damage, mostly due to ACoA aneurysm rupture. The reasons for the false-positive results are unclear. Classification and explicit memory capacity may have been issues: the patients lived at home and classification was based on interviews with relatives; one patient in the non-confabulating group was considered a possible 'latent confabulator'. Interestingly, mean time since injury of the confabulating patients was 43 months (range 3–98 months). This is an uncommonly long period for behaviourally spontaneous confabulation to continue, as we have seen in the last paragraph. Indeed, the long-term adaptations of behaviourally spontaneous confabulators are unknown; it is possible that classification becomes particularly tricky once a patient is integrated at his home. In addition, two non-confabulators had normal delayed recall in verbal memory testing. The impact of increased TCC on thinking in the presence of preserved explicit memory has never been studied. It would be interesting to know whether such patients can distinguish normally between memories referring to thoughts, dreams, and real events.

A situation in which TCC does not have a reliable predictive value for behaviour is degenerative *dementia*. We explored 23 patients with mild to moderate probable Alzheimer's disease (Mini Mental State Examination, 21.2 ± 3.7) (Joray *et al.* 2004); 52 per cent were disoriented. In contrast to our studies with patients recovering from acute brain lesions, TCC did not correlate with orientation and did not predict conspicuous behaviourally spontaneous confabulation. Among a series of cognitive measures, only general cognitive impairment significantly, albeit weakly, correlated with disorientation. A high variability of TCC values with no consistent behavioural association also suggested that the patients had difficulty in following task instructions. Indeed, occasional patients with dementia or severe focal *frontal dysfunction* simply fail to do the task and indicate familiarity with items irrespective of whether the familiarity relates to the items' previous occurrence in the same or an earlier run. The result then reflects impaired executive control rather than a failure of memory per se. To increase the probability that patients really do the task, we normally repeat task instructions several times during a run.

An increased susceptibility to the interference measured by our task was also described in *schizophrenic patients*. Badcock *et al.* (2005) and Waters *et al.* (2003) used a task with similar design to the one described in Figure 8.1, but composed of animal pictures. They found that schizophrenics having auditory hallucinations produced a similar number of false positives in the first run as schizophrenics with no auditory hallucinations and healthy controls. By contrast, they produced significantly more false positives in runs 2 to 4. Badcock *et al.* (2005) deduced from this finding the indication of

> a subtle interplay between inhibition and (episodic) memory in the genesis of [auditory hallucinations]. Thus, in patients currently experiencing hallucinations, failure to inhibit memories of prior events allows old memories to intrude into current events (i.e. to become functionally equivalent to perceptual representations of current events – the 'now') and become confused with ongoing reality.
>
> Badcock *et al.* (2005, p. 132)

Based on a comparison with our anatomical findings in behaviourally spontaneous confabulators, they even hypothesized on a possible role of the orbitofrontal cortex for the occurrence of auditory hallucinations. Indeed, abnormal patterns of posterior medial orbitofrontal gyri have recently been reported in schizophrenic patients (Nakamura *et al.* 2007). Even though the comparison is interesting, the reader may remember that behaviourally spontaneous confabulations have not been reported as a typical feature of schizophrenia (Chapter 4, pp. 127ff.). Such patients typically have largely intact verbal learning, so that TCC would not be expected to have a predictive value for the occurrence of behaviourally spontaneous confabulations. Nonetheless, schizophrenia represents a form of reality confusion, and patients act according to their delusional ideas.

It is possible that increased TCC has a different mechanism in dementia and schizophrenia than in patients with orbitofrontal lesions. Our clinical studies (and the imaging studies described below) pointed to the posterior orbitofrontal cortex as the critical area for the control of the interference measured by TCC. In behaviourally spontaneous confabulation, the damaged orbitofrontal cortex is thought to fail to exert its normal influence on activity in the neocortex. One might speculate that in degenerative dementia, possibly also in schizophrenia, a sick or developmentally abnormal neocortex failed to react normally to orbitofrontal signals.

Orbitofrontal memory selection seen with functional imaging

Our clinical studies highlighted the critical role of the anterior limbic system for the adaptation of thought to ongoing reality. But what precise conditions induce activation of this system in the healthy brain? And is it really the posterior orbitofrontal cortex, which is so important for selection of currently relevant memories?

To study these questions, we used functional imaging in healthy subjects. We chose $H_2[15]O$-PET (positron emission tomography using radio-labelled water) as the imaging method rather than functional MRI because the latter method usually has artefacts with signal dropout in the area of the orbitofrontal cortex (Ojemann *et al.* 1997). $H_2[15]O$-PET has a temporal resolution of approximately 45 seconds. Brain activity associated with a task of interest is usually determined by subtracting brain activation during a base-line task, which should have all components of the main task (type of stimuli, type of response etc.) except for the cognitive component of interest.

Our first attempt to obtain orbitofrontal activation was a failure. We had healthy subjects perform the same task – two runs of a continuous recognition task – as the one on which behaviourally spontaneous confabulators had failed (Figure 8.1). The break between the two runs was ten minutes. To our disappointment, this task did not yield any consistent brain activation in either run. Thus a task which had been so difficult for behaviourally spontaneous confabulators did not pose the slightest challenge to healthy subjects and did not induce activation of any specific brain area.

Obviously, the task had to be more difficult. So, a new, harder version was composed with colour photographs. Rather than presenting a few pictures five to eight times during a run, a higher number of pictures were repeated during a run, but only once or twice, thus requiring attention throughout the whole run (Schnider *et al.* 2000b). Rather than separating runs by a ten minutes' break, five runs were made in rapid succession, each lasting four minutes, separated by the time needed to restart the presentation program (approximately 90 seconds). Brain activation was measured during runs 1, 3, and 5, whereas runs 2 and 4 served as washout periods for radioactivity. The baseline task consisted of the repeated presentation of three pictures. Subjects had to indicate immediate picture repetitions, whose frequency was equal to the targets in the main task.

These adaptations had the desired effect. Finally, test subjects conceived the task as somewhat challenging, although performance remained virtually perfect.

Figure 8.8 displays the imaging results (Schnider *et al.* 2000b). The first run, in comparison to the baseline task, strongly activated medial temporal structures on both sides with main activation centred on the parahippocampal gyrus, that is, the cortex adjacent to the hippocampus (Figure 8.8a). In addition, there was activation of the middle part of the right gyrus rectus. An entirely different result was obtained in the later runs. In the third run, there was no medial temporal activation any more (similarly, there was no activation of the right gyrus rectus). In contrast, there was significant activation of the posterior medial orbitofrontal cortex on the left side (Figure 8.8b). In the fifth run, there was more restricted, bilateral activation of the orbitofrontal cortex (Figure 8.8c). In terms of cytoarchitecture, this activation corresponded to area 13 in Figure 4.2b, which is connected in a triangular way with the amgdala and the dorsomedial thalamic nucleus (Figure 4.1).

The results and the experimental adaptations needed to obtain them constituted more than just the confirmation of insights gained from the lesion studies. They had the following implications:

- ◆ The results confirmed dissociation between posterior and anterior limbic structures for the learning and selection of memories. The medial temporal lobe, that is, the posterior extension of the limbic system, was activated when new information had to be learned and subsequently recognized. In contrast, in the third and fifth run, when all items were familiar, so that familiarity judgements alone did not help to solve the

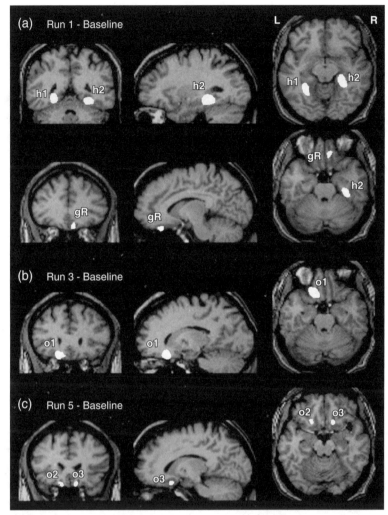

Figure 8.8 Memory selection by healthy subjects. H₂[15]O-positron emission tomography study using repeated runs of a continuous recognition task. (a) In the initial learning run, there was activation of parahippocampal cortex on both sides (h1, h2) and of the right middle rectal gyrus (gR). (b) In the third run, in which all items were already known, there was activation of the left posterior medial orbitofrontal cortex, corresponding to area 13 (o1); there was no activation of the medial temporal lobe. (c) In the fifth run, there was bilateral activation of posterior medial orbitofrontal cortex, area 13 (o2, o3). Whereas activation in regions h1, h2 and gR decreased from run to run, activation in regions o1, o2 and o3 increased from run to run. With permission from the Society for Neuroscience by Schnider et al. (2000b).

task, there was no medial temporal activation. In this situation, which demanded the ability to sort out those items that were repeated within the ongoing run, the posterior medial orbitofrontal cortex (area 13) was activated.

♦ The behavioural observations highlighted the efficacy of the suppression or filtering mechanism of interest. As we have seen in the previous chapters, damage of this mechanism has devastating effects on behaviour. Our new observations indicated that, in healthy subjects, this mechanism appears to be extremely efficient. The task had to be much more difficult than the clinical task to somewhat challenge the healthy subjects and to induce orbitofrontal activation.

♦ From a technical point of view, the result meant that we had found a task of sufficient difficulty to activate the orbitofrontal cortex in the way predicted by the lesion studies. This observation was crucial for devising an electrophysiological study on the time course of the suppression mechanism.

Early memory filtration indicated by evoked potentials

The conviction that behaviourally spontaneous confabulators, but also healthy subjects, hold in their concept of reality – the current time, place, and duties – suggests that the suppression or filtration capacity necessary to adapt thinking to ongoing reality is an early process, presumably preceding the conscious processing of upcoming memories.

We had healthy subjects do an adapted version of the task, which we had already used in the PET study described above (Schnider *et al.* 2000b). This time, their brain activity was registered using high resolution evoked potentials (Schnider *et al.* 2002). This method allows determining variations of cortical activity at very high temporal resolution. Subjects made two blocks consisting each of two runs of a continuous recognition task, which were composed of the same series of line drawings, during which some pictures were repeated once or twice, as in the task used with PET. The two blocks had different pictures and were separated by a 15-minute break. The two runs within each block were made in immediate succession. Data from the first and second runs of the two blocks were pooled into a total first and second run.

Our interest was to see when and in what way stimuli appearing for the first time in a run (distracters) differed from repeated items in the same run (targets). In the first run, this difference should reflect the distinction between new and familiar stimuli, a distinction depending on processes of learning and recognition mediated by the the medial temporal area (Figure 8.8a). In the second run, when all items are known and appear familiar, the distinction between distracters and targets should depend on the suppression (filtration) capacity, which had activated the orbitofrontal cortex in PET (Figure 8.8b, c). Our special interest in this study was to see how distracters of the second run would be processed. Behaviourally spontaneous confabulators had specifically failed on these stimuli, thinking that they had just seen them in the ongoing second run when, in fact, they had only seen them in the previous run (Schnider and Ptak 1999) (Figure 8.4). How does the healthy brain handle this interference?

Figure 8.9 gives a traditional view of the results, consisting of the evoked potential traces over three electrode positions commonly reported in studies on memory: midline electrodes at frontal (Fz), central (Cz), and parietal (Pz) position. As Figure 8.9a shows, processing of the four stimulus types (distracters and targets of runs 1 and 2) was very similar for the first 200 ms but then started to differ. Figure 8.9b gives the statistical comparison of the amplitudes between potentials induced by distracters and targets in the first run. The main difference appeared at about 400–480 ms over posterior

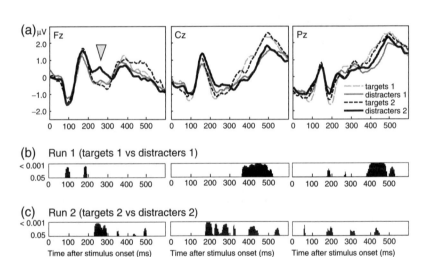

Figure 8.9 Evoked potential study on learning and memory selection.
(a) Electrocortical response to the four stimulus types. 'Distracters' denotes first occurrences of stimuli within a run, 'targets' denotes repeated presentation of items. Both are given four run 1 and run 2. The figure shows electrocortical potentials at electrode positions Fz, Cz, and Pz. The arrowhead points to the period between 200 and 300 ms, in which distracters of run 2 had a strikingly different electrocortical response. (b, c) Statistical difference of potential amplitudes shown in (a). (b) In run 1, first and repeated presentations of pictures (distracters as opposed to targets) induced marked amplitude differences between 400 and 500 ms over posterior electrode positions. (c) In run two, main amplitude differences were found between 200 and 300 ms in more anterior electrode positions. With permission from Schnider et al. (2002).

electrode positions. That is, learning and recognition, which are crucial for performance in the first run, appear to be cortically expressed at this relatively late period.

Figure 8.9c shows the comparison between distracters and targets in the second run, in which performance primarily depended on the suppression (filtration) capacity. The late difference over posterior electrodes was much less pronounced than in the first run. The main difference now emerged at the frontal electrode position between 200–300 ms, indicating that the selection of currently relevant memories is cortically expressed at this relatively early stage. The idea that this process really depends on suppression – as suggested by the clinical data – was supported by the potential forms induced by the four stimulus types at electrode Fz. It is immediately apparent from Figure 8.9a that distracters of run two underwent strikingly distinct processing: in contrast to all other stimuli, there was no negative deflection of the frontal potential in response to distracters of run 2 – the stimuli that behaviourally spontaneous confabulators had failed to suppress (Figure 8.9a, arrowhead).

Together, these data indicated that suppression or filtration of forthcoming memories according to their relation with ongoing reality occurs even before their precise content is recognized and probably re-encoded. In other words, even before we know what we think, the brain (or the orbitofrontal cortex) has already determined whether an upcoming thought relates to ongoing reality or not! This sequence of events also explains our capacity to distinguish between the memory of a thought and the memory of a real event. By the time these thoughts are again encoded (400–480 ms), their 'cortical format' has already been adapted according to their relation with ongoing reality by the filtration process at 200–300 ms.

The possible nature of preconscious memory filtration

These conclusions were drawn from the evoked potentials obtained at just three electrode positions, but the method applied in this study, with information from 123 electrodes, allowed going much further and performing pattern analyses of the cortical potential distribution (Michel *et al.* 2004). Such patterns do not randomly change but smoothly transgress from one pattern to the next. Techniques have been developed to separate stages characterized by relatively stable electrocortical potential configuration, which are thought to represent different processing stages (Lehmann 1987; Michel *et al.* 1999). When this technique – called segmentation – was applied to our data set, the first 600 ms after presentation of stimuli (distracters and targets of runs 1 and 2) could be split up into eight distinct electrocortical configuration maps. Figure 8.10a shows these eight map configurations.

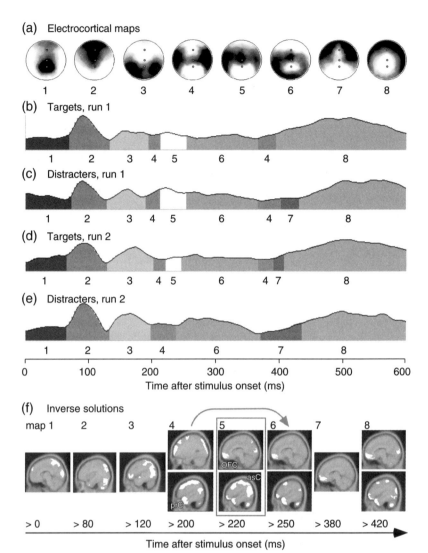

Figure 8.10 High resolution evoked potentials on learning and memory selection. The same study as in Figure 8.9, but with integration of 123 electrodes. (a–e) Result of segmentation procedure yielding eight different electrocortical configurations over 600 ms. (a) Potential distribution of the eight maps. Dark areas indicate a negative field potential. (b–e) Prevalent maps in the treatment of the four stimulus types. The amplitude of the curves indicates relative strength of the electrocortical configuration. Statistical analyses confirmed absence of map 5 in response to distracters of run 2 (e) Apparent map differences around 400 ms (maps 4, 7, 8) only related to different durations; there was no significant absence or presence of a map in any of the conditions. (f) Inverse solutions estimating the source of brain activity inducing the electrocortical maps shown in (a). Map 5, which was significantly absent in response to distracters of run 2 (e), apparently differed from the subsequent stage (map 6) by more activity in neocortical association areas. Thus, distracters of run 2 appeared to skip a stage characterized by extended neocortical synchronization. (a–e) With permission from Schnider et al. (2002); (f) With permission from Schnider (2003).

The question was to know how the four types of stimuli (distracters and targets of runs 1 and 2) differed from each other. Figure 8.10b–e shows the distribution of the prevalent maps over 600 ms after stimulus presentation (Schnider *et al.* 2002). There appeared to be two periods of marked difference between 200 and 300 ms and between 400 and 500 ms.

At about 220 ms, distracters of run 2 skipped map 5 and proceeded directly from map 4 to 6 (Figure 8.10e). Indeed, this is the period in which simple trace analysis showed that processing of distracters of run 2 did not induce the negative deflection that all other stimuli induced (Figure 8.9a, electrode Fz). Statistical analyses confirmed the result: Map 5 was not present in the processing of distracters of run 2. In other words, the suppression (filtering) of stimuli required for correctly processing the distracters of run 2 was characterized by the absence of a processing stage common to all other stimuli.

The second period of apparent difference occurred at around 400 ms. In this period, targets of run 1 seemed to skip map 7 (Figure 8.10b), whereas distracters of run 2 seemed to skip map 4 (Figure 8.10e). However, statistical analyses showed that, indeed, all maps were present in all conditions, although with varying intensity and duration. There was no specific absence or presence of a distinct map in response to any type of stimuli. In other words, learning and recognition in this experiment induced modulation of similar cortical networks rather than the activation of different networks (Schnider *et al.* 2002).

These data allowed us to go one step further and explore the very nature of the suppression or filtering process between 200 and 300 ms. It is possible to use the data obtained from 123 electrodes to estimate the source of the electrocortical potential distribution, a technique called 'inverse solution' (Michel *et al.* 2004). Figure 8.10f shows the inverse solutions of the electrocortical map configurations displayed in Figure 8.10a. This technique has a low spatial resolution with regards to activations emanating from deep midline structures such as the orbitofrontal cortex or the medial temporal lobe. Nonetheless, the analysis suggested early and continued activation of these areas starting at about 80 ms. The main difference between the maps appeared to concern neocortical activation. As we have seen above, treatment of distracters of run 2 was marked by the absence of map 5 (Figure 8.10e). When looking at the neocortical activation characterizing map 5 in comparison to map 6, it appears that the 'suppressed' (or filtered) stimuli skipped a processing stage with extended activation of neocortical association areas.

Although these data were somewhat tentative in that the topographical distribution differences lacked solid statistical confirmation, they suggested that the orbitofrontal cortex exerts the suppression or filtration of memories that do not pertain to ongoing reality – the process needed to adapt thought and behaviour to ongoing reality – by transiently inhibiting extended neocortical synchronization between about 200 and 300 ms (Schnider 2003).

Subcortical participation in memory selection

While the clinical and PET studies had indicated that the orbitofrontal cortex was critical for the selection of memories pertaining to ongoing reality, the evoked potential study showed that this selection process induced distinct alteration of electrocortical activity. So by what way, through what connections, does the orbitofrontal cortex communicate with the neocortex and influence the processing of thoughts and memories?

Anatomical studies have shown that discrete prefrontal areas are connected via segregated circuits with specific subcortical structures, which project back to the same prefrontal area (Alexander *et al.* 1986). The organizing principal of all loops is similar: the cortical area projects upon the striatum, then the pallidum and the substantia nigra (pars reticulata), which projects to the thalamic nucleus connected with the originating prefrontal area.

Of interest here is the loop originating in the orbitofrontal cortex, which projects to the ventral (limbic) part of the striatum, which then projects via the pallidum and the substantia nigra (pars reticulata) to the dorsomedial thalamic nucleus, which is the relay station to the whole prefrontal cortex, including the orbitofrontal cortex itself. Other loops originate in the dorsolateral prefrontal cortex, the anterior cingulate, the supplementary motor cortex, and the frontal eye field (Alexander *et al.* 1986). For our discussion of the orbitofrontal cortex influencing activity in wide areas of the neocortex, there are three observations of interest:

1. Although the circuits are anatomically segregated, there appears to be intense cross-communication on the level of the substantia nigra (Percheron *et al.* 1994). In this way, activity in one circuit might influence activation in the other circuits;

2. The loops are under modulatory influence from the dopaminergic system in the substantia nigra (pars compacta) and other structures in the midbrain. The orbitofrontal cortex not only participates in a cortico–subcortical loop, but also projects – via the limbic striatum – onto the dopaminergic system modulating the activity of the loops;

3. The projections coming from the limbic striatum have a much stronger influence on the other loops than vice versa (Joel and Weiner, 2000).

Our question, therefore, was whether there was evidence of subcortical participation in our task. We obtained such evidence when subjects made a variant of the task used in our previous PET study (Schnider *et al.* 2000b). In the new study, subjects made four blocks of a continuous recognition memory task (Treyer *et al.* 2003). Each block was made with a different type of stimuli: meaningful pictures, meaningful words, meaningless geometric designs, and meaningless words. Each block had three runs composed of the same pictures, arranged in different order each time, and was finished by the baseline task consisting of two repeatedly presented stimuli of the same type, among which subjects had to detect immediate picture repetitions. Brain activation was measured in the first run, third run, and during the baseline task of each block. Thus, this task not only had a higher statistical power than the previous study (four blocks rather than one), but potentially also a higher biological power in that different types of stimuli might possibly activate more components of the memory selection system of interest. A possible disadvantage was that the four blocks having the same design might create interference between each other, despite having different stimuli.

Overall, this new task yielded more extended activation than the previous one in diverse areas including medial temporal, visual and orbitofrontal areas, both in the first and third run (Treyer *et al.* 2003). Figure 8.11 shows the main results. Activation in the third run (compared with the baseline task) was of particular interest. As in our previous study, there was activation of the left posterior orbitofrontal cortex (Figure 8.11b). In this study, however, the activity was contiguous with subcortical activation including the ventral striatum, the body of the striatum down to the substantia nigra, then up to the medial thalamic area with the dorsomedial thalamic nucleus (Figure 8.11c). The study showed for the first time activation of an orbitofrontal–subcortical loop during a task demanding selection of currently relevant memories.

The need for suppression

According to our clinical studies, the ability to sort out memories of current relevance is of crucial importance for meaningful behaviour. In fact, it may be that the healthy brain has a constant need to filter forthcoming memories according to their relation with the 'now'. Think, for example, of a common working day. Most people work in places which look very similar from one day to the other. They enter the same office, meet the same people, and find the same desk every day; yet every morning, they have a feeling for the tasks they have to do on that day. Imaging studies have indicated that thinking about the future invokes very much the same cortical networks as thinking about the past (Addis *et al.* 2007). Within this flow of neural activity representing past experiences (memories of the past) and plans for the future (future memory), there must be some anchor retaining those thoughts that refer to the present.

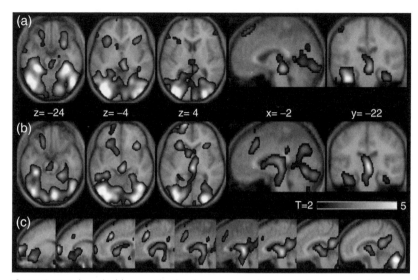

Figure 8.11 Subcortical loop activation in memory selection. Subjects made four blocks composed of three continuous recognition runs and one baseline task each. (a) The pooled first runs yielded activation of visual cortex, medial temporal areas and bilateral orbitofrontal cortex (area 13), stronger on the right side. (b) In the pooled third runs, there was stronger activation of the left orbitofrontal cortex (area 13), but markedly less activity in visual and medial temporal areas. (c) Sagittal cuts of activation in the pooled third runs, starting at the level of the left orbitofrontal activation (area 13) and proceeding to the right side. Activation of the left orbitofrontal cortex in the third run was contiguous with activation in the ventral striatum, body of the caudate, substantia nigra, and the medial thalamic area on the other side. x, y, and z values indicate the level of the images according to coordinates of the Montreal Neurological Institute. Adapted with permission from Treyer *et al.* (2003).

Sorting out the specifics of an individual day within a constant environment should theoretically pose a much harder problem for our brain than to learn the new pieces of information coming in every day.

Theoretically, any piece of information, any perception, may evoke memories and thoughts that give rise to action plans. Indeed, such associations are the very essence of creative thinking. But any attempt to retrieve a memory or thought also risks coactivating memories having no current relevance. So there may be a constant need to sort out memories that pertain to ongoing reality.

We searched for such coactivations using evoked potentials (Murray *et al.* 2004). Subjects made a continuous recognition task in which they saw a series of meaningful designs and had to indicate picture recurrences. To this point, the task was similar to the recognition tasks used in previous experiments. The trick of this new task was that half of the pictures were associated with a corresponding sound on initial presentation. Thus, the picture of a gun was associated with the typical 'bang' sound; an airplane was presented with no accompanying sound. The occurrence of such sounds was declared as irrelevant to the subjects; their only task was to look at the pictures and indicate repetitions within the run. Picture recurrences were purely visual, never accompanied by a sound. Our interest was to compare picture recurrences which had a history of being accompanied by a sound, and picture recurrences, which had no such history. Would there be an electrocortical correlate of this currently irrelevant memory of stimuli being previously associated with a sound? And what would be the electrophysiological correlate of the handling of such 'irrelevant associations'?

We found evidence for both questions (Murray *et al.* 2004). There was an initial period around 100–150 ms, in which stimuli, which had been accompanied by a sound on initial presentation, differed from pictures that had not. Hence, it appears that cues evoking a memory – in this case, the repeated presentation of pictures – may indeed induce currently irrelevant associations, which are expressed in early electrocortical activity. A second period with stronger amplitude differences occurred between 200 and 250 ms. In comparison with our earlier study on memory selection (Schnider *et al.* 2002), activity in this period might correspond to the filtering of such irrelevant associations. A third period with different amplitudes occurred at 320–400 ms. The study confirmed that in normal memory processing, early coactivation of currently irrelevant associations does indeed occur and is followed by electrocortical activity compatible with filtering of such associations.

The experiment was later performed using functional MRI (Murray *et al.* 2005). An interesting corollary result was that the processing of pictures previously associated with sounds also induced orbitofrontal activation.

Ubiquity of orbitofrontal memory selection

The tasks described so far – both in the clinical and functional imaging studies – used visual stimuli, but it appeared plausible that the same organizing principle with the posterior limbic system (medial temporal lobe) being involved in learning and recognition and the anterior limbic system (posterior orbitofrontal cortex) being crucial for the selection of currently relevant memories also applied to other modalities, such as hearing. We used $H_2[15]O$-PET to test this conjecture. Subjects made three runs of a continuous recognition task involving common spoken words presented over earphones (Treyer *et al.* 2006b). Half of them were concrete words (e.g., 'coffee'), the other half abstract words (e.g., 'project'). Subjects had to recognize word repetitions. Similar to the previous studies, the baseline task consisted of the repeated presentation of three words, among which subjects had to recognize immediate repetitions.

The result was similar to the study using visual stimuli (Schnider *et al.* 2000b) (Figure 8.8), with the exception of stronger activation of the auditory cortex in the temporal lobes (Treyer *et al.* 2006b). In the first run, there was medial temporal activation involving the posterior parahippocampal areas and the anteriorly situated perirhinal cortex. In the third run, activation of these areas was weaker. Conversely, there was now left posterior orbitofrontal activation centred on area 13, similar to the processing of visual stimuli. Thus, orbitofrontal filtering appears to intervene in auditory memory as much as in visual memory.

There may be other situations in which the orbitofrontal cortex might act as a filter, even when a task has not been designed to explore this capacity. Baseline tasks in functional imaging are usually similar to the target task (e.g., a memory task) in all aspects except the cognitive function under investigation. According to what has been said in the previous paragraphs, this similarity might possibly induce orbitofrontal filtering activity.

We explored this possibility in an extension to the imaging study, which had yielded activation of a frontal subcortical loop (Treyer *et al.* 2003). We compared brain activation in two groups of subjects, both performing four blocks of a continuous recognition task with different sitmuli (meaningful designs, meaningful words, meaningless geometric designs, meaningless words). One group performed the corresponding baseline task at the beginning of each block. The baseline task consisted of the repeated presentation of two pictures of the same type as the memory task; subjects had to indicate immediate picture repetitions. Thus, for these subjects, the baseline task introduced a new type of stimuli. The other group performed the baseline task at the end of each block and was, therefore, already familiar with the stimulus type when they performed the baseline task.

We found that the position of the baseline relative to the memory task had a profound impact on the apparent activation during the main task (Treyer *et al.* 2006a). When the baseline task was made before the main memory task, there was apparent activation in the right orbitofrontal cortex (area 13) during the memory task. In contrast, when the baseline task was performed after the main memory task, there was apparent activation of the parahippocampal areas during the memory task. Thus, although a memory task may seem well-designed and specific for a particular memory capacity, the brain switches between encoding of new information (medial temporal activation) and memory filtration (orbitofrontal activation) depending on the experience of a subject with the task and the context. The common habit of 'balancing' the position of baseline tasks with respect to main tasks does not resolve the problem but risks averaging dissociated processes.

Reality in thinking–model of the online filter

The clinical and imaging data presented in the previous chapters, and in particular in this chapter, allow one to formulate a theory on how the brain sorts out ongoing reality in thinking, how it figures out the 'now' in thinking and adapts behaviour to current reality. In this paragraph, I propose two models of this process: an anatomical and a functional one.

The anatomical model describes the contribution of the posterior and anterior limbic system to memory processing. Figure 8.12 describes the model. Regarding the *posterior limbic system*, it has been established beyond a doubt that the medial temporal lobe with the hippocampus and the surrounding cortex is important for retaining information in a durable way in memory. Additional lesion data (Figure 4.12) and functional imaging data (Figure 8.8) have been presented in this book. Failure of this capacity induces amnesia. Although there is some controversy about the precise role of the hippocampus in the retrieval of memories, it is generally believed that memories are stored and processed in distributed areas of the neocortex (Fuster 1995). The *neocortex* has the liberty to associate memories (thoughts) in every possible way – this is the essence of thinking. Thanks to such activity, we may plan meaningful acts or roam in fantasies. The data presented in this chapter and previous chapters indicate that it is the role of the *anterior limbic system*, in particular the posterior medial orbitofrontal and ventromedial cortex, to ensure at all time that the brain distinguishes between reality and fantasies (daydreams). This capacity allows us to act on the basis of thoughts (memories) that pertain

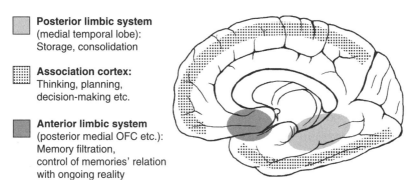

Posterior limbic system
(medial temporal lobe):
Storage, consolidation

Association cortex:
Thinking, planning,
decision-making etc.

Anterior limbic system
(posterior medial OFC etc.):
Memory filtration,
control of memories' relation
with ongoing reality

Figure 8.12 Anatomical model of the posterior and the anterior limbic contribution to memory.

to ongoing reality, rather than memories that do not – despite the liberty to engage in fantasies. Behaviourally spontaneous confabulators fail in this capacity. Of course, they may also fail in the first two capacities (storage and association of memories), but in this respect, they do not differ from non-confabulating amnesics.

The *functional model* describes the workings of the memory filter. It is supported by electrophysiological findings in healthy subjects. It is more hypothetical than the anatomical model because the significance of processing stages observed in evoked potentials is deduced from assumed task requirements; it is not yet possible to verify directly the influence of a distinct electrophysiological state on thoughts. In our studies, these assumptions were derived from the experimental tasks conducted with behaviourally spontaneous confabulators.

The model is illustrated in Figure 8.13. The traces show the electrophysiological evidence indicating that filtering – i.e., suppression of the interference by currently irrelevant memories – occurs at an early stage (Figure 8.9a, electrode Fz). Figure 8.13a shows the model for normal filtering of memories. It starts with the initiation of memory activation by a cue, be this a percept or a thought. As we have seen above (p. 263ff.), a cue may coactivate currently irrelevant associations. The idea is that, after 200–300 ms, upcoming memories pass through the (orbitofrontal) filter which checks whether an upcoming memory pertains to ongoing reality (reality) or not (fantasy). Memories that do not relate to ongoing reality skip a processing stage characterized by extended neocortical synchronization (Figure 8.10f.). This processing difference determines the 'format' of memories and characterizes them as reality or fantasy. As memories (thoughts) enter the phase of recognition and re-encoding (400–600 ms), they influence behaviour according to their format. This sequence also explains the capacity to distinguish between the memory of a real event and the memory of a fantasy; as the memories (thoughts) enter the stage of re-encoding, they have already the format characterizing them as a real experience or a fantasy.

Figure 8.13b shows the hypothetical dysfunction in behaviourally spontaneous confabulators. In this situation, memories are normally evoked by cues, as in healthy subjects. However, memories then do not normally pass through the filter at 200–300 ms, with the consequence that thoughts with no relation with ongoing reality have the same format as thoughts pertaining to 'now'. Depending on the cue, the evoked memories are sometimes in agreement with ongoing reality, sometimes not.

In this model, the orbitofrontal filter mechanism only determines a forthcoming memory's relation with ongoing reality, but not its content. Whether a patient has recurring, stable confabulatory themes or jumps from one idea to

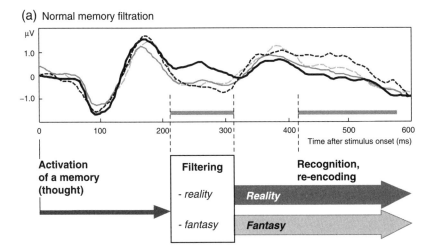

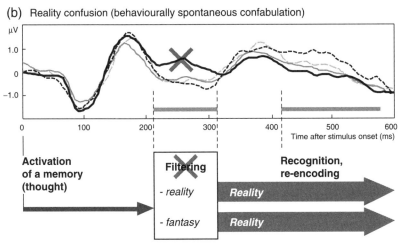

Figure 8.13 Functional model of memory filtration. The curves show electrocortical responses at electrode Fz (same as in Figure 8.9). The black curve shows the processing of distracters of run 2, i.e., stimuli needing filtration (suppression). The grey bar below the curves between 200 and 300 ms indicates the period of amplitude difference between distracters and targets in the second run of the task, i.e., the presumed period of memory filtration. The second bar between 400 and 600 ms indicates the period of significant amplitude difference between distracters and targets in the first run demanding learning and recognition. (a) Normal memory filtration, in which forthcoming memories are filtered according to their relation with ongoing reality at 200–300 ms. Thereafter, memories referring to current reality have a different format than those representing fantasies. (b) In behaviourally spontaneous confabulation, filtration after 200–330 fails (cross), so that all forthcoming memories have a format characterizing them as relating to ongoing reality when they enter the phase of recognition and re-encoding after 400–600 ms.

the other, depends on associative processes in the neocortex, which are independent of the orbitofrontal filter mechanism. Also, the mechanism does not determine whether a memory will be acted upon or not. In a strict sense, it does not even determine a subject's proclivity to verbally express his or her false ideas, that is, the tendency to confabulate. All it predicts is that, if subjects having a failure of this mechanism express their ideas – spontaneously or in response to questions – there will be confabulations, that is, objectively false statements, which agree with their (false) concept of reality.

The electrophysiological data underlying the model, in particular the source localizations (Figure 8.10f), suggest that the evocation of memories that do not relate to ongoing reality induces transient suppression (inhibition) of neocortical synchronization at 200–300 ms. However, the model allows such memories (fantasies, daydreams) to have full intensity thereafter – they just have a different format labelling them as thoughts that do not pertain to 'now'.

This model does not contradict the models of memory retrieval and confabulation discussed in the previous chapter, but gives neurophysiological meaning to them. The failure responsible for the reality confusion characterizing behaviourally spontaneous confabulation can be conceived as a defect in the 'construction' of memories. It can be seen as a defect of source monitoring–the ability to distinguish between memories relating to real events or thoughts. It can also be interpreted as a failure of retrieval monitoring, but in a very early phase of retrieval. Our electrophysiological data specify that the orbitofrontal contribution to monitoring precedes the recognition and re-encoding of memories, as far as monitoring concerns the filtration of memories according to their relation with the present. The model is also compatible with the observation that confabulations reflect a confusion of memories from different past events – the basic idea of temporal order hypotheses. Conversely, the model does not include aspects of personality and motivation. It might be that such factors influence the content of false memories, in that they bias the interpretation of cues or function as cues. In addition, personality and motivation might influence the way in which false memories are used and acted upon, but they do not explain the falsehood of the memories.

The main difference between our model and the cognitive models discussed in the previous chapter is that the latter introduced theoretical constructs of memory retrieval, which were then applied to diverse forms of confabulation. Our model is built upon electrophysiological and imaging data obtained with a paradigm specific for behaviourally spontaneous confabulation. Thus, the present model is physiologically more specific, but limited in scope to the sole confusion of ongoing reality, which characterizes behaviourally spontaneous confabulation. It does not extend to other forms of confabulation, such as (momentary) confabulations in tests of semantic memory.

Summary

The data presented in this chapter, together with the observations reported in the previous chapters, can be summarized as follows.

1. Behaviourally spontaneous confabulation represents a *confusion of reality*, which induces currently inappropriate ideas (confabulations and disorientation) and acts (typically the enactment of previous habits). The patients' reality is determined by elements of memories that do not relate to the present.

2. When behaviourally spontaneous confabulation results from focal brain damage, then damage involves *anterior limbic structures* (Figure 4.12). Damage may involve the posterior medial *orbitofrontal cortex* itself or structures having direct connections with it. According to lesion (Figure 4.12) and functional imaging data (Schnider *et al.* 2000b) (Figure 8.8), the functionally critical parts of the orbitofrontal cortex appear to be area 13 (Figure 4.2b) plus the ventromedial cortex.

3. Patients having the reality confusion typical of behaviourally spontaneous confabulation have a specific failure to distinguish between memories that pertain to ongoing reality and memories that do not (Schnider *et al.* 1996b). This failure is based on an inability to *suppress* the interference of memories that do not relate to 'now' (Schnider and Ptak 1999).

4. The failure to suppress (filter) the interference of currently irrelevant memories is also closely associated with *disorientation* (Schnider *et al.* 1996c) and appears to be a more important mechanism of disorientation in amnesic subjects than the difficulty to store enough information (Figure 8.3, see also Figure 5.3).

5. *Recovery* from behaviourally spontaneous confabulation, that is, the recovery of reality perception, is accompanied by the recovery of the ability to suppress the interference of memories that to not pertain to current reality (Schnider *et al.* 2000a). Most behaviourally spontaneous confabulators eventually regain the capacity to adapt behaviour and thought to ongoing reality; in some cases, this process may take many months. Most patients remain amnesic.

6. In the healthy brain, the need to exert such suppression (filtering) induces orbitofrontal activity centred on area 13 on both sides (Schnider *et al.* 2000b; Treyer *et al.* 2003) (Figure 8.8).

7. This *filtration* is a relatively *early process* occurring about 200–300 ms after stimulus presentation and precedes the stage of recognition and re-encoding (Schnider *et al.* 2002). That is, even before the content of a memory is recognized and re-encoded, the brain (orbitofrontal cortex) has already decided whether the forthcoming memory relates to ongoing reality or not. This sequence of events not only allows one to base behaviour on memories (thoughts) that pertain to ongoing reality, but also explains the capacity to distinguish between memories relating to previous real events and memories relating to thoughts.

8. Suppression of currently irrelevant memories (filtration) is cortically expressed by the absence of an electrocortical map configuration at 200–300 ms (Schnider *et al.* 2002). Source estimations suggest that suppression corresponds to the transient *inhibition of neocortical synchronization*, so that forthcoming memories having no relation with ongoing reality (fantasies) leave out a processing stage characterized by widespread neocortical synchronization (Schnider 2003).

9. An *orbitofrontal–subcortical loop* involving the ventral striatum, body of the striatum, substantia nigra and medial thalamus participates in the selection of currently relevant memories (Treyer *et al.* 2003) (Figure 8.11). Several of these structures are also part of the dopaminergic projection system.

10. Orbitofrontal area 13 is also activated in tasks involving other modalities (hearing) (Treyer *et al.* 2006b) and varying tasks performed in a constant environment, such as baseline tasks (Treyer *et al.* 2006a). The filtration of forthcoming memories appears to be a *ubiquitous* brain function.

11. The reality confusion underlying behaviourally spontaneous confabulation and disorientation probably results from the failure of this pre-conscious orbitofrontal memory filtering mechanism.

Chapter 9

Reward system and reality check

A hypothesis

The undeniable star of the last chapter has been the posterior medial orbitofrontal cortex. Our lesion data said that behaviourally spontaneous confabulation emanated from damage to the ventromedial prefrontal area and connected structures (Figure 4.12); functional imaging showed that the selection of currently relevant memories activates area 13. Thus, according to our data, it is this region, which filters upcoming memories according to their relation with ongoing reality.

How does it do it? What capacity allows the orbitofrontal cortex to check our thoughts' relation with the 'now?' On what basis does it interfere with the reactivation of our memories, outside the reach of conscious control?

In this chapter, I will review the anatomy and some of the functions of the orbitofrontal cortex. I will then propose an analogy between behaviourally spontaneous confabulation and a defect in extinction. Animal and human data will be taken to suggest that the adaptation of thought and behaviour to ongoing reality represents a capacity of the system commonly called the 'reward system'.

Anatomy of the orbitofrontal cortex

As we have seen in Chapter 4 (Figure 4.2b), the orbitofrontal cortex is not a homogenous area but has distinct components with different cytoarchitectonic structure, i.e., different composition of the cortical layers. The orbitofrontal cortex contains olfactory and gustatory cortex and has connections with diverse somatosensory and motor-related areas (Carmichael and Price 1995a). Of interest for our discussion is the posterior orbitofrontal cortex, a so-called agranular cortex, characterized by weak cellularity of layer IV. This region, often damaged in behaviourally spontaneous confabulators, encompasses areas 13, posterior area 11, area 14, 25, 32′ and 10′ in Figure 4.2b (Morecraft *et al.* 1992; Carmichael and Price 1994; Petrides and Pandya 1994; Öngür *et al.* 2003). It has strong connections with limbic structures – amygdala and the cortex adjacent to the hippocampus – and can be considered an anterior limbic extension (Carmichael and Price 1995b). It is phylogeneti-cally the oldest orbitofrontal component, which has the highest anatomical constancy (Chiavaras *et al.* 2001). The region extends into the anterior inferior insula, to which it is related by structure and connections (Carmichael and Price 1995b).

Within this posterior orbitofrontal area, two networks have been identified (Figure 9.1a): an *'orbital' prefrontal network* comprising areas 13, 11 and medial parts of area 47/12, and a *'medial' prefrontal network* involving areas 14, 10′, 32′, 25, and inferior area 24 (Carmichael and Price 1994, 1996; Price 2006). These networks have relatively little communication; parts of area 13 and 12 serve as points of interaction (Carmichael and Price 1996). Due to this position plus its connections with the amygdala and sensory areas, medial area 13 has been interpreted as a bridge between the amygdala and association areas (Haber *et al.* 1995).

Both networks have distinct, separate connections with the magnocellular portion of the *dorsomedial nucleus* of the thalamus and the amygdala (Figure 9.1b) (Ray and Price 1993; Price 2006). Thus the lateral limbic loop, which connects the orbitofrontal cortex in a triangle with the amygdala and the dorsomedial thalamic nucleus (Figures 4.1 and 9.1b), has a topographi-cally separate organization according to the originating ventromedial prefrontal network (Porrino *et al.* 1981).

Connections with the *hypothalamus* are also topographically specific (Figure 9.1c). Although details have been variously interpreted (Öngür *et al.* 1998; Rempel-Clower and Barbas 1998), it appears that the medial prefrontal network has particularly strong connections with the anterior and ventral hypothalamus. Readers may remember that damage to this area of the hypothalamus may also induce behaviourally spontaneous confabulation (Figure 4.10). The more lateral orbitofrontal cortex – the orbital prefrontal network – is preferentially connected with the lateral and posterior hypothalamus (Öngür *et al.* 1998; Rempel-Clower and Barbas 1998).

The networks also have separate projections upon the *ventral striatum* and the *pallidum* (Haber *et al.* 1995; Ferry *et al.* 2000), which then converge non-topographically on the dopaminergic part of the substantia nigra (pars compacta) (Figure 9.1d). As discussed on page 262, fibres emanating from this part of the substantia nigra, which has projections from the orbitofrontal cortex via the ventral striatum, may strongly influence activity in the frontal–subcortical loops emanating from other prefrontal areas (Percheron *et al.* 1994; Haber *et al.* 1995).

Thus, the different components of the posterior medial orbitofrontal area (medial and orbital networks) have extensive connections with other parts of

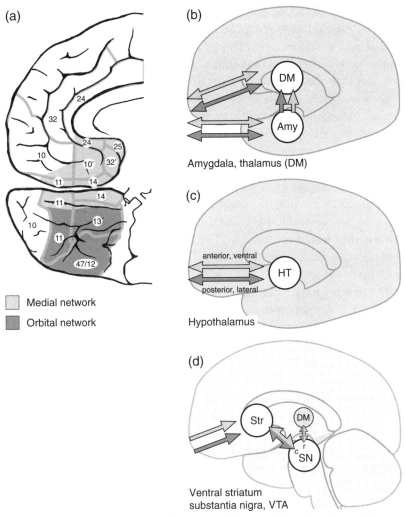

Figure 9.1 Ventromedial prefrontal networks. (a) Sagittal (above) and ventral view (bottom) of the prefrontal cortex. Extension of the cortical areas constituting a medial network and an orbital network. Numbers indicate cytoarchitectonic areas from the simplified schema in Figure 4.2; borders are indicated with grey lines. (b–d) Some important connections of the two networks. Parallel arrows indicate separate connections of the two networks, two-shade arrows indicate convergence of projections; arrow direction indicates direction of projections. The schemas do not reflect precise anatomical proportions. Abbreviations: Amy, amygdala; DM, dorsomedial nucleus of the thalamus; HT, hypothalamus; SN, substantia nigra (c, pars compacta; r, pars reticulata) plus ventral tegmental area (VTA); Str, ventral striatum.

the limbic system and the hypothalamus, and receive input from diverse cortical areas. For our forthcoming discussion, the connections of the two ventro-medial prefrontal networks through the striatum and pallidum upon the dopaminergic cells of the substantia nigra are particularly important. These cells and their connections are parts of the brain's reward system and may influence activity in wide areas of the neocortex. By way of the posterior medial orbitofrontal cortex, all areas damaged in behaviourally spontaneous confabulators may influence activity in this system.

Functions of the orbitofrontal cortex

Animal experiments with monkeys, which were performed in the 1960s, identified distinct behavioural changes after lesions of the orbitofrontal cortex. Once the animals had learned which one of two stimuli was associated with reward, they would continue to choose that stimulus even when reward contingencies changed and the other stimulus started being rewarded (Butter *et al.* 1963; Butter 1969; McEnaney and Butter 1969; Iversen and Mishkin 1970). In other words, the monkeys had a deficit of reversal learning – the ability to associate a previously unrewarded stimulus with reward in exchange for a previously rewarded one. In addition, they continued to act on stimuli which had been followed by reward in previous trials but which had then stopped being rewarded (Butter *et al.* 1963; Butter 1969). Thus, the animals had a deficit of extinction – the ability to learn that a previously rewarded stimulus is no more rewarded. The animals also displayed a continued interest in food beyond satiation (Butter *et al.* 1969). These behaviours did not simply reflect deficient response inhibition in the sense of perseverative behaviour as the animals had no deficit in go/no-go task, that is, when they had to refrain from reacting to specific stimuli (Goldman *et al.* 1971; Rosenkilde 1979; Dias *et al.* 1997).

With regard to *human behaviour*, the orbitofrontal cortex has long held a very discrete role in neuroscience and neurological teaching, as it was considered – like much of the prefrontal cortex – a silent, somehow superfluous part of the human brain, whose damage would not induce serious motor or sensory deficits. Nowadays, discussions of the orbitofrontal cortex fill entire volumes (Rolls 1999; Zald and Rauch 2006) and its impaired function is held accountable for sociopathy, poor decision-making, and disturbances of emotional processing.

Diverse researchers contributed to the increased awareness of consequences of orbitofrontal damage in humans. Among them were Antonio and Hanna Damasio, who revived the case of a patient presenting a dramatic, socially incapacitating personality change after prefrontal damage (Damasio 1994;

Damasio *et al.* 1994). The patient, Phineas Gage, had been described by Harlow (1848). Gage was 25 years old and working as a foreman in road building when he suffered a tragic accident, in which an iron rod shot through his left forehead and skull and destroyed most of his left frontal lobe. Gage did not lose consciousness and was able to speak and move normally. After weeks of protracted wound healing, he recovered, although Harlow described his behaviour as 'very childish'. In the following years, his behaviour turned out to be highly abnormal. In contrast to his perfect demeanour and reliability before the accident, he was now 'fitful, irreverent, indulging in the grossest profanity, manifesting but little deference for his fellows, ... capricious and vacillating, devising many plans of future operations, which ... [he soon] abandoned in turn for others' (From Harlow 1868, cited in Neylan 1999, p. 280).

Damasio and collaborators not only revived the case, but initiated an impressive research program on decision-making and sociopathy after orbitofrontal lesions. The basic tenet of their theory is that lesions of the orbitofrontal cortex, in particular the ventromedial prefrontal cortex, impair the ability to make advantageous and socially correct decisions because the anticipation of disadvantageous actions fails to evoke bodily signals – somatic markers – thought to guide decision-making (Damasio 1994; Bechara *et al.* 1997, 2000). Although aspects of the theory, including the specificity of the experimental approach (Maia and McClelland 2004), remain contested, diverse studies have established that lesions of the orbitofrontal cortex may induce socially inappropriate and personally disadvantageous behaviour (Eslinger and Damasio 1985). Even when recovery is excellent, the ability to make delicate moral judgements may be impaired (Koenigs *et al.* 2007). Damage during childhood may be associated with frank sociopathy in adult life, even when neuropsychological tests yield normal results (Price *et al.* 1990; Eslinger *et al.* 1992; Anderson *et al.* 1999). It should be noted, however, that many of these patients had lesions that involved large parts of the frontal lobes, not only the orbitofrontal cortex. In our patients with behaviourally spontaneous confabulation after ventromedial and orbitofrontal lesions, behavioural aberrations deserving the designation as 'socially inappropriate' have been a rarity; most patients had intact social manners in agreement with their premorbid social status. Group studies have provided ambiguous results (Bar-On *et al.* 2003; Hornak *et al.* 2003), in that the evidence for sociopathy and personality changes might well be interpreted as evidence for apathy and emotional blunting. Frank sociopathy may be as rare a consequence of orbitofrontal and ventromedial damage as behaviourally spontaneous confabulation.

Functional imaging has recently deepened the interest in the orbitofrontal cortex and reward processing in general. A rapidly growing literature has associated the orbitofrontal cortex, amygdala, and subcortical structures, in particular the striatum, with reward related functions (e.g., Elliott *et al.* 2000; Breiter *et al.* 2001; Critchley *et al.* 2001; Knutson *et al.* 2001b; O'Doherty *et al.* 2001; Gottfried *et al.* 2003). Even the sole feedback about the correctness of a decision may activate the orbitofrontal cortex (Elliott *et al.* 1997). Activations were also observed when subjects learned a series of complex designs, especially if some of the designs deviated from the rest (Petrides *et al.* 2002). We will come back to the imaging of reward processing later in this chapter.

Reality check and extinction

So, what would reward processing and extinction have to do with behaviourally spontaneous confabulation and thought adaptation?

The most impressive feature of behaviourally spontaneous confabulation is the incorrigibility of the patients' false reality; the patients fail to integrate contradicting information into their concept of reality. Mrs B, for example, obtained hospital care by nurses, passed numerous tests, and had regular therapy sessions, but still believed that she was a staff psychiatrist in our clinic and that she had to give a reception in the evening (Chapter 1). We have seen many other examples of such behaviour in this book. A 58-year-old woman remained convinced that she was at home, although she acknowledged that the hospital bedroom did not at all resemble the living room she had expected to find behind the room's door. Another patient was convinced that he was in Bordeaux, although he admitted that the town that he saw through the window looked entirely different (Pihan *et al.* 2004).

Why do these patients fail to integrate such information, which strikingly contradicts their convictions, into their concept of reality? Why does true reality fail to correct their false interpretation of reality? And how would the healthy brain react to information so flagrantly contradicting what was anticipated?

Figure 9.2a proposes a series of processing steps leading up to anticipations and – presumably – reality checking. In this schema, 'knowledge' denotes an individual's pool of memories. These memories can be evoked by cues, which may be external (perceptions) or internal (thoughts). A cue may not exclusively evoke the memory (thought) that leads up to the most appropriate action, but also associations that are not pertinent to current reality (fantasies). At this stage, decision-making processes may intervene, weighing benefits and risks, advantages and disadvantages. The main point is that the thoughts (memories) evoked by cues and their mental processing incite anticipations;

(a) Human anticipation and reality checking

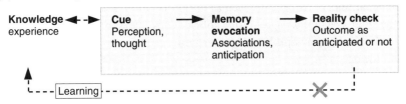

(b) Animal reward experiment

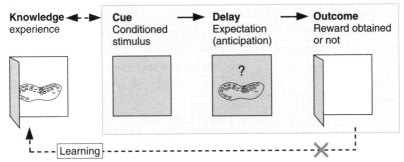

Figure 9.2 Reality checking and extinction. (a) Schema of human reality checking. Memories are thought to be evoked by cues and to induce mental associations leading to anticipations of future events. The appropriateness of memories for ongoing reality, i.e., reality checking, is performed by comparing the real outcome with the anticipation. (b) Typical animal experiment on reward processing. The animal updates its knowledge base and adapts behaviour in response to the outcome of a trial. The cross in (a) indicates the process that is presumably defective in behaviourally spontaneous confabulators if reality does not correspond to the anticipated course of events: Confabulators fail to adapt their thinking and behaviour to the fact that anticipated outcomes do not happen. The cross in (b) indicates the corresponding defect in animal experimentation: The animal fails to adapt its behaviour to the non-occurrence of the anticipated outcome (the reward). This deficit corresponds to deficient extinction.

there is no plan and no action that does not aim for a goal – an outcome. At some point in time, these anticipations either will be confirmed or negated; an anticipated outcome may occur or not. The cycle of cues evoking memories, mental associations inducing anticipations, and outcomes confirming or negating the anticipations, creates a new experience – a new memory added to the knowledge base. This process entails constant memory retrieval and learning.

The schema need not be limited to complex, consciously performed actions but may apply to any thought or anticipation, be it conscious or unconscious.

It may apply to long-term anticipations such as a career plan, but also to singular, short-term events, such as the anticipation of text being present on the other side of this page. Myriad anticipations (ideas) may be 'on hold' in the brain at any time and be checked against true reality at the appropriate moment.

Translating this schema to animal experimentation is straightforward. Figure 9.2b proposes such a translation. In a typical experiment, animals learn to associate a cue with an outcome. Outcomes are often pleasant and sweet – that is, 'rewards' – motivating the animal to continue working. The cue constitutes the conditioned stimulus, which arouses the expectation of a reward. When the animal has given the required response, the unconditioned stimulus – the reward – is either presented as reinforcement, or omitted. Trials of the latter type teach the animal not to associate the cue with the reward any more and, therefore, not to act on the cue any more. This learning process is called extinction.

Reversal learning is partly related to extinction. In this paradigm, animals first learn to associate a stimulus with a reward, whereupon the experimenter changes the contingencies so that another stimulus is associated with the reward. The animal has to abandon the previous stimulus and to associate the new one with the reward. Thus, reversal learning depends as much on the ability to form a new cue-reward association as on extinction. There are diverse forms of reversal learning. In object discrimination reversal, the association between distinct stimuli (objects) and the reward change. In spatial discrimination reversal, reward association depends on the spatial position of the cue. As we will see, these types of reversal learning have different anatomical bases (Butter 1969). It may be that extinction is more delicate than reversal learning because it requires knowledge about the time when an outcome should have occurred.

How does this schema apply to behaviourally spontaneous confabulation? As described above, the most striking feature of behaviourally spontaneous confabulators is their inability to adapt their concept of reality in the face of information disproving it; they maintain their idea of reality and continue to act according to it despite all evidence contradicting it. The problem of such patients is not that they fail to associate new situation with new outcomes; their problem is that they fail to integrate the absence of anticipated outcomes into their thinking. In the schema displayed in Figure 9.2, this corresponds to the situation where an animal continues to choose a cue in the expectation of a reward, even though the cue is not associated with reward anymore. Thus, my suggestion is that *the failure preventing behaviourally spontaneous confabulators from adapting their thinking to ongoing reality corresponds to deficient extinction in animal experimentation.* The only adaptation necessary to make this link is to extend the notion of reward processing to any type of anticipations and outcomes, including unconscious anticipations and outcomes that have no tangible reward value.

Anatomical basis of extinction in non-human primates

The type of extinction alluded to in this context concerns the ability to learn that a cue is no more associated with reward, which is probably different from fear extinction – the ability to learn that a previously threatening or harmful stimulus has no such negative association anymore. The reaction to fearful stimuli has a privileged influence on behaviour, including more direct anatomical connections (LeDoux 1996) and will not be reviewed here. Similarly, punishment – a negative outcome discouraging an animal from repeating the previous action – is not specifically treated here. Punishment constitutes a disadvantageous outcome, rather than absence of an outcome.

Few lesion studies have explored the anatomical basis of reward processing and extinction in non-human primates. Butter *et al.* (1963) compared monkeys having an orbitofrontal lesion with monkeys having dorsolateral prefrontal lesions on an extinction task. The animals first learned to press a lever to obtain a reward. Once they had learned this association, no reward was delivered when the animals pressed the lever. Animals with orbitofrontal lesions continued to press the lever, indicating that they had abnormal difficulty in suppressing strong, habitual modes of response.

A subsequent study by Butter (1969) explored in detail the impact of circumscribed prefrontal lesions on different types of reward associations. Five groups of monkeys with varying lesions were compared. The lesions are shown in Figure 9.3. The first experiment tested extinction. As in the previous study, animals learned to press a lever in response to the food pellet being illuminated. All animals learned to react to this stimulus. After this reinforcement training, extinction was tested, in that no reward was delivered upon pressing the lever. As it turned out, animals with extended orbitofrontal lesions (Figure 9.3b) and animals with posterior medial orbitofrontal lesions (Figure 9.3c) made significantly more errors than the other groups, continuing to press the lever. Thus, among all circumscribed prefrontal lesions, only posterior medial orbitofrontal lesions induced an extinction deficit, which was as severe as in the animals having extended orbitofrontal damage. As Figure 9.3c shows, the lesions of these animals were centred on area 13 bilaterally.

The other experiments underscored the specificity of the result. The second experiment tested spatial discrimination reversal. Animals learned whether they had to remove the cover of the right or the left food pellet in order to

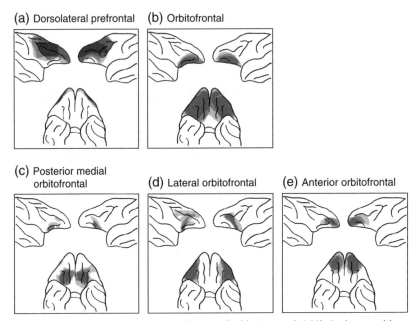

Figure 9.3 Lesion overlap in the monkeys studied by Butter (1969). Redrawn with permission.

obtain reward. Once they had learned the task, the rewarded pellet changed. Under this condition, animals with dorsolateral prefrontal lesions (Figure 9.3a) and those with lateral orbitofrontal lesions (Figure 9.3d) committed many more errors than the posterior medial, anterior orbitofrontal, and the control group.

In the third experiment, visual discrimination reversal was tested. Animals had to learn which one of two objects hid a reward. Reversal was tested on the following day. Under this condition, animals with extended orbitofrontal lesions and lateral orbitofrontal lesions (Figure 9.3d) made significantly more errors. Those with posterior medial orbitofrontal lesions made somewhat more errors than controls, whereas those with anterior orbitofrontal lesions were normal.

Taken together, Butter (1969) found that, among diverse focal lesions, dorsolateral damage selectively impaired spatial discrimination reversal, whereas a defect of object reversal learning (visual discrimination reversal) required lateral orbitofrontal damage. The most significant finding for our discussion, however, was that posterior medial orbitofrontal damage (Figure 9.3c) was the only partial prefrontal lesion that impaired extinction. Anterior orbitofrontal lesions (Figure 9.3e) induced no deficit in the studied processes.

The importance of the lateral orbitofrontal cortex for object alternation was confirmed by Iverson and Mishkin (1970). Animals with inferior frontal convexity lesions (similar to the lateral orbital lesions in Figure 9.3d) made many more errors in an initial series of object reversal trials than animals with medial orbital lesions (comparable to the posterior medial orbitofrontal lesions in Figure 9.3c). The animals with the latter lesions made more errors in subsequent reversal trial series. The authors concluded that:

> [It is very] likely… that the effects of the medial orbital lesion reflect an independent disorder in view of the many qualitative differences between the deficits of the [groups with lateral orbitofrontal and posterior medial orbitofrontal lesions] on the same tasks.
>
> Iversen and Mishkin (1970, p. 385)

Passingham (1972), too, supported the findings of Butter (1969): Animals with orbitofrontal lesions made more errors to the previously rewarded stimuli than animals with lateral frontal lesions in diverse reversal tasks, in this study also in spatial reversal.

Jones and Mishkin (1972) compared monkeys with extended orbitofrontal lesions and monkeys with temporal pole and amygdala lesions on object and place reversal learning. They found that the animals with combined temporal pole and amygdala lesions had major difficulty in the formation of new stimulus–reinforcement associations. In contrast, animals with orbitofrontal lesions had difficulty in suppressing the previously established habit and perseverated more than the other groups on already established stimulus–reinforcement associations.

The final study of interest for our discussion was conducted by Divac *et al.* (1967). These researchers examined the impact of selective, partial lesions of the caudate nucleus, which is a component of the striatum. They found that only monkeys with lesions of the ventrolateral part of the head of the caudate induced a deficit in object reversal. Interestingly, among the three parts of the caudate lesioned in this study, this is the only one which receives projections from the orbitofrontal, rather than dorsolateral prefrontal or inferotemporal area.

In summary, strong evidence indicates that circumscribed damage to the posterior medial orbitofrontal cortex, in particular area 13, may induce a specific deficit in extinction. In contrast, lateral orbitofrontal lesions appear to primarily induce a deficit in learning new stimulus–reward associations, which contradict previously established ones.

Single cell responses in extinction

Extinction in the sense discussed here – to learn that a previously rewarded stimulus is no more associated with reward – has not been the object of many studies. Extinction trials discourage the animals and therefore tend to be avoided. Of interest here is the question as to whether the orbitofrontal cortex, especially area 13, and structures connected with it have the neuronal apparatus to signal the non-occurrence of anticipated outcomes.

Rosenkilde *et al.* (1981) conducted probably the most detailed study on the topic. They analysed responses of neurons in two areas of the ventral prefrontal cortex: a medial region corresponding to area 13 and a lateral region near the inferior lateral convexity of the frontal lobes. Animals performed a delayed matching task (a working memory task) in which they had to retain either the colour or the spatial position of a stimulus. After a variable period of eight, ten, or 16 seconds, they had to choose the same stimulus from two stimuli. If the choice was correct, they received reward. Intermittently, however, no reward was delivered, although the animal had made the right choice. These extinction trials are of primary interest here.

The authors found three types of cells. Type I cells changed firing when reward was delivered following correct choice or when reward was delivered for free. Some neurons decreased firing when no reward was delivered. These cells appeared to encode the availability of reward. Type II cells increased activity when the anticipated reward was not delivered. In contrast, they were not affected by the delivery of an expected reward. Thus, these cells appeared to react to deviations from expectancy of reward. Type III cells exhibited comparable firing changes following reinforced and unreinforced choices and were, therefore, thought to encode termination of a trial sequence.

Of special interest here are type II cells. The behaviour of such a cell is shown in Figure 9.4a,b. This neuron did not change its firing rate when the expected reward was delivered in correct trials (Figure 9.4a). However, when the expected reward failed to be delivered after a correct choice, the cell transiently increased its firing rate, thus signalling the absence of the expected reward (Figure 9.4b). Of note, these cells were about three times more frequent in the medial region (area 13) than in the lateral ventral prefrontal cortex. By contrast, type I cells, which confirmed the occurrence of reward, were three times more frequent in the lateral region. Type III cells were equally frequent in both areas.

In conclusion, the study by Rosenkilde *et al.* (1981) showed that area 13 of the monkey contains neurons that specifically signal the non-occurrence of an anticipated reward at the time when the reward has previously been delivered. Thorpe and Rolls (1983), too, observed such neurons in area 13.

Reward-associated activity in subcortical structures connected with the medial orbitofrontal cortex was explored in a series of studies by Wolfram Schultz and collaborators. Delicate responses were found in dopaminergic

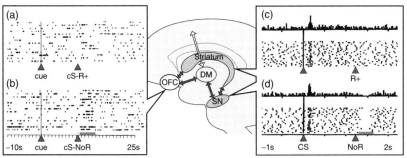

Figure 9.4 Single cell recordings of extinction trials. (a, b) Recording from an orbitofrontal neuron in area 13 (Rosenkilde *et al.* 1981). (a) Reinforced trials in a delayed matching task, starting with a cue. After a delay, the monkey had to choose the stimulus from two choice stimuli (cS). If the choice was correct, reward was delivered (R+). (b) Responses of the same neuron in extinction trials. These had the same design but no reward was delivered after correct choice (cS-NoR). (c, d) Responses of a dopaminergic neuron (Schultz *et al.* 1997). The conditioned stimulus (CS) predicted reward. (c) Reinforced trials with delivery of reward (R+). (d) Extinction trials, in which the expected reward failed to be delivered (NoR). In all displays, the lines of dots show discharges of the neuron during separate trials. Higher density of dots indicates increased firing. The grey bars on the time axes indicate the periods of interest when no reward was delivered, i.e., increased firing by the orbitofrontal neuron (b), decreased firing by the dopaminergic neuron (d). In (c) and (d), histograms of discharge frequencies are shown on top. The brain in the background schematically indicates the areas the recordings were made from. The schema does not reflect true anatomical proportions. Main connections of interest for the discussion are indicated. Abbreviations: DM, dorsomedial nucleus of the thalamus; OFC, orbitofrontal cortex, area 13; SN, substantia nigra and ventral tegmental area. (a) and (b) adapted with permission from Rosenkilde *et al.* (1981); (c) and (d) from Schultz *et al.* (1997).

neurons in the substantia nigra and the immediately adjacent ventral tegmental area (both located in the mesencephalon) and in their projection site, the striatum. Very much like the orbitofrontal neurons, dopaminergic neurons fired during the expectation and upon delivery of rewards (Schultz *et al.* 1997, 2000). A distinct quality of these neurons appeared to be, however, that they coded an error in the prediction of rewards (Schultz *et al.* 2000), including unexpectedly large or small rewards, coded as an increase or decrease of firing (Tobler *et al.* 2005), or temporal deviations of reward delivery (Hollerman and Schultz 1998). Most interesting for our discussion was their reaction to the absence of anticipated rewards. In contrast to the orbitofrontal type II neurons described by Rosenkilde *et al.* (1981), which increased firing when the expected reward was not delivered, dopaminergic neurons briefly (phasically) inhibited their firing (Schultz *et al.* 1997; Hollerman and Schultz 1998). Figure 9.4c, d displays the activity of such a neuron. Similar to the orbitofrontal neuron (Figure 9.4a), this dopaminergic neuron did not change firing when a predicted reward was delivered at the expected time (Figure 9.4c). However, when the reward failed to be delivered at the expected time, neuronal firing transiently decreased (Figure 9.4d).

The behaviour of dopaminergic neurons in reaction to deviations from reward expectancy has been the object of many more studies than the behaviour of orbitofrontal neurons. Accordingly, dopaminergic neurons have built themselves a special reputation for encoding expected rewards and signalling deviation of delivered from expected rewards. As far as the scarce data on orbitofrontal neurons in area 13 (Rosenkilde *et al.* 1981) and the mass of data on dopaminergic neurons can be compared in terms of experimental paradigm and data-analysis, the neurons seem to respond to quite similar events. Considering their different reactions to the absence of expected outcomes (increased firing in orbitofrontal neurons, depression in dopaminergic neurons), one could be tempted to speculate that the primary analysis of such non-events might as well occur in the orbitofrontal cortex as in dopaminergic neurons. According to this speculation, the signalling of the non-occurrence of anticipated outcomes by orbitofrontal neurons would transiently inhibit the activity of the dopaminergic neurons. More data, in particular on the behaviour of orbitofrontal neurons during extinction, would be necessary to clarify this point. Of course, this sequence of responses would be seamlessly compatible with our clinical data from behaviourally spontaneous confabulators and functional imaging data showing that the posterior medial orbitofrontal cortex including area 13 appears to be particularly important for the adaptation of thought to ongoing reality (Chapter 8). The idea that phasic inhibition of dopaminergic neurons might be critical for this capacity was one of our reasons – in addition to subcortical activation in imaging (Figure 8.11) – for trying dopamine antagonists in behaviourally spontaneous confabulators (p. 249) (Pihan *et al.* 2004). At the same time, it is clear that tonic inhibition of dopaminergic transmission, as induced by neuroleptics, cannot replace the phasic inhibition that dopaminergic neurons show upon the non-occurrence of anticipated events.

Outcome processing in humans

In contrast to a massive, rapidly growing imaging literature on human reward processing, very few studies have used reversal or extinction paradigms in patients with focal brain lesions. Patients with chronic orbitofrontal lesions typically had reversal deficits (Rolls *et al.* 1994; Freedman *et al.* 1998; Fellows and Farah 2003; Berlin *et al.* 2004; Hornak *et al.* 2004); apart from signs of impulsivity or disinhibition as revealed by questionnaires, no conse-quences on behaviour or memory were reported. An interesting clinical study by Czernecki *et al.* (2002) explored the influence of *L-dopa* on reversal learn-ing and extinction. L-dopa is metabolized to dopamine in the brain and is used to treat Parkinson's disease. Patients who had not had their medication for about 12 hours had difficulty in learning a simple association between one of two fractal images and a 'reward' in the form of a score. In addition, they were impaired on reversal of this association, but not on extinction. When the patients had taken their medication, reversal learning improved, in that omis-sion errors decreased. At the same time, however, extinction worsened due to an increase of perseveration errors. In agreement with the animal data discussed above, the study suggested a dissociation between reversal learning and extinction and a different implication of the dopaminergic system in these capacities. Dopamine also enhances the tendency to choose rewarding over non-rewarding outcomes (Frank *et al.* 2004).

Innumerable *imaging studies* with healthy subjects explored different facets of outcome processing. Activation of the orbitofrontal cortex was obtained when subjects received anticipated food reward (O'Doherty *et al.* 2002) or imagined good meals (Arana *et al.* 2003), but also in gambling or guessing tasks associated with monetary reward or punishment (Elliott *et al.* 1997; Thut *et al.* 1997; Elliott *et al.* 1999; Rogers *et al.* 1999; Elliott *et al.* 2000; Critchley *et al.* 2001; O'Doherty *et al.* 2001; Pochon *et al.* 2002; Kringelbach and Rolls 2004). Many studies reported activation of the striatum or amygdala in such tasks (Breiter *et al.* 2001; Knutson *et al.* 2001a; McClure *et al.* 2003; Ramnani *et al.* 2004; Yacubian *et al.* 2006).

Extinction in the sense of the omission of an anticipated reward was rarely studied. Ramnani *et al.* (2004) used a passive conditioning task, in which subjects learned that the presentation of one of two coloured circles would be followed two seconds later by the presentation of reward (image of a coin) or no-reward (empty circle). They found that the omission of expected rewards provoked activation of the frontal pole, area 10. In contrast, the unpredicted presentation of a reward induced late activation of the middle part of area 14. The anticipation of reward as opposed to the anticipation of no-reward activated the ventral striatum.

The striatum was also at the centre of the study by McClure *et al.* (2003), but with a different role. In this study, subjects learned that a flash of light would be followed six seconds later by the delivery of fruit juice. On some trials, juice delivery was delayed for four seconds, so that there was no juice at the expected time. When comparing the periods in which expected juice failed to be delivered and periods in which no juice delivery was expected, the authors found relatively decreased activation of the left putamen, a part of the striatum. Conversely, when subjects received unexpected reward, there was increased activation of the striatum. No orbitofrontal activation was reported. Yet another study (Yacubian *et al.* 2006) found that the striatum only encoded gain-related expected value, whereas loss-related expected value was encoded by the amygdala.

Even though imaging studies regularly reported activation of well-known reward-associated structures, the structures activated in the different studies also differed in significant ways, at times completely contradicting each other. To what degree such differences among studies are due to the relative weakness of functional MRI in picking up signal from the orbitofrontal area (Ojemann *et al.* 1997; Stenger 2006), differences in experimental paradigms, or different ways of analysis (selection of time windows; analysis of selected voxels) is unclear.

The described imaging studies only partially contribute to our discussion about the link between the reward system and the adaptation of thought to ongoing reality: virtually all studies used some form of tangible, explicitly defined reward as the outcome, be it fruit juice, money, or at least a score. Indeed, the orbitofrontal cortex has recently been suggested as a central structure for hedonic experience – the pleasure associated with an outcome (Kringelbach 2005). However the hypothesis described above, stating that the adaptation of thought to ongoing reality might depend on extinction, requires that the orbitofrontal cortex and connected structures also process outcomes having no tangible reward value.

We tested this prediction with a very simple anticipation task avoiding as far as possibly any connotation of reward (Schnider *et al.* 2005b). The general design is shown in Figure 9.5a (Main task design). Subjects had to decide behind which one of two red and green coloured rectangles an 'object' was hidden. The 'object' was a neutral drawing showing, for example, a button or a key. Immediately after the subject's decision, a fixation cross was shown in the chosen rectangle for 1.5 seconds, followed by presentation of the outcome, which was either the object or a grid indicating absence of the object. Most importantly, presentation of the outcome was not accompanied by any form of reward. There was no monetary reward, no score, not even a comment. The baseline task (Figure 9.5a, Baseline) had the same visual elements, presented for similarly long periods, but in reverse order, so that subjects first saw where the object actually was. Thus the baseline task demanded no anticipation or decision-making and provided no feedback.

In two conditions, subjects were asked to base their decision on the previous trial and to refrain from guessing, although the 'object' might occasionally

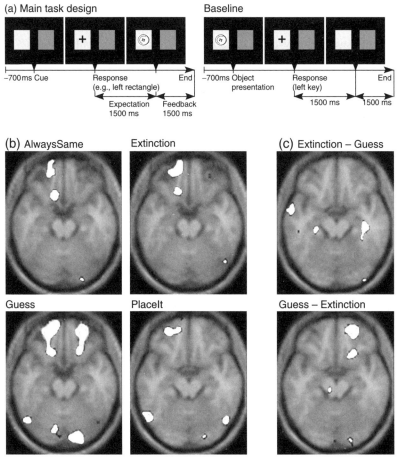

Figure 9.5 Anticipation and outcome processing. (a) Task design. The two rectangles were red and green. (b) Activation in the four main conditions in comparison with the baseline task. (c) Difference between conditions Extinction and Guess. White areas indicate clusters of significant activation. Adapted with permission from Schnider (2005b)

change position. In one of these conditions (AlwaysSame), the object never changed position (always behind the rectangle with the same colour) so that the prediction by the subject was always correct. Thus, this condition encompassed decision-making, anticipation, and processing of the outcome. As Figure 9.5b (AlwaysSame) shows, this simple task induced marked activation of orbitofrontal cortex, namely left area 13 plus frontal pole, corresponding to area 10. The second condition was similar to the AlwaysSame condition, but the object changed position on every second to fifth trial. Thus, this condition contained intermittent 'extinction' trials. As Figure 9.5b (Extinction) shows, activation was similar to AlwaysSame.

An amazing result was obtained in the third condition, called Guess. This condition was exactly similar to the Extinction condition. However, subjects were told that the object would change position randomly and that they should guess rather than base their decision on the previous trial. Subjects obviously believed in this instruction, as their performance significantly dropped. Figure 9.5b (Guess) shows that, in this condition, overall orbitofrontal activation was markedly stronger. Most significantly, however, there was additional activation of the right orbitofrontal cortex.

The fourth condition, called PlaceIt, had the same internal design as the previous conditions, but this time, subjects determined where they wanted the object to appear. Thus, this condition also contained decision-making and an anticipation phase, but the outcome was predefined by the subject and therefore never deviated from expectation. In this condition, there was only left frontal pole activation, but no posterior medial activation of area 13 (Figure 9.5b, PlaceIt).

In a direct comparison between the Extinction and the Guess condition, which had exactly the same design, the Guess condition differed by more right orbitofrontal activation (Figure 9.5c, Guess–Extinction). In contrast, the Extinction condition, in which the outcome had to be memorized for the next trial, induced more medial temporal activation involving the hippocampus and parahippocampal gyrus (Figure 9.5c, Extinction–Guess).

The study did not reveal any difference between the processing of the occurrence, as opposed to the non-occurrence of anticipated outcomes; the Extinction condition did not differ from the AlwaysSame condition (Figure 9.5b). PET, with its low temporal resolution of approximately 45 seconds, was probably not sensitive enough to pick up the specific treatment of the 30 per cent extinction trials differentiating the two conditions. In contrast to PET, an electrophysiological study using the same design and high resolution evoked potentials indicated that the extinction trials in this task undergo very distinct processing (Schnider et al. 2007). Extinction trials specifically induced a strikingly different electrocortical response than all other stimuli between 200–300 ms and again at 400–600 ms. When only the presented object was replaced (e.g., a key instead of the button), confirming nonetheless that the choice had been correct, electrocortical potentials were similar to the presentation of the expected, previously presented object. Thus, extinction trials, which were the only ones requiring behavioural adaptation (choice of the other rectangle in the next trial), passed through strikingly different early cortical processing at 200–300 ms. This is the same period, in which the suppression (filtering) of currently irrelevant memories seems to occur (Figures 8.9 and 8.10).

These results supported the idea that the orbitofrontal cortex also processes outcomes that have no appreciable reward value. It may thus function as a *generic outcome monitoring system* independent of the hedonic value of outcomes (Schnider *et al.* 2005b). Behaviourally relevant absence of anticipated outcomes (extinction trials) undergoes strikingly different electrocortical processing (Schnider *et al.* 2007).

In addition, the results suggested a simple model of the limbic and orbitofrontal contribution to *behavioural control*. The findings of the imaging study (Schnider *et al.* 2005b) were compatible with a prevalent role of the polar orbitofrontal cortex in the formation of new hypotheses and decision-making, of the medial temporal lobes in the storage of recent experience, and of the posterior medial orbitofrontal cortex (area 13) in the comparison of anticipated outcomes (hypotheses) with real outcomes (experiences).

Summary and discussion

More than previous chapters, this one has been speculative. Based on the observation that behaviourally spontaneous confabulators adhere to their false ideas even when true reality contradicts them, I derived an analogy with deficient extinction, the capacity to learn from the non-occurrence of antici-pated events. I invoked extinction rather than reversal learning for a reason: reversal learning occurs when there is an outcome, albeit inverse to expecta-tion. In contrast, extinction occurs when an anticipated outcome fails to happen. In normal thinking, many ideas (anticipations) never encounter an outcome. This may be the nature of fantasies: Fantasies differ from thoughts, which relate to ongoing reality, by the absence of real outcomes rather than unexpected outcomes. Behaviourally spontaneous confabulators cannot make this difference.

The idea that the reward system, by virtue of its extinction capacity, acts as a generic reality checking system requires that the concepts of reward and extinction be extended to unconscious anticipations and outcomes devoid of hedonic value. As regards the latter requirement, we have found strong activa-tion in orbitofrontal areas 13 and 10 when healthy subjects anticipated and monitored simple outcomes that had no tangible reward value (Schnider *et al.* 2005b). The extension of the reward concept to unconscious processing does not appear to be more difficult. In decision-making, somatic reactions (somatic markers) can be detected even before a subject has conscious knowl-edge about which choice would be advantageous (Bechara *et al.* 1997). Why should the same principle not apply to anticipation and outcome processing in general? To apply the notions of reward processing and extinction to human reality checking simply requires one to acknowledge that human thinking and anticipation underlie the same physiological principles as reward processing by non-human primates, although human thinking is much more complex.

The ventromedial prefrontal area with the orbitofrontal cortex provides the neural apparatus and the connections allowing it to check the non-occurrence of events and to signal it to other parts of the brain. Monkeys with lesions of area 13 had a specific deficit of extinction, whereas more lateral lesions in the inferior convexity of the frontal lobes induced a deficit of object reversal learning (Butter 1969). Single cell recordings from area 13 demonstrated the presence of neurons firing specifically in extinction trials, when rewards failed to be delivered at the expected time (Rosenkilde et al. 1981). Conversely, neurons in the lateral inferior prefrontal cortex preferentially signalled the detection of reward.

Behaviourally spontaneous confabulation occurs not only after damage to area 13 but the whole posterior ventromedial prefrontal area. Within this region, an orbital and medial network have been distinguished (Carmichael and Price 1996). Both networks have similar, albeit separate, connections with structures whose damage may induce behaviourally spontaneous confabulation and which are involved in reward processing.

Both the medial and orbital networks have connections with dopaminergic structures in the ventral striatum and the mesencephalon. Dopaminergic neurons code the non-occurrence of anticipated rewards by phasic decrease of their firing rate (Schultz et al. 1997). Whether this decrease reflects primary processing of non-events by these neurons or their inhibition by a signal from the medial orbitofrontal cortex, has not been resolved.

Single cell recordings have shown that area 13 has a particularly high density of neurons signalling the absence of rewards, while lateral orbitofrontal cortex has a particularly high density of neurons signalling the occurrence of rewards. However there is no strict separation; both areas contain both types of neurons (Rosenkilde et al. 1981). If the hypothesis is correct that the capacity to adapt thought and behaviour to ongoing reality critically depends on extinction, and hence on the presence of extinction cells, then the findings from single cell recordings might explain some clinical mysteries. As we have seen in Chapter 4, only a small minority of patients, who have the diseases and lesions commonly responsible for behaviourally spontaneous confabulation, will actually go on to have the syndrome of behaviourally spontaneous confabulation. This is true for ruptured aneurysms, diencephalic tumours, traumatic brain injury, and alcoholic Korsakoff syndrome. Could it be that these patients had the misfortune of concentrating their extinction cells in the critical area around the posterior medial orbitofrontal cortex? And could it be that the availability of extinction cells in surviving tissue determined the speed of recovery from behaviourally spontaneous confabulation? Finally, could it be that the propensity of patients to act out their false beliefs reflected goal-seeking behaviour, whose intensity depended on the density of reward-signalling neurons in undamaged orbitofrontal cortex? Thus, could there be an anatomical predisposition for losing the ability to adapt thought and behaviour to ongoing reality following posterior medial orbitofrontal damage?

The hypothesis exposed here seeks to explain the reality confusion that some patients experience after orbitofrontal damage, not necessarily the tendency to talk about the falsely perceived reality, that is, the intensity of the confabulations. In contrast to the observations described in the previous chapter, which were derived from controlled evidence obtained from behaviourally spontaneous confabulators, the hypothesis explained in this chapter awaits controlled exploration in patients who confuse reality.

For future studies on any type of confabulation, it will be crucial to characterize precisely the patients and their clinical course, analyse the circumstances inciting the confabulations, investigate the range of confabulatory themes, describe associated behaviours, and devise specific experimental procedures to test the physiological basis of the suggested mechanisms.

Korsakoff's (1891) call for research on confabulations is as justified nowadays as it was almost 120 years ago:

> Research on the connections among latent [memory] traces and the influence of latent (unconscious) traces on the flow of ideas might help to explain many interesting phenomena concerning normal and pathological psychology.
>
> Korsakoff (1891, p. 410)

References

Abe, K., Inokawa, M., Kashiwagi, A. and Yanagihara, T. (1998) Amnesia after a discrete basal forebrain lesion. *Journal of Neurology, Neurosurgery and Psychiatry* 65: 126–130.

Ackil, J. K. and Zaragoza, M. S. (1998) Memorial consequences of forced confabulation: age differences in susceptibility to false memories. *Developmenal Psychology* 34: 1358–1372.

Adair, J. C., Gilmore, R. L., Fennell, E. B., Gold, M. and Heilman, K. M. (1995) Anosognosia during intracarotid barbiturate anesthesia: unawareness or amnesia for weakness. *Neurology* 45: 241–243.

Adams, J. H. (1975) The neuropathology of head injury. In: *Handbook of clinical neurology, vol. 23: Head injury* (Vinken PJ and Bruyn GW, eds), pp. 35–65. Amsterdam: Elsevier Science.

Addis, D. R., Wong, A. T. and Schacter, D. L. (2007) Remembering the past and imagining the future: common and distinct neural substrates during event construction and elaboration. *Neuropsychologia* 45: 1363–1377.

Aggleton, J. P. (1992) The functional effects of amygdala lesions in humans: a comparison with findings from monkeys. In: *The amygdala. Neurobiological aspects of emotion, memory, and mental dysfunction* (Aggleton JP, ed.), pp. 485–503. New York: Wiley Liss Inc.

Aggleton, J. P. and Sahgal, A. (1993) The contribution of the anterior thalamic nuclei to anterograde amnesia. *Neuropsychologia* 31: 1001–1019.

Aggleton, J. P., McMackin, D., Carpenter, K., Hornak, J., Kapur, N., Halpin, S., Wiles, C. M. and Kamel, H. *et al.* (2000) Differential cognitive effects of colloid cysts in the third ventricle that spare or compromise the fornix. *Brain* 123: 800–815.

Alexander, G. E., DeLong, M. R. and Strick, P. L. (1986) Parallel organization of functionally segregated circuits linking basal ganglia and cortex. *Annual Review of Neuroscience* 9: 357–381.

Alexander, M. P., Stuss, D. T. and Benson, D. F. (1979) Capgras syndrome: a reduplicative phenomenon. *Neurology* 29: 334–339.

Alexander, M. P. and Freedman, M. (1984) Amnesia after anterior communicating artery aneurysm rupture. *Neurology* 34: 452–757.

Alexander, M. P., Hiltbrunner, B. and Fischer, R. S. (1989) Distributed anatomy of transcortical sensory aphasia. *Archives of Neurology* 46: 885–892.

Alexander, M. P., Stuss, D. T. and Fansabedian, N. (2003) California Verbal Learning Test: performance by patients with focal frontal and non-frontal lesions. *Brain* 126: 1493–1503.

Allen, J. S., Tranel, D., Bruss, J. and Damasio, H. (2006) Correlations between regional brain volumes and memory performance in anoxia. *Journal of Clinical and Experimental Neuropsychology* 28: 457–476.

Amarenco, P., Cohen, P., Roullet, E., Dupuch, K., Kurtz, A. and Marteau, R. (1988) Syndrome amnésique lors d'un infarctus du territoire de l'artère choroïdienne antérieure gauche. *Revue Neurologique (Paris)* 144: 36–39.

American Psychiatric Association (1994) *DSM-IV. Diagnostic and statistical manual of mental disorders*, 4th edn. Washington, DC: American Psychiatric Association.

Anderson, M. C. and Green, C. (2001) Suppressing unwanted memories by executive control. *Nature* 410: 366–369.

Anderson, M. C., Ochsner, K. N., Kuhl, B., Cooper, J., Robertson, E., Gabrieli, S. W., Glover, G. H. and Gabrieli, J. D. (2004) Neural systems underlying the suppression of unwanted memories. *Science* 303: 232–235.

Anderson, S. W., Bechara, A., Damasio, H., Tranel, D. and Damasio, A. R. (1999) Impairment of social and moral behavior related to early damage in human prefrontal cortex. *Nature Neuroscience* 2: 1032–1037.

Angelergues, R., Hécaen, H. and De Ajuriaguerra, J. (1955) Les troubles mentaux au cours des tumeurs du lobe frontal. A propos de 80 observations dont 54 avec troubles mentaux. *Annales Médico-Psychologiques* II: 577–642.

Angelergues, R. (1956) La valeur localisatrice du syndrome de Korsakow dans les tumeurs méso-diencéphaliques. *Neurochirurgie* 2: 232–233.

Anton, G. (1898) Ueber die Selbstwahrnehmung der Herderkrankungen des Gehirns durch den Kranken bei Rindenblindheit und Rindentaubheit. *Archiv für Psychiatrie und Nervenkrankheiten* 32: 86–127.

Apostolova, L. G., Dutton, R. A., Dinov, I. D., Hayashi, K. M., Toga, A. W., Cummings, J. L. and Thompson, P. M. (2006) Conversion of mild cognitive impairment to Alzheimer disease predicted by hippocampal atrophy maps. *Archives of Neurology* 63: 693–699.

Arana, F. S., Parkinson, J. A., Hinton, E., Holland A. J., Owen, A. M. and Roberts, A. C. (2003) Dissociable contributions of the human amygdala and orbitofrontal cortex to incentive motivation and goal selection. *Journal of Neuroscience* 23: 9632–9638.

Arnold, S. E., Hyman, B. T., Flory, J., Damasio, A. R. and Van Hoesen, G. W. (1991) The topographical and neuroanatomical distribution of neurofibrillary tangles and neuritic plaques in the cerebral cortex of patients with Alzheimer's disease. *Cerebral Cortex* 1: 103–116.

Aronsohn, O. (1909) Der Korsakowsche Symptomenkomplex nach Commotio cerebri. Ein Beitrag zur Kenntnis der akuten traumatischen Psychose. *Deutsche Medizinische Wochenschrift* 35: 1006–1008.

Artiola, L., Fortuny, I., Briggs, M., Newcombe, F., Ratcliff, G. and Thomas, C. (1980) Measuring the duration of post traumatic amnesia. *Journal of Neurology, Neurosurgery and Psychiatry* 43: 377–379.

Auld, D. S., Kornecook, T. J., Bastianetto, S. and Quirion, R. (2002) Alzheimer's disease and the basal forebrain cholinergic system: relations to beta-amyloid peptides, cognition, and treatment strategies. *Progress in Neurobiology* 68: 209–245.

Babinski, M. J. (1914) Contribution à l'étude des troubles mentaux dans l'hémiplégie organique cérébrale (anosognosie). *Revue Neurologique (Paris)* 27: 845–848.

Babinski, M. J. (1918) Anosognosie. *Revue Neurologique (Paris)* 31: 365–367.

Babinski, M. J. and Joltrain, E. (1924) Un nouveau cas d'anosognosie. *Revue Neurologique (Paris)* 40: 638–640.

Badcock, J. C., Waters, F. A., Maybery, M. T. and Michie, P. T. (2005) Auditory hallucinations: failure to inhibit irrelevant memories. *Cognitive Neuropsychiatry* 10: 125–136.

Baddeley, A. and Wilson, B. (1988) Frontal amnesia and the dysexecutive syndrome. *Brain and Cognition* 7: 212–230.

Baier, B. and Karnath, H. O. (2005) Incidence and diagnosis of anosognosia for hemiparesis revisited. *Journal of Neurology, Neurosurgery and Psychiatry* 76: 358–361.

Bancaud, J., Brunet-Bourgin, F., Chauvel, P. and Halgren, E. (1994) Anatomical origin of déjà vu and vivid 'memories' in human temporal lobe epilepsy. *Brain* 117: 71–90.

Bar-On, R., Tranel, D., Denburg, N. L. and Bechara, A. (2003) Exploring the neurological substrate of emotional and social intelligence. *Brain* 126: 1790–1800.

Barbizet, J., Degos, J. D., Louarn, F., Nguyen, J. P. and Mas, J. L. (1981) Amnésie par lésion ischémique bi-thalamique. *Revue Neurologique (Paris)* 137: 415–424.

Barrett, A. M., Eslinger, P. J., Ballentine, N. H. and Heilman, K. M. (2005) Unawareness of cognitive deficit (cognitive anosognosia) in probable AD and control subjects. *Neurology* 64: 693–699.

Bayley, P. J., Hopkins, R. O. and Squire, L. R. (2003) Successful recollection of remote auto-biographical memories by amnesic patients with medial temporal lobe lesions. *Neuron* 38: 135–144.

Bayley, P. J., Hopkins, R. O. and Squire, L. R. (2006) The fate of old memories after medial temporal lobe damage. *Journal of Neuroscience* 26: 13311–13317.

Bechara, A., Tranel, D., Damasio, H., Adolphs, R., Rockland C. and Damasio, A. R. (1995) Double dissociation of conditioning and declarative knowledge relative to the amygdala and hippocampus in humans. *Science* 269: 1115–1118.

Bechara, A., Damasio, H., Tranel, D. and Damasio, A. R. (1997) Deciding advantageously before knowing the advantageous strategy. *Science* 275: 1293–1295.

Bechara, A., Damasio, H. and Damasio, A. R. (2000) Emotion, decision making and the orbitofrontal cortex. *Cerebral Cortex* 10: 295–307.

Beck, E. (1949) A cytoarchitectural investigation into the boundaries of cortical areas 13 and 14 in the human brain. *Journal of Anatomy* 83: 147–157.

Bender, L. and Schilder, P. (1933) Encephalopathia alcoholica: polioencephalitis haemor-rhagica superior Wernicke. *Archives of Neurology and Psychiatry* 29: 990–1053.

Bender, L., Curran, F. and Schilder, P. (1938) Organization of memory traces in the Korsakoff syndrome. *Archives of Neurology and Psychiatry* 39: 482–487.

Benedek, L. and Juba, A. (1941) Korsakow-Syndrom bei den Geschwülsten des Zwischenhirns. *Archiv für Psychiatrie und Nervenkrankheiten* 114: 366–376.

Benon, R. and LeHuché, R. (1920) Traumatismes crâniens et psychose de Korsakoff. *Archives Suisses de Neurologie, Neurochirurgie et Psychiatrie* 7: 316–322.

Benson, D. F. and Geschwind, N. (1967) Shrinking retrograde amnesia. *Journal of Neurology, Neurosurgery and Psychiatry* 30: 539–544.

Benson, D. F., Gardner, H. and Meadows, J. C. (1976) Reduplicative paramnesia. *Neurology* 26: 147–151.

Benson, D. F. and Stuss, D. T. (1990) Frontal lobe influences on delusions: a clinical perspective. *Schizophrenia Bulletin* 16: 403–411.

Benson, D. F., Djenderedjian, A., Miller, B. L., Pachana, N. A., Chang, L., Itti, L., Eng, G. E. and Mena, I. (1996) Neural basis of confabulation. *Neurology* 46: 1239–1243.

Benton, A. L., Van Allen, M. W. and Fogel, M. L. (1964) Temporal orientation in cerebral disease. *The Journal of Nervous and Mental Diseases* 139: 110–119.

Berglund, M., Gustafson, L. and Hagberg, B. (1979) Amnestic-confabulatory syndrome in hydrocephalic dementia and Korsakoff's psychosis in alcoholism. *Acta Psychiatrica Scandinavica* 60: 323–333.

Berlin, H. A., Rolls, E. T. and Kischka, U. (2004) Impulsivity, time perception, emotion and reinforcement sensitivity in patients with orbitofrontal cortex lesions. *Brain* 127: 1108–1126.

Berlyne, N. (1972) Confabulation. *British Journal of Psychiatry* 120: 31–39.

Bernard, P. (1951) Essai psycho-pathologique sur le comportement dans le syndrome de Korsakoff. *La Raison* 2: 93–101.

Béthoux, L. (1935) Psychose polynévritique de Korsakoff au cours d'une tuberculose lympho-ganglionnaire suppurée évolutive. *Revue Neurologique (Paris)* 64: 748–754.

Betlheim, S. and Hartmann, H. (1925) Über Fehlreaktionen bei der Korsakoffschen Psychose. *Archiv für Psychiatrie und Nervenkrankheiten* 72: 257–286.

Bindschaedler, C., Assal, G. and de Tribolet, N. (1997) Troubles cognitifs séquellaires de la rupture d'anévrysmes de l'artère communicante antérieure et de l'artère cérébrale antérieure. Étude rétrospective de 56 cas. *Revue Neurologique (Paris)* 153: 669–678.

Bisiach, E., Vallar, G., Perani, D., Papagno, C. and Berti, A. (1986) Unawareness of disease following lesions of the right hemisphere: anosognosia for hemiplegia and anosognosia for hemianopia. *Neuropsychologia* 24: 471–482.

Bisiach, E. and Geminiani, G. (1991) Anosognosia related to hemiplegia and hemianopia. In: *Awareness of deficit after brain injury* (Prigatano GP, Schacter DL, eds), pp. 17–39. New York: Oxford University Press.

Bleuler, E. (1923) *Lehrbuch der Psychiatrie*. Berlin: Julius Spinger Verlag.

Bogousslavsky, J., Regli, F. and Uske, A. (1988) Thalamic infarcts: clinical syndromes, etiology, and prognosis. *Neurology* 38: 837–848.

Bogousslavsky, J. and Regli, F. (1990) Anterior cerebral artery territory infarction in the Lausanne stroke registry. Clinical and etiologic patterns. *Archives of Neurology* 47: 144–150.

Bonhoeffer, K. (1901) *Die akuten Geisteskrankheiten des Gewohnheitstrinkers. Eine klinische Studie.* Jena: Gustav Fischer.

Bonhoeffer, K. (1904) Der Korsakowsche Symptomenkomplex in seinen Beziehungen zu den verschiedenen Krankheitsformen. *Allgemeine Zeitschrift für Psychiatrie und psychisch-gerichtliche Medicin* 61: 744–752.

Bonhoeffer, K. (1911) Ueber psychische Störungen bei anämischen Psychosen. *Berliner Klinische Wochenschrift* 48: 2357.

Bowers, D., Verfallie, M., Valenstein, E. and Heilman, K. M. (1988) Impaired acquisition of temporal information in retrosplenial amnesia. *Brain and Cognition* 8: 47–66.

Bowman, K. M., Goodhart, R. and Jolliffe, N. (1939) Observations on the role of vitamin B1 in the etiology and treatment of Korsakoff psychosis. *The Journal of Nervous and Mental Diseases* 90: 569–575.

Braak, H. and Braak, E. (1991) Neuropathological stageing of Alzheimer-related changes. *Acta Neuropathol (Berl)* 82: 239–259.

Bradfield, A. L., Wells, G. L. and Olson, E. A. (2002) The damaging effect of confirming feedback on the relation between eyewitness certainty and identification accuracy. *Journal of Applied Psychology* 87: 112–120.

Brainerd, C. J. and Reyna, V. F. (2005) *The science of false memory*. Oxford: Oxford University Press.

Breiter, H. C., Aharon, I., Kahneman, D., Dale, A. and Shizgal, P. (2001) Functional imaging of neural responses to expectancy and experience of monetary gains and losses. *Neuron* 30: 619–639.

Brodmann, K. (1909) *Vergleichende Lokalisationslehre der Grosshirnrinde*. Leipzig: Barth.

Brooks, D. N., Aughton, M. E., Bond, M. R., Jones, P. and Rizvi, S. (1980) Cognitive sequelae in relationship to early indices of severity of brain damage after severe blunt head injury. *Journal of Neurology, Neurosurgery and Psychiatry* 43: 529–534.

Brown, M. W. and Aggleton, J. P. (2001) Recognition memory: what are the roles of the perirhinal cortex and hippocampus? *Nature Reviews Neuroscience* 2: 51–61.

Brown, R., Colter, N., Corsellis, J. A., Crow, T. J., Frith, C. D., Jagoe, R., Johnstone, E. C. and Marsh, L. (1986) Postmortem evidence of structural brain changes in schizophrenia. Differences in brain weight, temporal horn area, and parahippocampal gyrus compared with affective disorder. *Archives of General Psychiatry* 43: 36–42.

Brown, R. D., Jr and Kulik, K. (1977) Flashbulb memories. *Cognition* 5: 73–99.

Burgess, P. W. and Shallice, T. (1996) Confabulation and the control of recollection. *Memory* 4: 359–411.

Burgess, P. W. and McNeil, J. E. (1999) Content-specific confabulation. *Cortex* 35: 163–182.

Burke, J. M. and Schaberg, D. R. (1985) Neurosyphilis in the antibiotic era. *Neurology* 35: 1368–1371.

Butter, C. M., Mishkin, M. and Rosvold, H. E. (1963) Conditioning and extinction of a food–rewarded response after selective ablations of frontal cortex in Rhesus monkeys. *Experimental Neurology* 7: 65–75.

Butter, C. M. (1969) Perseveration in extinction and in discrimination reversal tasks following selective frontal ablations in *Macaca mulatta*. *Physiology and Behavior* 4: 163 –171.

Butter, C. M., McDonald, J. A. and Snyder, D. R. (1969) Orality, preference behavior, and reinforcement value of nonfood object in monkeys with orbital frontal lesions. *Science* 164: 1306–1307.

Cabeza, R., Mangels, J., Nyberg, L., Habib, R., Houle, S., McIntosh, A. R. and Tulving, E. (1997) Brain regions differentially involved in remembering what and when: a PET study. *Neuron* 19: 863–870.

Cabeza, R., Rao, S. M., Wagner, A. D., Mayer, A. R. and Schacter, D. L. (2001) Can medial temporal lobe regions distinguish true from false? An event-related functional MRI study of veridical and illusory recognition memory. *Proceedings of the National Academy of Science of the USA* 98: 4805–4810.

Capgras, J. and Reboul-Lachaux (1923a) L'illusion des 'sosies' dans un délire systématisé chronique. *Bulletin de la Société Clinique de Médecine Mentale* 11: 6–16.

Capgras, J. and Reboul-Lachaux (1923b) Société clinique de médecine mentale. Compte rendu de la séance du 10 Janvier 1923. L'illusion des 'sosies' dans un délire systématisé chronique. *Annales Médico-Psychologiques* 13: 186.

Carmichael, S. T. and Price, J. L. (1994) Architectonic subdivision of the orbital and medial prefrontal cortex in the macaque monkey. *Journal of Comparative Neurology* 346: 366–402.

Carmichael, S. T. and Price, J. L. (1995a) Sensory and premotor connections of the orbital and medial prefrontal cortex of macaque monkeys. *Journal of Comparative Neurology* 363: 642–664.

Carmichael, S. T. and Price, J. L. (1995b) Limbic connections of the orbital and medial prefrontal cortex in macaque monkeys. *Journal of Comparative Neurology* 363: 615–641.

Carmichael, S. T. and Price, J. L. (1996) Connectional networks within the orbital and medial prefrontal cortex of macaque monkeys. *Journal of Comparative Neurology* 371: 179–207.

Carota, A. and Schnider, A. (2005) Dramatic recovery from prolonged Wernicke–Korsakoff disease. *European Neurology* 53: 45–46.

Castaigne, P., Lhermitte, F., Buge, A., Escourolle, R., Hauw, J. J. and Lyon, C. O. (1981) Paramedian thalamic and midbrain infarcts: clinical and neuropathological study. *Annals of Neurology* 10: 127–148.

Celesia, G. G., Brigell, M. G. and Vaphiades, M. S. (1997) Hemianopic anosognosia. *Neurology* 49: 88–97.

Cermak, L. S. (1976) The encoding capacity of a patient with amnesia due to encephalitis. *Neuropsychologia* 14: 311–326.

Chaslin, P. (1912) *Eléments de sémiologie et clinique mentales.* Paris: Asselin et Houzeau.

Chiavaras, M. M., LeGoualher, G., Evans, A. and Petrides, M. (2001) Three-dimensional probabilistic atlas of the human orbitofrontal sulci in standardized stereotaxic space. *Neuroimage* 13: 479–496.

Christodoulou, G. N. (1976) Delusional hyper-identifications of the Fregoli type. Organic pathogenetic contributors. *Acta Psychiatrica Scandinavica* 54: 305–314.

Ciaramelli, E., Ghetti, S., Frattarelli, M. and Ladavas, E. (2006) When true memory availability promotes false memory: evidence from confabulating patients. *Neuropsychologia* 44: 1866–1877.

Ciaramelli, E. and Ghetti, S. (2007) What are confabulators' memories made of? A study of subjective and objective measures of recollection in confabulation. *Neuropsychologia* 45: 1489–1500.

Conway, M. A., Anderson, S. J., Larsen, S. F., Donnelly, C. M., McDaniel, M. A., McClelland A. G., Rawles, R. E. and Logie, R. H. (1994) The formation of flashbulb memories. *Memory and Cognition* 22: 326–343.

Conway, M. A. and Tacci, P. C. (1996) Motivated confabulation. *Neurocase* 2: 325–339.

Cooper, J. M., Shanks, M. F. and Venneri, A. (2006) Provoked confabulations in Alzheimer's disease. *Neuropsychologia* 44: 1697–1707.

Corkin, S., Amaral, D. G., Gonzalez, R. G., Johnson, K. A. and Hyman, B. T. (1997) H. M.'s medial temporal lobe lesion: findings from magnetic resonance imaging. *Journal of Neuroscience* 17: 3964–3979.

Corkin, S. (2002) What's new with the amnesic patient H. M.? *Nature Reviews Neuroscience* 3: 153–160.

Courbon, P. and Fail, G. (1927) Syndrome 'd'illusion de Frégoli' et schizophrénie. *Annales Médico-Psychologiques* 85: 289–290.

Courbon, P. and Tusques, J. (1932) Illusion d'intermétamorphose et de charme. *Annales Médico-Psychologiques* 90: 401–406.

Courville, C. B. (1945) *Pathology of the nervous system,* 2nd edn. Mountain View, CA: Pacific Press.

Crisp, J. (1995) Making sense of the stories that people with Alzheimer's tell: a journey with my mother. *Nursing Inquiry* 2: 133–140.

Critchley, H. D., Mathias, C. J. and Dolan, R. J. (2001) Neural activity in the human brain relating to uncertainty and arousal during anticipation. *Neuron* 29: 537–545.

Cubitt, A. W. (1930) Spontaneous subarachnoid hemorrhage, with Korsakoff's psychosis. *British Medical Journal* 2: 212–213.

Cummings, J., L, Tomiyasu, U., Read, S. and Benson, D., F (1984) Amnesia with hippocampal lesions after cardiopulmonary arrest. *Neurology* 34: 679–681.

Cummings, J. L. and Benson, D. F. (1992) *Dementia. A clinical approach*, 2nd edn. Boston, MA: Butterworth Heinemann.

Cummings, J. L. (1993) Frontal-subcortical circuits and human behavior. *Archives of Neurology* 50: 873–880.

Cunningham, J. M., Pliskin, N. H., Cassisi, J. E., Tsang, B. and Rao, S. M. (1997) Relationship between confabulation and measures of memory and executive function. *Journal of Clinical and Experimental Neuropsychology* 19: 867–877.

Curci, A. and Luminet, O. (2006) Follow-up of a cross-national comparison on flashbulb and event memory for the September 11th attacks. *Memory* 14: 329–344.

Cutting, J. (1978) Study of anosognosia. *Journal of Neurology, Neurosurgery and Psychiatry* 41: 548–555.

Czernecki, V., Pillon, B., Houeto, J. L., Pochon, J. B., Levy, R. and Dubois, B. (2002) Motivation, reward, and Parkinson's disease: influence of dopatherapy. *Neuropsychologia* 40: 2257–2267.

Dab, S., Morais, J. and Frith, C. (2004) Comprehension, encoding, and monitoring in the production of confabulation in memory: a study with schizophrenic patients. *Cognitive Neuropsychiatry* 9: 153–182.

Dalla Barba, G., Cipolotti, L. and Denes, G. (1990) Autobiographical memory loss and confabulation in Korsakoff's syndrome: a case report. *Cortex* 26: 525–534.

Dalla Barba, G. (1993a) Different patterns of confabulation. *Cortex* 29: 567–581.

Dalla Barba, G. (1993b) Confabulation: knowledge and recollective experience. *Cognitive Neuropsychology* 10: 1–20.

Dalla Barba, G., Parlato, V., Iavarone, A. and Boller, F. (1995) Anosognosia, intrusions and 'frontal' functions in Alzheimer's disease and depression. *Neuropsychologia* 33: 247–259.

Dalla Barba, G., Boisse, M. F., Bartolomeo, P. and Bachoud-Levi, A. C. (1997a) Confabulation following rupture of posterior communicating artery. *Cortex* 33: 563–570.

Dalla Barba, G., Mantovan, M. C., Cappelletti, J. Y. and Denes, G. (1998) Temporal gradient in confabulation. *Cortex* 34: 417–426.

Dalla Barba, G., Nedjam, Z. and Dubois, B. (1999) Confabulation, executive functions, and source memory in Alzheimer's disease. *Cognitive Neuropsychology* 16: 385–398.

Dalla Barba, G. F., Cappelletti, J. Y., Signorini, M. and Denes, G. (1997b) Confabulation: Remembering 'another' past, planning 'another' future. *Neurocase* 3: 425–436.

Dalla Barba, G. F. (2002) *Memory, consciousness and temporality*. Boston, MA: Kluwer Academic Publishers.

Damasio, A. R., Eslinger, P. J., Damasio, H., Van Hoesen, G. W. and Cornell, S. (1985a) Multimodal amnesic syndrome following bilateral temporal and basal forebrain damage. *Archives of Neurology* 42: 252–259.

Damasio, A. R., Graff Radford, N. R., Eslinger, P. J., Damasio, H. and Kassel, N. (1985b) Amnesia following basal forebrain lesions. *Archives of Neurology* 42: 263–271.

Damasio, A. R. (1994) *Descartes' error: Emotion, reason, and the human brain*. New York: Grosset/Putnam.

Damasio, H., Grabowski, T., Frank, R., Galaburda, A. M. and Damasio, A. R. (1994) The return of Phineas Gage: Clues about the brain from the skull of a famous patient. *Science* 264: 1102–1105.

Daniel, W. F., Crovitz, H. F. and Weiner, R. D. (1987) Neuropsychological aspects of disorientation. *Cortex* 23: 169–187.

Davis, C. C. (1932) Acute encephalitis and the Korsakoff symptom complex. *Lancet* I: 13 (March 26): 670–671.

Davis, K. L., Kahn, R. S., Ko, G. and Davidson, M. (1991) Dopamine in schizophrenia: a review and reconceptualization. *American Journal of Psychiatry* 148: 1474–1486.

Dayus, B. and van den Broek, M. D. (2000) Treatment of stable delusional confabulations using self-monitoring training. *Neuropsychological Rehabilitation* 10: 415–427.

de Beurmann, Roubinovitch, Gougerot (1906) Psychose polyneuritique chez un lépreux. *Revue Neurologique (Paris)* 14: 292–293.

de Pauw, K. W., Szulecka, T. K. and Poltock, T. L. (1987) Fregoli syndrome after cerebral infarction. *The Journal of Nervous and Mental Diseases* 175: 433–438.

Del Grosso Destreri, N., Farina, E., Calabrese, E., Pinardi, G., Imbornone, E. and Mariani, C. (2002) Frontal impairment and confabulation after herpes simplex encephalitis: A case report. *Archives of Physical Medicine and Rehabilitation* 83: 423–426.

Delay, J. and Brion, S. (1969) *Le Syndrome de Korsakoff*. Paris: Masson and Cie.

Delbecq-Derouesné, J., Beauvois, M. F. and Shallice, T. (1990) Preserved recall versus impaired recognition. *Brain* 113: 1045–1074.

Delis, D. C., Kramer, J. H., Kaplan, E. and Ober, B. A. (1987) *The California Verbal Learning Test*. New York: Psychological Corporation.

DeLuca, J. (1993) Predicting neurobehavioral patterns following anterior communicating artery aneurysm. *Cortex* 29: 639–647.

DeLuca, J. (2000) A cognitive neuroscience perspective on confabulation. *Neuropsychoanalysis* 2: 119–132.

DeLuca, J. and Cicerone, K. D. (1991) Confabulation following aneurysm of the anterior communicating artery. *Cortex* 27: 417–423.

DeLuca, J. and Diamond, B. J. (1995) Aneurysm of the anterior communicating artery: a review of neuroanatomical and neuropsychological sequelae. *Journal of Clinical and Experimental Neuropsychology* 17: 100–121.

DeLuca, J. and Locker, R. (1996) Cognitive rehabilitation following anterior communicating artery aneurysm bleeding: a case report. *Disability and Rehabilitation* 18: 265–272.

Demery, J. A., Hanlon, R. E. and Bauer, R. M. (2001) Profound amnesia and confabulation following traumatic brain injury. *Neurocase* 7: 295–302.

Derouesné, C., Thibault, S., Lagha-Pierucci, S., Baudouin-Madec, V., Ancri, D. and Lacomblez, L. (1999) Decreased awareness of cognitive deficits in patients with mild dementia of the Alzheimer type. *International Journal of Geriatric Psychiatry* 14: 1019–1030.

Devinsky, O., Morrell, M. J. and Vogt, B. A. (1995) Contributions of anterior cingulate cortex to behaviour. *Brain* 118: 279–306.

Dias, R., Robbins, T. W. and Roberts, A. C. (1997) Dissociable forms of inhibitory control within prefrontal cortex with an analog of the Wisconsin Card Sort Test: restriction to novel situations and independence from 'on-line' processing. *Journal of Neuroscience* 17: 9285–9297.

Divac, I., Rosvold, H. E. and Szwarcbart, M. K. (1967) Behavioral effects of selective ablation of the caudate nucleus. *Journal of Comparative and Physiological Psychology* 63: 184–190.

Dudai, Y. (2004) The neurobiology of consolidations, or, how stable is the engram? *Annual Review of Psychology* 55: 51–86.

Dusoir, H., Kapur, N., Byrnes, D. P., McKinstry, S. and Hoare, R. D. (1990) The role of diencephalic pathology in human memory disorder. *Brain* 113: 1695–1706.

Düzel, E., Yonelinas, A. P., Mangun, G. R., Heinze, H. J. and Tulving, E. (1997) Event-related brain potential correlates of two states of conscious awareness in memory. *Proceedings of the National Academy of Science of the USA* 94: 5973–5978.

Ellenberg, J. H., Levin, H. S. and Saydjary, C. (1996) Posttraumatic amnesia as a predictor of outcome after severe closed head injury. *Archives of Neurology* 53: 782–791.

Elliott, R., Friston, K. J. and Dolan, R. J. (2000) Dissociable neural responses in human reward systems. *Journal of Neuroscience* 20: 6159–6165.

Elliott, R., Frith, C. D. and Dolan, R. J. (1997) Differential neural response to positive and negative feedback in planning and guessing tasks. *Neuropsychologia* 35: 1395–1404.

Elliott, R., Rees, G. and Dolan, R. J. (1999) Ventromedial prefrontal cortex mediates guessing. *Neuropsychologia* 37: 403–411.

Ely, F. A. (1922) Memory defect of Korsakoff type, observed in multiple neuritis following toxaemia of pregnancy. *The Journal of Nervous and Mental Diseases* 56: 115–125.

Erdelyi, M. H. (2006) The unified theory of repression. *Behavioral and Brain Sciences* 29: 499–511 (with commentaries and references: 499–551).

Eslinger, J. P., Grattan, L. M., Damasio, H. and Damasio, A. R. (1992) Developmental consequences of childhood frontal lobe damage. *Archives of Neurology* 49: 764–769.

Eslinger, P. J. and Damasio, A. R. (1985) Severe disturbances of higher cognition after bilateral frontal lobe ablation: patient EVR. *Neurology* 35: 1731–1741.

Feinberg, T. E. and Roane, D. M. (1997a) Misidentification syndromes. In: *Behavioral neurology and neuropsychology* (Feinberg TE, Farah MJ, eds), pp. 391–397. New York: McGraw-Hill.

Feinberg, T. E. and Roane, D. M. (1997b) Anosognosia and confabulation. In: *Behavioral neurology and neuropsychology* (Feinberg TE and Farah MJ, eds), pp. 369–390. New York: McGraw-Hill.

Feinberg, T. E., Eaton, L. A., Roane, D. M. and Giacino, J. T. (1999) Multiple Fregoli delusions after traumatic brain injury. *Cortex* 35: 373–387.

Feinberg, T. E., Roane, D. M., Kwan, P. C., Schindler, R. J. and Haber, L. D. (1994) Anosognosia and visuoverbal confabulation. *Archives of Neurology* 51: 468–473.

Feinstein, A., Levine, B. and Protzner, A. (2000) Confabulation and multiple sclerosis: a rare association. *Multiple Sclerosis* 6: 186–191.

Fellows, L. K. and Farah, M. J. (2003) Ventromedial frontal cortex mediates affective shifting in humans: evidence from a reversal learning paradigm. *Brain* 126: 1830–1837.

Ferry, A. T., Öngür, D., An, X. and Price, J. L. (2000) Prefrontal cortical projections to the striatum in macaque monkeys: evidence for an organization related to prefrontal networks. *Journal of Comparative Neurology* 425: 447–470.

Fischer, R. S., Alexander, M. P., D'Esposito, M. and Otto, R. (1995) Neuropsychological and neuroanatomical correlates of confabulation. *Journal of Clinical and Experimental Neuropsychology* 17: 20–28.

Flament, J. (1957) La fabulation dans le syndrome de Korsakov d'étiologie traumatique. Considérations cliniques, psycho-pathologiques et neuro-pathologiques à propos d'une observation de fabulation à caractère mythopathique. *Acta Neurologica Belgica* 57: 119–161.

Flatau, E. (1921) Sur les hémorragies méningées idiopathiques. *Gazette des Hôpitaux (Paris)* 94: 1077–1081.

Fleminger, S. and Burns, A. (1993) The delusional misidentification syndromes in patients with and without evidence of organic cerebral disorder: a structured review of case reports. *Biological Psychiatry* 33: 22–32.

Folstein, M. F., Folstein, S. E. and McHugh, P. R. (1975) Mini mental state. A practical method for grading the cognitive state of patients for the clinician. *Journal of Psychiatric Research* 12: 189–198.

Förstl, H., Almeida, O. P., Owen, A. M., Burns, A. and Howard, R. (1991) Psychiatric, neurological and medical aspects of misidentification syndromes: a review of 260 cases. *Psychological Medicine* 21: 905–910.

Fotopoulou, A., Solms, M. and Turnbull, O. (2004) Wishful reality distortions in confabulation: a case report. *Neuropsychologia* 42: 727–744.

Frank, M. J., Seeberger, L. C. and O'Reilly R, C. (2004) By carrot or by stick: Cognitive reinforcement learning in Parkinsonism. *Science* 306: 1940–1943.

Frankland P. W. and Bontempi, B. (2005) The organization of recent and remote memories. *Nature Reviews Neuroscience* 6: 119–130.

Freedman, M., Black, S., Ebert, P. and Binns, M. (1998) Orbitofrontal function, object alternation and perseveration. *Cerebral Cortex* 8: 18–27.

Freud, S. (1915/1976) Verdrängung. In: *Psychologie des Unbewussten. Sigmund Freud – Studienausgabe* (Mitscherlich A, Richards A and Strachey J, eds), pp. 103–118. Zürich: Buchclub Ex Libris.

Friedman, H. M. and Allen, N. (1969) Chronic effects of complete limbic lobe destruction in man. *Neurology* 19: 679–690.

Friston, K. J., Liddle, P. F., Frith, C. D., Hirsch, S. R. and Frackowiak, R. S. J. (1992) The left medial temporal region and schizophrenia. A PET study. *Brain* 115: 367–382.

Fujii, T., Suzuki, M., Okuda, J., Ohtake, H., Tanji, K., Yamaguchi, K., Itoh, M. and Yamadori, A. (2004) Neural correlates of context memory with real-world events. *Neuroimage* 21: 1596–1603.

Fuster, J. M. (1995) *Memory in the cerebral cortex.* Cambridge, MA: MIT Press.

Fuster, J. M. (1997) *The prefrontal cortex. Anatomy, physiology, and neuropsychology of the frontal lobes,* 3rd edn. New York: Raven Press.

Gade, A. (1982) Amnesia after operations on aneurysms of the anterior communicating artery. *Surgical Neurology* 18: 46–49.

Gaffan, D. and Gaffan, E. A. (1991) Amnesia in man following transsection of the fornix. *Brain* 114: 2611–2618.

Gamper, E. (1928) Zur Frage der Polioencephalitis haemorrhagica der chronischen Alkoholiker. Anatomische Befunde beim alkoholischen Korsakow und ihre Beziehungen zum klinischen Bild. *Deutsche Zeitschrift für Nervenheilkunde* 102: 122–129.

Garoff-Eaton, R. J., Slotnick, S. D. and Schacter, D. L. (2006) Not all false memories are created equal: the neural basis of false recognition. *Cerebral Cortex* 16: 1645–1652.

Gentilini, M., De Renzi, E. and Crisi, G. (1987) Bilateral paramedian thalamic artery infarcts: report of eight cases. *Journal of Neurology, Neurosurgery and Psychiatry* 50: 900–909.

Georges, K. E. (1913–1918) *Ausführliches lateinisch-deutsches Handwörterbuch. Aus den Quellen zusammengetragen und mit besonderer Bezugnahme auf Synonymik und Antiquitäten unter Berücksichtigung der besten Hilfsmittel* (Reprint 1998). Hannover: Hahnsche Buchhandlung.

Geschwind, N. (1965) Disconnexion syndromes in animals and man. Part I and II. *Brain* 88: 237–294, 585–644.

Ghika-Schmid, F. and Bogousslavsky, J. (2000) The acute behavioral syndrome of anterior thalamic infarction: a prospective study of 12 cases. *Annals of Neurology* 48: 220–227.

Gilboa, A. and Moscovitch, M. (2002) The cognitive neuroscience of confabulation: a review and a model. In: *The handbook of memory disorders*, 2nd edn (Baddeley A, Kopelman MD and Wilson B, eds), pp. 315–342. West Sussex: John Wiley and Sons.

Gilboa, A., Alain, C., Stuss, D. T., Melo, B., Miller, S. and Moscovitch, M. (2006) Mechanisms of spontaneous confabulations: a strategic retrieval account. *Brain* 129: 1399–1414.

Gloor, P. (1997) *The temporal lobe and limbic system*. New York: Oxford University Press.

Goldenberg, G., Schuri, U., Gromminger, O. and Arnold, U. (1999) Basal forebrain amnesia: does the nucleus accumbens contribute to human memory? *Journal of Neurology, Neurosurgery and Psychiatry* 67: 163–168.

Goldflam, S. (1923) Beitrag zur Ätiologie und Symptomatologie der spontanen subarachnoidalen Blutungen. *Deutsche Zeitschrift für Nervenheilkunde* 76: 158–182.

Goldman, P. S., Rosvold, H. E., Vest, B. and Galkin, T. W. (1971) Analysis of the delayed-alternation deficit produced by dorsolateral prefrontal lesions in the rhesus monkey. *Journal of Comparative and Physiological Psychology* 77: 212–220.

Gordon, B., Selnes, O. A., Hart, J., Hanley, D. F. and Whitley, R. J. (1990) Long-term cognitive sequelae of acyclovir-treated herpes simplex encephalitis. *Archives of Neurology* 47: 646–647.

Gottfried, J. A., O'Doherty, J. and Dolan, R. J. (2003) Encoding predictive reward value in human amygdala and orbitofrontal cortex. *Science* 301: 1104–1107.

Graff-Radford, N. R., Tranel, D., Van, H. G. W. and Brandt, J. P. (1990) Diencephalic amnesia. *Brain* 113: 1–25.

Gritti, I., Mainville, L., Mancia, M. and Jones, B. E. (1997) GABAergic and other noncholinergic basal forebrain neurons, together with cholinergic neurons, project to the mesocortex and isocortex in the rat. *Journal of Comparative Neurology* 383.

Guberman, A. and Stuss, D. (1983) The syndrome of bilateral paramedian thalamic infarction. *Neurology* 33: 540–546.

Gundogar, D. and Demirci, S. (2006) Multiple sclerosis presenting with fantastic confabulation. *General Hospital Psychiatry* 28: 448–451.

Haber, S. N., Kunishio, K., Mizobuchi, M. and Lynd-Balta, E. (1995) The orbital and medial prefrontal circuit through the primate basal ganglia. *Journal of Neuroscience* 15: 4851–4867.

Halavaara, J., Brander, A., Lyytinen, J., Setala, K. and Kallela, M. (2003) Wernicke's encephalopathy: is diffusion-weighted MRI useful? *Neuroradiology* 45: 519–523.

Hall, A. (1929) Three cases of spontaneous subarachnoid hemorrhage: with especial reference to the occurrence of massive albuminuria and Korsakow's syndrome. *British Medical Journal* i: 1025–1028.

Hanley, J. R., Davies, A. D. M., Downes, J. J. and Mayes, A. R. (1994) Impaired recall of verbal material following rupture and repair of an anterior communicating artery aneurysm. *Cognitive Neuropsychology* 11: 543–578.

Hanse, A. (1928) Über einen eigenartigen Fall von Milzbrand-Meningo-Myelo-Encephalitis mit ungewöhnlichem Verlauf. *Deutsche Zeitschrift für Nervenheilkunde* 103: 67–77.

Harding, A., Halliday, G., Caine, D. and Kril, J. (2000) Degeneration of anterior thalamic nuclei differentiates alcoholics with amnesia. *Brain* 123: 141–154.

Harlow, J. (1848) Passage of an iron rod through the head. *Boston Medical and Surgical Journal* 39: 389–393.

Harlow, J. (1868) Recovery from the passage of an iron bar through the head. *Publications of the Massachusetts Medical Society* 2: 327–347.

Harris, R. J. (1973) Answering questions containing marked and unmarked adjectives and adverbs. *Journal of Experimental Psychology* 97: 399–401.

Harrison, P. J. (1999) The neuropathology of schizophrenia. A critical review of the data and their interpretation. *Brain* 122: 593–624.

Hashimoto, R., Tanaka, Y. and Nakano, I. (2000) Amnesic confabulatory syndrome after focal basal forebrain damage. *Neurology* 54: 978–980.

High, W. M., Levin, H. S. and Gary, H. E. (1990) Recovery of orientation following closed head injury. *Journal of Clinical and Experimental Neuropsychology* 12: 703–714.

Hirst, W. and Volpe, B. T. (1982) Temporal order judgments with amnesia. *Brain and Cognition* 1: 294–306.

Hirstein, W. (2005) *Brain fiction. Self-deception and the riddle of confabulation.* Cambridge, MA: The MIT Press.

Hodges, J. R. and Carpenter, K. (1991) Anterograde amnesia with fornix damage following removal of IIIrd ventricle colloid cyst. *Journal of Neurology, Neurosurgery and Psychiatry* 54: 633–638.

Holbourn, A. H. S. (1943) Mechanics of head injuries. *Lancet* II: 438–441.

Hollerman, J. R. and Schultz, W. (1998) Dopamine neurons report an error in the temporal prediction of reward during learning. *Nature Neuroscience* 1: 304–309.

Honea, R., Crow, T. J., Passingham, D. and Mackay, C. E. (2005) Regional deficits in brain volume in schizophrenia: a meta-analysis of voxel-based morphometry studies. *American Journal of Psychiatry* 162: 2233–2245.

Hooshmand H., Escobar, M. R. and Kopf, S. W. (1972) Neurosyphilis. A study of 241 patients. *Journal of the American Medical Association* 219: 726–729.

Hornak, J., Bramham, J., Rolls, E. T., Morris, R. G., O'Doherty, J., Bullock, P. R. and Polkey, C. E. (2003) Changes in emotion after circumscribed surgical lesions of the orbitofrontal and cingulate cortices. *Brain* 126: 1691–1712.

Hornak, J., O'Doherty, J., Bramham, J., Rolls, E. T., Morris, R. G., Bullock, P. R. and Polkey, C. E. (2004) Reward-related reversal learning after surgical excisions in orbito-frontal or dorsolateral prefrontal cortex in humans. *Journal of Cognitive Neuroscience* 16: 463–478.

Huppert, F. A. and Piercy, M. (1976) Recognition memory in amnesic patients: effect of temporal context and familiarity of material. *Cortex* 12: 3–20.

Inagaki, T., Shimitzu, Y., Tsubouchi, K., Momose, I., Miyaoka, T., Mizuno, S., Kishi, T., Yamamori, C. *et al.* (2003) Korsakoff syndrome following chronic subdural hematoma. *General Hospital Psychiatry* 25: 364–366.

Irle, E., Wowra, B., Kunert, H. J., Hampl, J. and Kunze, S. (1992) Memory disturbances following anterior communicating artery rupture. *Annals of Neurology* 31: 473–480.

Iversen, S. D. and Mishkin, M. (1970) Perseverative interference in monkeys following selective lesions of the inferior prefrontal convexity. *Experimental Brain Research* 11: 376–386.

Jackson, J. H. (1888) On a particular variety of epilepsy ('intellectual aura'), one case with symptoms of organic brain disease. *Brain* 11: 179–207.

Jackson, J. H. and Colman, W. S. (1898) Case of epilepsy with tasting movements and "dreamy state" – very small patch of softening in the left uncinate gyrus. *Brain* 21: 580–590.

James, W. (1890/1983) *The principles of psychology*, 1983 edn. Cambridge, MA: Harvard University Press.

Janowsky, J. S., Shimamura, A. P., Kritchevsky, M. and Squire, L. R. (1989a) Cognitive impairment following frontal lobe damage and its relevance to human amnesia. *Behavioral Neuroscience* 103: 548–560.

Janowsky, J. S., Shimamura, A. P. and Squire, L. R. (1989b) Memory and metamemory: comparisons between patients with frontal lobe lesions and amnesic patients. *Psychobiology* 17: 3–11.

Jaspers, K. (1973) *Allgemeine Psychopathologie*, 9th edn. Berlin: Springer-Verlag.

Jehkonen, M., Ahonen, J. P., Dastidar, P., Laippala, P. and Vilkki, J. (2000) Unawareness of deficits after right hemisphere stroke: double-dissociations of anosognosias. *Acta Neurologica Scandinavica* 102: 378–384.

Joel, D. and Weiner, I. (2000) The connections of the dopaminergic system with the striatum in rats and primates: an analysis with respect to the functional and compartmental organization of the striatum. *Neuroscience* 96: 451–474.

Johnson, M. K. and Raye, C. L. (1981) Reality monitoring. *Psychological Review* 88: 67–85.

Johnson, M. K., Hashtroudi, S. and Lindsay, D. S. (1993) Source monitoring. *Psychological Bulletin* 114: 3–28.

Johnson, M. K., O'Connor, M. and Cantor, J. (1997) Confabulation, memory deficits, and frontal dysfunction. *Brain and Cognition* 34: 189–206.

Johnson, M. K. and Raye, C. L. (1998) False memories and confabulation. *Trends in Cognitive Science* 2: 137–145.

Johnson, M. K., Hayes, S. M., D'Esposito, M. and Raye, C. L. (2000) Confabulation. In: *Handbook of neuropsychology, Vol. 2: Memory and its disorders*, 2nd edn (Boller F, Grafman J and Cermak LS, eds), pp. 383–407. Amsterdam: Elsevier Science.

Jolly, F. (1897) Ueber die psychischen Störungen bei Polyneuritis. *Charité-Annalen* 22: 579–612.

Jones, B. and Mishkin, M. (1972) Limbic lesions and the problem of stimulus–reinforcement associations. *Experimental Neurology* 36: 362–377.

Jones, E. G. (1985) *The thalamus*. New York: Plenum Press.

Jones, E. G. (2007) *The thalamus*, 2nd edn. Cambridge: Cambridge University Press.

Joray, S., Herrmann, F., Mulligan, R. and Schnider, A. (2004) Mechanism of disorientation in Alzheimer's disease. *European Neurology* 52: 193–197.

Kahn, E. A. and Crosby, E. C. (1972) Korsakoff's syndrome associated with surgical lesions involving the mammillary bodies. *Neurology* 22: 117–125.

Kalberlah, F. (1904) Ueber die acute Commotionspsychose, zugleich ein Beitrag zur Aetiologie des Korsakow'schen Symptomenkomplexes. *Archiv für Psychiatrie und Nervenkrankheiten* 38: 402–438.

Kapur, N. and Coughlan, A. K. (1980) Confabulation and frontal lobe dysfunction. *Journal of Neurology, Neurosurgery and Psychiatry* 43: 461–463.

Kapur, N., Barker, S., Burrows, E. H., Ellison, D., Brice, J., Illis, L. S., Scholey, K., Colbourn, C., *et al.* (1994) Herpes simplex encephalitis: long term magnetic resonance imaging and neuropsychological profile. *Journal of Neurology, Neurosurgery and Psychiatry* 57: 1334–1342.

Kapur, N., Turner, A. and King, C. (1988) Reduplicative paramnesia: possible anatomical and neuropsychological mechanisms. *Journal of Neurology, Neurosurgery and Psychiatry* 51: 579–581.

Karnath, H. O., Baier, B. and Nagele, T. (2005) Awareness of the functioning of one's own limbs mediated by the insular cortex? *Journal of Neuroscience* 25: 7134–7138.

Kaufer, D. I. and Cummings, J. L. (1997) Dementia and delirium: an overview. In: *Behavioral neurology and neuropsychology* (Feinberg TE and Farah MJ, eds), pp. 499–520. New York: McGraw-Hill.

Kauffmann, A. F. (1913) Zur Frage der Heilbarkeit der Korsakowschen Psychose. *Zeitschrift für die gesamte Neurologie und Psychiatrie* 20: 488–510.

Kern, R. S., Van Gorp, W. G., Cummings, J. L., Brown, W. S. and Osato, S. S. (1992) Confabulation in Alzheimer's disease. *Brain and Cognition* 19: 172–182.

Kesner, R. P., Hopkins, R. O. and Fineman, B. (1994) Item and order dissociation in humans with prefrontal damage. *Neuropsychologia* 32: 881–889.

Klein, R. and Kral, A. (1933) Zur Frage der Pathogenese und Psychopathologie des amnestischen Symptomenkomplexes nach Schädeltraumen. *Zeitschrift für die gesamte Neurologie und Psychiatrie* 149: 134–175.

Kleist, K. (1934) *Gehirnpathologie*. Leipzig: Johann Ambrosius Barth Verlag.

Knutson, B., Adams, C. M., Fong, G. W. and Hommer, D. (2001a) Anticipation of increasing monetary reward selectively recruits nucleus accumbens. *Journal of Neuroscience* 21: RC159.

Knutson, B., Fong, G. W., Adams, C. M., Varner, J. L. and Hommer, D. (2001b) Dissociation of reward anticipation and outcome with event-related fMRI. *Neuroreport* 12: 3683–3687.

Koehler, K. and Jacoby, C. (1978) Acute confabulatory psychosis: a rare form of unipolar mania? *Acta Psychiatrica Scandinavica* 57: 415–425.

Koenigs, M., Young, L., Adolphs, R., Tranel, D., Cushman, F., Hauser, M. and Damasio, A. (2007) Damage to the prefrontal cortex increases utilitarian moral judgements. *Nature* 446: 908–911.

Kopelman, M. D. (1987) Two types of confabulation. *Journal of Neurology, Neurosurgery and Psychiatry* 50: 1482–1487.

Kopelman, M. D. (1995) The Korsakoff syndrome. *British Journal of Psychiatry* 166: 154–173.

Kopelman, M. D. (1999) Varieties of false memory. *Cognitive Neuropsychology* 16: 197–214.

Kopelman, M. D., Hg, N. and Van den Brouke, O. (1997a) Confabulation extending over episodic, personal, and general semantic memory. *Cognitive Neuropsychology* 14: 683–712.

Kopelman, M. D., Stanhope, N. and Guinan, E. (1998) Subjective memory evaluations in patients with focal frontal, diencephalic, and temporal lobe lesion. *Cortex* 34: 191–207.

Kopelman, M. D., Stanhope, N. and Kingsley, D. (1997b) Temporal and spatial context memory in patients with focal frontal, temporal lobe, and diencephalic lesions. *Neuropsychologia* 35: 1533–1545.

Környey, S. (1932) Aufsteigende Lähmung und Korsakowsche Psychose bei Lymphogranulomatose. *Deutsche Zeitschrift für Nervenheilkunde* 125: 129–141.

Korsakoff, S. S. (1889) Etude médico-psychologique sur une forme des maladies de la mémoire. *Revue Philosophique* 20: 501–530.

Korsakoff, S. S. (1890a) Ueber eine besondere Form psychischer Störung, combiniert mit multipler Neuritis. *Archiv für Psychiatrie und Nervenkrankheiten* 21: 669–704.

Korsakoff, S. S. (1890b) Eine psychische Störung combiniert mit multipler Neuritis (Psychosis polyneuritica seu Cerebropathia psychica toxaemica). *Allgemeine Zeitschrift für Psychiatrie und psychisch-gerichtliche Medicin* 46: 475–485.

Korsakoff, S. S. (1891) Erinnerungstäuschungen (Pseudoreminiscenzen) bei polyneuritischer Psychose. *Allgemeine Zeitschrift für Psychiatrie und psychisch-gerichtliche Medicin* 47: 390–410.

Korsakoff, S. S. (1955, original 1889) Psychic disorder in conjunction with peripheral neuritis (translation by M. Victor, P. I. Yakovlev). *Neurology* 5: 394–406.

Kraepelin, E. (1886) Ueber Erinnerungsfälschungen (1/3). *Archiv für Psychiatrie und Nervenkrankheiten* 17: 830–843.

Kraepelin, E. (1887a) Ueber Erinnerungsfälschungen (2/3. Fortsetzung). *Archiv für Psychiatrie und Nervenkrankheiten* 18: 199–239.

Kraepelin, E. (1887b) Ueber Erinnerungsfälschungen (3/3. Fortsetzung und Schluss). *Archiv für Psychiatrie und Nervenkrankheiten* 18: 395–436.

Kraepelin, E. (1899) *Psychiatrie. Ein Lehrbuch für Studirende und Aerzte*, 6th edn. Leipzig: Johann Ambrosius Barth Verlag.

Kraepelin, E. (1909) *Psychiatrie. Ein Lehrbuch für Studierende und Ärzte. I. Band: Allgemeine Psychiatrie*, 8th edn. Leipzig: Johann Ambrosius Barth Verlag.

Kraepelin, E. (1910) *Psychiatrie. Ein Lehrbuch für Studierende und Ärzte. II. Band: Klinische Psychiatrie, I. Teil*, 8th edn. Leipzig: Johann Ambrosius Barth Verlag.

Kraepelin, E. (1921) *Einführung in die Psychiatrische Klinik*, 4th edn. Leipzig: Johann Ambrosius Barth Verlag.

Kraepelin, E. (1926) The problems presented by general paresis. *The Journal of Nervous and Mental Diseases* 63: 209–218.

Kreczmanski, P., Heinsen, H., Mantua, V., Woltersdorf, F., Masson, T., Ulfig, N., Schmidt-Kastner, R., Korr, H., et al. (2007) Volume, neuron density and total neuron number in five subcortical regions in schizophrenia. *Brain* 130: 678–692.

Kringelbach, M. L. and Rolls, E. T. (2004) The functional neuroanatomy of the human orbitofrontal cortex: evidence from neuroimaging and neuropsychology. *Progress in Neurobiology* 72: 341–372.

Kringelbach, M. L. (2005) The human orbitofrontal cortex: linking reward to hedonic experience. *Nature Reviews Neuroscience* 6: 691–702.

Kuwert, T., Homberg, V., Steinmetz, H., Unverhau, S., Langen, K. J., Herzog, H. and Feinendegen, L. E. (1993) Posthypoxic amnesia: regional cerebral glucose consumption measured by positron emission tomography. *Journal of the Neurological Sciences* 118: 10–16.

Lebrun, Y. (1987) Anosognosia in aphasics. *Cortex* 23: 251–263.

LeDoux, J. (1996) *The emotional brain. The mysterious underpinnings of emotional life.* New York: Simon and Schuster.

Lehmann, D. (1987) Principles of spatial analysis. In: *Handbook of electroencephalography and clinical neurophysiology. Volume 1: Methods of analysis of brain electrical and magnetic signals* (Gevins AS and Rémond A, eds), pp. 309–354. Amsterdam: Elsevier.

Leonhard, K. (1986) *Aufteilung der endogenen Psychosen und ihre differenzierte Ätiologie.* Berlin: Akademie-Verlag.

Levine, D. N., Calvanio, R. and Rinn, W. E. (1991) The pathogenesis of anosognosia for hemiplegia. *Neurology* 41: 1770–1781.

Liddle, P. F., Friston, K. J., Frith, C. D., Hirsch, S. R., Jones, T. and Frackowiak, R. S. J. (1992) Patterns of cerebral blood flow in schizophrenia. *British Journal of Psychiatry* 160: 179–186.

Lim, C., Alexander, M. P., LaFleche, G., Schnyer, D. M. and Verfaellie, M. (2004) The neurological and cognitive sequelae of cardiac arrest. *Neurology* 63: 1774–1778.

Lindqvist, G. and Norlén, G. (1966) Korsakoff's syndrome after operation on ruptured aneurysm of the anterior communicating artery. *Acta Psychiatrica Scandinavica* 42: 24–34.

Linke, P. (1918) *Grundfragen der Wahrnehmungslehre*. Munich: Reinhardt.

Lipowski, Z. J. (1985) Delirium (acute confusional state). In: *Handbook of clinical neurology, vol. 46: Neurobehavioural disorders* (Frederiks JAM, ed.), pp. 523–559. Amsterdam: Elsevier Science.

Lishman, W. A. (1981) Cerebral disorders in alcoholism. Syndromes of impairment. *Brain* 104: 1–20.

Lobosky, J. M., Vangilder, J. C. and Damasio, A. R. (1984) Behavioural manifestations of third ventricular colloid cysts. *Journal of Neurology, Neurosurgery and Psychiatry* 47: 1075–1080.

Loftus, E. F. (1979/1996) *Eyewitness Testimony*. Cambridge, MA: Harvard University Press.

Loftus, E. F. (1992) When a lie becomes memory's truth: memory distorsion after exposure to misinformation. *Current Directions in Psychological Science* 1: 121–123.

Loftus, E. F. (1997) Memory for a past that never was. *Current Directions in Psychological Science* 6: 60–65.

Loftus, E. F. and Palmer, J. C. (1974) Reconstruction of automobile destruction: an example of the interaction between language and memory. *Journal of Verbal Learning and Verbal Behavior* 13: 585–589.

Logue, V., Durward, M., Pratt, R. T. C., Piercy, M. and Nixon, W. L. B. (1968) The quality of survival after rupture of an anterior cerebral aneurysm. *British Journal of Psychiatry* 114: 137–160.

Lu, L. H., Barrett, A. M., Schwartz, R. L., Cibula, J. E., Gilmore, R. L., Uthman, B. M. and Heilman, K. M. (1997) Anosognosia and confabulation during the Wada test. *Neurology* 49: 1316–1322.

Maia, T. V. and McClelland J. L. (2004) A reexamination of the evidence for the somatic marker hypothesis: what participants really know in the Iowa gambling task. *Proceedings of the National Academy of Science of the USA* 101: 16075–16080.

Mair, W. G., Warrington, E. K. and Weiskrantz, L. (1979) Memory disorder in Korsakoff's psychosis: a neuropathological and neuropsychological investigation of two cases. *Brain* 102: 749–783.

Marcel, A. J., Tegner, R. and Nimmo-Smith, I. (2004) Anosognosia for plegia: specificity, extension, partiality and disunity of bodily unawareness. *Cortex* 40: 19–40.

Marková, I. S. and Berrios, G. E. (2000) Paramnesias and delusions of memory. In: *Memory disorders in psychiatric practice* (Berrios GE and Hodges J, eds), pp. 313–337. Cambridge: Cambridge University Press.

Marshall, J. C., Halligan, P. W. and Wade, D. T. (1995) Reduplication of an event after head injury? A cautionary case report. *Cortex* 31: 183–190.

Mayes, A. R., Meudell, P. R., Mann, D. and Pickering, A. (1988) Location of lesions in Korsakoff's syndrome: neuropsychological and neuropathological data on two patients. *Cortex* 24: 367–388.

McClure, S. M., Berns, G. S. and Montague, P. R. (2003) Temporal prediction errors in a passive learning task activate human striatum. *Neuron* 38: 339–346.

McEnaney, K. W. and Butter, C. M. (1969) Perseveration of responding and nonresponding in monkeys with orbital frontal ablations. *Journal of Comparative and Physiological Psychology* 68: 558–561.

McKenna, P. J., P., M. A. and Laws, K. (2000) Memory in functional psychosis. In: *Memory disorders in psychiatric practice* (Berrios GE and Hodges J, eds), pp. 234–267. Cambridge: Cambridge University Press.

McKhann, G. M., Albert, M. S., Grossman, M., Miller, B., Dickson, D. and Trojanowski, J. Q. (2001) Clinical and pathological diagnosis of frontotemporal dementia: report of the Work Group on Frontotemporal Dementia and Pick's Disease. *Archives of Neurology* 58: 1803–1809.

McKhann, G., Drachman, D., Folstein, M., Katzman, R., Price, D. and Stadlan, E. M. (1984) Clinical diagnosis of Alzheimer's disease: Report of the NINCDS-ADRDA Work Group under the auspices of Department of Health and Human Services Task Force on Alzheimer's disease. *Neurology* 34: 939–944.

Mega, M. S. and Cummings, J. (1997) The cingulate and cingulate syndromes. In: *Contemporary behavioral neurology* (Trimble MR and Cummings J, eds), pp. 189–214. Boston, MA: Butterworth Heinemann.

Melo, B., Winocur, G. and Moscovitch, M. (1999) False recall and false recognition: an examination of the effects of selective and combined lesions to the medial temporal lobe/diencephalon and frontal lobe structures. *Cognitive Neuropsychology* 16: 343–359.

Mendez, M. F. and Cummings, J. L. (2003) *Dementia. A clinical approach*, 3rd edn. Boston, MA: Butterworth Heinemann.

Mercer, B., Wapner, W., Gardner, H. and Benson, D. F. (1977) A study of confabulation. *Archives of Neurology* 34: 429–433.

Mesulam, M. M. and Mufson, E. J. (1982) Insula of the old world monkey. Part III: Efferent cortical output and comments on function. *Journal of Comparative Neurology* 212: 38–52.

Metcalf, K., Langdon, R. and Coltheart, M. (2007) Models of confabulation: A critical review and a new framework. *Cognitive Neuropsychology* 24: 23–47.

Meyer, E. and Raecke, J. (1903) Zur Lehre vom Korsakow'schen Symptomencomplex. *Archiv für Psychiatrie und Nervenkrankheiten* 37: 1–44.

Meythaler, J. M., Peduzzi, J. D., Eleftheriou, E. and Novack, T. A. (2001) Current concepts: diffuse axonal injury-associated traumatic brain injury. *Archives of Physical Medicine and Rehabilitation* 82: 1461–1471.

Michel, C. M., Murray, M. M., Lantz, G., Gonzalez, S., Spinelli, L. and Grave de Peralta, R. (2004) EEG source imaging. *Clinical Neurophysiology* 115: 2195–2222.

Michel, C. M., Seeck, M. and Landis, T. (1999) Spatio-temporal dynamics of human cognition. *News in Physiological Sciences* 14: 206–214.

Michon, A., Deweer, B., Pillon, B., Agid, Y. and Dubois, B. (1994) Relation of anosognosia to frontal lobe dysfunction in Alzheimer's disease. *Journal of Neurology, Neurosurgery and Psychiatry* 57: 805–809.

Miller, E. K. and Cohen, J. D. (2001) An integrative theory of prefrontal cortex function. *Annual Review of Neuroscience* 24: 167–202.

Milner, B., Corkin, S. and Teuber, H. L. (1968) Further analysis of the hippocampal amnesic syndrome: 14-year follow-up study of H. M. *Neuropsychologia* 6: 215–234.

Milner, B., Corsi, P. and Leonard, G. (1991) Frontal-lobe contribution to recency judgements. *Neuropsychologia* 29: 601–618.

Minski, L. (1936) Non-alcoholic polyneuritis associated with Korsakow syndrom. *Journal of Neurology and Psychopathology* 16: 219–224.

Moll, J. (1915) The "amnestic" or "Korsakow's" syndrome with alcoholic etiology: an analysis of thirty cases. *The Journal of Mental Science* 61: 424–443.

Morecraft, R. J., Geula, C. and Mesulam, M.-M. (1992) Cytoarchitecture and neural afferents of orbitofrontal cortex in the brain of the monkey. *Journal of Comparative Neurology* 323: 341–358.

Morris, M. K., Bowers, D. W., Chatterjee, A. and Heilman, K. M. (1992) Amnesia following a discrete basal forebrain lesion. *Brain* 115: 1827–1847.

Moscovitch, M. (1989) Confabulation and the frontal systems: strategic versus associative retrieval in neuropsychological theories of memory. In: *Varieties of memory and consciousness. Essays in honour of Endel Tulving* (Roediger HLI and Craik FIM, eds), pp. 133–160. Hillsdale, NJ: Lawrence Erlbaum Associates.

Moscovitch, M. (1995) Confabulation. In: *Memory distortion. How minds, brains, and societies reconstruct the past* (Schacter DL, ed.). Cambridge, MA: Harvard University Press.

Moscovitch, M. and Melo, B. (1997) Strategic retrieval and the frontal lobes: evidence from confabulation and amnesia. *Neuropsychologia* 35: 1017–1034.

Moscovitch, M. and Winocur, G. (2002) The frontal cortex and working with memory. In: *Principles of frontal lobe function* (Stuss DT and Knight RT, eds), pp. 188–209. New York: Oxford University Press.

Moscovitch, M., Rosenbaum, R. S., Gilboa, A., Addis, D. R., Westmacott, R., Grady, C., McAndrews, M. P., Levine, B., et al. (2005) Functional neuroanatomy of remote episodic, semantic and spatial memory: a unified account based on multiple trace theory. *Journal of Anatomy* 207: 35–66.

Moulin, C. J., Conway, M. A., Thompson, R. G., James, N. and Jones, R. W. (2005) Disordered memory awareness: recollective confabulation in two cases of persistent déjà vecu. *Neuropsychologia* 43: 1362–1378.

Murray, M. M., Michel, C. M., Grave de Peralta, R., Ortigue, S., Brunet, D., Gonzalez Andino, S. and Schnider, A. (2004) The sound and the memory: Rapid, incidental discrimination of visual and multisensory memories. *NeuroImage* 21: 125–135.

Murray, M. M., Foxe, J. J. and Wylie, G. R. (2005) The brain uses single-trial multisensory memories to discriminate without awareness. *Neuroimage* 27: 473–478.

Nadel, L. and Moscovitch, M. (1997) Memory consolidation, retrograde amnesia and the hippocampal complex. *Current Opinion in Neurobiology* 7: 217–227.

Nadel, L., Samsonovich, A., Ryan, L. and Moscovitch, M. (2000) Multiple trace theory of human memory: computational, neuroimaging, and neuropsychological results. *Hippocampus* 10: 352–368.

Nakamura, M., Nestor, P. G., McCarley, R. W., Levitt, J. J., Hsu, L., Kawashima, T., Niznikiewicz, M. and Shenton, M. E. (2007) Altered orbitofrontal sulcogyral pattern in schizophrenia. *Brain* 130: 693–707.

Nakano, K., Kayahara, T., Tsutsumi, T. and Ushiro, H. (2000) Neural circuits and functional organization of the striatum. *Journal of Neurology* 247 Suppl 5: V1–15.

Nathaniel-James, D. A. and Frith, C. D. (1996) Confabulation in schizophrenia: evidence of a new form? *Psychological Medicine* 26: 391–399.

Neary, D., Snowden, J. S., Gustafson, L., Passant, U., Stuss, D., Black, S., Freedman, M., Kertesz, A. *et al.* (1998) Frontotemporal lobar degeneration: a consensus on clinical diagnostic criteria. *Neurology* 51: 1546–1554.

Nedjam, Z., Dalla Barba, G. and Pillon, B. (2000) Confabulation in a patient with frontotemporal dementia and a patient with Alzheimer's disease. *Cortex* 36: 561–577.

Nedjam, Z., Devouche, E. and Dalla Barba, G. (2004) Confabulation, but not executive dysfunction discriminate AD from frontotemporal dementia. *European Journal of Neurology* 11: 728–733.

Nelson, J., Parisi, J. and Schochet, S. (eds) (1993) *Principles and Practice of Neuropathology.* St Louis: Mosby.

Neylan, T. (1999) Frontal lobe function: Mr. Phineas Gage's famous injury. *Journal of Neuropsychiatry and Clinical Neurosciences* 11: 280–283.

Nolde, S. F., Johnson, M. K. and D'Esposito, M. (1998) Left prefrontal activation during episodic remembering: an event- related fMRI study. *Neuroreport* 9: 3509–3514.

Nys, G. M., van Zandvoort, M. J., Roks, G., Kappelle, L. J., de Kort, P. L. and de Haan, E. H. (2004) The role of executive functioning in spontaneous confabulation. *Cognitive and Behavioral Neurology* 17: 213–218.

O'Doherty, J., Kringelbach, M. L., Rolls, E. T., Hornak, J. and Andrews, C. (2001) Abstract reward and punishment representations in the human orbitofrontal cortex. *Nature Neuroscience* 4: 95–102.

O'Doherty, J. P., Deichmann, R., Critchley, H. D. and Dolan, R. J. (2002) Neural responses during anticipation of a primary taste reward. *Neuron* 33: 815–826.

Ojemann, J. G., Akbudak, E., Snyder, A. Z., McKinstry, R. C., Raichle, M. E. and Conturo, T. E. (1997) Anatomic localization and quantitative analysis of gradient refocused echo-planar fMRI susceptibility artifacts. *Neuroimage* 6: 156–167.

Öngür, D., An, X. and Price, J. L. (1998) Prefrontal cortical projections to the hypothalamus in macaque monkeys. *Journal of Comparative Neurology* 401: 480–505.

Öngür, D., Ferry, A. T. and Price, J. L. (2003) Architectonic subdivision of the human orbital and medial prefrontal cortex. *Journal of Comparative Neurology* 460: 425–449.

Papagno, C. and Baddeley, A. (1997) Confabulation in a dysexecutive patient: implication for models of retrieval. *Cortex* 33: 743–752.

Papez, J. W. (1937) A proposed mechanism of emotion. *Archives of Neurology and Psychiatry* 38: 725–743.

Parfitt, D. N. (1934) Psychoses associated with pernicious anaemia with a report of two cases. *Journal of Neurology and Psychopathology* 15: 12–19.

Parkin, A. J. and Hunkin, N. M. (1993) Impaired temporal context memory on anterograde but not retrograde tests in the absence of frontal pathology. *Cortex* 29: 267–280.

Parkin, A. J., Bindschaedler, C., Harsent, L. and Metzler, C. (1996) Pathological false alarm rates following damage to the left frontal cortex. *Brain and Cognition* 32: 14–27.

Parkin, A. J., Ward, J., Bindschaedler, C., Squires, E. J. and Powell, G. (1999) False recognition following frontal lobe damage: the role of encoding factors. *Cognitive Neuropsychology* 16: 243–265.

Passingham, R. E. (1972) Non-reversal shifts after selective prefrontal ablations in monkeys (*Macaca mulatta*). *Neuropsychologia* 10: 41–46.

Penfield, W. and Perot, P. (1963) The brain's record of auditory and visual experience. A final summary and discussion. *Brain* 86: 595–696.

Percheron, G., Yelnik, J., François, C., Fenelon, G. and Talbi, B. (1994) Analyse information-nelle du système lié aux ganglions de la base. *Revue Neurologique (Paris)* 150: 614–626.

Perret, E. (1974) The left frontal lobe of man and the suppression of habitual responses in verbal categorical behavior. *Neuropsychologia* 12: 323–330.

Petrides, M. and Pandya, D. (1994) Comparative architectonic analysis of the human and macaque frontal cortex. In: *Handbook of neuropsychology* (Grafman J, and Boller F, eds), pp. 17–58. Amsterdam: Elsevier Science.

Petrides, M., Alivizatos, B. and Frey, S. (2002) Differential activation of the human orbital, mid-ventrolateral, and mid-dorsolateral prefrontal cortex during the processing of visual stimuli. *Proceedings of the National Academy of Science of the USA* 99: 5649–5654.

Pfeifer, B. (1928) Zur Syptomatologie der progressiven Paralyse (Korsakowsche Psychose und delirante Zustände). *Journal für Psychologie und Neurologie* 37: 274.

Pick, A. (1876) Zur Casuistik der Erinnerungstäuschungen. *Archiv für Psychiatrie und Nervenkrankheiten* 6: 568–574.

Pick, A. (1903a) On reduplicative paramnesia. *Brain* 26: 260–267.

Pick, A. (1903b) Ueber eine neuartige Form von Paramnesie. *Jahrbücher für Psychiatrie und Neurologie* 20: 1–35.

Pick, A. (1905) Zur Psychologie der Confabulation. *Neurologisches Centralblatt* 24: 509–516.

Pick, A. (1921) Neues zur Psychologie der Konfabulation. *Monatsschrift für Psychiatrie und Neurologie* 49: 314–321.

Pihan, H., Gutbrod, K., Baas, U. and Schnider, A. (2004) Dopamine inhibition and the adaptation of behavior to ongoing reality. *Neuroreport* 15: 709–712.

Pillemer, D. B. (1984) Flashbulb memories of the assassination attempt on President Reagan. *Cognition* 16: 63–80.

Pochon, J. B., Levy, R., Fossati, P., Lehericy, S., Poline, J. B., Pillon, B., Le Bihan, D. and Dubois, B. (2002) The neural system that bridges reward and cognition in humans: an fMRI study. *Proceedings of the National Academy of Science of the USA* 99: 5669–5674.

Poeck, K. (1984) Neuropsychological demonstration of splenial interhemispheric disconnection in a case of 'optic anomia'. *Neuropsychologia* 22: 707–713.

Poeck, K. (1985) The Klüver-Bucy syndrome in man. In: *Handbook of clinical neurology, vol 45: Clinical neuropsychology* (Frederiks JAM, ed), pp. 257–263. Amsterdam: Elsevier Science.

Poreh, A., Winocur, G., Moscovitch, M., Backon, M., Goshen, E., Ram, Z. and Feldman, Z. (2006) Anterograde and retrograde amnesia in a person with bilateral fornix lesions following removal of a colloid cyst. *Neuropsychologia* 44: 2241–2248.

Porrino, L. J., Crane, A. M. and Goldman-Rakic, P. S. (1981) Direct and indirect pathways from the amygdala to the frontal lobe in rhesus monkeys. *Journal of Comparative Neurology* 198: 121–136.

Pötzl, O. (1924) Über Störungen der Selbstwahrnehmung bei linksseitiger Hemiplegie. *Zeitschrift für die gesamte Neurologie und Psychiatrie* 93: 117–168.

Price, B. H., Daffner, K. R., Stowe, R. M. and Mesulam, M. M. (1990) The comportmental learning disabilities of early frontal lobe damage. *Brain* 113: 1383–1393.

Price, J. L., Carmichael, S. T. and Drevets, W. C. (1996) Networks related to the orbital and medial prefrontal cortex; a substrate for emotional behavior? *Progress in Brain Research* 107: 523–536.

Price, J. L. (2006) Connections of orbital cortex. In: *The orbitofrontal cortex* (Zald DH, Rauch SL, eds), pp. 39–55. Oxford: Oxford University Press.

Ptak, R., Gutbrod, K. and Schnider, A. (1998) Association learning in the acute confusional state. *Journal of Neurology, Neurosurgery and Psychiatry* 65: 390–392.

Ptak, R. and Schnider, A. (1999) Spontaneous confabulations after orbitofrontal damage: The role of temporal context confusion and self-monitoring. *Neurocase* 5: 243–250.

Ptak, R., Birtoli, B., Imboden, H., Hauser, C., Weis, J. and Schnider, A. (2001) Hypothalamic amnesia with spontaneous confabulations: A clinicopathologic study. *Neurology* 56: 1597–1600.

Ptak, R. and Schnider, A. (2004) Disorganized memory after right dorsolateral prefrontal damage. *Neurocase* 10: 52–59.

Raisman, G., Cowan, W. M. and Powell, T. P. S. (1966) An experimental analysis of the efferent projection of the hippocampus. *Brain* 89: 83–108.

Ramnani, N., Elliott, R., Athwal, B. S. and Passingham, R. E. (2004) Prediction error for free monetary reward in the human prefrontal cortex. *Neuroimage* 23: 777–786.

Rapcsak, S. Z., Reminger, S. L., Glisky, E. L., Kazniak, A. W. and Comer, J. F. (1999) Neuropsychological mechanisms of false facial recognition following frontal lobe damage. *Cognitive Neuropsychology* 16: 267–292.

Ray, J. P. and Price, J. L. (1993) The organization of projections from the mediodorsal nucleus of the thalamus to orbital and medial prefrontal cortex in macaque monkeys. *Journal of Comparative Neurology* 337: 1–31.

Reed, L. J., Marsden, P., Lasserson, D., Sheldon, N., Lewis, P., Stanhope, N., Guinan, E. and Kopelman, M. D. (1999) FDG-PET analysis and findings in amnesia resulting from hypoxia. *Memory* 7: 599–612.

Regard, M., Strauss, E. and Knapp, P. (1982) Children's production on verbal and non verbal fluency tasks. *Perceptual and Motor Skills* 55: 839–844.

Rempel-Clower, N. L. and Barbas, H. (1998) Topographic organization of connections between the hypothalamus and prefrontal cortex in the rhesus monkey. *Journal of Comparative Neurology* 398: 393–419.

Ries, M. and Marks, W. (2006) Heightened false memory: a long-term sequela of severe closed head injury. *Neuropsychologia* 44: 2233–2240.

Robertson, R. T. and Kaitz, S. S. (1981) Thalamic connections with limbic cortex. I. Thalamocortical projections. *Journal of Comparative Neurology* 195: 501–525.

Roediger, H. L., III and McDermott, K. B. (1995) Creating false memories: Remembering words not presented in lists. *Journal of Experimental Psychology: Learning, Memory and Cognition* 21: 803–814.

Roediger, H. L., III., Watson, J. M., McDermott, K. B. and Gallo, D. A. (2001) Factors that determine false recall: a multiple regression analysis. *Psychonomic Bulletin and Review* 8: 385–407.

Roemheld, L. (1906) Ueber den Korsakow'schen Symptomencomplex bei Hirnlues. *Archiv für Psychiatrie und Nervenkrankheiten* 41: 703–711.

Rogers, R. D., Owen, A. M., Middleton, H. C., Williams, E. J., Pickard, J. D., Sahakian, B. J. and Robbins, T. W. (1999) Choosing between small, likely rewards and large, unlikely rewards activates inferior and orbital prefrontal cortex. *Journal of Neuroscience* 19: 9029–9038.

Rolls, E. T. (1999) *The brain and emotion*. Oxford: Oxford University Press.

Rolls, E. T., Hornak, J., Wade, D. and McGrath, J. (1994) Emotion-related learning in patients with social and emotional changes associated with frontal lobe damage. *Journal of Neurology, Neurosurgery and Psychiatry* 57: 1518–1524.

Rosen, H. J., Gorno-Tempini, M. L., Goldman, W. P., Perry, R. J., Schuff, N., Weiner, M., Feiwell, R., Kramer, J. H. *et al.* (2002) Patterns of brain atrophy in frontotemporal dementia and semantic dementia. *Neurology* 58: 198–208.

Rosenkilde, C. E. (1979) Functional heterogeneity of the prefrontal cortex in the monkey: a review. *Behavioral and Neural Biology* 25: 301–345.

Rosenkilde, C. E., Bauer, R. H. and Fuster, J. M. (1981) Single cell activity in ventral prefrontal cortex of behaving monkeys. *Brain Research* 209: 375–394.

Ruff, R. L. and Volpe, B. T. (1981) Environmental reduplication associated with right frontal and parietal lobe injury. *Journal of Neurology, Neurosurgery and Psychiatry* 44: 382–386.

Rugg, M. D., Fletcher, P. C., Chua, P. M. and Dolan, R. J. (1999) The role of the prefrontal cortex in recognition memory and memory for source: An fMRI Study. *Neuroimage* 10: 520–529.

Russchen, F. T., Amaral, D. G. and Price, J. L. (1985) The afferent connections of the substantia innominata in the monkey, *Macaca fascicularis*. *Journal of Comparative Neurology* 242: 1–27.

Russchen, F. T., Amaral, D. G. and Price, J. L. (1987) The afferent input to the magnocellular division of the mediodorsal thalamic nucleus in the monkey, *Macaca fascicularis*. *Journal of Comparative Neurology* 256: 175–210.

Russel, W. R. (1932) Cerebral involvement in head injury. *Brain* 55: 549–603.

Russel, W. R. and Smith, A. (1961) Post-traumatic amnesia in closed head injury. *Archives of Neurology* 5: 4–17.

Russel, W. R. (1971) *The traumatic amnesias.* New York: Oxford University Press.

Salazar-Fraile, J., Tabares-Seisdedos, R., Selva-Vera, G., Balanza-Martinez, V., Martnez-Arn, A., Catalan, J., Baldeweg, T., Vilela-Soler, C. *et al.* (2004) Recall and recognition confabulation in psychotic and bipolar disorders: evidence for two different types without unitary mechanisms. *Comprehensive Psychiatry* 45: 281–288.

Sawa, A. and Snyder, S. H. (2002) Schizophrenia: diverse approaches to a complex disease. *Science* 296: 692–695.

Schacter, D. L. (2001) *The seven sins of memory. How the mind forgets and remembers.* Boston, MA: Houghton Mifflin Company.

Schacter, D. L. and Slotnick, S. D. (2004) The cognitive neuroscience of memory distortion. *Neuron* 44: 149–160.

Schacter, D. L., Buckner, R. L., Koutstaal, W., Dale, A. M. and Rosen, B. R. (1997) Late onset of anterior prefrontal activity during true and false recognition: an event-related fMRI study. *Neuroimage* 6: 259–269.

Schacter, D. L., Curran, T., Galluccio, L., Milberg, W. P. and Bates, J. F. (1996a) False recognition and the right frontal lobe: A case study. *Neuropsychologia* 34: 793–808.

Schacter, D. L., Norman, K. A. and Koutstaal, W. (1998a) The cognitive neuroscience of constructive memory. *Annual Review of Psychology* 49: 289–318.

Schacter, D. L., Reiman, E., Curran, T., Yun, L. S., Bandy, D., McDermott, K. B. and Roediger, H. L. I. (1996b) Neuroanatomical correlates of veridical and illusory recognition memory: evidence from positron emission tomography. *Neuron* 17: 267–274.

Schacter, D. L., Verfaellie, M. and Pradere, D. (1996c) The neuropsychology of memory illusions: false recall and recognition in amnesic patients. *Journal of Memory and Language* 35: 319–334.

Schacter, D. L., Verfaellie, M., Anes, M. D. and Racine, C. (1998b) When true recognition suppresses false recognition: evidence from amnesic patients. *Journal of Cognitive Neuroscience* 10: 668–679.

Scheid, W. (1934) Zur Pathopsychologie des Korsakow-Syndroms. *Zeitschrift für die gesamte Neurologie und Psychiatrie* 151: 346–369.

Schmolck, H., Buffalo, E. A. and Squire, L. R. (2000) Memory distortions develop over time: recollections of the O. J. Simpson trial verdict after 15 and 32 months. *Psychological Science* 11: 39–45.

Schnider, A. (2000) Spontaneous confabulations, disorientation, and the processing of 'now'. *Neuropsychologia* 38: 175–185.

Schnider, A. (2001) Spontaneous confabulation, reality monitoring, and the limbic system – a review. *Brain Research Reviews* 36: 150–160.

Schnider, A. (2003) Spontaneous confabulation and the adaptation of thought to ongoing reality. *Nature Reviews Neuroscience* 4: 662–671.

Schnider, A. (2004) *Verhaltensneurologie. Die neurologische Seite der Neuropsychologie. Eine Einführung für Ärzte und Psychologen*, 2nd edn. Stuttgart: Thieme.

Schnider, A. and Gutbrod, K. (1997) Possible role of insular damage for behavioral features of amnesia. *Journal of Neuropsychiatry and Clinical Neurosciences* 9: 147 (abstract).

Schnider, A. and Ptak, R. (1999) Spontaneous confabulators fail to suppress currently irrelevant memory traces. *Nature Neuroscience* 2: 677–681.

Schnider, A., Benson, D. F. and Scharre, D. W. (1994a) Visual agnosia and optic aphasia: are they anatomically distinct? *Cortex* 30: 445–457.

Schnider, A., Bonvallat, J., Emond, H. and Leemann, B. (2005a) Reality confusion in spontaneous confabulation. *Neurology* 65: 1117–1119.

Schnider, A., Gutbrod, K., Hess, C. W. and Schroth, G. (1996a) Memory without context. Amnesia with confabulations following right capsular genu infarction. *Journal of Neurology, Neurosurgery and Psychiatry* 61: 186–193.

Schnider, A., Gutbrod, K., Ozdoba, C. and Bassetti, C. (1995) Very severe amnesia with acute onset after isolated hippocampal damage due to systemic lupus erythematosus. *Journal of Neurology, Neurosurgery and Psychiatry* 59: 644–646.

Schnider, A., Mohr, C., Morand S. and Michel, C. M. (2007) Early cortical response to behaviorally relevant absence of anticipated outcomes: A human event-related potential study. *NeuroImage* 35: 1348–1355.

Schnider, A., Ptak, R., von Däniken, C. and Remonda, L. (2000a) Recovery from spontaneous confabulations parallels recovery of temporal confusion in memory. *Neurology* 55: 74–83.

Schnider, A., Regard, M. and Landis, T. (1994b) Anterograde and retrograde amnesia following bitemporal infarction. *Behavioural Neurology* 7: 87–92.

Schnider, A., Treyer, V. and Buck, A. (2000b) Selection of currently relevant memories by the human posterior medial orbitofrontal cortex. *Journal of Neuroscience* 20: 5880–5884.

Schnider, A., Treyer, V. and Buck, A. (2005b) The human orbitofrontal cortex monitors outcomes even when no reward is at stake. *Neuropsychologia* 43: 316–323.

Schnider, A., Valenza, N., Morand S. and Michel, C. M. (2002) Early cortical distinction between memories that pertain to ongoing reality and memories that don't. *Cerebral Cortex* 12: 54–61.

Schnider, A., von Däniken, C. and Gutbrod, K. (1996b) The mechanisms of spontaneous and provoked confabulations. *Brain* 119: 1365–1375.

Schnider, A., von Däniken, C. and Gutbrod, K. (1996c) Disorientation in amnesia: A confusion of memory traces. *Brain* 119: 1627–1632.

Schnider, A., von Däniken, C. and Gutbrod, K. (1997) Mechanisms of human amnesia: information storage and temporal context confusion. *Journal of the International Neuropsychological Society* 4: 44 (abstract).

Schultz, W., Dayan, P. and Montague, P. R. (1997) A neural substrate of prediction and reward. *Science* 275: 1593–1599.

Schultz, W., Tremblay, L. and Hollerman, J. R. (2000) Reward processing in primate orbitofrontal cortex and basal ganglia. *Cerebral Cortex* 10: 272–284.

Schulz, W. (1908) Korsakoff'sches Syndrom bei CO-Vergiftungen. *Berliner Klinische Wochenschrift* 45: 1621–1623.

Scoville, W. B. and Milner, B. (1957) Loss of recent memory after bilateral hippocampal lesions. *Journal of Neurology, Neurosurgery and Psychiatry* 20: 11–21.

Segal, J. (1916) Über das Vorstellen von Objekten und Situationen. *Münchener Studien zur Psychologie und Philosophie* 4: 298–655.

Servan, J., Verstichel, P., Catala, M. and Rancurel, G. (1994) Syndromes amnésiques et fabulations au cours d'infarctus du territoire de l'artère cérébrale postérieure. *Revue Neurologique (Paris)* 150: 201–208.

Shapiro, B. E., Alexander, M. P., Gardner, H. and Mercer, B. (1981) Mechanisms of confabulation. *Neurology* 31: 1070–1076.

Sharot, T., Martorella, E. A., Delgado, M. R. and Phelps, E. A. (2007) How personal experience modulates the neural circuitry of memories of September 11. *Proceedings of the National Academy of Science of the USA* 104: 389–394.

Shimamura, A. P. and Squire, L. R. (1987) A neuropsychological study of fact memory and source amnesia. *Journal of Experimental Psychology: Learning, Memory and Cognition* 13: 464–473.

Shimamura, A. P., Janowsky, J. S. and Squire, L. R. (1990) Memory for the temporal order of events in patients with frontal lobe lesions and amnesic patients. *Neuropsychologia* 28: 803–813.

Shoqeirat, M. A. and Mayes, A. R. (1991) Disproportionate incidental spatial-memory and recall deficits in amnesia. *Neuropsychologia* 29: 749–769.

Signer, S. F. (1992) Psychosis in neurologic disease: Capgras syndrome and delusions of reduplication in neurologic disorders. *Neuropsychiatry, Neuropsychology and Behavioral Neurology* 5: 138–143.

Simpson, J. and Done, D. J. (2002) Elasticity and confabulation in schizophrenic delusions. *Psychological Medicine* 32: 451–458.

Sittig, O. (1912) Ein Fall von Korsakowscher Psychose auf Grund diabetischer Acidose. *Monatsschrift für Psychiatrie und Neurologie* 32: 241–251.

Snodgrass, J. G. and Vanderwart, M. (1980) A standardized set of 260 pictures: norms for name agreement, image agreement, familiarity, and visual complexity. *Journal of Experimental Psychology: Human Learning and Memory* 6: 174–215.

Squire, L. R. and Alvarez, P. (1995) Retrograde amnesia and memory consolidation: a neurobiological perspective. *Current Opinion in Neurobiology* 5: 169–177.

Squire, L. R. and Bayley, P. J. (2007) The neuroscience of remote memory. *Current Opinion in Neurobiology* 17: 185–196.

Squire, L. R. and Shimamura, A. P. (1986) Characterizing amnesic patients for neurobehavioral study. *Behavioral Neuroscience* 100: 866–877.

Squire, L. R. and Zola-Morgan, S. (1991) The medial temporal lobe memory system. *Science* 253: 1380–1386.

Squire, L. R., Amaral, D. G., Zola-Morgan, S., Kritchevsky, M. and Press, G. (1989) Description of brain injury in the amnesic patient N. A. based on magnetic resonance imaging. *Experimental Neurology* 105: 23–35.

Squire, L. R., Zola-Morgan, S., Cave, C. B., Haist, F., Musen, G. and Suzuki, W. A. (1990) Memory: organization of brain systems and cognition. *Cold Spring Harbor Symposium of Quantitative Biology* 55: 1007–1023.

Starkstein, S. E., Vazquez, S., Migliorelli, R., Teson, A., Sabe, L. and Leiguarda, R. (1995) A single-photon emission computed tomographic study of anosognosia in Alzheimer's disease. *Archives of Neurology* 52: 415–420.

Starkstein, S. E., Sabe, L., Chemerinski, E., Jason, L. and Leiguarda, R. (1996) Two domains of anosognosia in Alzheimer's disease. *Journal of Neurology, Neurosurgery and Psychiatry* 61: 485–490.

Stefanacci, L., Buffalo, E. A., Schmolck, H. and Squire, L. R. (2000) Profound amnesia after damage to the medial temporal lobe: A neuroanatomical and neuropsychological profile of patient E. P. *Journal of Neuroscience* 20: 7024–7036.

Stenger, V. A. (2006) Technical considerations for BOLD fMRI of the orbitofrontal cortex. In: *The orbitofrontal cortex* (Zald DH and Rauch SL, eds), pp. 423–446. Oxford: Oxford University Press.

Sturm, W. and Willmes, K. (1995) *NVLT bzw. VLT – Nonverbaler und Verbaler Lerntest.* Mödling: Dr. G. Schuhfried GmbH.

Stuss, D. T., Alexander, M. P., Lieberman, A. and Levine, H. (1978) An extraordinary form of confabulation. *Neurology* 28: 1166–1172.

Stuss, D. T., Alexander, M. P., Floden, D., Binns, M. A., Levine, B., McIntosh, A. R., Rajah, N. and Hevenor, S. J. (2002) Fractionation and localization of distinct frontal lobe processes: evidence from focal lesions in humans. In: *Principles of frontal lobe function* (Stuss DT and Knight RT, eds), pp. 392–407. New York: Oxford University Press.

Suzuki, W. (1996) Neuroanatomy of the monkey entorhinal, perirhinal and parahippocampal cortices: Organization of cortical inputs and interactions with amygdala and striatum. *Seminars in the Neurosciences* 8: 3–12.

Talland G. A. (1961) Confabulation in the Wernicke–Korsakoff syndrome. *The Journal of Nervous and Mental Diseases* 132: 361–381.

Talland G. A. (1965) *Deranged memory. A psychonomic study of the amnesic syndrome.* New York: Academic Press.

Talland G. A., Sweet, W. H. and Ballantine, H. T. (1967) Amnesic syndrome with anterior communicating artery aneurysm. *The Journal of Nervous and Mental Diseases* 145: 179–192.

Tallberg, I. M. and Almkvist, O. (2001) Confabulation and memory in patients with Alzheimer's disease. *Journal of Clinical and Experimental Neuropsychology* 23: 172–184.

Tanaka, Y., Miyazawa, Y., Akaoka, F. and Yamada, T. (1997) Amnesia following damage to the mamillary bodies. *Neurology* 48: 160–165.

Tarachow, S. (1939) The Korsakoff psychosis in spontaneous subarachnoid hemorrhage. Report of three cases. *American Journal of Psychiatry* 95: 887–899.

Tatemichi, T. K., Desmond, D. W., Prohovnik, I., Cross, G. T. I., Mohr, J. P. and Stern, Y. (1992) Confusion and memory loss from capsular genu infarction. *Neurology* 42: 1966–1979.

Tekin, S., Mega, M. S., Masterman, D. M., Chow, T., Garakian, J., Vinters, H. V. and Cummings, J. L. (2001) Orbitofrontal and anterior cingulate cortex neurofibrillary tangle burden is associated with agitation in Alzheimer disease. *Annals of Neurology* 49: 355–361.

Terry, R. D., Masliah, E., Salmon, D. P., Butters, N., DeTeresa, R., Hill, R., Hansen, L. A. and Katzman, R. (1991) Physical basis of cognitive alterations in Alzheimer's disease: Synapse loss is the major correlate of cognitive impairment. *Annals of Neurology* 30: 572–580.

Teuber, H. L., Milner, B. and Vaughan, H. G. (1968) Persistent anterograde amnesia after stab wound of the basal brain. *Neuropsychologia* 6: 267–282.

Thaiss, L. and Petrides, M. (2003) Source versus content memory in patients with a unilateral frontal cortex or a temporal lobe excision. *Brain* 126: 1112–1126.

Thompson, J. C., Stopford, C. L., Snowden, J. S. and Neary, D. (2005) Qualitative neuropsychological performance characteristics in frontotemporal dementia and Alzheimer's disease. *Journal of Neurology, Neurosurgery and Psychiatry* 76: 920–927.

Thompson, P. M., Mega, M. S., Woods, R. P., Zoumalan, C. I., Lindshield, C. J., Blanton, R. E., Moussai, J., Holmes, C. J. *et al.* (2001) Cortical change in Alzheimer's disease detected with a disease-specific population-based brain atlas. *Cerebral Cortex* 11: 1–16.

Thorpe, S. J., Rolls, E. T. and Maddison, S. (1983) The orbitofrontal cortex: neuronal activity in the behaving monkey. *Experimental Brain Research* 49: 93–115.

Thurstone, L. L. and Thurstone, T. G. (1963) *Chicago test of primary mental abilities.* Chicago, IL: Research Associates.

Thut, G., Schultz, W., Roelcke, U., Nienhusmeier, M., Missimer, J., Maguire, R. P. and Leenders, K. L. (1997) Activation of the human brain by monetary reward. *Neuroreport* 8: 1225–1228.

Tiling, T. (1890) Ueber die bei der alkoholischen Neuritis multiplex beobachtete Geistesstörung. *Allgemeine Zeitschrift für Psychiatrie und psychisch-gerichtliche Medicin* 46: 233–257.

Tiling, T. (1892) Ueber die amnestische Geistesstörung. *Allgemeine Zeitschrift für Psychiatrie und psychisch-gerichtliche Medicin* 48: 549–565.

Tobler, P. N., Fiorillo, C. D. and Schultz, W. (2005) Adaptive coding of reward value by dopamine neurons. *Science* 307: 1642–1645.

Torgovnick, J., Arsura, E. L. and Lala, D. (2000) Cytomegalovirus ventriculoencephalitis presenting as a Wernicke's encephalopathy-like syndrome. *Neurology* 55: 1910–1913.

Toth, C., Voll, C. and Macaulay, R. (2002) Primary CNS lymphoma as a cause of Korsakoff syndrome. *Surgical Neurology* 57: 41–45.

Tranel, D. and Hyman, B. T. (1990) Neuropsychological correlates of bilateral amygdala damage. *Archives of Neurology* 47: 349–355.

Treyer, V., Buck, A. and Schnider, A. (2003) Orbitofrontal-subcortical loop activation during suppression of memories that do not pertain to ongoing reality. *Journal of Cognitive Neuroscience* 15: 610–618.

Treyer, V., Buck, A. and Schnider, A. (2006a) Effects of baseline task position on apparent activation in functional imaging of memory. *Neuropsychologia* 44: 462–468.

Treyer, V., Buck, A. and Schnider, A. (2006b) Selection of currently relevant words: an auditory verbal memory study using PET. *Neuroreport* 17: 323–327.

Trillet, M., Fischer, C., Serclerat, D. and Schott, B. (1980) Le syndrome amnésique des ischémies cérébrales postérieures. *Cortex* 16: 421–434.

Tsiminakis, Y. (1934) Über einen Fall von postencephalitischem Korsakoffschem Syndrom. *Zeitschrift für die gesamte Neurologie und Psychiatrie* 150: 323–327.

Turnbull, O. H., Berry, H. and Evans, C. E. (2004a) A positive emotional bias in confabulatory false beliefs about place. *Brain and Cognition* 55: 490–494.

Turnbull, O. H., Jenkins, S. and Rowley, M. L. (2004b) The pleasantness of false beliefs: an emotion-based account of confabulation. *Neuropsychoanalysis* 6: 5–16.

Turner, M. S., Cipolotti, L., Yousry, T. A. and Shallice, T. (2007) Confabulation: Damage to a specific inferior medial prefrontal system. *Cortex* (in press).

Valenstein, E., Bowers, D., Verfaellie, M., Heilman, K. M., Day, A. and Watson, R. T. (1987) Retrosplenial amnesia. *Brain* 110: 1631–1646.

Van der Horst, L. (1932) Über die Psychologie des Korsakowsyndroms. *Monatsschrift für Psychiatrie und Neurologie* 83: 65–84.

Van Hoesen, G. W. (1982) The parahippocampal gyrus. New observations regarding its cortical connection in the monkey. *Trends in Neuroscience* 5: 345–350.

Vermelin, H. and Louyot, J. (1936) Vomissements incoercibles; syndrome de Korsakoff. *Bulletin de la Société d'Obstétrique et de Gynécologie* 25/I: 91–95.

Victor, M. and Agamanolis, D. (1990) Amnesia due to lesions confined to the hippocampus: a clinical-pathologic study. *Journal of Cognitive Neuroscience* 2: 246–257.

Victor, M. and Yakovlev, P. I. (1955) SS. Korsakoff's Psychic disorder in conjunction with peripheral neuritis. A translation of Korsakoff's original article with brief comments on the author and his contribution to clinical medicine. *Neurology* 5: 394–406.

Victor, M., Adams, R. D. and Collins, G. H. (1989) *The Wernicke–Korsakoff syndrome*, 2nd edn. Philadelphia, PA: F. A. Davis.

Victor, M., Angevine, J. B., Mancall, E. L. and Fisher, C. M. (1961) Memory loss with lesions of the hippocampal formation. *Archives of Neurology* 5: 244–263.

Vilkki, J. (1985) Amnesic syndromes after surgery of anterior communicating artery aneurysms. *Cortex* 21: 431–444.

Volpe, B. T. and Hirst, W. (1983) The characterization of the amnesic syndrome following hypoxic ischemic injury. *Archives of Neurology* 40: 436–440.

Von Cramon, D. and Säring, W. (1982) Störung der Orientierung beim hirnorganischen Psychosyndrom. In: *Hirnorganische Psychosyndrome im Alter* (Bente D, Coper H and Kanowski S, eds), pp. 38–49. Berlin: Springer.

Von Cramon, D. Y., Hebel, N. and Schuri, U. (1985) A contribution to the anatomical basis of thalamic amnesia. *Brain* 108: 993–1008.

Von Cramon, D. Y., Hebel, N. and Schuri, U. (1988) Verbal memory and learning in unilateral posterior cerebral infarction. A report on 30 cases. *Brain* 111: 1061–1077.

Von Cramon, D. Y., Markowitsch, H. J. and Schuri, U. (1993) The possible contribution of the septal region to memory. *Neuropsychologia* 31: 1159–1180.

Von Hösslin, R. (1905) Die Schwangerschaftslähmungen der Mütter. *Archiv für Psychiatrie und Nervenkrankheiten* 40: 445–576.

Vuilleumier, P., Mohr, C., Valenza, N., Wetzel, C. and Landis, T. (2003) Hyperfamiliarity for unknown faces after left lateral temporo-occipital venous infarction: a double dissociation with prosopagnosia. *Brain* 126: 889–907.

Vuilleumier, P. (2004) Anosognosia: the neurology of beliefs and uncertainties. *Cortex* 40: 9–17.

Wade, K. A., Garry, M., Read, J. D. and Lindsay, D. S. (2002) A picture is worth a thousand lies: using false photographs to create false childhood memories. *Psychonomic Bulletin and Review* 9: 597–603.

Walton (1953) The Korsakov syndrome in spontaneous subarachnoid haemorrhage. *The Journal of Mental Science* 99: 521–530.

Waters, F. A., Badcock, J. C., Maybery, M. T. and Michie, P. T. (2003) Inhibition in schizophrenia: association with auditory hallucinations. *Schizophrenia Research* 62: 275–280.

Wechsler, D. (1945) A standardized memory scale for clinical use. *Journal of Psychology* 19: 87–95.

Weinstein, E. A. and Kahn, R. L. (1950) The syndrome of anosognosia. *Archives of Neurology and Psychiatry* 64: 772–791.

Weinstein, E. A., Kahn, R. L. and Sugarman, L. A. (1952) Phenomenon of reduplication. *Archives of Neurology and Psychiatry* 67: 808–814.

Weinstein, E. A. and Kahn, R. L. (1955) *Denial of illness. Symbolic and physiological aspects.* Springfield, IL: Charles C Thomas.

Weinstein, E. A. and Lyerly, O. G. (1968) Confabulation following brain injury. Its analogues and sequelae. *Archives of General Psychiatry* 18: 348–354.

Weinstein, E. A. (1987) The functions of confabulation. *Psychiatry* 50: 88–89.

Wells, G. L. and Bradfield, A. L. (1998) 'Good, you identified the suspect': Feedback to eyewitnesses distorts their reports of the witnessing experience. *Journal of Applied Psychology* 83: 360–376.

Wells, G. L. and Olson, E. A. (2003) Eyewitness testimony. *Annual Review of Psychology* 54: 277–295.

Wernicke, C. (1900) *Grundriss der Psychiatrie in klinischen Vorlesungen.* Leipzig: Thieme.

Wernicke, C. (1906) *Grundriss der Psychiatrie*, 2nd edn. Leipzig: Thieme.

Whitley, R. J., Alford, C. A., Hirsch, M. S., Schooley, R. T., Luby, J. P., Aoki, F. Y., Hanley, D., Nahmias, A. J. *et al.* (1986) Vidarabine versus acyclovir therapy in herpes simplex encephalitis. *New England Journal of Medicine* 314: 144–149.

Whitlock, F. (1981) Some observations on the meaning of confabulation. *British Journal of Medical Psychology* 54: 213–218.

Whitty, C. W. and Lewin, W. (1960) A Korsakoff syndrome in the post-cingulectomy confusional state. *Brain* 83: 648–653.

Williams, H. W. and Rupp, C. (1938) Observations on confabulation. *American Journal of Psychiatry* 95: 395–405.

Williams, M. and Pennybacker, J. (1954) Memory disturbances in third ventricle tumours. *Journal of Neurology, Neurosurgery and Psychiatry* 17: 115–123.

Wilson, B. A., Evans, J. J., Emslie, H. and Malinek, V. (1997) Evaluation of NeuroPage: a new memory aid. *Journal of Neurology, Neurosurgery and Psychiatry* 63: 113–115.

Wilson, B. A., Emslie, H. C., Quirk, K. and Evans, J. J. (2001) Reducing everyday memory and planning problems by means of a paging system: a randomized control crossover study. *Journal of Neurology, Neurosurgery and Psychiatry* 70: 477–482.

Yacubian, J., Glascher, J., Schroeder, K., Sommer, T., Braus, D. F. and Buchel, C. (2006) Dissociable systems for gain- and loss-related value predictions and errors of prediction in the human brain. *Journal of Neuroscience* 26: 9530–9537.

Yoneoka, Y., Takeda, N., Inoue, A., Ibuchi, Y., Kumagai, T., Sugai, T., Takeda, K. and Ueda, K. (2004) Acute Korsakoff syndrome following mammillothalamic tract infarction. *American Journal of Neuroradiology* 25: 964–968.

Young, A. W., de Haan, E. H. and Newcombe, F. (1990) Unawareness of impaired face recognition. *Brain and Cognition* 14: 1–18.

Zald, D. H. and Rauch, S. L., eds (2006) *The orbitofrontal cortex*. Oxford: Oxford University Press.

Zaragoza, M. S., Payment, K. E., Ackil, J. K., Drivdahl, S. B. and Beck, M. (2001) Interviewing witnesses: forced confabulation and confirmatory feedback increase false memories. *Psychological Science* 12: 473–477.

Zola-Morgan, S., Squire, L. R. and Amaral, D. G. (1986) Human amnesia and the medial temporal region: enduring memory impairment following a bilateral lesion limited to field CA1 of the hippocampus. *Journal of Neuroscience* 6: 2950–2967.

Zorrilla, L. T., Aguirre, G. K., Zarahn, E., Cannon, T. D. and D'Esposito, M. (1996) Activation of the prefrontal cortex during judgments of recency: a functional MRI study. *Neuroreport* 7: 2803–2806.

Author Index

Subject Index